THE ELECTIONS
OF 1984

THE ELECTIONS
OF 1984

Michael Nelson, editor
Vanderbilt University

CQ PRESS

a division of
Congressional Quarterly Inc.
1414 22nd St. N.W., Washington, D.C. 20037

Printed in the United States of America

Library of Congress Cataloging in Publication Data

The Elections of 1984.

    Includes index.
    1. Presidents — United States — Election — 1984 — Addresses, essays, lectures.
2. United States. Congress — Elections, 1984 — Addresses, essays, lectures. I. Nelson, Michael. II. Title.

JK1968 1984	324.973'0927	85-444

ISBN 0-87187-342-7
ISBN 0-87187-330-3 (pbk.)

To my mother and father

Herta F. Nelson
Walter C. Nelson

TABLE OF CONTENTS

Figures and Tables   xi

Preface   xiii

1. A Critical Realignment? The New Politics, the
   Reconstituted Right, and the Election of 1984   1
   Benjamin Ginsberg and Martin Shefter

   The Collapse of America's Postwar Regime   1
   Building a New Political Order   5
   Electoral Strategies: The New Politics Movement   10
   Electoral Strategies: The Reconstituted Right   19
   A Critical Realignment?   23

2. The Nomination Process: Vicissitudes of
   Candidate Selection   27
   Gary R. Orren

   A Season of Surprises   27
   Short-Term Forces and the Nomination Process   31
   Long-Term Forces and the Nomination Process   65
   The Democratic Convention   69
   The Republicans in 1984   71
   Conclusion   72

3. The Election: Candidates, Strategies,
   and Decisions   83
   Paul C. Light and Celinda Lake

   The Strategic Climate   83
   Candidates and Strategies   88
   The Campaign   95
   Decisions   103
   Conclusion   109

4. **The Media Campaign: Struggle for the Agenda**   111
Thomas E. Patterson and Richard Davis

News versus Politics   113
A Concluding Note: Disorganized Politics   124

5. **Foreign Policy: Dominance and Decisiveness
in Presidential Elections**   129
Stephen Hess and Michael Nelson

Foreign Policy Dominance in Presidential Campaigns   130
Foreign Policy Decisiveness in Presidential Elections   140
The Election of 1984   145

6. **The Economy: Economists, Electoral Politics,
and Reagan Economics**   155
Paul J. Quirk

Presidents, Voters, and Economists   156
Electoral Politics and Reagan Economics   161
Reagan Economics and the 1984 Presidential Campaign   170
Democracy and Economic Policy   178

7. **The Presidency: Reagan and the Cycle of
Politics and Policy**   189
Erwin C. Hargrove and Michael Nelson

Cycles of Politics and Policy   190
Ford, Carter, Reagan, and the Cycle   195
Prospects for Reagan's Second Term   206
Conclusion   210

8. **Congress: Politics after a Landslide
without Coattails**   215
Gary C. Jacobson

A Landslide without Coattails   215
The National Campaigns   220
Senate Results   224
Interpreting the Election   225
Prospects for the 99th Congress   229
1986 and Beyond   234

9. **The Courts: 40 More Years?**   239
Robert H. Birkby

The Court and the Campaign   239
The Court and the President   240

Supreme Court Appointments 242
Lower Court Appointments 250
The Solicitor General 253

10. Implications: What Americans Wanted 259
Nicholas Lemann

Constituencies 259
Technique 265
Policy 268
Conclusion 274

11. An Aligning Election, A Presidential Plebiscite 277
Theodore J. Lowi

The Campaign: A Four-Year Stretch 278
Out of the Polling Booth, Into the Polling Agency 288
Search for Meaning: What Was Decided? 291
The Legacy of Ronald Reagan: R.I.P 297

Contributors 303

Index 307

FIGURES AND TABLES

Figure 2.1   Number of Democratic Presidential Primaries and Proportion of Democratic Convention Delegates Chosen in Primaries, 1912-1984   34

Figure 2.2   Average Proportion of State Spending Limits Spent by Democratic Candidates, 1984   45

Figure 2.3   Cumulative Proportions of the Overall Spending Limit Expended by Democratic Candidates, and Delegates Apportioned over Time, 1983-1984   47

Figure 2.4   Cumulative Proportions of Each Democratic Candidate's Total Expenditures and Delegates Apportioned over Time, 1983-1984   48

Figure 5.1   The Partisan Effects of Voter Attitudes to Presidential Elections, 1952-1980   141

Figure 5.2   Public Opinion on Political Parties and Peace, 1952-1980   144

Figure 11.1   Presidential Approval Ratings from Harry S. Truman to Ronald Reagan: Nationwide Responses to the Gallup Poll Question, "Do you approve or disapprove of the way President _____ is handling his job as president?"   282

Figure 11.2   A Profile of Ronald Reagan's Presidential Popularity, 1983-1984: Nationwide Responses to the Harris Survey Question, "How would you rate the job Reagan is doing as president— excellent, pretty good, only fair, or poor?"   283

Table 2.1   1984 Democratic Primary Results   37

Table 2.2	1984 Democratic Caucus Results, First Round	38
Table 2.3	Popular Vote and Delegates Won in 1984 Democratic Presidential Primaries	39
Table 2.4	Popular Vote and Delegates Won in 1984 Democratic Presidential Primaries, by Type of Primary	39
Table 2.5	Popular Vote and Delegates Won in 1984 First-Round Democratic Caucuses	40
Table 2.6	Actual and Hypothetical Delegate Totals for Democratic Candidates in 1984	41
Table 2.7	Spending in the 1984 Democratic Nomination Contest	49
Table 2.8	Relationship between Spending and Outcomes in 1984 Democratic Nomination Contests	50
Table 2.9	Presidential Balloting at the 1984 Democratic Convention	64
Table 2.10	Group Support for Candidates in the 1984 Democratic Primaries	67
Table 3.1	Official 1984 Presidential Election Results	104
Table 3.2	ABC News Exit Poll, Voting for President	106
Table 4.1	News References to Mondale, Hart, and Cranston, January and February 1984	114
Table 4.2	News Coverage of Hart's and Mondale's Themes and Issues, January and February 1984	117
Table 4.3	News Stories Involving Polls in the *New York Times*, October 31-November 6, 1984	124
Table 5.1	Presidential Election Returns, 1952-1984	131
Table 8.1	Coattails in Landslide Elections, 1956-1984	216
Table 8.2	House Elections, 1984	223
Table 8.3	Senate Election Results by State, 1984	226
Table 11.1	Voter Preferences on Election Day, Results of the *New York Times*/CBS News Exit Poll of November 6, 1984	290

PREFACE

American political campaigns often produce florid prose, and "Campaign '84" was no exception. Consider, for example, one journalist's vivid account of the Republican convention at the moment of its candidate's nomination for president:

> Whole delegations mounted their chairs and led the cheering which instantly spread to the galleries and deepened into a roar fully as deep and deafening as the voice of the Niagara.... The air quivered, the lights trembled and the walls fairly shook. The flags were stripped from the gallery and stage and frantically raised, while hats, umbrellas, handkerchiefs and other personal belongings were tossed to and fro like bubbles over the great dancing sea of human heads.... [Republican liberals] applauded with the tips of their fingers, held immediately in front of their noses.[1]

A Republican clergyman, caught up in the passion of the cause, soon after defined the upcoming election as "not between the two great parties but between the brothel and the family, between decency and indecency, between law and lust."

The Democratic candidate for president, who said his campaign policy would be "Above all, tell the truth," was not without articulate defenders of his own. A New York newspaper pithily endorsed him on the following four grounds: "1. He is an honest man; 2. He is an honest man; 3. He is an honest man; 4. He is an honest man." More colorfully, this same newspaper headlined its report on the Republican nominee's dinner with some of New York's wealthiest men as "Hobnobbing with the Mighty Money Kings ... Monopolists and Millionaires Seal Their Allegiance ... While the Country Sorrows."

If these accounts seem familiar in what they say but a bit archaic in how they say it, it is because the Campaign '84 they describe is Campaign 1884, which matched Democrat Grover Cleveland against Republican James G. Blaine. All American elections embody certain common traits, even as each is distinctive. (In 1884, for example, the Democrat won.)

The main purpose of *The Elections of 1984* is to analyze this blend of the universal and the particular, which marks every election. The book assesses the races of 1984, especially the presidential contest, both in their own right and in historical and theoretical context. To this end the volume is organized to provide description and analysis of the election (and elections) in Chapters 1, 2, 3, and 4; the interrelationship of electoral politics and public policy in Chapters 5 and 6; the consequences of the campaigns and voting for the three branches of the national government in Chapters 7, 8, and 9; and the long-term consequences for American politics in Chapters 10 and 11.

The authors of the essays were selected for their well-established expertise in the broad topics of their chapters and also for their demonstrated capacity to write clearly and engagingly in a way that illuminates recent political events with well-grounded historical and theoretical understanding. All the authors began work on their chapters a year or more before the elections and continued until significant post-election analyses and data were in.

No reader will agree with all of the interpretations; indeed, no reader could, since the perspectives of different authors on the same events are as diverse as they are insightful and provocative. This is as it should be: elections are not so one-dimensional as to be captured easily by any one line of interpretation. Better that readers should experience a variety of viewpoints than that they should have a single one imposed upon them.

I would like to thank the entire staff of CQ Press for their help in producing this book, including Joanne D. Daniels, director of the press; David R. Tarr, director of the book department; Nancy Blanpied and Carolyn McGovern, who compiled the index; and Rhodes Cook, who provided valuable research assistance. Barbara R. de Boinville, Carolyn Goldinger, Nola Healy Lynch, Carolyn McGovern, and John L. Moore worked tirelessly and well to help edit the final drafts of the individual chapters. Nancy Lammers, the project editor for the book, made the entire editorial process pleasant and productive, despite my best efforts to be cantankerous. My greatest thanks are to my wife, Linda E. Nelson, and my son, Michael, Jr., for supporting their husband and daddy even when he wrote and edited under the Christmas tree.

Michael Nelson
Nashville, Tennessee
January 1985

1. All historical quotes in this preface appear in: Paul F. Boller, Jr., *Presidential Campaigns* (New York: Oxford University Press, 1984), Chapter 25.

1. A CRITICAL REALIGNMENT?
THE NEW POLITICS, THE RECONSTITUTED RIGHT,
AND THE 1984 ELECTION

Benjamin Ginsberg and Martin Shefter

The 1984 election was an episode—perhaps a climactic episode—in a conflict that has been central to American politics during the past 15 to 20 years, a conflict between what has been called the "New Politics" coalition and what we will call the "Reconstituted Right." The struggle between these coalitions has engulfed the entire political system—not just the electoral arena but also the courts, Congress, executive branch, and communications media. For the most part, the forces of the New Politics have sought to influence American politics through the Democratic party, while the Republican party has served as the partisan base of the Reconstituted Right.

The Collapse of America's Postwar Regime

The New Politics and Reconstituted Right coalitions emerged from the wreckage of the regime that governed the United States during the two decades that followed World War II. The foundations of that regime were laid by Franklin D. Roosevelt in the 1930s. His New Deal coalition was composed of unionized labor, urban ethnics, southerners, northern blacks, middle-class liberals, and businessmen in technologically advanced sectors of the economy with high capital-to-labor ratios, such as oil and banking.[1] Because firms in these sectors were internationally competitive they benefited from the Roosevelt administration's free trade policies, and because their labor costs were relatively low they could easily afford Roosevelt's concessions to labor. The New Deal was opposed by businessmen in sectors that were not internationally competitive and that had relatively high labor costs. In addition to small businesses, this included heavy industries, such as steel and automobiles, which had both high labor and high capital costs. Many businessmen in these industries bitterly resented the New Deal's labor policies, which had helped bring about the unionization of their employees. One legacy of the

1

1930s, then, was an important break in the political unity of American business.

After World War II the Democrats reached an accommodation with their former opponents in heavy industry and also with the new defense industries that had been created during the war. Heavy industry was reconciled to the New Deal because the wartime destruction of the European and Japanese economies enabled even American firms with high labor costs to dominate world markets. In addition, the federal government's efforts to expand their markets at home (by pursuing Keynesian fiscal policies and enacting social entitlement programs) and abroad (through free trade) permitted heavy industries to amortize their enormous fixed capital costs over a wider base of production.[2] As for the defense industries, they supported America's postwar regime because the nation's policy of rearmament during the Truman administration brought them healthy profits.

Conditions of Regime Stability

The stability of America's postwar regime depended upon three conditions that largely characterized the national and international political economies during the two decades that followed World War II. The first was that the magnitude of the various costs associated with building and maintaining the system of international alliances and protectorates that the United States constructed in the postwar period—such as the North Atlantic Treaty Organization (NATO) and the Southeast Asia Treaty Organization (SEATO)—not undermine domestic political support for a foreign policy of "internationalism." One of these costs was economic. The permanent military establishment that the United States maintained during the cold war years had to be financed by some combination of taxation, government borrowing, and inflation, but so long as the economy grew at a reasonable rate—which it did, for the most part, throughout the postwar period—the burdens this imposed upon the electorate were not onerous. Another cost of empire was conscription, but to the extent that children of the middle and upper classes could avoid military service through student deferments the draft did not threaten the most politically influential segments of the population.

The second precondition for the survival of America's postwar regime was that American industry retain its competitiveness in world markets. Financial and commercial interests with a stake in international trade could only coexist in the same political coalition with the owners and employees of industrial firms if the trade policies promoted by the former group did not cost the latter their profits or their jobs. In addition, to win the support of the rest of the remarkably heterogeneous coalition that also included labor, agriculture, middle-class liberals, and the beneficiaries of social entitlement programs, the postwar regime relied upon a policy of universal payoffs, or in Theodore Lowi's terminology, "interest group liberalism." [3] This was a costly strategy. Politicians who practiced it could retain the acquiescence of these selfsame interests in their capacity as taxpayers and consumers only if the economy grew at a sufficient pace to enable Washington to avoid higher tax rates and highly inflationary fiscal and monetary policies. In the international regime of free trade promoted by the United States during the postwar period, this economic growth in turn was contingent upon the ability of American firms to compete successfully with foreign firms in markets both at home and abroad.

Third and finally, a coalition composed both of southern whites and northern blacks and liberals could endure only so long as the issue of race was submerged. Franklin Roosevelt had succeeded in doing this during his lifetime, but Democratic party and congressional leaders found it an increasingly difficult issue to manage during the late 1940s and the 1950s.

Breakdown of the Postwar Regime

During the 1960s and 1970s changes in the national and international political and economic systems, which in part were brought about by the very policies of America's postwar regime, violated these three conditions and ultimately shattered the nation's governing coalition. Conflicts and cleavages over race, the Vietnam War, and the fiscal and regulatory policies of the national government were political manifestations of these changes.

Race-related issues were the first to emerge, partly because of New Deal and postwar agricultural policies that had been enacted by the Democrats to win the support of farmers (and also organized labor).[4] These policies stimulated the mechanization, consolidation, and internationalization of American agriculture, which in turn drove millions of black sharecroppers from the rural South to northern cities, where they were able to vote. To win these votes northern Democrats took up the cause of civil rights for blacks in the South.[5] In addition, Washington's efforts in the 1960s to expand American influence in the Third World, where the British and French empires had recently disintegrated, were seriously embarrassed by the system of racial segregation in the South. This gave presidents John F. Kennedy and Lyndon B. Johnson another reason to bring the federal government into the campaign for black civil rights,[6] but their actions led many southern whites to abandon the Democratic party in presidential elections—the first major element of the New Deal coalition to do so.

3

So long as the crusade for civil rights was confined to the South, it enjoyed widespread support among all elements of the Democratic coalition in the North. That state of affairs was short-lived, however. The sight of their brothers and sisters rising up against oppressive conditions in the South encouraged blacks in northern cities to do the same. Their political mobilization, in turn, provided northern liberals with an opportunity to increase their influence relative to other elements of the Democratic coalition—urban machine politicians, labor leaders, and working-class and lower-middle-class ethnics. This alliance between upper-middle-class liberals and blacks was consummated through the various urban programs of the New Frontier and Great Society. These provided federal funds to finance "innovative" programs that would help the "culturally disadvantaged" in inner-city neighborhoods—circumventing local governments and municipal bureaucracies that were castigated for being insensitive and unresponsive to the needs of the "community." [7] The working-class and lower-middle-class ethnics who controlled and staffed municipal governments and bureaucracies in most northern cities fully understood that these euphemisms meant the redistribution of public benefits at their expense. This led many of them to turn against Democratic presidential candidates.

Opposition to the Johnson administration's policies in Southeast Asia generated the second major cleavage in America's postwar governing coalition. The Vietnam War was a logical consequence of the nation's postwar foreign policy: wars and indigenous uprisings are natural concomitants of empire building, and the United States had fought just such a war in Korea in the early 1950s. The Korean War had not been especially popular at home, but public unease with it never escalated into active resistance and disruption. What helped turn the intense but initially limited opposition to America's involvement in Vietnam into one of the largest and most disruptive mass movements in American history was a shift in the Johnson administration's conscription policies. Precisely because the administration was committed to civil rights, it was embarrassed by the charge that a disproportionate number of American soldiers and war casualties in Vietnam were black. In seeking to be fair by limiting college-student deferments, the Johnson administration helped create an antiwar constituency that included a substantial segment of the middle class—students (and the parents of students) at Kent State and Colorado State, not just Berkeley and Harvard. Finally, in order to avoid further undermining domestic political support for his administration, President Johnson decided not to raise taxes to finance the war. This helped accelerate the rate of inflation, which also weakened middle-class support for the Democrats.

Finally, the erosion of America's dominant position in the world economy contributed to the collapse of the nation's postwar regime. Again, policies pursued by Washington helped bring this about. The United States had helped its allies in Europe and Japan rebuild their economies after World War II—most notably, through the Marshall Plan—in order to increase their ability to resist Soviet military pressure and to prevent local Communist parties from gaining internal influence.[8] By so doing, Washington helped create the very competitors that later were to challenge the preeminent position of American firms in many world markets. Moreover, by assuming the role of defender of the free world, the United States saddled its economy with military costs that were proportionately greater than those borne by its trading partners. More recently, the 1973 price increase by the Organization of Petroleum Exporting Countries (OPEC) and the decade of stagflation it precipitated in the world economy made it difficult for American firms producing new products to absorb the workers who had lost their jobs in industries that no longer were competitive. The OPEC increase was also a consequence in part of American national security policy. The Nixon administration had indicated to OPEC that it would tolerate a steep price increase because the revenues it generated could finance weapons purchases that would enable the Shah of Iran to serve as policeman of the Persian Gulf— a role that the administration wanted him to play but that Congress was unwilling to underwrite.[9]

The difficulties the American economy experienced in the 1970s placed great strains on the postwar coalition. Both businessmen and workers in industrial sectors that no longer were internationally competitive abandoned their prior commitment to a central tenet of that coalition—free trade. Middle-class taxpayers and businessmen no longer believed that they, their firms, and the nation as a whole could afford to fight a war on poverty—a conviction whose most dramatic expression was the tax-revolt movement of the late 1970s.

Building a New Political Order

The developments that weakened the attachment of many members of the postwar coalition to the political accommodations and policy settlements that had bound them together also increased their willingness to sit out an election, to defect to the opposition (including a third-party candidate such as George Wallace), or to seek political influence through nonelectoral channels. Out of this disarray there emerged in the late 1960s and the 1970s two major efforts to create a successor to America's postwar regime—the New Politics movement and the Reconstituted Right.

The New Politics Movement

The New Politics movement was the first to appear. It was spear-headed by young members of the upper-middle class for whom the civil rights and antiwar movements were formative experiences, just as the Great Depression and World War II had been for their parents. The crusade against racial discrimination and the Vietnam War led these young men and women to define themselves as a political force in opposition to the public policies, political actors, and governmental institutions of the nation's postwar regime.

The various components of the New Politics movement enjoyed a remarkable degree of success during the late 1960s and early 1970s in securing the enactment of policies they favored and in undermining the powers and prerogatives of many members of the postwar governing coalition. Opponents of the war in Vietnam ultimately forced the withdrawal of American forces from Southeast Asia. Through the War Powers Act, the Foreign Commitments Resolution, the Arms Control Export Act, and stricter scrutiny of the Central Intelligence Agency (CIA), they also imposed some limits on the president's ability to use American troops, intelligence operatives, and weapons to prop up anticommunist regimes abroad. The result was to restrain, albeit not entirely reverse, a central thrust of American foreign policy during the cold war. New Politics activists also played a major role in securing the enactment of environmental, consumer, and occupational health and safety legislation that significantly restricted the prerogatives of capitalists as a class by imposing limits on the goods they could produce and the ways they could produce them, and requiring business to invest capital in equipment needed to promote a cleaner environment, less dangerous products, and safer working conditions.[10] This legislation represented a dramatic change in federal regulatory policy, whose primary function previously had been to restrict price competition, enabling firms in regulated industries to reap monopoly profits and pay above-market wages to their employees. In addition, environmental and community activists defeated numerous public works projects designed to channel public resources to coalitions of local officials, business interests, and construction unions. Along with antinuclear activists, they have worked to bring the multibillion-dollar nuclear power industry to its knees.

In more recent years these same political forces have secured the enactment of bottle-return and antismoking regulations that seek to regulate—and stigmatize—the behavior of the working- and lower-middle classes in a manner similar to that of the Prohibition movement. And despite the failure of the campaign to ratify the Equal Rights Amendment, feminists have enjoyed considerable success in the congressional arena. For example, they won the passage of legislation, opposed by the insurance industry, that increased the pension benefits of women and have gained some official recognition for the doctrine of equal pay for jobs of "comparable worth."

In addition to winning the enactment of these public policies, political actors associated with the New Politics movement successfully attacked the political institutions and procedures upon which the power of their opponents rested, then altered them in ways that would enhance their own influence. The best-known example is the McGovern-Fraser Commission, which changed the Democratic party's presidential nomination procedures in ways that reduced the influence of the party's traditional power brokers.[11] In addition, because they commanded considerable legal talent and enjoyed support within the judiciary, the environmental and consumer movements drafted regulatory legislation that provided manifold opportunities for public interest law firms to sue executive officials who were not enforcing these laws to their satisfaction.[12] And organizations such as Common Cause pressed for the enactment of the Freedom of Information Act and various "sunshine laws" that would enable them to make the most of their access to the mass media.

Although elections are the most visible arena for political change, they have been only one arena—and not the most important—in which the New Politics movement has sought to exercise influence. Indeed, the movement has experienced far less success in its efforts to construct majority coalitions in national elections than from its cultivation of alliances with three major institutions—the national news media, the federal judiciary, and Congress. The most spectacular example of this alliance in action was Watergate. In that episode, investigations conducted by the national news media (most importantly, the *Washington Post* and the *New York Times*) and a special prosecutor recruited from the Harvard Law School (Archibald Cox), which were provided with their definitive evidence by the Supreme Court (in its decision requiring release of the White House tapes) and were publicized by a congressional committee (the Ervin Committee) on national television, drove President Richard Nixon from office.

What accounts for the emergence of these alliances between the New Politics movement and the national news media, the federal judiciary, and many senators and representatives? Mutual self-interest animates all three partnerships. The national news media have enabled the movement to depict its causes as contests between the public interest and selfish interests that sought to enrich themselves by despoiling the environment, subjecting consumers to the risks of cancer, or bribing public officials with cash or campaign contributions. This goes a long way toward explaining how the clean air and clean water acts of the early 1970s, which imposed billions of dollars in costs on industries and local governments, nonetheless were enacted by Congress with nearly unanimous votes.

The media's motives for publicizing the causes of the consumer, environmental, and antiwar movements in the 1960s and early 1970s were as much economic as political. CBS, under the leadership of its president Frank Stanton, a sociologist by training, pioneered in the use of sophisticated market research techniques to assess the demographic character of audiences for various types of programming. Market research revealed that the audience for news and public affairs programs had a higher level of education and income—and therefore a greater attraction to advertisers—than the audience for any other type of programming and that during prime time the members of this upscale audience tended to remain with the network whose evening news program they had watched. Market research also revealed that this audience had particular tastes in the news: it liked news analysis and critical programming. It wanted to know what *really* went on in Washington and in Vietnam, not simply what the White House press secretary and the generals said in news briefings. CBS responded to these findings with alacrity—it invented the genre of televised investigative journalism—and the other networks followed its lead.

The alliance between the New Politics movement and the federal courts also has provided benefits for both sides. A remarkable number of activists and sympathizers in the consumer, environmental, and feminist movements are lawyers. From their perspective, the judiciary is a valuable ally because it provides a channel for exerting political influence that is not (at least in the short run) contingent upon victories in the electoral arena. From the perspective of the judiciary, the alliance is valuable because the New Politics movement can defend the Supreme Court in its struggles with opponents in the other two branches of government who might seek to limit the Court's enforcement power or its jurisdiction over one or another controversial issue. This helps explain why, despite the more conservative ideologies of its members, the Burger Court has gone considerably farther than the Warren Court in protecting the rights of women, exempting the media from the law of libel, and increasing the liability of executive officials in civil suits.

Finally, many senators and representatives found it politically advantageous in the 1960s and 1970s to take up one or another cause of the antiwar, consumer, or environmental movements because, by conducting televised hearings on such issues, they were able to mobilize national constituencies, become national figures, and in a number of instances become serious contenders for their party's presidential nomination.

Senate committee hearings led by William Fulbright on the Vietnam War, George McGovern on hunger, Edmund Muskie on environmental issues, and Edward Kennedy on national health insurance are cases in point.

The Reconstituted Right

The victories that the New Politics movement achieved through its alliances with the media, courts, and Congress contributed to the alienation of a number of political forces that formerly had supported the nation's postwar governing coalition. These joined together to form what can be called the Reconstituted Right. In particular, industrialists whose firms were unable to compete successfully in world markets attributed many of their problems to recently implemented regulatory policies that increased their production costs and to burgeoning social welfare expenditures that directly increased their tax burden and indirectly increased their labor costs. Even firms that remained internationally competitive had reason to oppose these regulatory and social expenditure policies on the grounds that they contributed to inflation and reduced American productivity relative to that of its trading partners, with adverse consequences for the level of interest and foreign exchange rates and for the health of the American economy as a whole.

In the 1970s, then, some of the divisions that had characterized the nation's business community from the 1930s through the 1960s began to heal. This political reunification and revitalization of American business was expressed through the organization of the Business Roundtable, which successfully fought both the efforts of consumer groups to establish a consumer protection agency and the efforts of the American Federation of Labor (AFL) to reform the nation's labor laws; through the increased willingness of businessmen to finance institutions, such as the American Enterprise Institute and the Heritage Foundation, that propounded the principles of free enterprise; and through the phenomenal growth in the late 1970s of business political action committees (PACs).

During the 1960s and 1970s the Democratic party also suffered defections on the mass level as a result of its identification with racial minorities and with the New Politics movement. In presidential elections between 1964 and 1980, a substantial proportion of the southern white electorate abandoned the Democrats for the Republicans or for George Wallace's independent candidacy in 1968, largely because of the party's stand on racial issues. Moreover, these voters, as well as many Catholics and evangelical Protestants from other regions of the country, were deeply offended by the stances of national Democratic politicians on abortion, school prayer, gay rights, and other social or family issues. These sentiments led to additional defections from the party.

Finally, a striking regional division became increasingly evident in American electoral politics during the 1970s. Voters in regions of the country least affected by the declining competitiveness of American heavy industry—that is, the South and the West—not surprisingly found the case for a free market economy more persuasive than their counterparts in the midwestern and northeastern industrial belt. This made them likely prospects for mobilization by conservative opponents of the regulatory and social welfare programs enacted by the Democrats.[13] These voters, along with those unhappy with the Democratic positions on racial and social issues, provided the Republicans with their margins of victory in the presidential elections of 1968, 1972, and 1980.

Electoral Strategies: The New Politics Movement

The political forces that emerged from the wreckage of the postwar coalition have experimented with various electoral strategies over the past 16 years. Between 1968 and 1984 elements of the New Politics movement pursued strategies of independence (1968), alliance with blacks and minorities in a coalition of the disaffected (1972), reconstitution of the New Deal coalition under New Politics leadership (1976), boycott (1980), and alliance with labor in a coalition of antagonists (1984). In the 1984 elections, moreover, the outlines of a sixth strategy began to emerge, namely, the construction of a grand coalition of the middle class.

1968: The Strategy of Independence

The first of these strategies, independence, was pursued by New Politics forces in the 1968 presidential election. During that campaign antiwar activists supported efforts by Sen. Eugene McCarthy to secure the Democratic nomination without making any sustained effort to build electoral alliances with other political and social forces. As an independent force, the movement proved powerful enough to dissuade Johnson from seeking renomination. Moreover, the reluctance of this increasingly important component of the Democratic party to support the eventual Democratic nominee, Hubert Humphrey, helped to seal Humphrey's doom. New Politics activists learned in 1968 that, acting as an independent political force, they could undermine the electoral chances of their rivals within the Democratic party but could not secure the election of their friends.

1972: The Coalition of the Disaffected

The results of the 1968 election convinced leaders of the New Politics movement that they could not hope to win power without constructing alliances with other groups and forces. From their perspective, the most likely coalition partners were blacks. But in the view of New Politics leaders, blacks were very much the junior partners in this alliance—the mass base of support for a movement led by upper-middle-class professionals.

Prior to the 1972 election, supporters of the New Politics on the McGovern-Fraser Commission essentially rewrote the rules of the Democratic presidential nominating process in two ways that worked to their own advantage. First, the alliance introduced new procedures, in particular open caucuses and proportional representation primaries, that were designed to increase the weight of New Politics adherents in the nominating process. Second, the alliance introduced rules regarding delegate quotas and credentials designed to increase the role of blacks and minorities at the party convention. The result was the nomination of McGovern, a leader of the New Politics movement and, not coincidentally, the chairman of the party committee that rewrote the rules.

In the 1972 presidential election McGovern was decisively defeated by Nixon. The causes of this defeat were complex; however, five merit particular emphasis. First, the McGovern candidacy drove large numbers of blue-collar voters out of the Democratic ranks, essentially because many of the goals of the New Politics movement were directly at odds with the interests of the American working class. A major portion of the cost of reducing air, water, and noise pollution, cutting defense production, and redressing two centuries of racial injustice would be borne by the white working class in the form of lost jobs and lost income. This conflict of interest was exacerbated by the disdain—verging on class hatred—often exhibited by the upper-middle-class proponents of the New Politics toward members of the working class. Second, the alliance between the New Politics movement and blacks increased the rate of desertion of white southern voters from the Democratic party.

A third reason McGovern lost is that his positions on issues of national security were antithetical to the interests of those segments of the defense industry that normally were aligned with the Democratic party. McGovern promised substantial and long-term reductions in military construction and procurement—reductions that posed a direct threat to the industry's economic well-being. Fourth, McGovern's advocacy of programs that would redistribute income was not well received by either middle-class or working-class taxpayers, who were beginning to feel the economic effects of inflation induced by the Vietnam War.

Finally, the electoral alliance between blacks and the New Politics movement upon which the McGovern candidacy was based proved to be a rather shaky partnership. McGovern generated little enthusiasm among blacks, who correctly perceived that the McGovern candidacy was oriented mainly to the political and social concerns of a segment of the American upper-middle class. The overwhelming majority of blacks who voted in 1972 voted for McGovern. But blacks did not turn out in the numbers anticipated by Democratic strategists. Thus, an important lesson that New Politics strategists learned, or thought they learned, in 1972 was that blacks were not the most reliable of coalition partners. On the one hand, black voters seemed lukewarm in their support for New Politics candidates; on the other, appeals made to win the support of blacks tended to alienate at least some white voters. Another important lesson that New Politics leaders drew from the 1972 experience was that they could expect little support from working-class voters. This sense of alienation from the working class was to play an important part in the future electoral strategies of New Politics groups.

Of all the lessons drawn from the 1972 debacle, the most significant was that the electoral arena, at least at the presidential level, was not the political battleground most congenial to the fortunes of the New Politics movement. Many activists concluded that the executive branch, which had been regarded as the commanding height of the American political terrain, might not in the immediate future be accessible to the forces they represented. This conclusion prompted New Politics groups to concentrate their efforts more heavily in other arenas of American politics, including Congress, the media, and the courts.

In these three arenas, New Politics groups were able to achieve considerable success through lobbying, public relations efforts, and legal action—tactics that were attractive, first, because they capitalized on the talents and resources most readily available to the movement's upper-middle-class adherents and, second, because they did not require the movement to seek alliances with other social forces. Even more significant than the immediate programmatic gains that stemmed from New Politics successes in Congress, the courts, and the national media, the movement found that from these new positions of strength it could lay siege to its enemies in the executive branch. Indeed, the movement fashioned a new "iron triangle" of congressional inquiry, media disclosure, and judicial process (later institutionalized in the form of the court-appointed special prosecutor, aimed at deposing or at least neutralizing one or more executive branch officials).

Nevertheless, the movement was not ready to abandon electoral politics. It sought, instead, to construct electoral alliances with other forces in the hope of obtaining at least a foothold in the executive branch. In 1976 this tactic was initially—albeit temporarily—successful.

1976: The Reconstitution of the New Deal Coalition

In 1976 the New Politics movement played a major role in an effort to reunite the coalition of forces that had made the Democratic party the dominant political force in the United States during the prewar and postwar years. The success of this strategy depended upon identifying a candidate who satisfied two criteria. First, the candidate could not be tied closely to any of the established and now mutually antagonistic party factions. Second, it was essential that the candidate have some appeal to traditionally Democratic voters, particularly southern whites and northern blue-collar workers, who had deserted the party in huge numbers in 1968 and 1972. A candidate with precisely these qualities emerged in the person of James Earl Carter. The very fact that Carter was an unknown commodity meant that he could be supported, albeit without great enthusiasm, by all factions of the Democratic party.

In the general election campaign, the media associated with the New Politics movement showed Carter in a far more favorable light than his opponent, Gerald R. Ford. Carter was portrayed, or was allowed to portray himself, as a nuclear engineer and successful small businessman, even though neither description was entirely accurate. Ford, on the other hand, was depicted as a genial bumbler, ostensibly unable to chew gum and walk simultaneously—this despite Ford's more extensive governmental experience. This media effort reached its peak in the reaction to the second debate between the two candidates. A rather inconsequential gaffe by Ford was seized upon by the media as conclusive evidence of his lack of fitness for the presidency. The furor surrounding what amounted to Ford's slip of the tongue on Soviet domination of Poland sealed his electoral fate.

Carter's chief virtue as a candidate, namely, that he had no firm political base, proved to be a severe handicap when he assumed office. Virtually every effort Carter made to build a political constituency by linking himself to one or more factions of the Democratic coalition angered the rival factions, which thought that they deserved preferential treatment from the new administration. Consequently, Carter found it impossible to build a legislative coalition capable of enacting his major proposals.

In the end, Carter actively courted environmental, conservation, feminist, and other New Politics groups by sponsoring many of the

13

programs they advocated. However, he was unable to translate these goals into federal policy. From the perspective of the New Politics movement, Carter's failure not only indicated that he was personally unworthy of its support, but also demonstrated the limits of the party unity strategy. If their participation in a winning electoral coalition could only produce an administration too weak to deliver much in the way of legislative and administrative payoff, then such electoral participation was not particularly worthwhile. This lesson set the stage for 1980.

The 1980 Interlude: A Political Boycott

In 1980 two of the forces that had cooperated to bring Carter into office in 1976 turned against him and one another. Organized labor sought to block Carter's renomination by supporting Edward Kennedy. Many New Politics activists had no interest in Carter but little love for Kennedy either. But with dim prospects for fielding a candidate with the potential to defeat both Kennedy and Carter, New Politics forces essentially boycotted the Democratic primary campaign, content to let Kennedy and Carter bloody one another. This boycott continued into the 1980 general election, with a curious difference, namely, "the Anderson difference." John Anderson was an obscure Republican representative from Illinois with little national reputation, political following, or known accomplishments. His independent presidential candidacy seemed to be another of those quixotic campaigns that are among the favorite topics of American humorists. But Anderson did have one special political attraction: he told audiences what they neither expected nor wanted to hear. In the pretelevision era Anderson's pleasant eccentricity might have received scant attention. But in the age of the electronic media, Anderson's "difference" made him news. Virtually overnight, he moved from obscurity to celebrity.

All this would have been merely another commentary on the behavior of the media in American politics, but for one fact. In 1980 many supporters of New Politics causes were disenchanted with Carter and the party unity coalition he nominally led—so disappointed, in fact, that they were not prepared to support the Democratic ticket even though the result would be to virtually guarantee a victory by Ronald Reagan. In fact, some felt, a Reagan victory might have the virtue of demonstrating to other Democrats that they could not hope to win without New Politics support. These adherents of the New Politics movement boycotted the 1980 election by throwing their votes to Anderson. The movement's rivals within the Democratic party learned the lesson. Ronald Reagan won the election.

1984: The Alliance of Antagonists

In 1984 Walter F. Mondale sought to build an alliance between the two central forces that are nominally linked with the Democratic party—labor and the New Politics movement. The electoral alliance of 1976 between labor and the New Politics had been unsatisfactory to both and was short-lived. However, the alliance that Mondale sought to construct was to be different. Labor and the New Politics movement had united behind Carter because he was tied to neither; they deserted Carter because he could serve neither. Mondale, on the other hand, was clearly and closely linked with organized labor. But he ardently courted the support of New Politics groups, promising to press the causes of feminism, environmentalism, and demilitarization if elected. From the perspective of New Politics groups, Mondale's close ties with organized labor, though disconcerting, could be advantageous if he could be trusted to keep his promises. Because of his firm labor support, Mondale potentially could succeed as president where Carter had failed and could secure the enactment and implementation of New Politics programs.

In 1983 Mondale actively sought public endorsements from both labor and New Politics groups to demonstrate publicly that he was allied with both. At the same time, he gave his stamp of approval to a concept that, while masquerading as an economic doctrine, was actually a political contract or treaty between organized labor and the New Politics movement. This concept was known as "industrial policy." Industrial policy has many variants, but Mondale's basic idea was that the federal government should take a greater hand in long-range economic planning and should, in particular, supervise what was said to be the inevitable transformation of the American industrial base from obsolescent smokestack industries to the high-technology, energy-efficient, and nonpolluting industries that purportedly were the wave of the future. Government intervention was said to be essential to this transformation in order to minimize the human and social costs that otherwise would accompany massive changes in employment and investment.

Whatever its economic merits, industrial policy can be viewed politically as a compact between the New Politics movement, which would gain influence over the allocation of capital, and organized labor, whose members are promised protection against lost jobs and income during the period of transition as well as job retraining for the high-technology industries of the future. These promises were accompanied by the discovery of a pressing need to repair the American "infrastructure" of roads, bridges, railways, and the like—the 1984 equivalent of New Deal public works programs for displaced workers. The validity of industrial policy as an economic doctrine is questionable. The new jobs that may become available to members of the working class in high-technology industries are more likely to be found in Singapore than Detroit. As a political doctrine, however, industrial policy was more promising, at least at the outset of the 1984 campaign. With the support of organized labor and the endorsement of a number of important New Politics groups, including the National Organization for Women (NOW), Mondale appeared to have a firm grasp upon the Democratic nomination even before the first caucus or primary. However, this appearance proved illusory.

Taken together, the candidates who entered the race for the 1984 Democratic nomination could be seen as representing the geological strata of the postwar Democratic party. The oldest stratum, representing the New Deal Democratic party, consisted of Sen. John Glenn, Sen. Ernest Hollings, and Gov. Reubin Askew—the first speaking for the northeastern industrial quadrant and the latter two for the white South. The next stratum included Sen. Alan Cranston and McGovern, representing the New Politics of antimilitarism that emerged in the late 1960s. Next in terms of geological sequence was Jesse Jackson, speaking for the forces of black protest. Next came Mondale, the personification of the labor-New Politics alliance that appeared to be the dominant theme of Democratic politics in 1984. Then came Gary Hart, purporting to speak for a new generation. If Mondale represented the Democratic party of the present and the others, the Democratic party of the past, Hart claimed to speak for the Democratic party of the future—a future in which the party would be substantially reshaped. Although Hart was unsuccessful in 1984, it is important to examine the character of the coalition he sought to build, because Hart's efforts indicate the likely future direction of the New Politics movement.

Hart was first and foremost a New Politics candidate. Among his campaign themes was the by now conventional New Politics wisdom concerning the merits of clean air and clean water. However, to these familiar themes Hart added "new ideas." The most significant of these were: (1) the need to streamline social services and defense programs; (2) a version of industrial policy that, unlike Mondale's, attached little importance to the costs that would be borne by blue-collar workers during the transition to high-technology industry; and (3) the urgent need to enhance the economic and political status of women through methods such as the substitution of comparable worth for market mechanisms of wage determination. Conspicuously absent from Hart's new ideas were any having to do with the working class or blacks.

Hart's campaign was significant not so much for the intrinsic merit of his ideas as for the shape of the political coalitions to which they pointed. In essence, Hart's new ideas amounted to a New Politics campaign that neglected both blacks and the working class in favor of women and the middle class. Hart's new ideas on social services and defense were important to the middle-class tax rebels who had helped bring Reagan to power in 1980. To advocate streamlining social services is basically a polite way to advocate welfare cuts. Similarly, to call for a more efficient defense program is to call for more economical ways of killing the enemy. Hart's ideas on feminism were designed to gain the support of millions of female voters whose hostility to Reagan, it was believed, had already resulted in the "gender gap." According to proponents of this notion, women had become increasingly dissatisfied with Republican and especially Reaganite policies and positions on domestic and international affairs. By exploiting this dissatisfaction, the theory goes, the Democratic party again could make itself the nation's majority party. Moreover, the group within the Democratic party that was best able to take advantage of the gender gap and build a political alliance with women would become the party's dominant faction.

In point of fact, the theory of the gender gap so often put forth since 1980 included more than a little wishful thinking both by Democrats and by feminists anxious to portray themselves as a powerful force. The actual political gender gap that developed during the 1980 presidential election resulted less from women's disavowal of Reagan and love for the Democrats than from the fact that (while both men and women left the Democratic party in large numbers) more male Democrats deserted than female Democrats. Reagan, it should be noted, won more votes from women in 1980 than Carter: according to the *New York Times*/CBS News poll, Reagan captured 47 percent of the women's vote to Carter's 45 percent (7 percent went to Anderson); among white women Reagan won 52 percent to Carter's 39 percent.[14] Thus, the development of a political gender gap in 1980 actually represented a major shift away from the Democrats by white males: Carter won only 32 percent of the white male vote to Reagan's 59 percent. Nevertheless, orthodox Democratic doctrine prior to the 1984 election held that women's votes, presumed to be pouring across the gender gap, were the key to the party's electoral resurgence. By emphasizing the strength of his commitment to feminism, Hart sought to link himself to this new Democratic constituency.

Thus, with his politics of new ideas, Hart proposed to form a coalition substantially different from any previous Democratic alliance. It was to be a coalition of middle-class taxpayers, politically conscious women, and New Politics groups—in essence, a grand coalition of the middle class without significant black or working-class representation. In theory, at least, such a coalition may have posed a serious challenge to the

Reagan regime. However, this prospect was not tested in 1984 because Hart was unable to secure the Democratic nomination. Although at the outset Hart's challenge appeared to have little chance of success (Mondale had already secured promises of support from the New Politics groups that were the core of any potential Hart campaign), Hart's strong showings in Iowa and New Hampshire gave him the momentum (a magical property that the media confer upon candidates) of a serious contender. Very quickly, Mondale's carefully nurtured New Politics following began to desert him and to support Hart. New Politics activists helped Hart sweep the New England primaries.

Unfortunately, however, from the perspective of the Hart candidacy, the two groups he courted heavily—middle-class taxpayers and women — are far more important in the general elections than in the Democratic primaries. Middle-class taxpayers, in particular, already had deserted the Democratic party by the millions. The two groups he did not bother to court, on the other hand—blacks and workers—vote in large numbers in Democratic primaries. Thus, once outside the New Politics movement's New England stronghold, the Hart candidacy began to falter. Ultimately Mondale was able to secure the Democratic nomination. Once having done so, though, he moved to conciliate New Politics Democrats by designating a woman—Rep. Geraldine A. Ferraro of New York—as his vice presidential running mate and by making platform and rules concessions to New Politics forces. Indeed, Mondale was far more willing to make such concessions to New Politics groups than to the other major dissident group in the 1984 Democratic campaign, blacks. The reasons for this differential treatment of blacks and New Politics Democrats are simple. Major concessions to black voters can alienate important groups in the white electorate, a lesson of the 1972 election reinforced by the black-Jewish rift of 1984. In addition, despite threats by Jackson and other black leaders, the probability that blacks would refuse to support the Democratic ticket was far lower than the likelihood that New Politics voters would repeat their 1980 boycott of the general election if they were dissatisfied with the party's actions. The upper-middle-class adherents of the New Politics were better prepared than blacks to tolerate four more years of Reaganism if that were the price of compelling the Democratic party to heed their wishes.

Thus, after several false starts, the Democratic party entered the 1984 election led by a candidate who sought to unite its labor and New Politics wings. However, this alliance of antagonists was unable to defeat the powerful coalition of forces led by Reagan, a coalition to which we shall now turn.

Electoral Strategies: The Reconstituted Right

The second major coalition of forces to emerge from the wreckage of the New Deal order, the Reconstituted Right, also has sought to create a new political regime in the United States. This coalition eventually came to consist of a politically reunified American business community, including the defense industry; social and religious conservatives who were initially mobilized by George Wallace; and southern whites, northern blue-collar workers, and large segments of the suburban middle class. The formation of this coalition took place over a period of roughly 20 years and in two phases. The first of these, comprising the Nixon years, was the electoral era of the "silent majority." The second phase, coinciding with the ascendancy of Reagan, was the era of the fully Reconstituted Right.

1968 and 1972: The Silent Majority

In 1968 and 1972 Nixon assembled a coalition, as described by two observers at the time, of "the unyoung, the unpoor and the unblack." [15] The coalition, in other words, consisted of the various groups that were offended by or opposed to the policies that had become linked to the Democratic party. Two aspects of this Nixon coalition are notable. First, the coalition was not, at least not yet, united by philosophical or ideological principles, beyond opposition to the New Politics and the Democrats. Nixon aides aptly named this coalition the "silent majority." It was, in fact, silent on matters of philosophy, led by a politician whose world view and vision were decidedly pragmatic. In 1968 the Nixon coalition won a narrow victory over the fragmented Democrats. In 1972 the triumph of the New Politics forces within the Democratic party led to the exodus of millions more unyoung, unpoor, unblack, and unhappy Democratic voters and to a landslide victory for Nixon. Through these two elections, Nixon's majority continued to be silent. Indeed, the Nixon administration's policies in most domestic and international areas hardly diverged from those of his Democratic predecessors. In particular, social spending skyrocketed during Nixon's presidency. Nixon had constructed a successful electoral coalition but without uniting voters around any affirmative ideology or program.

The second noteworthy aspect of the Nixon coalition was the role of business. The American business community united for Nixon against McGovern in 1972, but it had not been unanimous in its enthusiasm for Nixon in 1968 nor would it be in its support for Ford in 1976. Nixon's actions in office, particularly in the area of trade policy, were less than popular with many sectors of American business. Internationally competitive segments of the business community, such as multinational corporations and the banking industry, which had been identified with the Democratic party since the New Deal regime, were not yet ready to abandon the Democrats completely during the Nixon era. Instead, businessmen in these sectors pursued a strategy of studied bipartisanship, symbolized by the formation of the Trilateral Commission, and bided their time.

By the time of the 1976 presidential election, the Nixon coalition was fragmented. Many of its members, chastened by the Watergate revelations, returned to the Democratic party they had abandoned in 1972. Other members of Nixon's silent majority deepened their silence by remaining home on election day. But despite the Republican defeat in 1976, Nixon's silent coalition continued to be an important element in American electoral politics. In 1980 it was remobilized, reinforced, and finally given a voice—a loud voice—by Reagan.

1980 and 1984: Reconstitution of the Right

In 1980 Reagan successfully sought to rebuild and expand the Nixon coalition. But rather than relying exclusively upon the common dislike for the groups and policies associated with the Democratic party upon which Nixon had based a coalition, Reagan presented a set of affirmative proposals designed to link the targeted forces to one another and to his presidential campaign. Thus, Reagan first promised middle-class suburbanites that he would trim social programs, cut taxes, and bring inflation under control—whatever the cost in blue-collar unemployment. Second, he told social and religious conservatives that he would support antiabortion and school prayer legislation. Third, Reagan pledged to white southerners and other opponents of the civil rights revolution an end to federal support for affirmative action, minority quotas, and other programs designed to aid blacks. Fourth, Reagan promised American business that he would relax the environmental rules and other forms of regulation that New Politics groups had succeeded in enacting during the 1970s. Finally, he offered the defense industry greatly increased rates of military spending—this under the rubric of the need to respond to a growing Soviet threat.

Each of Reagan's themes—tax cuts, social service reductions, expanded military spending, relaxation of business regulations, and so on—was designed to establish a link between him and a major national political force. The main problem faced by the Reaganites was that these themes, whatever the case for them individually, seemed contradictory. The most important of these apparent contradictions was between Reagan's promise of substantial tax relief for the middle class and his pledge to increase defense spending dramatically. This was not merely a problem of contradictory campaign promises, but reflected a potentially serious conflict within the coalition that Reagan sought to assemble. At the elite level of the nascent Reagan coalition, the defense industry wanted major spending increases. On the other hand, the millions of middle-class suburbanites whom Reagan sought to woo demanded tax relief. To construct a new conservative coalition, Reagan somehow needed to satisfy both.

At this juncture, the Reaganites presented a political theory that, like the Democrats' industrial policy, masqueraded as economic doctrine. The theory was called "supply-side economics." The economic details of the theory need not concern us; indeed, most economists ridiculed it. However, like industrial policy, supply-side economics was far more important as a political theory than as an economic theory. Supply-side theory purported to show that it was possible to cut taxes and increase spending simultaneously. Thus, in promising to introduce supply-side economics, Reagan was asserting that he could and would pursue policies that worked to the advantage of the two major groups in his proposed constituency whose interests had seemed most likely to clash.

Resolution of this problem, coupled with Reagan's promise to eviscerate Democratic regulatory programs, set the stage for the political reunification of American business under Republican auspices. This reunification was a critical element in the 1980 election as well a significant portent for the future of American politics. The enthusiastic support of business gave the Republican party access to virtually unlimited campaign funds—sometimes laundered through conservative foundations and organizations—for national, state, and even local races. These campaign funds, in turn, gave the Republicans a decisive edge in the use of the expensive new political technologies—computers, phone banks, polls, and television advertising—that are the keys to political success in the 1980s. The Republicans' mastery of the new political technology not only played an important role in 1980 but later proved crucial in preventing a Republican disaster in the 1982 midterm elections. The support of the reunited American business community for the Republicans promises to be a major influence in American electoral politics for years to come.

Under Reagan's leadership, the Republican party scored a decisive victory in the 1980 presidential election, won control of the Senate, and substantially increased its representation in the House. Once in office Reagan sought to fashion a legislative program that would implement his campaign promises and solidify his relationship with the various groups that had helped bring him to power. Thus, in the first half of his term, he moved to cut taxes, reduce inflation, slash social programs, increase defense outlays, reduce federal regulatory interference with business, and diminish federal efforts on behalf of blacks and other minorities. In addition, Reagan gave his support—although more in word than deed—to social and religious conservatives who were determined to ban abortion and return prayer to the public schools.

Reagan's legislative efforts encountered a number of obstacles. First, efforts to reduce spending on domestic social problems were hampered by the effective defense of these programs by powerful political constituencies. This was especially true in the case of Social Security, precisely the area where spending cuts might have yielded substantial budgetary savings. Second, Reagan's efforts to reduce regulatory interference with business, especially by placing limits on the federal agencies charged with environmental protection, encountered stiff resistance from New Politics activists. These forces responded to Reagan's attacks on "their" agencies by mobilizing the iron triangle of congressional investigation, media disclosure, and judicial process that had become such a potent political weapon during the past decade. This counterattack by New Politics forces not only brought about the ouster of several Reagan appointees—most notably, the head of the Environmental Protection Agency and the secretary of the interior—but succeeded in limiting the effectiveness of Reagan's offensive against federal regulation of business. The third problem that Reagan faced was the budget deficits and the resultant decline of business confidence in his administration. The supply-side concept that Reagan had championed as a candidate was a brilliant political theory, but when he actually increased defense spending and simultaneously cut taxes, while failing to realize substantial budgetary savings in domestic social spending, the result was an enormous federal deficit, high interest rates, and considerable unease in business and financial circles.

Despite deficits and other problems, Reagan was able to fulfill many of his campaign promises during his first term in office. The upper and upper-middle classes realized substantial savings from Reagan's tax reduction programs.[16] Inflation was brought under control, although the cost of doing so was the deepest recession since the 1930s. Arms outlays increased dramatically. The federal regulatory climate became somewhat more favorable to business. The rate of increase in domestic social spending diminished. The federal government's efforts on behalf of minorities and the poor were reduced. Finally, legislation was enacted to promote school prayer, various federal agencies reduced their backing for abortion, and Reagan personally continued to offer moral support and encouragement to the various groups of social and religious conservatives who had championed his candidacy.

As a result of this record, Reagan's support among the forces that had initially elected him to office increased. In the 1984 election, Reagan's share of the vote rose within all of the major segments of the electorate that had backed him in 1980. According to the *New York Times*/CBS News exit poll, Reagan's support between the 1980 and 1984 elections increased among southern whites by 11 points to 72 percent; among Catholics by 6 points to 55 percent; among white born-again Christians by 17 points to 80 percent; among middle- and upper-income voters by 7 points to 65 percent; and among the elderly—many of whom live on fixed incomes and thus are extremely sensitive to inflation—by 9 points to 63 percent. (Moreover, the gender gap of 1980 was largely closed in 1984: Reagan won 57 percent of the women's vote to Mondale's 42 percent, and among white women Reagan was supported by 64 percent to Mondale's 36 percent—a stunning 28-point Republican advantage.)[17] These increases enabled Reagan to win 59 percent of the popular vote in 1984, and to carry 49 states. This was an impressive electoral triumph, but potentially more important than Reagan's margin of victory was his ability to consolidate and reinforce an alliance among traditionally Republican and traditionally Democratic voting blocs. If this coalition were to endure, it would mark the end of one era in American politics and the beginning of a new one—that is, a critical realignment.

A Critical Realignment?

The question left open by the 1984 election returns is whether Reagan's success merely reflects his personal popularity or portends a permanent realignment of political forces. The former view is supported by the Republicans' failure to increase their strength in Congress significantly in 1984; the latter is buttressed by Reagan's winning of 60 percent support among first-time voters in this election and by a substantial increase, particularly evident among young voters, in the percentage of the electorate claiming a Republican-party identification. In any event, the durability of the Reagan alignment depends less upon the votes cast in 1984 than upon the president's success during his second term in institutionalizing his electoral coalition.

In America's last successful episode of political realignment, Franklin Roosevelt institutionalized his coalition by enacting a set of policies that gave his supporters an enduring stake in the New Deal regime. In this way, Roosevelt turned the combination of his extraordinary personal popularity and voter distress over the economic legacy of his predecessor into political links that endured for a generation after his death. Several policies enacted or supported by the Reagan administration may institutionalize the coalition of the Reconstituted Right in a similar way. For example, the indexing of federal income tax rates to inflation has turned the 1981 Reagan tax cut into an entitlement program for the middle and upper classes; to defend their entitlements these voters will have an incentive to support the Republican party in years to come. Similarly, the administration's proposed tuition tax credits for the parents of parochial and private school pupils could provide millions of Catholics and evangelical Protestants—and perhaps millions of other middle-class voters as well—with a lasting stake in the regime that enacted and defends such a program. Another example is the Reagan administration's proposed "Star Wars" antimissile program. Despite its problematic military value, the Star Wars project could be quite worthwhile politically; for, were this trillion-dollar, decade-long effort to be undertaken, it would enable Reagan to extend and institutionalize the political linkages between the Republican party and firms throughout American industry. If through these and similar programs Reagan is able to follow Roosevelt's example, then the elections of 1980 and 1984, like those of 1932 and 1936, may come to be seen as a critical turning point in American political history.

It should be noted, however, that a realignment in the electoral arena would not necessarily mean the total victory of the Reconstituted Right over the New Politics. Even if they continue to be denied control of the presidency, these forces are hardly without influence in American politics. New Politics activists have demonstrated time and again that their power in Congress, the federal courts, and the media is sufficient to thwart their opponents' programs, secure favorable treatment for themselves, and initiate damaging attacks upon the president and his subordinates. Thus, the existing conflict between the forces of the New Politics and the Reconstituted Right may become less a clash *within* the national electoral arena than a conflict over just how decisive the electoral arena is to be.

Notes

1. Thomas Ferguson, "From Normalcy to New Deal: Industrial Structure, Party Competition, and American Public Policy in the Great Depression," *International Organization* 38 (Winter 1984): 42-94.
2. Peter Gourevitch, *The Changing International Division of Labor: The Politics of Policy Response* (Ithaca, N.Y.: Cornell University Press, forthcoming), Chapter 3.
3. Theodore J. Lowi, *The End of Liberalism*, 2d ed. (New York: W. W. Norton, 1979), Chapter 3.

4. Karen Orren, "Union Politics and Postwar Liberalism, 1946-1979." Unpublished paper, Department of Political Science, University of California, Los Angeles.
5. Frances Fox Piven and Richard Cloward, *Poor People's Movements* (New York: Vintage Books, 1979), Chapter 4.
6. To be sure, northern liberals found southern racial practices morally abhorrent, and for this reason they had supported antilynching legislation in Congress in the 1930s. But they were prepared to risk shattering the Democratic coalition with a crusade against segregation only when additional considerations led them in this direction. For an excellent analysis of these issues, see C. Vann Woodward, *The Strange Career of Jim Crow* (New York: Oxford University Press, 1974).
7. Martin Shefter, "Party, Bureaucracy, and Political Change in the United States," in *Political Parties: Development and Decay*, ed. Louis Maisel and Joseph Cooper, Sage Electoral Studies Yearbook 4 (Beverly Hills: Sage Publications, 1978), 243-254.
8. Franz Schurmann, *The Logic of World Power* (New York: Pantheon Books, 1974), 127.
9. Immanuel Wallerstein, "Friends as Foes," *Foreign Policy* 40 (Fall 1980): 119-131.
10. David Vogel, "The Power of Business in America: A Reappraisal," *British Journal of Political Science* 13 (January 1983): 19-44.
11. Nelson Polsby, *Consequences of Party Reform* (New York: Oxford University Press, 1983).
12. David Vogel, "The Public Interest Movement and the American Reform Tradition," *Political Science Quarterly* 95 (Winter 1980-1981): 607-627.
13. Walter Dean Burnham, *The Current Crisis in American Politics* (New York: Oxford University Press, 1982), Chapter 9.
14. *New York Times*, November 8, 1984, A19.
15. Richard Scammon and Ben Wattenberg, *The Real Majority* (New York: Coward-McCann, 1970).
16. John Palmer and Isabel Sawhill, eds., *The Reagan Experiment* (Washington, D.C.: Urban Institute, 1982).
17. *New York Times*, November 8, 1984, A19. Other polls showed a larger gender gap, but all agreed that Reagan carried the women's vote by a substantial margin.

2. THE NOMINATION PROCESS: VICISSITUDES OF CANDIDATE SELECTION

Gary R. Orren

"Elect who you will to office," said Boss Tweed, "just let me pick the candidates." Here Tweed put his finger on an essential truth of American politics: selecting the candidates who will appear on the November ballot is at least as important as choosing between them. Indeed, some maintain that the nomination is the most critical stage of presidential selection, since it is then that the major screening of candidates takes place.[1] Nearly 90 million people meet the Constitution's age, residency, and citizenship requirements for the presidency, yet a mere handful seek the nomination of one of the two major parties, and only two are nominated.

Although the nomination process is also important abroad, only in the United States is the public given such a strong voice in the selection of candidates. The citizens of other democracies may have the final say over which party will rule, but the selection of candidates for chief executive generally is viewed as an internal party decision. In Great Britain, for example, members of Parliament select their parties' candidates for prime minister. Other European countries follow a similar practice.[2]

This distinctive aspect of American presidential politics has received close scrutiny from scholars, political pundits, and politicians alike. Especially in recent years, dissatisfaction with the products of the process—the major party nominees—has directed the attention of would-be reformers to the ad hoc nature of the existing procedures and has inspired many proposals for change. No doubt the events of 1984 will prove no exception; the Democratic party's nomination race included all the bolts from the blue, twists of fate, and rolls of the dice that typify candidate selection in the United States.

A Season of Surprises

An element of unpredictability in the 1984 Democratic race was evident from the first primary. On the eve of the February 28 balloting in

New Hampshire, the media were poised to coronate Walter F. Mondale as the inevitable Democratic nominee. And no wonder: the former vice president had racked up the most impressive list of preprimary endorsements from interest groups and party leaders since Lyndon B. Johnson in 1964 (including an unprecedented declaration of support from the AFL-CIO), he had collected more campaign contributions than any of his opponents, and he held a commanding lead in all the national polls. One savvy political analyst concluded that "for once, conventional wisdom seems correct. This is a two-man race [Mondale versus Glenn] and Mondale is ahead," indeed, he ventured, "far ahead." [3] The conventional wisdom was summed up by the *New York Times*. On the morning of the New Hampshire primary a front page article announced that "with Senator John Glenn continuing to fade and no new challenger emerging strongly, Walter F. Mondale now holds the most commanding lead ever recorded this early in a presidential nomination campaign by a nonincumbent." [4]

In that day's voting, Sen. Gary Hart of Colorado upset Mondale 37 percent to 28 percent. For the next few weeks Mondale's campaign teetered on the brink of disaster, and Hart rose to front-runner status from the rear of the pack, a pack that included, in addition to Glenn, Sen. Ernest Hollings of South Carolina, former Florida governor Reubin Askew, California senator Alan Cranston, the Reverend Jesse Jackson, and former senator George McGovern. In short order the pundits began preparing obituaries for the Mondale campaign. After a string of losses to Hart in New England and the South, Mondale's candidacy seemed to be doomed. But he recovered, surprising by his success almost as many people as he had with his early losses.

Other elements of the race were equally unanticipated, including a strong showing by the first serious black candidate for president, Jackson, and the eventual selection of the first woman as a major party's vice-presidential nominee, Rep. Geraldine A. Ferraro of New York. Perhaps the earliest surprise of the 1984 nomination season had come in December 1982, when Sen. Edward M. Kennedy withdrew from the race. After his impassioned speech at the 1980 Democratic convention and his active role in the deliberations of the party's Hunt Commission, which had rewritten the rules for the 1984 caucuses and primaries, he had been widely considered a leading contender for the nomination.

The Constancy of Unpredictability

The surprises of 1984 were merely the most recent installment of a long and continuing story. Unpredictability has become the hallmark of the nomination process. Although the modern campaign arsenal—polls, targeting, computers, direct mail, and so on—has extended our prophetic powers, the future in a nomination contest still can be perceived only dimly.

Consider the last three Democratic contests. In 1972 the early favorites were former vice president Hubert Humphrey and Sen. Edmund Muskie. Looking back four years to Humphrey's 1968 success against Sen. Eugene McCarthy, most experts predicted that the party would nominate a centrist candidate. But it was McGovern, favored by only 3 percent of rank-and-file Democrats in a January poll and running a blatantly ideological campaign, who carried the day. After the "lesson" of 1972, the conventional wisdom suggested that in 1976 ideological candidates who could rally fellow activists to participate in the primaries and caucuses would enjoy an edge. Yet a virtual unknown, former Georgia governor Jimmy Carter, built a coalition of diverse interests around a nonideological theme ("Trust me") and was victorious. In 1980 no one was surprised when Edward Kennedy challenged President Carter's bid for renomination. What was surprising was that after trailing Kennedy by more than 2 to 1 in the polls, Carter suddenly rebounded to win the nomination.

One kind of surprise has become so prevalent as to be almost predictable: the strength of "outsider" candidates—mavericks, insurgents, relatively weak partisans, even newcomers to the party. In the eight presidential elections prior to 1984 the party establishment candidate of the out party—the party that does not control the White House—won the nomination only twice.[5] In 1952 Dwight D. Eisenhower successfully challenged "Mr. Republican," Sen. Robert Taft; in 1960 a young upstart senator, John F. Kennedy, defeated such Democratic luminaries as Senate majority leader Lyndon Johnson, Sen. Stuart Symington, former Illinois governor Adlai Stevenson, and then-senator Humphrey; in 1964 Sen. Barry Goldwater won the nomination against more orthodox Republicans like Gov. Nelson Rockefeller, Gov. William Scranton, and Ambassador Henry Cabot Lodge; in 1972 McGovern triumphed over Sen. Henry Jackson, Muskie, and Humphrey; four years later Carter beat a field of Democratic stalwarts, including Jackson, Rep. Morris Udall, and Sen. Birch Bayh; and former governor Ronald Reagan won the 1980 Republican contest against Ambassador George Bush, Sen. Robert Dole, and Sen. Howard Baker. The only two times the out party turned to the candidate backed by the party establishment were in 1956, when the Democrats nominated Stevenson, and in 1968, when the Republicans selected former vice president Richard Nixon.

Outsider candidates of the party that controls the White House (the in party) naturally have not fared as well because incumbency exerts a strong unifying influence. Still, they sometimes have been strong contenders: Sen. Estes Kefauver against Stevenson in 1952, McCarthy against Humphrey in 1968, and Reagan against President Gerald R. Ford in 1976.

In 1984 Hart and Jackson were the latest in a long line of outsider candidates to exploit two age-old political sentiments that have grown increasingly potent among voters: suspicion of established politicians and traditional party ways, and fascination with new faces and antiestablishment ideas. In light of recent history, the real surprise of 1984 was not that Hart came close to defeating Mondale but that Mondale, the insider, was able to make a comeback.

The Sources of Surprise

How can we explain why surprise—the confounding of expert predictions—has dominated the nominating contests of 1984 and previous elections? The answer lies beyond the events of any particular year. It lies instead in the analytical distinction between two types of influences on electoral outcomes: short-term and long-term forces.[6]

General elections between the Republican and Democratic nominees for president are principally arenas for the expression of long-term forces, influences that were shaped before and extend beyond the immediate campaign: the distribution of party loyalties among voters, their underlying interests and concerns, their general feelings of well-being or dissatisfaction, degrees of political interest or apathy, and so on. To be sure, short-term forces—the candidates' personalities, their campaign strategies, their oratorical triumphs and verbal blunders, the impressions they convey over the airwaves—often are important. And weakening party ties among voters, along with the replacement of eroding party machines by ad hoc candidate organizations and electronic media, have surely accentuated the importance of short-term forces. However, the November balloting typically hinges on longer-standing factors. Thus, the 1984 general election was decided mostly by things such as gradual shifts in partisan alignment that have been under way since 1968 and the public's retrospective appraisal of the incumbent president's performance in comparison with that of other administrations. The two candidates' personalities, their telegenic qualities, and their campaign virtuosity or ineptitude were less important.[7]

Because they are dominated by long-term forces, general elections usually offer few surprises. The surprises that did occur in 1984—the Mondale organization functioned less smoothly than expected, the Ferraro selection turned out to be less consequential than many imagined, and Reagan was a less effective debater than his reputation predicted—were minor tremors that hardly registered on the otherwise steady political seismograph. The Gallup poll recorded the relative constancy of public support for Reagan and Mondale. From June through November, Reagan's margin over Mondale varied only a little: 19 percent, 14 percent, 12 percent (after the Democratic convention), 11 percent, 15 percent, 18 percent, 17 percent, 20 percent, 17 percent, and 18 percent.[8]

In contrast, the nomination process is dominated by volatile short-term forces. The most powerful long-term force, party allegiance, is by definition less relevant—these are *intra*party contests. In further contrast to the general election, the length of the nomination process is 18 months or longer, not 2 months, and instead of one national election on a single day there are more than 50 primaries or caucuses held on many days. All of this magnifies the unpredictable and invites surprises, so much so that the authors of a recent book on the nomination process considered giving it the title *Random Selection*.[9]

Short-Term Forces and the Nomination Process

If we are to understand the presidential nomination process, then, we must turn the spotlight to the short-term forces that dominate it. Four stand out as most important: delegate selection rules, money, media coverage, and candidate strategy. As we shall see, many of the political and social changes of the last 30 years or so (some deliberate, some beyond anyone's immediate control) have heightened the importance of these short-term forces in the selection of party nominees. Indeed, each of them, as our analysis will demonstrate, plays a more important role in the nomination process than in the general election.

Delegate Selection Rules

The Constitution spells out in meticulous detail the rules for conducting general elections for president. To be sure, these rules hold strategic implications for the candidates—for example, the electoral college method of apportioning and counting the votes makes the large states crucial battlegrounds. But the same strategic implications apply to each candidate, and, because the electoral college procedure has escaped amendment, they remain constant from election to election.[10] Moreover, the rules of the electoral college have had little direct influence on the final election outcome. With three exceptions, the most recent in 1888, the electoral college winner has been the popular vote winner as well.

In contrast, the rules for choosing the parties' nominees are an "orphan of constitutionalism," their invention left almost entirely to the political parties and state legislatures.[11] Unlike general election procedures, nomination rules have undergone frequent and radical revision, which has profoundly affected the electoral fortunes of different candidates for nomination.

Historically, the presidential nomination process has evolved through four basic stages: the congressional caucus, party conventions, a mixed system of conventions and primaries, and the current primary-centered system.[12] In the first three decades after the signing of the Constitution, the candidates were nominated by partisan caucuses of congressmen. In the 1830s, after a brief period when candidates were selected by state legislatures or local conventions, the parties instituted a new system: national party conventions. The selection of delegates to these conventions was dominated by state party leaders; the conventions themselves served as forums for these leaders to forge agreements and rally the various state organizations behind a single candidate. Around the turn of the century the Progressive movement introduced another innovation—delegate selection by means of primary elections—in an effort to break the power of the party bosses.[13] By 1916 both parties were selecting more than half of their delegates in primaries. But soon thereafter, the importance of primaries declined until the parties were swept by a new wave of reforms after 1968. As late as 1960, Hubert Humphrey could say, "You have to be crazy to go into a primary." In 1968 he won the Democratic nomination without contesting a single primary.[14]

Since 1968 the rules governing presidential nominations have been changed so dramatically as to constitute a fourth selection period.[15] Delegate selection reforms that were adopted by the Democrats between 1968 and 1980 had a twofold purpose: to broaden the base of public participation in candidate selection, thereby making the process more representative of rank-and-file views, and to render public officials more directly accountable to the voters. The reforms substituted proportional representation in caucuses and primaries for winner-take-all representation, bound delegates to vote at the convention for the candidates they were elected to support, phased out primaries that were open to voters registered in the opposition party, and adopted affirmative action requirements for minorities and women.

Change has been ongoing since this latest round of reforms began after 1968. For example, despite the requirement that presidential candidates be represented in state delegations to the national convention in proportion to their popular vote, new rules that were adopted after the 1972 election permitted winner-take-all results through "loophole" primaries in which a candidate who won a plurality of votes in a congressional district could claim all the district's delegates. This meant that a candidate with broad appeal could sweep all the delegates in a state despite relatively strong performances by other contenders. After 1976 the

Democrats banned these loophole primaries and required that delegates list their candidate preference on the ballot and run as part of a slate rather than as individuals. Candidates who received more than a specified percentage of the vote (which ranged from 15 to 25 percent in 1980) were allocated at least some of the delegates on their slate.[16]

Between 1968 and 1980 the number of primaries and the proportion of convention delegates selected in them almost doubled (*Figure 2.1*). Although the reformers intended no such increase, it seems fairly clear that the rules changes, along with strong encouragement from the media and some local pressures, touched off the explosion.[17] What is even more clear is that primaries have become the heart of the selection process, thereby transforming nomination politics.

Several studies have demonstrated the influence of specific delegate selection rules on recent nominations by showing that different sets of rules would have altered the candidates' strategic situations at important junctures of the process.[18] But the new rules have affected far more than the fates of individual candidates. By stripping state and local party leaders of their control over the nomination process, they weakened the traditional party apparatus. By enhancing the power of citizens and minimizing that of party leaders, the reforms also have enhanced the media's role as a critical link between candidates and voters.[19]

In 1980, dissatisfied with the products of 12 years of reform, the Democrats established their fourth rules commission since 1968, under the leadership of North Carolina governor James B. Hunt, Jr. The Hunt Commission pursued two main goals, the first made public, the other, for the most part, kept private: to strengthen the party and to diminish the chances of outsider candidates.[20] As in all previous efforts at rules reform, short-term political interests significantly shaped the commission's work. Because Mondale and Kennedy, the party's leading contenders for the 1984 nomination, were involved intimately in the deliberations, the coming election was never far from the minds of the rulemakers.

The new rules aimed to fortify the party in several ways. The convention was expanded to include 568 "superdelegates" (14 percent of the convention total), who were permitted to attend and vote without declaring their presidential preferences in advance. This group included up to 191 senators and representatives (who were to be selected by the Democratic congressional caucuses), state party chairs, governors, mayors, and other elected officials. It was argued that the superdelegates would inject professional judgment, peer review, flexibility, and deliberation into the convention. Also, it was thought that the process of seeking the support of congressional leaders would prove valuable in governing if the party's nominee won in November. Finally, it was presumed that the super-

Figure 2.1 Number of Democratic Presidential Primaries and Proportion of Democratic Convention Delegates Chosen in Primaries, 1912–1984

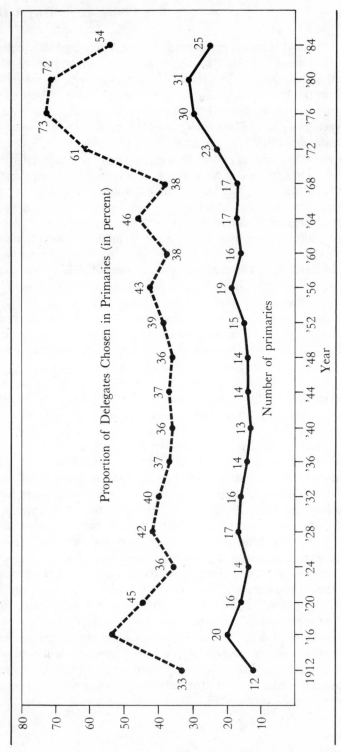

Note: Includes only primaries that choose or allocate delegates. Excludes "beauty contest," or nonbinding, primaries. The District of Columbia and Puerto Rico are counted as states. The Republican party trend has followed the Democratic trend very closely.

Source: Stephen J. Wayne, *The Road to the White House* (New York: St. Martin's Press, 1984), 12; David Price, *Bringing Back the Parties* (Washington: CQ Press, 1984), 208-209; *Congressional Quarterly Weekly Report*, July 5, 1980, 1873; *Congressional Quarterly Weekly Report*, June 16, 1984, 1443.

delegates would have stronger ties with established candidates than with outsiders. In a further effort to increase maneuvering room at the convention, all delegates were given the right to vote as they pleased, despite their initial pledges. In all, the hope was that the nomination would not be sewn up after just the first few, smaller primaries and caucuses and that the importance of the later contests would grow.

The new rules postponed the beginning of the delegate selection season by about five weeks and set the February 20 Iowa caucuses and the New Hampshire primary a week apart (instead of five weeks, as in 1980). It was thought that the compressed period would favor more established candidates, who could command greater campaign resources at the outset and therefore finance organizations and media advertising in several states at once. Several modifications in the system of proportional representation also were made to give well-known candidates a greater edge over outsiders. Each state was permitted to adopt a winner-take-more system, in which a bonus delegate would be awarded to the winning candidate in each congressional district. In 1984 six caucus and four primary states chose this plan, as did Puerto Rico. Moreover, loophole primaries were revived, and the seven states that selected this option included five of the largest: California, Florida, Illinois, New Jersey, and Pennsylvania. Finally, the party raised the minimum percentage of the vote that a candidate needed in order to win delegates from 15 percent to 20 percent in most states and districts.

After much discussion the Hunt Commission decided not to interfere with the practice of "front loading," in which states schedule their primaries as early as possible to prevent them from becoming irrelevant to the final outcome. Some reformers hoped that the reintroduction of loophole primaries would permit larger states to gain an important role without having to move to the front of the calendar. Nonetheless, several large states that traditionally had held their primaries late in the year moved up their dates to recover the influence they had lost. The most important of these were New York, Pennsylvania, Michigan, and Ohio.

Another vexing problem that the Hunt Commission ducked was the growing number of primaries. Even so, between 1980 and 1984, six states voluntarily switched from a primary to a caucus system, and no state moved the other way. The proportion of Democratic delegates chosen in caucuses grew from 28 percent in 1980 to 32 percent four years later; the new superdelegates accounted for another 14 percent. Consequently, only 54 percent of the 1984 Democratic delegates were chosen in primaries, a substantial decline from 1980 and the first such decline since 1968 (*Figure 2.1*).

In terms of influencing the fortunes of the individual candidates, rules changes probably played a larger role in 1984 than before. For a time it appeared that the famous "law of unintended consequences" had returned to haunt the rulemakers. When Hart's electoral prospects suddenly soared after the New Hampshire primary, it looked as if the shortened and front-loaded delegate selection schedule would help, rather than hinder, the outsider candidate. The bunching of early contests could make it difficult for other candidates to recoup and halt Hart's momentum (or "prairie fire," in the favored image of 1984). One adviser to the Hunt Commission had outlined a possible dark horse scenario two years before the primaries:

> A dark horse, regionally based, "outsider" candidate with time to spare will surprise the experts and do well in Iowa, win in New Hampshire just a week later, carry his momentum into the caucus and big primary states in March and April, and, combined with a solid base of delegates from his own region, lock up the nomination before the convention. Sound familiar?[21]

But the "familiar" did not happen in 1984. (Complete primary and caucus results are reported in Tables 2.1 and 2.2.) Mondale, the party establishment candidate, found salvation in the new delegate selection rules. Nearly all of the Hunt Commission reforms worked to Mondale's benefit, and their cumulative effect was crucial to his victory. Mondale's popular-vote lead over Hart in the primaries was less than 3 percentage points—less than 430,000 votes out of nearly 18 million. In fact, Hart actually won more primaries (16 to 11) and more caucuses (13 to 10) than Mondale. Yet Mondale was able to parlay his 39 percent of the primary vote into 49 percent of the pledged delegates chosen in the primaries (*Table 2.3*).[22] Hart's share of the delegates was roughly equal to his share of the popular vote in the primaries, 36 percent. And Jackson, who earned 19 percent of the primary vote, got only 10 percent of the delegates selected through primaries.

Mondale built his wide delegate lead by taking advantage of the new winner-take-more and winner-take-all primary rules, the increased number of caucuses, and the new group of superdelegates. Mondale did well in primaries whose rules transformed a narrow popular-vote victory into a huge delegate harvest (*Table 2.4*). He won six of the seven loop-hole primaries and four of the five winner-take-more primaries. His 40 percent of the popular vote in these primaries yielded 53 percent of the delegates. In Pennsylvania, Mondale's 45 percent of the vote translated into a full 80 percent of the pledged delegates. The Mondale victory in New Jersey produced a delegate bonanza: 45 percent of the popular vote won him 102 of the 107 delegates. Hart, by and large, won

Table 2.1 1984 Democratic Primary Results

State	Estimated Turnout	Hart	Jackson	Mondale	Others	Uncommitted
N.H. (2/28)	101,131	37.3%*	5.3%	27.9%	29.5%	
Vt. (3/6)[a]	74,059	70.0*	7.8	20.0	2.2	
Ala. (3/13)	428,283	20.7	19.6	34.6*	24.1	1.0%
Fla. (3/13)	1,160,713	40.0*	12.4	32.1	15.5	
Ga. (3/13)	684,541	27.3	21.0	30.5*	20.8	0.4
Mass. (3/13)	630,962	39.0*	5.0	25.5	29.7	0.8
R.I. (3/13)	44,511	45.0*	8.7	34.4	10.9	1.0
Puerto Rico (3/18)	143,039	0.6		99.1*	0.3	
Ill. (3/20)	1,659,425	35.2	21.0	40.5*	3.3	
Conn. (3/27)	220,842	52.6*	12.0	29.1	5.4	0.9
N.Y. (4/3)	1,387,950	27.4	25.6	44.8*	2.2	
Wis. (4/3)[a]	635,768	44.4*	9.9	41.1	3.5	1.1
Pa. (4/10)	1,656,294	33.3	16.0	45.1*	5.6	
D.C. (5/1)	102,731	7.1	67.3*	25.6		
Tenn. (5/1)	322,063	29.1	25.3	41.0*	2.5	2.1
La. (5/5)	318,810	25.0	42.9*	22.3	3.7	6.1
Ind. (5/8)	716,955	41.8*	13.7	40.9	3.6	
Md. (5/8)	506,886	24.3	25.5	42.5*	4.6	3.1
N.C. (5/8)	960,857	30.2	25.4	35.6*	4.2	4.6
Ohio (5/8)	1,444,797	42.1*	16.4	40.3	1.2	
Neb. (5/15)	148,855	58.2*	9.1	26.6	3.0	3.1
Ore. (5/15)	397,892	58.7*	9.3	27.7	4.3	
Idaho (5/22)[a]	54,722	58.0*	5.7	30.1	2.2	4.0
Calif. (6/5)[b]	2,724,248	41.2*	19.6	37.4	1.8	
N.J. (6/5)	676,561	29.7	23.6	45.2*	1.5	
N.M. (6/5)	187,403	46.8*	11.8	36.1	4.5	0.8
S.D. (6/5)	52,561	50.7*	5.2	39.0	2.6	2.5
W.Va. (6/5)	369,245	37.3	6.7	53.8*	2.2	
N.D. (6/12)[a]	33,555	85.2*		2.8	12.0	
National Primary Total	17,845,659	36.2	18.3	38.6	6.2	0.7

[a] Nonbinding primary, delegates selected by caucus process.

[b] No Democratic preference vote was held. The vote for each candidate's most popular delegate in each congressional district was aggregated to get a statewide total.

Note: Asterisk (*) indicates winner.

Source: *Congressional Quarterly Weekly Report,* June 16, 1984, 1443, updated by Congressional Quarterly.

Table 2.2 1984 Democratic Caucus Results, First Round

State	Estimated Turnout	Hart	Jackson	Mondale	Others	Uncom-mitted
Iowa (2/20)	85,000	16.5%	1.5%	48.9%*	23.7%	9.4%
Me. (3/4)	16,830	50.2*	0.4	45.4	0.8	3.2
Wyo. (3/10)	3,526	60.4*	0.4	35.9	0.3	3.0
Hawaii (3/13)	2,830		4.2	32.3		63.5*
Nev. (3/13)	5,000	52.3*	0.6	37.7	2.2	7.2
Okla. (3/13)	42,800	43.3*	3.7	38.9	4.0	10.1
Wash. (3/13)	75,000	52.6*	3.0	33.2	1.6	9.6
Del. (3/14)	2,856	29.8	9.6	60.1*		0.5
Alaska (3/15)	2,200	43.6*	10.6	27.7		18.1
Ark. (3/17)	22,202	30.3	19.9	44.0*		5.8
Mich. (3/17)	132,002	32.2	16.7	50.4*	0.2	0.5
Miss. (3/17)	20,000	11.0	26.9	30.3		31.8*
S.C. (3/17)	40,000	12.7	25.0	9.1		53.2*
Minn. (3/20)[a]	66,000	7.0	2.0	62.0*		29.0
Kan. (3/24)	11,553	41.8	3.3	48.7*		6.2
Va. (3/24, 26)	25,505	14.7	26.7	30.4*		28.2
Mont. (3/25)	13,895	49.1*	5.2	35.5	0.3	9.9
N.D. (3/14-28)	5,000	35.8*	2.8	29.9		31.5
Ky. (3/31)	16,000	15.2	18.5	30.4		35.9*
Wis. (4/7)	33,719	30.4	10.2	57.7*		1.7
Ariz. (4/14)	34,173	44.4*	15.7	38.5		1.4
Mo. (4/18)	40,000	19.8	18.5	58.0*		3.7
Vt. (4/24)	2,000	48.2*	14.0	33.2		4.6
Utah (4/25)	9,506	50.5*	3.1	19.5	0.6	26.3
Texas (5/5)[b]	200,000	27.0	16.9	49.7*		6.4
Colo. (5/7)	50,000	80.9*	4.1	9.4		5.6
Idaho (5/24)[c]	—	57.5*	2.4	33.6		6.5

[a] Based on results from 150 precincts, tabulated to form a weighted sampling of the state.

[b] Results with about 70 percent of precincts reporting.

[c] No turnout figure was available.

Note: Asterisk (*) indicates winner.

Source: *Congressional Quarterly Weekly Report,* June 2, 1984, 1317, updated by the author and Congressional Quarterly.

in states that divided delegates proportionately, giving no premium for winning.

Mondale also benefited from the expanded number of caucuses, which accounted for nearly one-third of the delegates (*Table 2.5*). Although Hart won more caucuses than Mondale, they were mostly in smaller states. All told, Mondale accumulated 242 more pledged caucus delegates than Hart. In both the primaries and the caucuses Mondale did best in the more solidly Democratic areas. Delegates are apportioned to states (and to districts within states) according to their voting records. The most loyally Democratic congressional districts often elect seven, eight, or

Table 2.3 Popular Vote and Delegates Won in 1984 Democratic Presidential Primaries

	Mondale	Hart	Jackson	Other
Popular Vote				
Initial contests (Feb. 28-March 13)	30%	35%	14%	21%
Mist clearing (March 18-April 10)	44	34	18	4
Home stretch (May 1-June 5)	38	38	19	5
Total	39	36	19	6
Delegates	49	36	10	5

Notes: Based on voting in 25 primaries. Excludes nonbinding primaries where delegates were selected in caucuses (Vermont, Wisconsin, Idaho, North Dakota, and Montana). Delegates are those pledged at the time of the state primaries. Unpledged superdelegates are excluded.

Source: Popular vote calculated from data reported in *Congressional Quarterly Weekly Report*, June 16, 1984, 1443, updated by Congressional Quarterly. Pledged delegate totals are from Congressional Quarterly reports following each primary.

Table 2.4 Popular Vote and Delegates Won in 1984 Democratic Presidential Primaries, by Type of Primary

	Primary Vote			Pledged Delegates Won		
	Mondale	Hart	Jackson	Mondale	Hart	Jackson
Winner-take-all (loophole)	40%	36%	18%	53%	32%	7%
Winner-take-more (bonus)	41	32	21	53	33	14
Proportional representation	32	39	17	38	45	11
Total	39	36	19	49	36	10

Source: Calculated from data reported in *Congressional Quarterly Weekly Report*, June 16, 1984, 1443, updated by Congressional Quarterly. Pledged delegate totals are from Congressional Quarterly reports following each primary.

Table 2.5 Popular Vote and Delegates Won in 1984 First-Round
Democratic Caucuses

	Mondale	*Hart*	*Jackson*	*Other*
Popular vote	43%	31%	12%	14%
Pledged delegates	52	33	11	4

Source: Popular vote computed from data reported in *Congressional Quarterly Weekly Report,* June
2, 1984, 1317, updated by Congressional Quarterly. It is a best approximation since the exact number
of votes cast by caucus participants often is not kept by the states. Many states report only an estimate
of caucus turnout. In several states the data reported by Congressional Quarterly have been updated
with information provided by Democratic state parties. Delegate figures are from Congressional
Quarterly reports following each caucus and from data supplied by the Mondale campaign. The
above data exclude caucuses in Guam, the Virgin Islands, Latin America, American Samoa, and
Democrats abroad. They also exclude the Idaho caucuses, where turnout figures were unavailable.

nine delegates, while marginal or Republican districts elect as few as
three. Hart ran best in the latter.

Finally, Mondale won the overwhelming majority—around 500—of
the superdelegates, leaving only a few for Hart and Jackson. Despite the
Hunt Commission's expectation that these formally unpledged delegates
would help prolong the contest and perhaps even provide for a more
deliberative convention, many of them publicly endorsed candidates in
January, almost a month before the first state contest. Throughout the
primaries, news reports of Mondale's wide lead among the superdelegates
belied any impression of a competitive race. In fact, even in five of the
states where Hart won the primary—Massachusetts, Rhode Island,
Indiana, Ohio, and New Mexico—Mondale's support among superdelegates gave him control of the delegation at the convention.

The major candidate most adversely affected by the 1984 rules was
Jackson, who, as we saw in Table 2.3, received only 10 percent of the pri-
mary-selected delegates for his 19 percent of the primary vote. Jackson's
disadvantage was that his vote was concentrated in heavily black precincts
and congressional districts. In these districts he usually won many more
votes than he needed to capture all the delegates. In other congressional
districts he fell below the threshold necessary for obtaining a delegate
(often 20 percent or higher). Jackson fared poorly in caucus states,
winning only 12 percent of the votes. Furthermore, like Hart, Jackson did
well in districts with few delegates. The number of delegates that had
been allocated to Jackson strongholds on the basis of their voting in

previous elections did not reflect the heavy voter turnout that he was able to generate for his own candidacy in 1984.

Without the Hunt Commission rules, Mondale probably would have become locked in a tight race with Hart by the time of the final primaries. A hypothetical replay of the Democratic nomination contest shows what might have happened if the convention delegates had been divided among the candidates strictly in proportion to the votes they received in each state (*Table 2.6*). All else being equal, Mondale would have finished nearly 400 votes short of the 1,967 needed for nomination, with Hart fewer than 300 votes behind him. Jackson still would have run third, but with almost twice his actual number of delegates.[23]

The nomination calendar also aided Mondale's campaign. Front loading has increased steadily since 1968. In that year only 7 percent of Democratic delegates were selected through the first Tuesday in April. That proportion grew to 17 percent in 1972, 33 percent in 1976, 42 percent in 1980, and 52 percent in 1984.[24] The Hunt Commission did not like front loading but decided not to forbid it, partly in response to pressure from the Mondale campaign, which was seeking to wrap up the nomination early and which greeted early scheduling with enthusiasm. "We're all for front loading and are encouraging it whenever we can," one Mondale aide acknowledged.[25]

For a time it seemed that the front-loaders would be victimized by their own cleverness as the Hart bandwagon suddenly gathered momentum. Ultimately, however, front loading proved a bane to Hart, who was unable to maintain his momentum from New Hampshire long enough to wrap up the nomination. In the manner of previous long-shot candidates,

Table 2.6 Actual and Hypothetical Delegate Totals for Democratic Candidates in 1984

	Mondale	*Hart*	*Jackson*	*Uncommitted and Others*
Actual delegate count	2,061	1,248	384	240
Delegate count under hypothetical statewide proportional representation	1,591	1,307	645	390

Note: The number of delegates required to win the nomination was 1,967.

Source: Actual count compiled by United Press International on June 27, 1984, as reported in *Congressional Quarterly Weekly Report*, June 30, 1984, 1570. The hypothetical figures were calculated by Congressional Quarterly and appeared in *Congressional Quarterly Weekly Report*, June 23, 1984, 1505.

such as McGovern in 1972 and Carter in 1976, Hart vaulted quickly from obscurity to the front of the pack on the strength of his early successes. But for McGovern and Carter the primaries had been arranged like stepping stones. The early contests were staggered over two months, with the larger states' primaries scheduled on scattered dates later in the spring. In fact, neither McGovern nor Carter faced more than two primaries on any single day until May, when their leads were fairly secure. Thus by the time the big states began voting, the nomination was largely settled. In 1984, however, Iowa and New Hampshire were quickly followed by contests in states such as Illinois, New York, Pennsylvania, and Michigan.[26] By April 10, four of the seven largest delegations to the Democratic convention had been chosen.

The early scheduling of states with large blocs of staunchly Democratic voters and strong labor unions helped Mondale revive his faltering candidacy. To score his initial breakthrough, Hart had been forced to concentrate his limited time and money on Iowa and New Hampshire. But once successful, he suddenly had to wage simultaneous campaigns in several large industrial states. Mondale won all these states, and even though he split the remaining contests with Hart (see the "home stretch" May/June period in Table 2.3), he still won the nomination.

In 1984, as in every other contentious nomination campaign in recent years, the rules themselves became an issue. Hart and Jackson complained bitterly that the deck had been stacked against them because they were not the candidates of the party establishment. In a bid to maintain harmony at the convention and into the fall campaign, reminiscent of similar compromises at the 1968 and 1980 conventions, the Mondale forces accepted demands by the two runners-up that the party convene yet a fifth panel, dubbed the Fairness Commission, to review and rewrite the delegate selection rules for 1988. The convention also approved a sweeping package of nonbinding recommendations for the new rules commission, which included cutting the number of superdelegates in half and deferring their selection until after the first primary or caucus; requiring states with primaries or caucuses in the first half of the nomination calendar to award delegates in proportion to the popular vote; and rolling back the threshold needed to win a share of the delegates to no more than 15 percent in most places. In this newest round of rulemaking, contestants for the 1988 Democratic nomination undoubtedly will push hard for changes they think will most benefit their candidacies.

Money

The United States stands out among the world's democracies in the extent to which private wealth can be converted into political influence.[27]

Nonetheless, money has played a much smaller role in our presidential elections than most people imagine. In few general elections has the financial advantage of one party over the other been decisive.[28] The importance of money was diminished even further by the passage of campaign finance legislation after the 1972 election. Now major-party presidential nominees are financed automatically by the U.S. Treasury.[29]

Campaign spending is a short-term force that, like electoral rules, has a greater influence on the nomination process than on general elections. In the spring more than in the fall, spending is needed to gain visibility, establish an organization that can compete effectively in the various states, and get supporters to the polls without the pull of party allegiance. Although recent campaign finance regulations have reduced the influence of money in the general election, they have heightened its role in the nomination contest.[30]

In recent years the costs of campaigning for a party's nomination have skyrocketed. The greater number of primaries and caucuses, combined with new delegate selection rules that make it imperative for candidates to campaign actively in nearly all 50 states, has put increasing pressure on the candidates' financial resources. The Federal Election Campaign Act (FECA) amendments of 1974 instituted a system of federal matching funds in the nomination period, which alleviates this burden somewhat, but the accompanying limits on the size of individual and group donations have forced candidates to develop elaborate fund-raising operations. Under the act, the U.S. Treasury will match each candidate's private contributions dollar for dollar, but those contributions must be raised in amounts no larger than $1,000 from an individual and $5,000 from a group, and only the first $250 of each individual contribution is matched.

These limits force candidates to spend a great deal of time scrambling to raise seed money early in the campaign, since donations must be relatively small. This is especially true for outsider candidates whose opponents have more established political bases. As a result, the nomination calendar has grown longer. Campaigning must begin well before the first balloting, because the candidates must build a broad financial base as soon as they can. Hence "unemployed" candidates (those who hold no office to distract them from campaigning) are advantaged. As Bush's 1980 general counsel reported, the campaign finance law discriminates in favor of those who can spend two and a half years before the election organizing and fund raising.[31]

The contribution limits affect candidate strategy in the later stages of the contest as well. Before FECA, candidates could enter the primaries late in the game and still compete. For example, Robert Kennedy entered the 1968 primaries in March and still was able to raise $11 million in only 11 weeks. Now the contribution limits and other rules all but prohibit late starters.

While FECA has forced outsider candidates to work harder and longer to raise money, in another respect it has benefited them. In 1976, if the better-known candidates with connections to traditional wealthy Democratic givers, such as Henry Jackson, had been able to accept large contributions, Jimmy Carter might have been swamped in the early primaries. Also, Carter and other dark horse candidates could not have survived without federal matching funds.

In addition to restricting and matching contributions, FECA limits the amount that candidates can spend both in each state's primary or caucus, based on the state's population, and over the course of the entire nomination season.[32] Because the total spending ceiling ($24.2 million in 1984) is much lower than the sum of the individual state ceilings ($60.2 million), the spending limits color almost every facet of a campaign. The expectations of the press and delegate selection rules such as proportional representation encourage candidates to wage a strong effort nearly everywhere, but FECA requires that they pick and choose. To stay within spending limits, campaigns must decide very early to mount only partial efforts in certain states and to bypass others altogether.

The candidates tend to concentrate their resources on the earliest primaries and caucuses. Because the press assigns great significance to these first skirmishes, the candidates regard them as strategically crucial and spend all the money they can. (Since New Hampshire's spending limit is the same as Guam's, the campaigns are forced to resort to a good deal of creative accounting to do so, inventing ingenious ways to allocate spending from one state to another so as not to exceed state limits.) In circular fashion, this spending inflates the importance of the early states even further, often to the detriment of voters in later states. Since the spending ceilings have not kept pace with spiraling campaign contests, it is not surprising that presidential candidates often exhaust most of their allowance early in the delegate selection season. By the end of April 1980, for example, the four leading presidential candidates had spent, on average, 74 percent of the legal maximum, even though only 51 percent of the delegates had been selected.[33]

The low spending ceiling in early states such as Iowa and New Hampshire, like the contribution limits and the availability of federal matching funds, has helped long-shot candidates by preventing their more established opponents from overwhelming them early in the delegate selection season. Spending limits in the primaries and caucuses (and in the general election as well) also enhance the importance of independent expenditures, spending that is not coordinated with a candidate's organization and thus is not subject to any limitations. Campaigns may circumvent the legal limits by taking advantage (albeit at arm's length) of organizations that wish to mount spending barrages on behalf of candidates. In 1980, for example, the Fund for a Conservative Majority spent more than $60,000 in New Hampshire on behalf of Ronald Reagan at a time when his own campaign was fast approaching the state's $294,000 spending limit.[34]

In 1984 many of these patterns were repeated. As before, the candidates spent heaviest in the early contests, at the expense of the later ones (*Figure 2.2*). Mondale spent between 90 and 100 percent of the legal maximum in the early Iowa and Maine caucuses and the New Hamp-

Figure 2.2 Average Proportion of State Spending Limits Spent by Candidates (in percent)

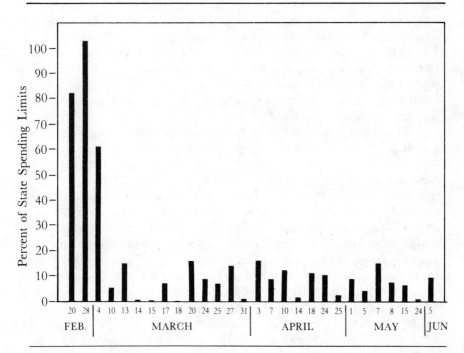

Note: Includes spending by Glenn, Hart, Jackson, or Mondale in states where they won 10 percent or more of the vote.

Source: Candidate expenditures from reports filed with the Federal Election Commission: "Allocation of Primary Expenditures by State for a Presidential Candidate," October 20, 1984 (for financial activity through September 30, 1984).

shire primary. Two weeks later he spent about 40 percent of the limit in Alabama and Massachusetts and 28 percent in Georgia. Thereafter Mondale never spent more than 26 percent of the limit in any state. In fact, Mondale's spending reached 20 percent of the legal limit in only 10 states. In the crucial Illinois, New York, and Pennsylvania primaries his campaign spent about 12 percent of the individual state limits. Although to a lesser extent, Hart also spent a large portion of his state allotment only in early contests. Hart spent nearly 67 percent of the limit in Iowa, 90 percent in New Hampshire, and 34 percent in Massachusetts. His outlay was less than 20 percent of the allowable level in more than half of the states.

Mondale's formidable opening thrust was part of his "early knock-out" strategy. Taking advantage of his fund-raising strength, and setting what one aide called a "fast and vicious pace" long in advance of the first caucuses and primaries, the Mondale brigade hoped to force the competition to travel and campaign extensively and thus to exhaust their more limited resources early. Mondale also hoped to solidify his image as the inevitable winner. But when he failed to eliminate the competition early, his strategy almost backfired as he ran up against the overall spending ceiling. Excluding spending for fund raising, by the end of February Mondale had spent more than half of the overall spending allowance, with all but 2 percent of the delegates still to be chosen (*Figure 2.3*). The shortage of funds required Mondale to scale down his campaign spending and reduce the size and salaries of his staff.

The common tendency of both Hart and Mondale to approach state spending ceilings only in the early states masks some substantial differences between the two campaigns. Financially speaking, the Hart campaign was teetering on the ropes during the long "invisible primary" that preceded the first state contests. Hart was a long shot, unable to raise or spend much money. He even was forced to take out a second mortgage on his home, and just weeks before the New Hampshire primary his campaign was unable to cover the rent on its Manchester office. Following Hart's surprise victory in New Hampshire, however, money flowed more freely; unlike Mondale, who had almost exhausted his allowable funds early, Hart was legally free to spend his new money. By the time Mondale had expended half the limit, Hart had spent barely 11 percent. In March his campaign spent more than $5 million, compared with less than $2 million by Mondale, an expenditure that represented 44 percent of Hart's overall campaign treasury (excluding money used for fund raising). Over time, then, Hart's spending pattern looked rather different from Mondale's. Hart allocated his money in closer proportion to the number of delegates at stake (*Figure 2.4*).

Figure 2.3 Cumulative Proportions of the Overall Spending Limit Expended by Democratic Candidates, and Delegates Apportioned over Time, 1983-1984

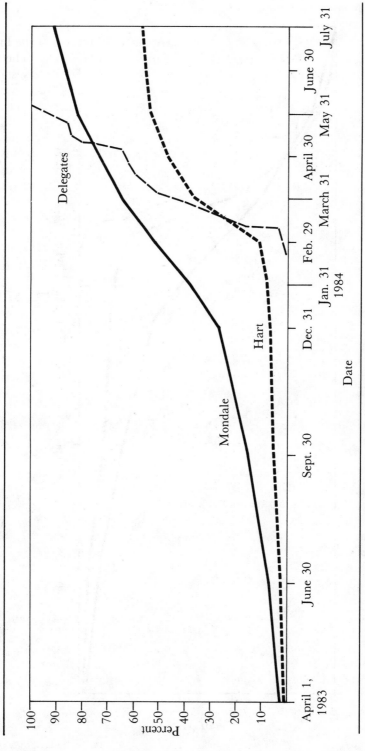

Note: Excludes fund-raising expenditures. Therefore, the $20.2 million spending limit applies.

Source: Federal Election Commission

Figure 2.4 Cumulative Proportions of Each Democratic Candidate's Total Expenditures and Delegates Apportioned over Time, 1983-1984

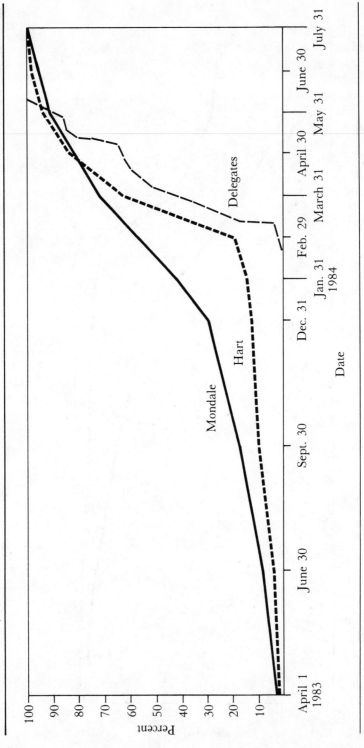

Note: Excludes fund-raising expenditures.
Source: Federal Election Commission

Hart spent about $10 million in the primary and caucus states, Mondale only $7 million (*Table 2.7*). Indeed, Hart outspent Mondale in 33 of the 50 states, including nearly all the large ones. He more than doubled Mondale's expenditures in New Jersey, Ohio, Pennsylvania, and New York and nearly doubled them in Illinois. But in "nonallocated" expenditures—money spent at the national headquarters on planning, media, polling, delegate hunting, and fund raising—the Mondale campaign expended nearly $12 million and the Hart campaign only $1.4 million. The Hart campaign took great pride in the fact that they concentrated their fire power out in the field and not in Washington. This huge disparity reflects both the more centralized nature of the Mondale campaign and the enormous sums expended by it before the primaries and caucuses. The difference also reflects its virtuosity in clever accounting techniques. From the outset, the Mondale forces paid painstaking attention to accounting schemes that would permit them to attribute expenditures to the national side of the ledger so that they would not approach the state spending ceilings.

In the end, Mondale spent $23 million, or about 95 percent of the overall limit, and Hart spent almost $14 million, or about 56 percent. But although fund-raising and spending decisions clearly affected the strategies of the candidates, it is much less clear that the power of the purse af-

Table 2.7 Spending in the 1984 Democratic Nomination Contest (in Millions of Dollars)

	Mondale	*Hart*	*Jackson*
Allocated expenditures (spending in the states)	$ 7.2	$10.2	$2.5
Nonallocated expenditures (spending at the national headquarters)	11.7	1.4	2.9
Fund-raising costs	4.1	2.0	0.6
Subtotal[a]	23.0	13.6	6.0
Legal and accounting costs	1.9	0.3	0.4
Grand Total	$24.9	$13.9	$6.4

[a] Subject to an overall spending limit of $24.24 million.

Source: From reports filed by each campaign with the FEC: "Allocation of Primary Expenditures by State for a Presidential Candidate," October 20, 1984 (for financial activity through September 30, 1984).

fected the final outcome. Money may guarantee exposure, but it does not guarantee success at the polls. In the past some of the biggest spenders, including Nelson Rockefeller in 1964 and 1968 and John Connally in 1980, have gone down in defeat.[35]

In the primaries and caucuses of 1984 there were 26 events in which the winner outspent the loser and 26 events in which the loser outspent the winner (*Table 2.8*). Mondale spent more in several early contests, winning some of them (the Iowa caucus, the Alabama primary) and losing

Table 2.8 Relationship between Spending and Outcomes in 1984 Democratic Nomination Contests

Winner Outspent Loser			*Loser Outspent Winner*		
Mondale Won	*Hart Won*	*Jackson Won*	*Mondale Won*	*Hart Won*	*Jackson Won*
Iowa $198	**Calif. $271**	D.C. $71	**N.Y. $622**	**Me. $276**	La. $34
Minn. 189	**Conn.** 247		**N.J.** 479	**Mass.** 195	S.C.[a] 13
Ala. 152	**Ohio** 222		**Pa.** 412	Okla. 130	
Miss.[a] 91	**Fla.** 220		**Ill.** 279	Wash. 52	
Ark. 64	**Ind.** 134		Mo. 244	**N.H.** 51	
Hawaii[a] 1	Colo. 107		**Texas** 208	Vt. 44	
	Wis.[b] 62		Va. 177	Alaska 3	
	Mont. 51		Tenn. 170		
	Ariz. 42		Md. 116		
	Neb. 29		**Ga.** 69		
	Wyo. 21		Wis.[b] 62		
	Nev. 18		**Mich.** 37		
	Ore. 14		Kan. 34		
	R.I. 10		N.C. 25		
	N.M. 8		Ky.[a] 21		
	Utah 8		Del. 5		
	S.D. 7		W.Va. 4		
	Idaho 6				
	N.D. 2				

[a] Four caucus states were won by "uncommitted." They are categorized above according to the second-place finisher.

[b] Wisconsin held a nonbinding primary, which Hart won, and a binding caucus, which Mondale won. Therefore the state is listed twice.

Note: The above figures represent the spending gap between the top two candidates (in thousands of dollars). The politically most important contests are in boldface type.

Source: Spending data from reports filed by each campaign with the FEC: "Allocation of Primary Expenditures by State for a Presidential Candidate," October 20, 1984 (for financial activity through September 30, 1984).

others (the New Hampshire and Massachusetts primaries, the Maine caucus). Hart won in 19 states where he outspent Mondale, but most of them were western states where Mondale was not a serious challenger. In 17 states, including many of the larger states, Hart spent more than Mondale but lost. If we consider only the most politically important contests, the picture remains muddied: in seven (Iowa, Alabama, Florida, Connecticut, Indiana, Ohio, and California) the winner spent more than the losers, while in ten (New Hampshire, Maine, Massachusetts, Georgia, Illinois, Michigan, New York, Pennsylvania, Texas, and New Jersey) the losers spent more. Such mixed results hardly suggest that money determined who won and who lost.

A partial explanation for this anomaly, especially for Hart's losing efforts in several large states where he had an enormous financial advantage, may be that some of the spending on behalf of Mondale was not charged against him. Since 1974 candidates have shown great ingenuity in circumventing FECA's fund-raising and spending limitations. First came independent expenditures, then "soft money"—money spent by state party organizations that is exempt from limitations—then the use of money by labor unions to "educate" their own members.

A Mondale innovation was to use "delegate committees." In 1980 the Federal Election Commission allowed individuals who were running as delegates to the national conventions to form committees to raise money for grass-roots campaigning on behalf of their own candidacies. The law stipulated that the activities of these committees had to be uncoordinated with the candidates' campaigns. While few delegate committees formed in 1980, about 130 groups of Mondale delegates were established in 1984. They raised and spent about $600,000, most of it from labor union political action committees (PACs). None of this counted against Mondale's own spending limits, even though the money went for activities that were virtually indistinguishable from those organized directly by the Mondale campaign and Mondale had pledged he would accept no PAC contributions. Moreover, these delegate committees received guidance from the Mondale campaign.

Hart seized upon this "tainted delegates" issue in an effort to demonstrate that Mondale was a tool of the special interests. He contended that "the treasury of organized labor has virtually become the treasury of the Mondale campaign," [36] taunted Mondale to "give the money back, Walter," and threatened to challenge all 587 committee-supported delegates' credentials at the convention. Later Mondale was able to reach a compromise with Hart, and the issue did not surface at the convention.[37]

Thus, in the 1984 nomination race money and its regulation profoundly shaped the conduct of the campaign. But neither seems to have affected the final result in a decisive way.

Media

The media constitute another important short-term force in the nomination process. Like delegate selection rules and campaign finance practices, the media have changed substantially in recent years. The combined effects of all three sets of changes in turn have transformed the political landscape. The adoption of new delegate rules and the proliferation of primaries have spurred nomination candidates to pump more and more money into the media. Because the public, which under the new rules effectively chooses the nominee, would know very little about the candidates and their campaign without the media, most presidential contenders believe that the media—particularly television—are the main determinant of their success or failure. That belief influences how they allocate their campaign resources, plan their schedules, define their themes, and select their strategy. The result, in political scientist Thomas Patterson's words, is that "today's presidential campaign is essentially a mass media campaign." [38]

The media have a far greater influence on the nomination process than on the general election. The primary season is more ambiguous and complex than the general election: several state contests occur on the same day; contests may have many candidates; candidates run in certain states but not in others; the different states have a confusing variety of rules and procedures; and so on. Thus the public must rely on the media to keep score—to define the standards of victory and interpret the results—far more than during the general election. During the primaries, moreover, the voters' knowledge of the candidates is often scant, and their main guide for interpreting political information in other situations—their partisan allegiance—is not available. The voters are therefore more susceptible than in the fall to both the candidates' paid advertising and the stories that the media choose to emphasize in their news coverage.[39] As Donald Matthews observes, a "struggle over the content of political news has become the core of presidential nominating politics." [40]

In recent years the news media have shaped this content by selectively emphasizing certain primaries and caucuses, focusing on certain candidates, and placing more importance on the contest itself than on issues. News coverage, like the delegate rules and finance laws, tilts strongly toward the early contests. Candidates who do well in Iowa and New Hampshire receive a flood of news coverage that can buoy them from invisibility to prominence while the losers drown in obscurity.[41] Later in the season, when primaries are being held three and four at a time, the media usually decide to stress certain states and ignore others. The states favored for coverage are typically those where a hotly contested race is in doubt, where the delegate selection process is less complicated, or where there are fewer candidates on the ballot.[42]

The ambiguity of nomination contests also gives the media more discretion in how they treat candidates. For example, the media's criterion for declaring Muskie a loser in the 1972 New Hampshire primary— although he actually won—was that he failed to win with a clear majority, which some journalists thought was the necessary showing for a front-runner from New England. The news media tend to pay more attention to front-runners but to treat them more harshly than challengers.[43]

Finally, the media emphasize the "horse race" dimension of the nomination season. They concentrate on who's ahead, who's behind, strategies and tactics, and staff intrigues, instead of on the candidates' issue positions or leadership qualities.[44] Since many reporters rely on the same sources, they usually agree on which candidate is leading and which ones are fading. Horse race journalism thus fosters a homogeneity that amplifies the effects of the reporting.

Many of these patterns of media coverage and candidate response were evident in the early weeks of the 1984 nomination contest. The first balloting took place on February 20, when about 85,000 people attended the Iowa caucuses. Mondale won an overwhelming victory: 45 percent to Hart's 15 percent, McGovern's 13 percent, and Glenn's 5 percent. Yet despite Mondale's overwhelming victory, and despite the tiny size of the Iowa electorate, the media verdict was swift and unequivocal: the contest had become a two-man race between Mondale and Hart, and Glenn's candidacy had been dealt a nearly fatal blow. In the week that followed, Mondale's share of media attention shrank, while Hart's coverage, spurred by his support from a mere 12,600 Iowa voters, grew to the same level as Mondale's—10 times what had been reported the week before on NBC.[45] More important, the national coverage of Hart was "virtually free of any harsh criticism, unflattering issues, or cynical commentary," [46] thus prompting shifts in voter preference from Mondale and other candidates to Hart in the next state, New Hampshire.[47]

After his victory in New Hampshire, Hart was christened the new front-runner. Then, suddenly, the networks' coverage of Hart turned sour. Having inflated his image, they proceeded to deflate it. In a daily series of biting critiques that lasted through the eve of the next big round of primaries and caucuses on March 13, "Super Tuesday," all three networks attacked Hart's credibility. Not surprisingly, voters who made up their minds in the last few days before Super Tuesday were far less likely to favor Hart than those who had decided soon after the New Hampshire primary.

If on February 20 the media had vastly exaggerated Hart's performance and undervalued Mondale's, on Super Tuesday they turned the tables. Five states held primaries, and four states held caucuses. Although Hart was soundly defeated in Alabama, he won the popular vote in Massachusetts, Rhode Island, and Florida convincingly, nearly won in Georgia (Jimmy Carter's home state), and clinched three caucus states (Nevada, Oklahoma, and Washington). That day the overall popular vote went 35 percent for Hart, 31 percent for Mondale.

The media message was that this was a Mondale victory, or at least a split decision. The networks downplayed the caucus results, which were harder to report and slower to come in from the West. The Mondale campaign had been successful in defining expectations, convincing the media that all Mondale had to do that evening was survive, while Hart needed to maintain his momentum and score a complete victory. The media probably accepted this definition on the basis of events from previous years. Unlike Johnson in 1968 or Muskie in 1972, Mondale had avoided being knocked out. Since he was still on the ropes, he was declared the winner.[48]

On the whole, regular news coverage in 1984 appears not to have determined the outcome of the nomination contest between Hart and Mondale; both were able to overcome and thus reshape media expectations on more than one occasion. More influential were the televised debates—in all, nearly a dozen—that took place among the candidates. One observer called these confrontations the spine of the nomination campaign. The debates, with a variety of formats and a variety of sponsors, provided the campaign's most important media moments. In Iowa Hart asked Mondale to name a single major domestic issue on which he disagreed with the AFL-CIO, and Mondale did not answer. In Atlanta Mondale challenged the significance of Hart's new ideas, asking, "Where's the beef?" The debates in Illinois, Pennsylvania, and New York affected the outcome in those state primaries. Although the debates themselves were seen by a relatively small audience, the subsequent news coverage of them greatly magnified their importance.

Political advertising, the form of media exposure most under the control of candidates, was apparently not crucial in influencing votes during the 1980 nomination season, and it probably was not a major force in 1984. A possible exception in 1984 was Mondale's "red telephone" ad, which pointedly questioned whether Hart was experienced and dependable enough to be entrusted with the "most awesome, powerful responsibility in the world." The ad showed a red phone blinking on the president's desk while a somber voice warned of the dangers of having an "unsure . . . unsteady . . . untested" hand on the receiver.

In several other instances political commercials figured significantly in the primaries, not because their messages directly affected the voters but because each generated a self-inflicted wound by Hart that stirred up a media storm. Five days before the Illinois primary, the Hart campaign heard that Mondale had put some insinuating commercials on the air and demanded that they be retracted. In fact, the ads had never been shown, and Hart was forced to issue a formal apology. Also in Illinois, internal snafus within the Hart campaign permitted an ad that personally attacked Cook County Democratic boss Ed Vrdolyak and his support for Mondale to be aired against Hart's wishes. Hart insisted that the ad be pulled off, but it continued to be shown over a weekend, prompting Mondale to ask how Hart could run the country if he could not pull his own commercial off the air. Hart's answer to the red telephone ad caused a flap during the New York primary. It was a political commercial that showed a fuse burning while the voice-over suggested that Mondale would risk another Vietnam in Central America by leaving U.S. troops there and using "our sons as bargaining chips." During the televised debate that preceded the New York primary, Mondale indignantly attacked Hart for using "those ads that suggest I'm out trying to kill kids" and demanded that they be taken off the air.

The influence of the media on election outcomes cannot, of course, be gauged with much precision. For one thing it is difficult to separate the effects of actual campaign events from the effects of the same events as filtered through the media. Some aspects of campaign coverage in 1984 were clearly significant, particularly the media's interpretations of the early primaries and caucuses and the televised debates. But in determining the final outcome, the media appear to have played a far smaller role than the rules although a somewhat greater role than money.

Strategy

The impression one gets from following a general election campaign in the daily press is that the outcome turns heavily on the candidates' strategies. This "top down" view of the fall campaign exaggerates the importance of short-term forces such as money, the media, and candidate strategy. Actually, the two parties' nominees for president have surprisingly little freedom in drawing battle plans to oppose each other. They are constrained by both the distribution of party loyalties in the electorate and the performance of previous administrations—whether their own, their predecessors', or their opponent's. They are limited by their party's positions, past and present, on the burning issues of the day. As noted earlier, the electoral college dictates a fairly rigid strategic blueprint; because it makes the large states the main battlegrounds, that is where the candidates must spend most of their time and money. It is no accident that in recent elections the parties' game plans have followed a similar outline or that the influence of their strategies on the final outcomes has been minimal.

The nomination process is altogether different. In recent nomination campaigns the styles and approaches of candidates have contrasted sharply, and it is largely these differences that have separated the victors from the vanquished.[49] The strategies candidates followed in 1984 shaped not only the season's major turning points but also the final results.

Some of those turning points came early. According to political scientist John Kessel, nomination politics proceeds through four stages: the early days between the midterm election and the selection of the first delegates; the initial contests, when the long-awaited first caucuses and primaries finally take place; "mist clearing," that time when doubts about the outcome are dispelled by the results of crucial contests; and the convention, which confirms the nomination of the primaries-and-caucuses winner and signals the beginning of the fall campaign.[50] In 1984 the strategies of the four main Democratic contenders—Mondale, Glenn, Hart, and Jackson—varied through these stages in ways that influenced the final results.

Mondale, Glenn, and Hart: Early Days and Initial Contests.
The events of 1984 fit neatly into Kessel's four-stage temporal pattern, with one amendment: the early days began long before the midterm election of 1982. Mondale began his quest for the nomination immediately after the 1980 election. His strategy was to outplan and outorganize the opposition to such an extent that he would win the nomination virtually before a single caucus or primary vote was cast. Mondale and his aides assembled one of the most professional political organizations in American history. They raised enough funds to fill a bulging campaign treasury and worked hard to persuade the party to adopt new delegate selection rules that would benefit their campaign. After Kennedy withdrew from the race, Mondale easily won the formal endorsements of the largest Democratic interest groups—the AFL-CIO, the National Organization for Women (NOW), and the National Education Association (NEA)—and the private support of hundreds of Democratic elected officials and other party leaders. The Mondale team elevated the importance of the straw polls that were conducted at various state party conventions and fund-raisers in 1983, then won most of them, including one in Maine, where Mondale dispatched some 100 campaign workers and spent around

intensify the new generation-new ideas message and to counterpose it starkly with the Mondale approach. A campaign that from the beginning had lacked a practical political plan for implementing its themes suddenly revised its tactics with a bold move. Hart invested thousands of scarce dollars in Iowa, not in field organization but in a media blitz.

The abrupt shift in strategy initially worked. Although Hart finished way behind Mondale and barely ahead of third-place finisher McGovern in Iowa, he was propelled to the status of Mondale's main opponent by a media corps that was eager for a competitive race to cover and privately suspicious that Mondale's popular support might be soft. A tidal wave then hit upper New England, as Hart won smashing victories in New Hampshire, Vermont, and Maine. As in 1976 and 1980, the out party in 1984 had attracted a large field of candidates. Mondale had assumed that some of them would remain viable in the initial contests, fragmenting the non-Mondale vote. But except for Hart and Jackson, all the other candidates dropped out of the competition quickly.

Jackson's Strategy. Jackson stayed in the race through the convention balloting. Like the other long-shot candidates he emphatically denied that he was running to enhance his or his followers' influence in the party, to amass enough delegates to play a power broker at the convention, to maneuver for the second spot on the ticket, or to lay the groundwork for a 1988 bid. He was running, he said, to win the nomination. Regardless of his intent, the Jackson campaign created a historically important movement for black electoral power: an opportunity for nearly one-fourth of Democratic voters to send party leaders a message and to gain more influence in the political process.

Jackson's most important strategic decision was simply to run, knowing that he would face some serious obstacles. Jackson would have to challenge the black political establishment, which frowned on his candidacy; most eventually sided with Mondale. He then would have to wage a nationwide campaign without much money or knowledge of the campaign finance laws, the delegate selection rules, or other details of presidential politics. Jackson did not care; his strategy sought to create a grass-roots movement, a crusade that enlisted younger black leaders, the black religious community, and, most important, rank-and-file black voters. The strategy assumed that blacks' enthusiasm and pride would be roused by having one of their own contend seriously for the highest office in the land, an arousal one journalist called "the Joe Louis effect."

In the early days of his campaign Jackson harbored some hope of assembling a "rainbow coalition" of blacks, Hispanics, women, young people, lower-income whites, and activists from various liberal causes.

There were signs, especially upon Jackson's return from Syria in January after he negotiated the release of Navy Lt. Robert Goodman, that this may not have been an impossible dream. These hopes were soon dashed, however, by two incidents touching on black-Jewish relations.

The first was when Jackson, thinking he was speaking off the record with a reporter, referred to Jews as "Hymies" and to New York as "Hymietown." The second involved a series of incendiary comments by his ally Louis Farrakhan of the Nation of Islam, a Black Muslim sect, who denounced Jews and Judaism and threatened to harm those who hurt Jackson's candidacy. Both episodes touched off a firestorm in the press, and the Jackson campaign was divided about how to respond. At first Jackson denied having made the Hymie remark, then another two weeks went by before he apologized for it, and months passed before he repudiated the most flagrant excesses of Farrakhan. In the meantime, these events caused irreparable damage to Jackson's hopes of a rainbow coalition. In New Hampshire, where his campaign had been drawing large, enthusiastic crowds of young people and registering many new voters, the controversy over the Hymie comment erased this possibility. By some estimates, it cost Jackson an additional 10 percent share of the vote in New Hampshire. (He actually received 5 percent.) As the primary season wore on, the Jackson campaign continued to call for a broad multiracial coalition, but it concentrated its full energies on winning the black vote.

Mondale and Hart: Mist Clearing. The next important strategic move of the campaign was Mondale's response to the Hart prairie fire. Shortly after New Hampshire, the Mondale campaign decided to launch an unrelenting offensive on Hart's personal and public record, with an emphasis on the personal. They hoped to make Hart himself the issue by raising doubts about his character and suitability for the presidency. The attack, they thought, also would demonstrate "Fighting Fritz's" toughness and backbone. The press scrutinized Hart's character with persistent questions about changes he had made in his stated age (from 47 to 46), last name (Hartpence to Hart), and signature. Meanwhile the Mondale campaign fixed on the alleged paucity of Hart's new ideas with the taunting refrain "Where's the beef?" and raised doubts about his character in the ominous red telephone ad. After New Hampshire, Mondale never really offered himself as a positive alternative; his main message was anti-Hart. Although Hart's campaign message was slightly less hostile, his candidacy too became fundamentally negative. Consequently, the votes he received were more anti-Mondale than pro-Hart.[56]

As Mondale moved from his "early knockout" strategy to his negative, "raise the stakes" campaign, he did not scrap all of the initial battle plan. Although his strong reliance on organized labor and the party establishment had made him especially vulnerable to Hart's outsider critique, it was to them that he turned in his hour of greatest need, just after the New Hampshire debacle. The party leaders and unions came to his rescue. Mondale received crucial help from Bert Lance (the Democratic state chair in Georgia), Birmingham mayor Richard Arrington and the Alabama Democratic Conference (the state's major black political organization), the Cook County Democratic machine in Illinois, and Gov. Mario Cuomo and his political apparatus in New York. AFL-CIO members served as an effective army in the Michigan caucuses and the Illinois, New York, and Pennsylvania primaries. At a time when the Mondale campaign was fast approaching the overall spending limit, the unions provided essential money for the field organization, polls, advertising, and the rest.

Hart's go-for-broke strategy had brought sudden success in New England but also created problems. Almost overnight his ill-funded, locally oriented campaign grew into a national crusade. The need to fight a full-scale conventional war everywhere instead of limited guerrilla insurgencies here and there put a tremendous strain on the campaign staff. The atmosphere in the Hart brigade was frenzied. To make matters worse, the staff was wracked with internal disputes generated primarily by a contest for control of the campaign between Caddell and others. These conditions were not conducive to rational strategic thinking during the crucial phase of the campaign.

The Mondale campaign exploited Hart's organizational weakness to the fullest. Having narrowly avoided elimination on Super Tuesday (March 13), Mondale faced severe tests in several large industrial states. His campaign advisers thought that their relentless attacks on Hart might force him and his inexperienced and feuding staff into making mistakes. They were right. During the mist clearing primaries in Illinois, New York, and Pennsylvania, the Hart campaign committed several major blunders. First came the snafus in Illinois—Hart's complaint about Mondale ads that never aired, and the continued showing of the Hart commercial that linked Mondale to Chicago's machine politics. The allegations about Hart's character and stability in Mondale's ads seemed to be confirmed by reports on the nightly news. Hart looked inexperienced, unsteady, and ineffective.

The Hart campaign temporarily lost its strategic gyroscope and compass. In the initial contests Hart had campaigned successfully as an outsider, a maverick running against the special interests and party professionals. His behavior and tone in Illinois belied that image. The flaps over the television ads sounded like old-fashioned politics as usual. Hart had gone into Illinois with a commanding lead; it evaporated during the course of a week, and he lost by 5 percentage points.

In the New York primary Hart did further damage to his carefully cultivated image as a new-generation candidate. While he was criticizing Mondale as a special interest politician, Hart spent his time pandering to ethnic minorities and other groups, debating with Mondale over which of the two had been the first to promise to move the U.S. embassy in Israel to Jerusalem (which appeared to be a shift in Hart's position), and courting Irish-Americans over the issue of Northern Ireland. Hart also forsook his coalitional, anti-ideological banner for a more familiar ideological approach.[57] Hammering away in particular on the Central America issue, Hart stressed that he would pull out American combat troops but that Mondale would not. The "burning fuse" ad, which explicitly raised the memory of Vietnam and all but called Mondale a warmonger, was meant to arouse younger voters and cut into Mondale's liberal support. But in provoking a left-right debate, Hart necessarily de-emphasized his new ideas theme. The public, intrigued as usual by a fresh face and receptive to the call for new ideas, wanted to know what new ideas he favored. But Hart did not clearly, simply, and crisply spell them out.

During the 1984 primary season three Democratic candidates tried to exploit the electability issue, each with little success. During the campaign's early days, before the New Hampshire primary, and again before the May 8 Ohio primary, Mondale spent most of his time contrasting his policy positions with Reagan's and emphasizing his own virtues as a candidate in the upcoming general election.[58] But turning his wrath on Reagan instead of Hart brought Mondale defeat in both primaries; Democratic voters had their minds on the present contest and were not yet ready to think seriously about the fall. Glenn also had billed himself as the strongest candidate against Reagan, but this too apparently held little sway among the voters.

The electability theme was a constant weapon in Hart's campaign arsenal but he invoked it with varying emphasis. One of the puzzling features of the mist clearing period is that Hart did not try to capitalize on the electability issue in March. The polls were on his side, and it was widely acknowledged, even by the White House and many Mondale supporters, that Hart probably would be the stronger Democratic candidate in the fall.[59] Although the electability issue has never proved a powerful vote-getter, the animus of many liberal Democratic primary voters toward Reagan might have made them receptive to such an appeal in 1984. It was also an issue on which Hart could appeal to strong

Democratic partisans, claiming to be the only candidate who could save the party.

The Hart campaign rediscovered its strategic bearings later in the primaries. Toward the end of April, Hart returned to the themes of new ideas, the challenge of shaping the future, and the danger of nominating someone too beholden to special interests. But Hart's problems with campaign miscues recurred. The most costly gaffe, perhaps, was a casual complaint that while his wife was in California he had to campaign in New Jersey. The comment did not help his chances in the New Jersey primary, which was widely identified by the media as the most important contest of the final day of the delegate selection season.

As much as the rules, and more than money and the media, Hart's strategic errors, coupled with Mondale's strategic master strokes from Super Tuesday in March through Pennsylvania in April, were decisive in the 1984 Democratic nomination process. One final point seals the case for Mondale's strategic superiority. From the outset, the Mondale forces understood that the nomination battle was at base a contest for delegates. A central part of their overall strategy was the delegate hunt. Mondale's chief delegate tracker worked full-time on this operation with a staff of two dozen scouts and an almost unlimited budget. In contrast, the Hart campaign had no serious delegate-gathering program. Plagued early on by limited resources and a flawed political strategy, the Hart campaign had failed even to fill delegate slates in many states, including Florida and Pennsylvania. In the closing days of the fight, Hart tried to argue that his smashing victories in Ohio, Nebraska, Oregon, and California demonstrated his vote-getting ability in states that would be essential in the fall campaign. But for Hart in 1984—as for Jerry Brown and Frank Church, who had won states in the late stages of 1976—the currency of the nomination game was delegates. *Newsweek* called the final contest of the 1984 season the "telephone primary." It took place on the morning of June 6, when Mondale called 50 delegates and won the pledges of support that put him over the top that day. When the roll was called on July 19 at the Democratic convention in San Francisco, the tally was: Mondale 2,191, Hart 1,200.5, Jackson 465.5, others and abstentions 66 (*Table 2.9*).

A Competition between Short-Term Forces

Of the four short-term forces discussed here, rules and candidate strategy were especially influential in the 1984 nomination race, the media and money somewhat less so.[60] Between rules and strategy, the latter probably was more important. The Mondale campaign's careful investment in defining the rules and its virtuosity in exploiting them was not sufficient protection against Hart's assault in the initial contests. It was

Table 2.9 Presidential Balloting at the 1984 Democratic Convention

State	Totals	Mondale	Hart	Jackson	Other	Abstained
Alabama	62	39	13	9	1	0
Alaska	14	9	4	1	0	0
Arizona	40	20	16	2	0	2
Arkansas	42	26	9	7	0	0
California	345	95	190	33	0	27
Colorado	51	1	42	1	0	7
Connecticut	60	23	36	1	0	0
Delaware	18	13	5	0	0	0
District of Columbia	19	5	0	14	0	0
Florida	143	82	55	3	0	2
Georgia	84	40	24	20	0	0
Hawaii	27	27	0	0	0	0
Idaho	22	10	12	0	0	0
Illinois	194	114	41	39	0	0
Indiana	88	42	38	8	0	0
Iowa	58	37	18	2	1	0
Kansas	44	25	16	3	0	0
Kentucky	63	51	5	7	0	0
Louisiana	69	26	19	24	0	0
Maine	27	13	13	0	1	0
Maryland	74	54	3	17	0	0
Massachusetts	116	59	49	5	3	0
Michigan	155	96	49	10	0	0
Minnesota	86	63	3	4	16	0
Mississippi	43	26	4	13	0	0
Missouri	86	55	14	16	0	0
Montana	25	11	13	1	0	0
Nebraska	30	12	17	1	0	0
Nevada	20	9	10	1	0	0
New Hampshire	22	12	10	0	0	0
New Jersey	122	115	0	7	0	0
New Mexico	28	13	13	2	0	0
New York	285	156	75	52	0	0
North Carolina	88	53	19	16	0	0
North Dakota	18	10	5	1	2	0
Ohio	175	84	80	11	0	0
Oklahoma	53	24	26	3	0	0
Oregon	50	16	31	2	0	0
Pennsylvania	195	177	0	18	0	0
Puero Rico	53	53	0	0	0	0
Rhode Island	27	14	12	0	0	0
South Carolina	48	16	13	19	0	0
South Dakota	19	9	10	0	0	0
Tennessee	76	39	20	17	0	0
Texas	200	119	40	36	2	0
Utah	27	8	19	0	0	0
Vermont	17	5	8	3	0	1
Virginia	78	34	18	25	0	0
Washington	70	31	36	3	0	0
West Virginia	44	30	14	0	0	0
Wisconsin	89	58	25	6	0	0
Wyoming	15	7	7	0	0	1
Latin America	5	5	0	0	0	0
Democrats Abroad	5	3	1.5	0.5	0	0
Virgin Islands	6	4	0	2	0	0
American Samoa	6	6	0	0	0	0
Guam	7	7	0	0	0	0
Totals		2,191	1,200.5	465.5	26	40

Note: Ten delegates were absent.
Source: *Congressional Quarterly Weekly Report,* July 21, 1984, 1799.

only after he had provoked Hart into stumbling that Mondale was able to recover and win.

Because Mondale and Hart conceived of the Democratic party differently, they varied in the way they waged their nomination fight in terms of rules and strategy. In a sense, the 1984 nomination contest was a competition between these two dominant short-term forces. Mondale emphasized delegate selection, the insider's game. Through organizational prowess rather than a fetching message or vision, he set out to capture a majority of delegates in the primaries and caucuses and among the unpledged superdelegates. In contrast, Hart built his campaign not on delegate selection but on a message. The goal was to define a compelling theme that would portray Mondale as a captive of special interests who was mired in the past and inadequate to the tasks that lay ahead. Because the Hart people regarded the party as a power vacuum, they assumed that it would be impossible to assemble a winning coalition out of power blocs within the party. They may have been right: only after Hart had lost control over his thematic strategy did he lose the advantage to Mondale.

In a world of computers, polls, direct mail technology, and slick political commercials, the Democratic nomination boiled down to a human drama involving the two candidates and the people around them. The dramatic conflict was resolved by the personal strengths and weaknesses of the combatants and their relationships with their advisers: the capacity of Mondale and his staff to absorb crushing defeats and bounce back with even greater self-control, and the inability of Hart to manage either his sudden momentum or the internecine wars that rent his organization. When short-term forces are in command, as they are in the nomination process, victories are won mainly by default; one side prevails by disorienting the other, forcing it to make mistakes, then capitalizing on those errors. The news media and paid advertising constitute the vehicles through which the campaigns talk to each other and try to force mistakes.

Long-Term Forces and the Nomination Process

While short-term forces dominate the topsy-turvy world of nomination politics, longstanding social and political conflicts are more consequential in general elections. But long-term forces are usually at work in the nomination stage as well. In the 1984 nomination contest, three long-term forces stood out: generational divisions, blacks' struggle for equality, and debate over the role of interest groups in society.

Generational Divisions

For many years there have been signs of a growing political division along generational lines. Young adults (representing the postwar baby boom) and the elderly (benefiting from great improvements in health care) constitute increasingly visible and powerful segments of the electorate. Each group has its own distinctive political outlook. Unlike the older generation, whose political views were formed during the Great Depression and the New Deal, the younger generation came of age challenging established institutions and leaders, rejecting traditional politics, and valuing political independence. The new generation also grew up with greater opportunities for higher education, social and occupational mobility, and affluence than did their parents, and this too has shaped their political perspective.

This generational schism became especially prominent in the 1984 Democratic primaries. (In fact, a new word entered the political lexicon: "Yuppie," or young urban professional.) Despite the tortuous path of the nomination contest, generational (and other demographic) voting patterns showed remarkable stability throughout. Analysts from the *New York Times* therefore were able to combine results from exit polls in 24 separate primaries into a single survey, as if there had been one extended national primary election (*Table 2.10*).

The polls showed that nearly half the primary votes were cast by people below the age of 45, most of them in the 30-to-44 age group. In some primaries (such as New Hampshire) younger voters made up almost 60 percent of the total. Mondale's vote increased steadily with the age of the voters: those 60 and over gave him twice the support of those under 30. Support for Hart and Jackson dwindled with increasing age.[61] Furthermore, this generation gap cut across class, religious, union, and ideological lines. Young union members voted for Hart, older ones for Mondale; young liberals were for Hart, older liberals preferred Mondale.[62]

The generational cast of the voting in 1984 also was reflected in the differential support for Mondale and Hart among other categories of voters, such as those with varying levels of formal education and those with strong or weak partisan ties. (Hart did consistently better among college-educated voters and weak partisans.) In primaries, the full force of most voters' Democratic or Republican allegiance is attenuated since these are intraparty contests. However, the *strength* of the voters' partisanship is increasingly important in nomination contests, as it was in 1984.

Mondale won handily among hard-core Democrats; Hart carried the less strongly partisan voters. Overall, one in five Democratic primary voters was a self-described independent (more than one in three in New Hampshire and Massachusetts), and Hart enjoyed a 16-point advantage over Mondale with them. Hart scored better than Mondale among independents in every state, and he won a plurality of their votes in 21 of the 24 primaries. In fact, he owed to independents his margin of victory in

Table 2.10 Group Support for Candidates in the 1984 Democratic Primaries

	Share of Primary Electorate	Vote for Mondale	Vote for Hart	Vote for Jackson
Age				
18-29	17%	26%	39%	26%
30-44	30	30	38	23
45-59	24	41	34	18
60 and over	28	52	31	10
Education				
Less than high school	14	51	26	18
High school graduate	33	43	34	16
Some college	27	33	38	21
College graduate	26	31	41	20
Ideology				
Liberal	27	34	36	25
Moderate	47	41	37	15
Conservative	21	37	34	16
Party				
Democrat	74	42	33	20
Independent	20	28	44	16
Race				
White	78	42	43	5
Black	18	19	3	77
Sex				
Male	46	38	36	17
Female	54	39	35	20
Union household	33	45	31	19

Source: Adam Clymer, "The 1984 National Primary," *Public Opinion*, August-September 1984, 53. The table combines data from exit polls in 24 states (conducted by *New York Times*/CBS News, CBS News alone, NBC News, and ABC News) plus vote totals from secretaries of state.

several states that permitted independents or Republicans to pick up Democratic ballots.[63] These included New Hampshire and Indiana, where he ran just even with Mondale among Democrats, and Ohio, where he won the primary even though he lost the Democratic vote. In the end, Hart's victories came in a collection of distinctly non-Democratic states: he won Indiana, Ohio, Wisconsin, Maine, New Hampshire, Vermont,

Connecticut, and Florida, and he made a clean sweep in the West (Mondale carried only two states west of Missouri). Only two of Hart's states, Massachusetts and Rhode Island, have a strong Democratic lineage.

Hart's appeal among weak or even antipartisan voters is reminiscent of Carter's similar support in the 1976 primaries.[64] One of the great ironies of the 1984 election was that Mondale, a loyal partisan insider— the heir of Hubert Humphrey—was also associated in the public mind with Jimmy Carter, an insurgent Democratic outsider. Thus Mondale faced the Sisyphean task of defending two pasts: the outmoded past of Humphrey's politics of party regulars and interest group coalitions and the embarrassing past of Carter's discredited presidency.

Blacks' Struggle for Equality

The 1984 nomination contest provided a stage for another long-term issue: the drive for greater equality by blacks. Unlike women's rights, which did not play a major role until the convention, issues of racial equality were never far from the top of the agenda throughout the primary season. Jackson won 77 percent of the black vote but only 5 percent of the white vote. Hart, by contrast, carried the white vote in all but seven states yet won only 3 percent of the black vote. It was Mondale who was consistently able to attract both white and black votes, an ability that saddled his opponents with an insurmountable obstacle.

The Role of Interest Groups

Finally, a continuing issue in the primaries was the proper role of organized interest groups. According to Mondale and his allies, the proliferation of such groups is one of the glories of pluralistic America. Early in the campaign a Mondale aide argued that the debate over special interests was strictly a reporters' issue and of little concern to the voters. Not true, as it turned out. For example, although most Americans admire the accomplishments of organized labor, they resent the unions' heavy involvement in politics. Campaign events—Mondale's acceptance of union endorsements, attacks by Glenn and then Hart on Mondale's unquestioning union ties and his back-door financial support from unions—and campaign issues—merit pay for teachers, trade protectionism, the Carter administration's Chrysler bailout—kept the voters' opposition to union involvement alive. Nationally, one out of three Democratic voters was from a union household, although this figure ranged from 13 percent in North Carolina to 45 percent in Pennsylvania. Mondale beat Hart 45 percent to 33 percent among union voters overall, and in every state outside of New England and the South. Mondale's support was especially concentrated in blue-collar unions, whose vote he got in all but one state; Hart, on the other hand, won among white-collar unionists in eight states.

The Democratic Convention

During most of American history, national party conventions were arenas for the interplay of many short-term forces—the rules, the power of state party leaders and favorite sons, the bargaining skills of the candidates, and the occasional interventions of the press—that combined in byzantine ways to produce a nominee. But in the era of television and reformed party rules, the conventions have operated less as juries than as assemblies that ratify the verdict of the primaries and caucuses.

The modern convention serves two main functions. First, because it is telecast to a national viewing audience, it is a stage for introducing the party's presidential nominee to the public. More than ever, this makes conventions an important short-term force in the general election. Conventions are the first occasions for many voters to scrutinize the candidates.

Second, the convention is a window through which the public (if it is interested) and the political community (which always is interested) can be reminded of the compelling long-term issues that divide each of the parties. The convention reveals the major intraparty political fault lines by gathering together in one place representatives of disparate party factions and points of view—such as political activists who care deeply about certain issues and others who have more pragmatic or personal concerns—to debate what the party represents, which issues it will accent and which it will duck, and who shall gain or lose power.

The same long-term issues that had colored the Democratic primaries and caucuses pervaded the party's July convention in San Francisco. The most profound split at the 1984 convention was not ideological but generational.[65] As the previous section demonstrated, Hart had exposed a sensitive nerve in the party—the sharp differences in outlook between young and old. The majority of delegates endorsed an approach that looked for guidance from the past; they hoped to rebuild the old New Deal coalition and reclaim the venerable themes of equity and fairness. Representing this view in his keynote address, Governor Cuomo urged the party to look to the future by recalling the past: "Make this nation remember how futures are built," he said. But two nights later Hart warned the party that theirs must not be "the party of memory." They "must disenthrall themselves from the policies of the comfortable past that do not answer the challenges of tomorrow" and instead "offer a new generation of ideas to a new generation." This generational schism was never repaired. In the November election, around one-third of the Democrats who had preferred Hart defected to Reagan, according to a

New York Times/CBS News election-day poll. Fully two-thirds of the independents who had supported Hart rejected Mondale and voted for Reagan. Others probably stayed home.

The 1984 Democratic convention was awash in racial and other equality issues. In keeping with the party's affirmative action rules, 50 percent of the delegates were women and 18 percent were black. Six percent of the delegates were Hispanic. All told, more than six out of every ten delegates were women or minorities. The San Francisco convention was a watershed in the history of group political gains. Those present heard an address by Jackson, the first serious black candidate to seek a major party's presidential nomination, and nominated Ferraro, the first woman vice-presidential candidate of a major party. From gavel to gavel convention oratory rang with references to equality: self-congratulation on having opened the doors of opportunity to women and frequent attacks on Reagan's generosity to the rich and parsimony to the poor.

The convention further fueled the debate over the third long-term issue to pervade the 1984 nomination process—the role of special interest groups in the party. In deciding on his vice-presidential running mate, Mondale borrowed a page from Jimmy Carter. Beginning in mid-June he invited seven potential candidates to come to his home in Minnesota for private interviews. The Mondale campaign thought that this procedure would undermine Hart's continuing challenge, demonstrate Mondale's willingness to open up the process to previously excluded groups (the interviewees included three women, two blacks, and one Hispanic), and show that Mondale was strong enough to choose a running mate on his own.

This method had worked well in 1976, when Mondale was selected, because it had built the outsider Carter a bridge to established party leaders. But the insider Mondale's use in 1984 of the same approach was greeted as another example of how this indecisive candidate pandered to special interests. NOW reinforced this perception by warning publicly that if Mondale did not choose a woman as his running mate, there would be a "thunderstorm."

On the eve of the convention a storm did develop, but over another incident. The Mondale forces tried to replace Charles Manatt, chair of the Democratic National Committee, with Bert Lance, chair of the Georgia state Democratic party and Carter's director of the Office of Management and Budget. In the face of enormous opposition based on Manatt's popularity and Lance's history of legal problems, Mondale dropped the effort—but not before the question of trying to appease interest groups (in this case, southerners unhappy about the selection of a northern liberal woman for the second spot on the ticket) was raised again.

The composition of the convention was itself a point of controversy. Whereas many party regulars viewed with pride a convention that included many union members (25 percent of the delegates, 11 percent of them from the AFL-CIO alone), teachers (16 percent, 7 percent of them from the NEA), and feminists (more than 6 percent from NOW and the National Women's Political Caucus), others feared the balkanization of the party.

Most recent Democratic conventions have been fractious affairs. In 1984 few discordant notes were struck during the convention itself, and it adjourned in a festival of harmony. Nevertheless, the convention, like the primaries and caucuses before it, was a reminder that nagging long-term questions about generational differences, the demands of blacks and women for greater equality, and the proper role of interest groups remained unresolved.

The Republicans in 1984

The Democrats took the 1984 prize for high drama in nomination politics, but the Republican nomination process also was important. The historical significance of the Republican story is that there *was* no story. This was the first time a party had had no contest for the nomination, not even a token one, since Eisenhower's renomination in 1956. Considering the embattled incumbent presidents of recent years—Johnson, who was forced to withdraw from the race in 1968, and Ford (1976) and Carter (1980), who had to battle right through to their conventions in order to win renomination—this was no mean feat.

The Republicans' unanimity in renominating Reagan was a harbinger of their fortunes in the general election. In fact, party unity in the nomination process has always worked this way. All the twentieth-century presidents who were defeated in their reelection bids—Taft, Hoover, Ford, and Carter—faced significant and sometimes bitter opposition for renomination. Their weakness as candidates sowed dissent within their own parties, so that the renomination challenges they faced were as much a symptom of their vulnerability as a cause of it.

Despite their unanimity in 1984, the Republicans were far from dormant during the primaries and caucuses. They used that time to prepare for the upcoming general election. Reagan was entitled to receive federal matching funds for his renomination candidacy, and his campaign spent about $24 million, 99 percent of the maximum. Much of that money went for a sophisticated voter registration campaign concentrated in Sun Belt states. According to most reports, the Republican efforts enabled them to more than match the Democrats at adding new voters to the rolls.

The Reagan campaign also used the primary season to organize for the fall campaign, especially by making peace between the moderate and conservative wings of the party; to direct public attention to Reagan's positions on noneconomic policies such as educational excellence and women's rights; to orchestrate presidential trips to China, Ireland, France, and elsewhere to capture media and public attention; and to urge state Republican party committees to see to it that approximately half the delegates to the convention were women.

Although the Republican convention was predestined to recoronate Reagan, the platform fights, speech making, and general politicking that occurred there revealed that party unity extended only as far as the choice of a nominee. The ideological strains ran from the moderates to the laissez-faire Old Right to the more populist New Right. There were supply-side true believers, crusaders for legislating traditional moral and social values, and innumerable shades in between.

Ronald Reagan's popularity and conservatism, as well as the Republicans' strong urge to maintain control of the White House, kept these intramural rivalries from getting out of hand in 1984. But like the Democrats, the Republicans are beset by generational wars (young, antiestablishment conservatives versus older, established party leaders), polarization on social issues (abortion and religion), and disputes over special interest groups (such as how closely to align with big business).

Conclusion

The 1984 presidential election will surely rekindle the debate over the nomination process.[66] As the Democrats dig out from under the rubble of their landslide defeat, their situation looks grim. They have lost six of the last nine elections, five of them catastrophically. Their only two victories since 1960 were tied to special circumstances: the aftermath of an assassination (1964) and the wake of Watergate (1976). Indeed, they nearly lost the 1976 election even though they were challenging a weak, unelected incumbent.

Many now blame the party's condition in part on the nomination process, just as they did after the previous defeats. Carter's loss in 1980 prompted complaints that the party's post-1968 reformed rules had led to the nomination of two successive outsider candidates, one of whom turned out to be an ineffective general election candidate (McGovern), the other widely regarded as an ineffective president (Carter).

The election of 1984 has introduced some puzzling new developments that will complicate the current round of party soul-searching. In

1980 the candidate who made it through the Republican nomination process was an outsider whose credentials for governing the country seemed flimsy. Four years later this outsider looked like an impressively effective president, in both political and policy terms, especially when compared with his recent predecessors. Ironically, when the Hunt Commission rewrote the Democratic rules in 1982 to diminish the chances of outsider candidates and put the nomination more into the hands of party professionals, they reduced the possibility that the party's nomination could go to anyone as unestablished as Reagan was in 1980. Democrats nominated a consummate insider in 1984, just as they had planned, then went down in ignominious defeat.

Some will warn against too much generalizing about insiders, outsiders, and the nomination process on the basis of what happened in 1984. Perhaps it was the peculiarities of the day that accounted for Reagan's good luck (oil gluts, rich food harvests) and Mondale's misfortune (the memory of Carter). The election did not show that insiders cannot win; Mondale was just the wrong insider and 1984 was the wrong year. Others will point to the kind of arguments raised in this chapter and note that the nomination system, even with the Hunt Commission reforms, is dominated by a multitude of short-term forces that is bound to yield unpredictable twists and turns. In 1984 the rules were important, but probably less important than the candidates' strategic decisions, especially Hart's strategic mistakes.

Elections always involve the interplay of both long-term and short-term forces. To disregard long-term influences is to risk losing any sense of purpose, direction, and continuity in elections. To disregard short-term forces is to jeopardize the ability to respond to the concerns of the day. A good system must permit calm deliberation and inject elements of the past into the process but not snuff out all excitement or fail to test candidates' abilities to withstand sudden pressures. Both established political insiders and dark horse challengers should have the opportunity to compete effectively. The enormous challenge facing those who would redesign the electoral system is to create the proper balance between long-term and short-term forces so as to achieve these varied and often competing goals.

Notes

1. Donald Matthews, "Presidential Nominations: Process and Outcomes," in *Choosing the President,* ed. James David Barber (Englewood Cliffs, N.J.:

Prentice-Hall, 1974), 36; Austin Ranney, *Channels of Power: The Impact of Television on American Politics* (New York: Basic Books, 1983), 92-93.

2. Anthony King, "How Not to Select Presidential Candidates: A View from Europe," in *The American Elections of 1980,* ed. Austin Ranney (Washington, D.C.: American Enterprise Institute, 1981), 307-320; Austin Ranney, "Candidate Selection," in *Democracy at the Polls,* ed. David Butler, Howard E. Penniman, and Austin Ranney (Washington, D.C.: American Enterprise Institute, 1981), 75-106. Only in Canada does the degree of rank-and-file participation even remotely approach that in the United States.

3. Morton Kondracke, "In like Fritz," *New Republic,* December 19, 1983, 19.

4. Hedrick Smith, "Mondale Lead over Nearest Rival in Poll Sets Nonincumbent Record," *New York Times,* February 28, 1984, 1.

5. Outsider candidates are not an exclusively post-1952 phenomenon. The American Republic was born in a climate of antipartisanship, and antiparty, antipolitics, and antiestablishment themes have run throughout our history. In the early twentieth century, for example, both the Republicans and the Democrats turned to men not closely allied with the party regulars, Theodore Roosevelt in 1904 and Woodrow Wilson in 1912. In 1940 the Republicans nominated Wendell Willkie, a former Democrat who had virtually no prior national political experience and who bucked orthodox Republicanism. However, most party nominees in the first half of this century were strong party loyalists—men like Franklin D. Roosevelt, Al Smith, Warren G. Harding, and Calvin Coolidge. Since 1952 major changes in the social and political environment have made the nomination process more receptive to outsiders.

6. Some years ago political scientist Philip Converse suggested that we might think of the vote decision in general elections as consisting of two components, an underlying, or normal, vote based on partisanship and a vote based on the circumstances of the specific election. Partisanship is by far the most durable political force. Thus one can interpret voting as the combination of long-term forces, operationally defined as the vote that would occur if party identification were the sole influence, and short-term forces—particular candidates and campaign issues—that cause some voters to turn their backs temporarily on their party. Philip Converse, "The Concept of a Normal Vote," in *Elections and the Political Order,* ed. Angus Campbell et al. (New York: John Wiley and Sons, 1966), 9-39. Expanded from Converse's technical usage to a somewhat more colloquial usage, this distinction between long- and short-term forces is applied in this chapter to an analysis of the nomination process.

7. This interpretation conflicts with the view often heard as the events unfolded. The 1984 election was seen by many as turning on personality and the media. The voters reelected Reagan, according to House majority leader Jim Wright, because "they like him, they like his personality." Political columnist David Broder complained that issues were overshadowed in the campaign by Reagan's personality. House Speaker Thomas P. O'Neill, Jr., blamed the

news media, especially television, for painting an unfavorable impression of Mondale. Reagan, a master image maker, was at home with television. Many, including Mondale himself in a candid post-mortem after the election, suggested that Mondale lost because he could not communicate effectively on television. In truth, the 1984 election turned less on personality or the media than on the economic and international state of the nation over the previous eight years, Reagan's record compared with Carter's.

8. Also, most Americans (some two-thirds) usually decide whom to vote for by the time of the party conventions, long before the fall campaign gets rolling. In 1984 the public may have decided even earlier. In a *Los Angeles Times* poll, nearly half the voters reported that they had decided how to vote in the general election even before the primaries began in February. Furthermore, citizens who remain undecided generally have a minimal interest in politics and are not apt to follow the fall campaign closely.

9. Scott Keeter and Cliff Zukin, *Uninformed Choice: The Failure of the New Nominating System* (New York: Praeger, 1983), vii.

10. For a discussion of the big-state effect of the electoral college in recent presidential campaigns see Herbert Asher, *Presidential Elections and American Politics* (Homewood, Ill.: Dorsey Press, 1984), 271-277.

11. "Primary Lunacy," *New Republic,* March 26, 1984, 6.

12. On the history of nomination procedures see James Ceaser, *Presidential Selection: Theory and Development* (Princeton, N.J.: Princeton University Press, 1979); Paul T. David, Ralph M. Goldman, and Richard Bain, *The Politics of National Party Conventions* (Washington, D.C: Brookings Institution, 1960); Gerald Pomper, *Nominating the President* (New York: Norton, 1966); Louise Overacker, *The Presidential Primary* (New York: Macmillan, 1926); and James W. Davis, *Presidential Primaries: Road to the White House* (New York: Thomas Y. Crowell, 1967).

13. Most political reformers in the early twentieth century shared Nebraska senator George Norris's view: "One of the objections that is always made to the direct primary is that it takes away party responsibility and breaks down party control. But this objection thus given against the direct primary I frankly offer as one of the best reasons for its retention." Quoted in Pope McCorkle and Joel L. Fleishman, "Political Parties and Presidential Nominations: The Intellectual Ironies of Reform and Change in the Mass Media Age," in *The Future of American Political Parties,* ed. Joel L. Fleishman (Englewood Cliffs, N.J.: Prentice-Hall, 1982), 142.

14. During this period of mixed conventions and primaries, primary elections were little more than a footnote to the nomination process. Candidates could win primaries and fail to gain their party's nomination, as did Theodore Roosevelt in 1912 and Estes Kefauver in 1952. Occasionally the primaries provided a testing ground in which to demonstrate electoral appeal when this was in doubt. For example, John F. Kennedy sought a victory in Protestant West Virginia in order to prove to Democratic leaders that his religion would not be a liability in the fall. Although successful candidates

sometimes competed in a few primaries, most concentrated on winning the favor of the party leaders who controlled delegate selection.

15. For detailed descriptions and analyses of these rules reforms between 1968 and 1980 see Austin Ranney, *Curing the Mischiefs of Faction* (Berkeley: University of California Press, 1975); Byron Shafer, *Quiet Revolution: The Struggle for the Democratic Party and the Shaping of Post-Reform Politics* (New York: Russell Sage Foundation, 1983); and David E. Price, *Bringing Back the Parties* (Washington, D.C.: CQ Press, 1984).

16. The substantial changes mandated by the Democrats spilled over into Republican delegate selection as well. In response to pressure to broaden public participation and improve minority representation, the 1972 Republican convention adopted a resolution urging the state parties to encourage participation by women, youth, ethnic groups, and racial minorities. The national Republican party, unlike the Democratic party, did not undertake to dictate to the states the standards for delegate selection, but many reforms in these procedures were forced on the Republicans by Democratic-controlled state legislatures that adopted statutes applying to both parties.

17. Whether the proliferation of primaries can be attributed directly to the rules reforms has been hotly debated. See Kenneth A. Bode and Carol F. Casey, "Party Reform: Revisionism Revised," in *Political Parties in the Eighties*, ed. Robert A. Goldwin (Washington, D.C.: American Enterprise Institute, 1980), 16-18; Nelson Polsby, *Consequences of Party Reform* (New York: Oxford University Press, 1983), 55-59, 62-64; Price, *Bringing Back the Parties*, 207, 210. For a discussion of the influence of the media on the increase in primaries see Richard Rubin, *Press, Party and Presidency* (New York: Norton, 1981), 191-196.

18. William Cavala, "Changing the Rules Changes the Game: Party Reform and the 1972 California Delegation to the Democratic National Convention," *American Political Science Review* (March 1974): 27-42; James I. Lengle and Byron Shafer, "Primary Rules, Political Power, and Social Change," *American Political Science Review* (March 1976): 25-40; Gerald M. Pomper, "New Rules and New Games in the National Conventions," *Journal of Politics* (August 1979): 784-805; Louis Maisel and Gerald J. Lieberman, "The Impact of Electoral Rules on Primary Elections: The Democratic Primaries in 1976," in *The Impact of the Electoral Process*, ed. Louis Maisel and Joseph Cooper (Beverly Hills, Calif.: Sage Publications, 1977), 39-80.

19. For a thorough discussion of the effects of rules changes on political and governmental institutions and the governing process see Polsby, *Consequences of Party Reform*.

20. The best summary and analysis of the Hunt Commission reforms is contained in Price, *Bringing Back the Parties*, 159-183. Price, who served as staff director of the commission, emphasizes the theme of party renewal (see pp. 162, 182-183). Lanny Davis, a member of the technical advisory committee of the commission, has stressed the second theme: "It was

principally the memory of Jimmy Carter's 1976 campaign and nomination that brought party regulars and reformers, elected officials, labor representatives, and Mondale and Kennedy supporters to the same conclusion in 1982: new reforms were needed to prevent an outsider from using the primaries to lock up the nomination without the support of the party establishment and before the national convention could meet." Davis, "Reforming the Reforms," *New Republic,* February 17, 1982, 8.

21. Davis, "Reforming the Reforms," 13.

22. Mondale's share of the delegates exceeded his popular vote in every primary state except California (where the winner-take-all procedure benefited Hart).

23. Pennsylvania illustrates how this different method of distributing delegates would have yielded vastly different results. Mondale won 45 percent of the popular vote there, compared with Hart's 33 percent and Jackson's 16 percent. If the delegates had been divided in exact proportion to the primary vote, the delegate count would have been 88 for Mondale, 65 for Hart, and 31 for Jackson. However, with its winner-take all system (Pennsylvania was a loophole state) and superdelegates, Mondale claimed a total of 160 delegates (82 percent), compared with 18 for Jackson and 17 for Hart.

24. Figures for 1968-1980 from Price, *Bringing Back the Parties,* 225.

25. Quoted in Ibid., 227.

26. These four states not only scheduled early contests, they each adopted delegate selection procedures well suited to the Mondale campaign: loophole primaries in Illinois and Pennsylvania, a bonus primary in New York, and a caucus in Michigan.

27. See Sidney Verba and Gary R. Orren, *Equality in America: The View from the Top* (Cambridge: Harvard University Press, 1985), chapters 1 and 10; Thomas B. Edsall, *The New Politics of Inequality* (New York: Norton, 1984).

28. Republican candidates outspent their Democratic opponents in 17 of the 19 presidential elections between 1900 and 1972 yet won the White House only 10 times. Wilson was outspent in both of his elections, Franklin D. Roosevelt was outspent in all four of his, and Kennedy and Johnson were outspent in each of their elections. In the twentieth century the spending of the two parties is virtually uncorrelated with their shares of the presidential vote. For presidential campaign spending data see Herbert E. Alexander, *Financing Politics* (Washington, D.C.: CQ Press, 1980), 5; Herbert E. Alexander, "Making Sense about Dollars in the 1980 Presidential Campaigns," in *Money and Politics in the United States,* ed. Michael J. Malbin (Washington, D.C.: American Enterprise Institute, 1984), 11-37; and Asher, *Presidential Elections and American Politics,* 182. This is not to say that money has never influenced the final outcome. The spending gap in 1968 ($25 million to $11 million) may well have figured in Nixon's eyelash victory over Humphrey. But that is the exception.

29. In 1984, for example, Reagan and Mondale each received $40.4 million from the government to run their fall campaign. Party and private organizations

were permitted to raise additional money to be spent under certain restrictions. Although Reagan supporters raised more of this supplemental money than the Democrats in both 1980 and 1984, Carter and Mondale had sufficient funds to mount highly visible and active campaigns. Reagan's landslide victories cannot be attributed to his financial advantages.

30. This discussion of the role of money in the nomination process draws upon a more extensive analysis in Gary R. Orren, "Presidential Campaign Finance: Its Impact and Future," *Commonsense* (No. 2, 1983): 50-66.

31. Ibid., 55. Mondale, of course, was just that sort of "unemployed" candidate, as were Carter in 1976 and Reagan in 1980.

32. Candidates who accept public matching funds must abide by certain spending restrictions. In 1984 a candidate could spend no more than $20.2 million during the entire prenomination period, plus an additional 20 percent for fund-raising costs, making the overall spending ceiling $24.2 million. Candidates were permitted to spend unlimited amounts on legal and accounting fees necessary for complying with the law. Each candidate also was subject to separate spending limits in each state. In 1984 the individual state limits (including an inflation factor) were set at 32.3 cents per eligible voter, with a minimum state spending limit of $404,000.

33. Only a third of the Republican delegates had been chosen in 1980 by the time Reagan had spent about three-fourths of his allowance. If Reagan had faced a more serious challenge from George Bush, his campaign would have been in serious trouble. In 1980 both the Reagan and the Carter campaigns bumped up against the overall spending limit by the end of the primaries, as did Ford and Carter in the 1976 primaries.

34. Maxwell Glen, "Free Spenders—the 'Other' Campaign for Reagan Chooses Its Targets," *National Journal*, September 13, 1980, 1513.

35. One study found that in 25 presidential primaries in 1976 the winner outspent the loser in 15 of the Republican contests but in only 6 of the Democratic ones. Joel H. Goldstein, "The Influence of Money on the Prenomination Stage of the Presidential Selection Process: The Case of the 1976 Election," *Presidential Studies Quarterly* (Spring 1978): 164-179.

36. Maxwell Glen, "Another Campaign, Another Loophole—This Time, It's Delegate Committees," *National Journal*, May 5, 1984, 873.

37. Hart decided not to pursue the issue at the convention. Historically, however, credentials challenges often have been used by outsider candidates to wrest the nomination from the grip of party regulars. Some have failed, as did Theodore Roosevelt in his challenge of the credentials of William Howard Taft's delegates in 1912. Others have succeeded, including McGovern in his crucial 1972 challenge of the credentials committee's ruling on the California delegation, and Eisenhower in his instrumental 1952 challenge of the credentials of many delegates pledged to Sen. Robert Taft.

   During the 1984 primaries Mondale ordered that the delegate committees be disbanded, promised to refund excess contributions, and agreed to treat the spending of the committees as spending by his own campaign, subject to the limits of the campaign finance laws. After the general election the Federal Election Commission ruled that the Mondale campaign had acted improperly in its use of delegate committees. The ruling required that the Mondale campaign reimburse the Treasury for the amount of money that was contributed to delegate committees in excess of federal limits and ordered the campaign to pay a small fine.

38. Thomas E. Patterson, *The Mass Media Election: How Americans Choose Their President* (New York: Praeger, 1980), 3.

39. For evidence on the surprisingly weak effect of both paid advertising and news coverage on voters during presidential general elections, see Sidney Kraus and Dennis Davis, *The Effects of Mass Communications on Political Behavior* (University Park: Pennsylvania State University Press, 1976), 48-109; Michael Robinson, "The Media in 1980: Was the Message the Message?" in Ranney, *The American Elections of 1980,* 177-211; Gary Jacobson, "The Impact of Broadcast Campaigning in Electoral Outcomes," *Journal of Politics* (August 1975): 769-793; and Thomas E. Patterson and Robert McClure, *The Unseeing Eye: The Myth of Television Power in National Elections* (New York: G. P. Putnam's Sons, 1976), 109-139. On the stronger influence of the media during the nomination period, see Jacobson, "The Impact of Broadcast Campaigning in Electoral Outcomes," 781; and Robinson, "The Media in 1980," 183.

40. Donald Matthews, "Winnowing: The News Media and the 1976 Presidential Nominations," in *Race for the Presidency: The Media and the Nominating Process,* ed. James David Barber (Englewood Cliffs, N.J.: Prentice-Hall, 1978), 55. Also see Thomas R. Marshall, "The News Verdict and Public Opinion during the Primaries," in *Television Coverage of the 1980 Presidential Campaign,* ed. William C. Adams (Norwood, N.J.: Ablex Publishing, 1983), 49-67.

41. On the inflated news coverage of the early contests and its powerful influence on the voters see Michael Robinson, "TV's Newest Program: The 'Presidential Nominations Game,' " *Public Opinion,* May-June 1978, 41-45; Michael Robinson, "Media Coverage in the Primary Campaign of 1976: Implications for Voters, Candidates, and Parties," in *The Party Symbol,* ed. William Crotty (San Francisco: W. H. Freeman and Company, 1980), 178-191; Michael Robinson and Margaret Sheehan, *Over the Wire and on TV: CBS and UPI in Campaign '80* (New York: Russell Sage, 1980), 174-178; and Keeter and Zukin, *Uninformed Choice,* 68, 86, 136, 141-142, 151-155. As Rep. Morris Udall, who ran in the 1976 Democratic primaries, put it: "It's like a football game, in which you say to the first team that makes a first down with ten yards, 'hereafter, your team has a special rule. Your first downs are five yards. And if you make three of those you get a two yard first down. And we're going to let your first touchdown count twenty-one points. Now the rest of you bastards play catch-up under the regular rules.' " Quoted in Jules Witcover, *Marathon: The Pursuit of the Presidency 1972-1976* (New York: Viking Press, 1977), 692-693.

42. Thus, for example, in 1976 the media chose to emphasize in their primary

coverage Wisconsin rather than New York, Oregon rather than five other primaries on the same day, and Ohio rather than New Jersey or California.

43. Robinson and Sheehan, *Over the Wire and on TV,* 90, 116-139, 243.

44. Patterson and McClure, *The Unseeing Eye,* 27-46; Patterson, *The Mass Media Election,* 21-30; and Robinson and Sheehan, *Over the Wire and on TV,* 140-166, 207-208.

45. William C. Adams, "Media Coverage of Campaign '84: A Preliminary Report," *Public Opinion,* April-May 1984, 10-11.

46. Ibid., 11.

47. David Moore, "The Death of Retail Politics in New Hampshire," *Public Opinion,* February-March 1984, 56-57.

48. There were other instances in 1984 when the media chose to play up certain contests and gloss over others—such as the limited coverage they gave to the nonbinding Wisconsin primary, which Hart unexpectedly won (Mondale won the binding Wisconsin caucus, but that event attracted only 30,000 voters compared with 700,000 in the primary), or the emphasis they placed on Mondale's June 5 victory in New Jersey at the expense of Hart's win that same day in California.

49. In *Presidential Campaign Politics* (Homewood, Ill.: Dorsey Press, 1984), 143-218, John Kessel describes candidate strategies and their consequences in recent presidential nomination contests. Also see John H. Aldrich, *Before the Convention: Strategies and Choices in Presidential Nomination Campaigns* (Chicago: University of Chicago Press, 1980), 100-197; and Gary R. Orren, "Candidate Style and Voter Alignment in 1976," in *Emerging Coalitions in American Politics,* ed. Seymour Martin Lipset (San Francisco: Institute for Contemporary Studies, 1978), 127-181.

50. Kessel, *Presidential Campaign Politics,* 3-12.

51. Cranston also latched onto the straw polls in his strategy. His plan was to do well in these preliminary tests and emerge from the crowded field as the leading liberal alternative to Mondale and Glenn.

52. For example, Hamilton Jordan, Carter's former campaign manager and chief of staff, publicly offered a strong dose of advice: Mondale must shake the special interest albatross or his candidacy was doomed. Jordan, "Mondale's Choice," *New Republic,* June 6, 1983, 15-19.

53. Three years before the primaries James Johnson, Mondale's campaign manager, had emphasized in a memo to Mondale that the candidate must "renew and refurbish yourself substantively, so you can articulate new ideas, outline new approaches, provide a vision of the future." Quoted in Sidney Blumenthal, "Steel and Roses," *New Republic,* April 30, 1984, 10. Mondale did some retooling, what he called "The Re-Education of Walter Mondale" in a *New York Times Magazine* article (November 8, 1981, 67, 110-115, 165). But the fruits of his efforts were not prominent in his subsequent campaign.

54. In the fall of 1983 the Glenn campaign aired a five-minute advertisement that intoned, "At a time when most politicians are caught up in the policies of the past or the issue of the moment . . . only one man is talking about the fu-

ture.... He doesn't play to the special interests, he doesn't play the old political game.... Believe in the future again."

55. Quoted in Sidney Blumenthal, "Over and Out," *New Republic,* February 13, 1984, 15.

56. Hart voters were less likely than Mondale voters to strongly favor their own candidate, but more likely to disfavor his chief opponent. One of Hart's main constituencies, as we shall see, was young voters. Yet Hart's favorability rating showed almost no variation with age, whereas Mondale's declined steadily from older to younger voters. As William Schneider observed, "Opposition to Mondale appeared to be the key factor in the Hart vote." Schneider, "This Time, the Division in the Democratic Party Is along Generational Lines," *National Journal,* March 10, 1984, 489. Hart himself substantiated this conclusion in a *Newsweek* interview during the primaries: "Mondale thinks I'm his problem. I'm not his problem. He's his problem." Quoted in William Schneider, "Half a Realignment," *New Republic,* December 3, 1984, 21.

57. On the contrast between coalitional and ideological styles see Orren, "The Changing Styles of American Party Politics," in *The Future of American Party Politics,* 6-10.

58. An analysis of Mondale's speeches confirms that he concentrated more on Reagan at these two points in the primaries. Paul Light, "Mondale's Message," *Public Opinion,* June-July 1984, 15-16.

59. Just before the Illinois primary two national polls reported Hart and Reagan to be neck and neck, and another found Hart with a slight lead. Throughout March the gap between Hart and Reagan in various polls was about 10 to 15 points narrower than the gap between Mondale and Reagan.

60. Other short-term forces are important, including voter turnout. Although there is a long-term, stable component of voter turnout, which reflects an underlying status difference (higher status citizens participate more in politics) and historical and cultural patterns (for example, voter turnout is consistently higher in northern states where the Progressive movement flourished than in southern states), there is also a short-term component that reflects election-specific factors: the nature of the candidates and issues, the degree of competition, group mobilization patterns, and election rules. Voter turnout in Democratic primaries was higher in 1984 than in 1980, in virtually every state. That was particularly true in states where Jackson's candidacy inspired a surge of black registration and voting. But part of the increased turnout can be traced to the absence of a Republican contest, which led many independents (and a few Republicans) to pick up Democratic ballots.

61. This age division recurred in state after state, beginning with Iowa, where a *Los Angeles Times* exit poll showed Mondale's support dropping precipitously with younger voters. He won 67 percent of the votes of those 65 and over, 54 percent of those 45 to 64, 40 percent of those 30 to 44, and only 28 percent of those 18 to 29.

62. I have used the word "generational" loosely. Not all age differences warrant

a generational explanation. Political scientists distinguish between two sources of age differences: generational effects and life-cycle effects. The former refers to distinctive outlooks that people of roughly the same age share because they were exposed to similar formative social experiences. The latter refers to distinctive political views that are associated with particular stages in one's life. Generational effects endure throughout a lifetime; life-cycle effects change as one matures. It is too soon to know whether generational or life-cycle forces account for the differences among age groups in the 1984 primary voting, but the answer has profound implications for the permanence of age-related conflict in the Democratic party. See Paul Allen Beck, "Young vs. Old in 1984: Generational and Life States in Presidential Nomination Politics," *PS* (Summer 1984): 515-524.

63. This underscores the importance of what is happening in the other party's primary on election day. In New Hampshire there were few important contests on the Republican ballot. As a result, twice as many independents voted in the Democratic primary in 1984 as in 1980. Without them Hart probably would have lost. On the other hand, in Illinois moderate senator Charles Percy faced a New Right challenger in the Republican primary. This contest attracted many independents who otherwise might have voted for Hart.

64. Like Hart, Carter ran against the "special interests" and the party regulars in 1976, and his public support closely resembled Hart's in many ways: "Democratic regulars reacted to Carter's antipartisanship predictably: they did not like him for it. Voters who supported him in the primaries were not distinguished by partisan loyalty. In primary after primary, he drew stronger support from Democrats who had defected to Nixon than from those who voted Democratic in 1972. He scored his widest primary margins in the typically Republican areas of upstate New York, western Massachusetts, and southern Illinois." Orren, "Candidate Style and Voter Alignment in 1976," 148.

65. William Schneider, "The Dividing Line between Delegates Is Age," *National Journal Convention Daily*, July 16, 1984, 4.

66. The debate in the political arena has spilled over into academe. Studies most critical of the 1968-1980 reforms include: James W. Ceaser, *Reforming the Reforms: A Critical Analysis of the Presidential Selection Process* (Cambridge, Mass: Ballinger, 1982); Ranney, *Curing the Mischiefs of Faction*; Jeane J. Kirkpatrick, *Dismantling the Parties: Reflections on Party Reform and Party Decomposition* (Washington, D.C.: American Enterprise Institute, 1978); and Polsby, *Consequences of Party Reform*. More sanguine views of the new nominating system are William Crotty, *Decision for the Democrats: Reforming the Party Structure* (Baltimore: Johns Hopkins University Press, 1978); William Crotty, *Party Reform* (New York: Longman, 1983); Bode and Casey, "Party Reform"; and Michael Nelson, "The Presidential Nominating System: Problems and Prescriptions," in *What Role for Government? Lessons from Policy Research,* ed. Richard Zeckhauser and Derek Leebaert (Durham, N.C.: Duke University Press, 1982), 34-51.

3. THE ELECTION:
CANDIDATES, STRATEGIES, AND DECISIONS

Paul C. Light and Celinda Lake

From the beginning the 1984 election was Ronald Reagan's to lose. With unemployment and inflation down, Grenada and the Olympics in the forefront, and the repeated bombings in Beirut, Lebanon, strangely unimportant, Reagan led from start to finish. In what was surely the longest campaign in history—running almost two years from Walter F. Mondale's formal announcement of candidacy—there was little doubt that Reagan would win. The only question was by how much. Mobilizing all the advantages of incumbency, with few of the problems that recent incumbent presidents have faced, Reagan reversed the apparent trend toward one-term presidencies.

No matter how hard Mondale might have tried he could not have won the 1984 election without Reagan's help. But Reagan ran a masterful campaign. Repeating his campaign theme from 1980, he asked voters if they were better off now than they were four years ago. The economy was still the voters' main concern, and by election day 59 percent of them apparently had concluded that they were better off. That figure had increased throughout the fall campaign. Reagan dominated the issues that mattered most to voters—the economy and a strong defense—and was able to neutralize his weaknesses—arms control, budget deficits, and Social Security.

Mondale, on the other hand, asked voters whether they would be better off four years into the future and hoped they would say no. In the terminology of political science, Mondale's only chance of winning rested on a "prospective" strategy, in contrast with Reagan's "retrospective" one. Mondale had to get the voters to think ahead, to cast their ballots on the basis of their fears of another recession, a nuclear war, continued budget deficits, and growing environmental spoils. Unfortunately for Mondale, the voters' minds apparently stayed very much in the recent past or present. They wondered about Mondale's leadership qualities, remembering his connection to the Carter administration. They wondered about his obligations to special interest groups, recalling the many endorsements he had received and promises he had made during the long nomination campaign. They asked themselves how they were doing today and felt good. Although some voters did worry about prospective issues and about the fairness of Reagan's policies, these issues never did matter to them as much as their short-term self-interest. Besides, Mondale's campaign failed to give the voters a clear sense of what he stood for or of how he would fulfill his promises to build a different future.

Indeed, according to the public opinion polls, Mondale never closed to striking distance, which left Reagan with little need to address the prospective issues. Compared with the remarkable volatility of the spring primaries, the general election was hardly dramatic. Allowing for the natural statistical error that comes from representing 100 million voters with a very small random sample, Mondale never came within nine percentage points of Reagan after August. Moreover, most voters decided early, giving Mondale the added problem of shaking voters loose from their initial choices. Even following the first debate—a debate in which the president was clearly tired, confused, and poorly prepared—Reagan suffered only a slight loss in support. Although some voters expressed doubts about his knowledge and age, the second debate reassured most of them, as evidenced by a boost in support for the president. For all intents, the election was over almost three weeks before the actual balloting.

The Strategic Climate

To understand the fall campaign, it is first necessary to grasp the central elements in voting decisions. What are the ingredients that determine voter choice? What is the role of party identification? Issues? Candidate images? Next, it is important to understand how the two candidates designed their campaigns. Reagan and Mondale had very different ideas about how voters mix those ingredients and make their choices. As the incumbent, Reagan wanted them to look *back* over four years of declining inflation and vote retrospectively; Mondale wanted them to look *ahead* to four years of growing budget deficits and nuclear tension and vote prospectively. Finally, it is important to look at how candidate strategies and voter decisions were played out in the day-to-day dynamics of the 1984 campaign.

Party Identification

Past work on voting behavior has shown that there are three major factors that influence voters' decisions: party identification, issues, and the candidates' images.[1] Each election involves a somewhat different combination of these factors. Some elections emphasize traditional party differences; others center on the candidates' personalities. The relative influence of the three factors depends on the candidates who run, the issues currently in the headlines and on the voters' minds, the differences between the candidates and their campaign strategies. If, for example, voters see no real choice on the issues they care about most, the election is likely to turn on party identification or candidate images.

Historically, party identification has proven to be the most stable predictor of elections. Party identification is the psychological attachment that voters feel toward one or the other political party; it is rooted in their childhood political learning and their later contact with issues and candidates. When voters have no other information about candidates or issues, they can only make their choice on the basis of party identification. However, in the highly visible campaign season, voters now are bombarded with information about the candidates from both paid and free media. In that kind of highly informed environment, voters increasingly defect from their party. One strategic decision that presidential candidates must make is whether to try to reinforce or dilute party identification in order to increase or decrease its importance in the vote.

In 1984 Mondale wanted to reinforce Democratic party identification, while Reagan wanted to weaken it. Since Democrats still outnumber Republicans, Mondale wanted to make sure his partisans stayed with him. In contrast, Reagan, already assured of Republican support, openly invited Democrats to defect, reminding them that he was once a Democrat and only broke with the party when it lost touch with the mainstream. Thus, Mondale often talked about the leadership and heritage of the Democratic party, while Reagan emphasized nonpartisan themes such as patriotism and a strong economy and referred frequently in his speeches to Democratic heroes like Franklin D. Roosevelt and John F. Kennedy.

Independents also make up an increasingly large part of the American electorate. Although most independents actually lean toward one party or the other, they generally vote on the basis of the candidate or the issues, not the party, and often split their ballots between the presidential ticket and lower-level contests. Mondale faced the formidable task of persuading Democrats to support him as the candidate of his party, while asking independents to support him as the candidate of the issues or of leadership.

Incumbency Advantage

Mondale's task was certainly complicated by his running against an incumbent. To be sure, incumbent presidents have not done well in recent elections. Counting Reagan's reelection in 1984, only two of the past five

85

incumbents have won a second full term. Lyndon B. Johnson decided not to run for reelection in 1968 because of problems with his Vietnam policy and a poor showing in the New Hampshire primary. President Gerald R. Ford barely won nomination against a challenger named Reagan in 1976 and was ultimately defeated on economic issues and Watergate. Jimmy Carter also struggled for renomination, and he too was defeated on economic issues.

Still, incumbent presidents have significant advantages in reelection campaigns. First, they carry the mantle of leadership. They occupy the strongest office in the free world and have all the perquisites that go with it. Challengers must compose their own theme songs; presidents campaign to the tune of "Hail to the Chief." Second, incumbents often have highly seasoned campaign staffers already on the White House payroll. Reagan hired most of his 1980 campaign aides for administrative slots and had no trouble reassembling a powerful reelection team for 1984. Third, the White House machinery offers great electoral advantages, including instant media coverage for presidential events. The Office of Public Liaison, for example, is dedicated to cultivating interest group support for the president, which can be translated into reelection support. Fourth, the president has the political loyalty and support of the vice president. In recent years, the vice president has become a much more important White House player and now occupies a highly visible campaign role, especially in midterm elections. With the vice president and other surrogates, including cabinet secretaries, on the road during the term, presidents enter the election year at some advantage. Even if challengers convince the voters that they would be just as good as the incumbent, voters usually prefer to maintain the status quo. Other things being equal, continuity is favored over change and certainty over uncertainty.

Other things, however, seldom are equal. If there is to be an incumbency advantage, it must lie in the president's record and in his ability to persuade the voters that the record is good. In incumbent contests, at least, the Reagan campaign's theory of voting behavior usually applies: voters choose on the basis of their retrospective judgments.[2] They look back, not ahead. In 1980 the voters remembered high inflation and the hostage crisis in Iran. In 1984 they remembered low inflation, a strong national defense, and the successful invasion of Grenada. Moreover, one legacy of the Carter years was an increase in voter concern for presidential leadership. Voters had decided that promises are meaningless without effective leadership.

In making these retrospective judgments, voters usually concentrate on the economy first, defense second, and foreign affairs a distant third. They tend to draw their conclusions on the basis of what they see as the general condition of the country and not on their own personal experience; they also, however, vote in their self-interest.[3] In short, they ask how the nation is doing and then vote on the basis of what they think will happen to them. Although voters do care about what is happening to others—minorities, the poor, the elderly—those concerns generally do not outweigh their personal stake. Mondale asked middle-class voters to ignore their current condition, think of others in need, and vote on the future. Reagan asked them to look at their own situations, assume that most others were enjoying similar good times, and vote on the recent past.

Indeed, research shows that voters have very short memories in making their retrospective judgments, looking back only at economic performance during the past year or so. With the economy expanding in November 1984, for example, American voters apparently chose to forget that, just two years earlier, their economy had been suffering its most serious decline since the Great Depression of the 1930s. Presidential candidates, of course, try to remind voters of the events and conditions that will help win the election. Mondale wanted to remind them of the recession, Reagan's 1981 attack on Social Security, fairness, and the Beirut bombings; Reagan of low inflation, Grenada, and a resurging patriotic pride in national strength.

This, then, was the strategic climate that Mondale faced in the summer of 1984. His choices were limited—long shots at best. He could not stress party identification too heavily, or he would alienate independent voters. As for the issues and candidates, it is virtually impossible to change voters' perceptions of what has happened to them. If people feel good, it is hard to convince them to feel bad. Thus, Mondale could not hope to win the election by convincing voters that the economy was failing or by getting them to dislike Reagan. Mondale had to take what few concerns voters did have about Reagan—the budget deficits, for example—and convince them to think about the future, persuading the public that America could not afford four more years of the incumbent. While acknowledging the good economic news and peaceful times, Mondale had to show voters that the glad tidings would not continue if the deficits were not cut and if the arms race were accelerated into the heavens by Reagan's proposed "Star Wars" defense. He had to show voters that Reagan was unlikely to make much progress on either issue, that even if times were good for another four years it would be at tremendous cost for their future and their children's future.

The Reagan campaign, in contrast, spent much of its resources trying to reassure the public. Because Mondale never gave a clear sense of where he wanted to go in the future, beyond a few specific proposals, and because voters did not believe in him as a leader who could get them there anyway, Reagan's campaign had little trouble answering the long-term questions. Further, the American system rewards short-term strategies. Presidents are encouraged to produce immediate gains, even if they shortchange future generations. Voters prefer tangible benefits to uncertain promises.

Like other challengers, however, Mondale could try to change the weights that voters gave to party identification, issues, and candidate images. He could try to elevate the importance of the fairness issue, of arms control, and of Reagan's connection to the religious right and its leader, the Reverend Jerry Falwell. If he could shift the campaign to those issues and reinforce traditional party loyalties, he would have a chance. Yet, as his campaign staff knew, those issues would have a hard time competing against a prosperous economy, a strong defense, and peace.

Candidates and Strategies

Presidential candidates are not fools. They are highly skilled politicians, electoral survivors. Whatever they may do once in office, they surely know how to get elected. They work with the very best pollsters, policy staffers, media consultants, and fund raisers available. They know how a campaign works. Mondale, for example, had won two Senate elections, the vice presidency, and a number of primaries before taking on Reagan in 1984. Although he had not run for office on his own as a nonincumbent since his junior year in high school (he had been appointed to the Senate), Mondale was a skilled political strategist. Reagan had won two terms as governor, the presidency, and the uncontested renomination for a second term before entering his final campaign. Each had met dozens of challengers over their careers, losing against some, prevailing against most.

Although political observers sometimes question presidential candidates' tactics, all nominees are trying to win. In doing so, they must make political choices. They must decide where to travel, what to spend, who to hire, what to say. Whatever the abstract models of voting behavior may suggest about their chances, candidates confront the real world of building a campaign. Even if the odds are against them—as they were against Mondale in 1984—candidates must act. They carry the party's mantle into battle and often feel responsible for the full slate of party candidates. Mondale, for example, was aware of the lengthening Reagan coattails in September and mounted an effort to save Democratic congressional seats.

Candidates try ideally to maximize their strengths and minimize their weaknesses. In reality, limited campaign resources and the strategic climate may reduce their ability to do either. Reagan, for example, had to counter the Democratic edge in party identification, while calming fears about his uneven record in foreign policy and his staggering budget deficits. Mondale had to neutralize the huge Republican margin in fund raising and Reagan's incumbency advantages, while downplaying his connection to Carter and cutting his losses from the long battle for the nomination against Sen. Gary Hart. Both candidates had to design strategies to fit their needs, but clearly Reagan had many more advantages at the onset.

Reagan's Strengths

Ultimately, presidents must defend their records. If the economy has not done well, if the nation remains involved in an unpopular war, if the public believes that things are getting worse rather than better, no amount of incumbency perquisites or vice presidential campaigning will help. (Think of Ford or Carter.) In Reagan's case, however, most of the politically relevant indicators were moving up at the start of the campaign—especially the four that mattered most to voters. The economy was improving, and public support for the president's policies was rebounding. Reagan was viewed as a strong leader, and he certainly was liked by potential voters.

The Economy. Most theories of voting behavior emphasize the importance of economic issues in elections. Pocketbook issues both reinforce traditional party loyalties and act as separate influences on final votes. Among the wide range of economic concerns, however, some are easier for voters to understand than others. Inflation, for example, hits voters whenever they buy gas or food. They can tell if prices are getting higher or lower and can actually calculate the effects. Unemployment also hits close to home. Although joblessness directly affects relatively small numbers of voters, workers at steel mills and auto plants know whether their jobs are in jeopardy, whether their friends and neighbors have been hurt. Both issues are easy to translate into campaign imagery—candidates appear at new factories or closed mills; they talk with unemployed workers or new job-holders; they hold up to the camera loaves of bread that cost more or less. A third easily understood economic issue is high interest rates. In this credit-card economy, voters have no trouble recognizing increasing rates.

Other economic issues are more difficult to comprehend. Although many economists agree that massive budget deficits are dangerous, it is hard to make voters understand just why or to link deficits directly to day-to-day experience. Will deficits add to the price of that loaf of bread? The very concept of a $200 billion annual deficit is hard to explain. What does it look like? Why does it matter? The same is true of international trade deficits. The issue is certainly important but hard to translate into concrete information for voters. Why should they care about massive trade deficits? How can the concept be captured in a 30-second commercial?

Reagan's great strength in 1984, of course, was that he was doing very well on the "easy" economic issues. Inflation was down from double-digit levels in 1980 to just over 4 percent in 1984. Unemployment had surged to more than 10 percent in 1982, but it was moving steadily downward by 1984 and hovered just above 7 percent throughout the fall campaign. (This downward trend was important: no matter what the actual unemployment rate, when it is rising, it scares both the unemployed and those who fear they may be next; when it is falling, its effect is confined mainly to the unemployed themselves.) Interest rates also were down from 1980. In contrast with the good news on the easily translated issues, Reagan's major economic troubles were limited to the "hard" issues—those that voters found difficult to understand and thus to use in making their vote choices. Still, Reagan was obviously in some trouble on budget deficits in 1984. After initially promising a balanced budget by 1984, he added almost as much to the national debt in four short years as had all presidents before him combined. Further, the international trade deficit was at record levels throughout 1984, hitting $190 billion by the end of the fiscal year.

It was the easy economic issues that translated into votes in 1984. Voters had little information on the hard issues and so did not blame Reagan. The problems did not fit their preconceived notions about the candidates or their parties, which made Democratic attacks all the more difficult. After all, are not Republicans the party of balanced budgets? The issues were further clouded by divided party control of government. Reagan could easily blame the Democratic House of Representatives for the record deficits. He was a Republican and a known fiscal conservative. Although the Mondale campaign succeeded in educating voters about some of these hard issues, Reagan was strong on the easy items, those that the voters could actually touch and feel, those they cared about.

Political Support.   Like all presidents, Reagan faced a period of decreasing influence at the beginning of his first term. His public approval was bound to decline, rebounding if at all during the reelection campaign. During this time, Reagan was sure to find it increasingly difficult to win legislative victories in Congress, and his party predictably would lose seats in the midterm elections. Depending on how much of his support returned in the fourth year, Reagan would face an easy or a tough reelection campaign. As it happened, most of the indicators either had stabilized or were moving up by mid-1984.

On the positive side, when asked by the Gallup poll whether they approved or disapproved of the way Reagan was handling his job as president, 60 percent of the poll respondents said they approved in September 1981. This fell to a low of 35 percent in February 1983 but rose to 55 percent a year later. When asked by the *Washington Post*/ABC News poll about Reagan's general handling of the economy, 59 percent approved at the beginning of the term, falling to 38 percent by February 1982, but rising back to 53 percent by July 1984. Asked whether they thought the economy was getting better, getting worse, or staying the same, only 9 percent had said it was getting better in early 1981. By mid-1984, 46 percent said it was getting better, a remarkable increase. And while 54 percent had said it was getting worse in 1981, only 20 percent said it was still falling in July 1984.

On the negative side, public approval of Reagan's handling of foreign affairs and his dealing with the Soviet Union had fallen during the term but was stabilizing by 1984. Reagan's most persistent problem was the budget deficit, an issue on which he received only 35 percent approval in mid-1984 in a *Washington Post*/ABC News poll. Even here, however, Reagan's weakness was not serious. Ironically, the voters who cared most about budget deficits were also the least likely to support Mondale: Republican men. They simply did not find the Democrats credible on this issue.

When considered together, the polling evidence suggested that Reagan had what his vice president, George Bush, once had called "Big Mo," or momentum. On economic issues he was moving up; on foreign policy he had stopped falling.

Leadership. Regardless of the specific policy issues, Reagan also benefited from overwhelming public approval of him as a leader. According to *Washington Post*/ABC News polls, 72 percent said the president had "strong leadership qualities." Only 49 percent said that about Mondale.

That the public saw Reagan as a strong leader was particularly important because of Mondale's effort to raise the future as a campaign issue. Even if voters thought about the threat of tax increases and nuclear war, their view of Reagan as a strong leader worked in his favor. Indeed, the more uncertain the future seems to voters, the greater their potential support for a strong president.[4] Facing a cloudy future, why not stick with a proven leader?

Popularity. Voters who disagreed with Reagan's handling of certain issues still found him a very appealing person. Consider their responses to the following *Washington Post*/ABC News poll question that was asked at various times during the first term: "Which of the following four statements most closely reflects your own feelings?":

A. I like Ronald Reagan personally, and I mostly approve of his policies.
B. I like Ronald Reagan personally, but I mostly disapprove of his policies.
C. I dislike Ronald Reagan personally, and I mostly disapprove of his policies.
D. I dislike Ronald Reagan personally, but I mostly approve of his policies.

The answers showed striking support of Reagan across his term. On the average, only around 10 percent of the public said they agreed with statement D, while another 20 percent or so said they agreed with statement C. The other 70 percent liked Reagan personally, while dividing almost evenly between approving and disapproving of his policies. With such a reservoir of personal approval, Reagan entered the campaign with a seemingly easy task: to convince about half of those who liked him personally to ignore his policies and to vote for him. Mondale would have to convince a much larger number that he was just as likeable as Reagan or at least that such personal images should not outweigh policy stances.

Mondale's Troubles

Despite Reagan's clear strengths, there were some vulnerable areas left for Mondale to attack. The president suffered on the fairness issue, the notion that he was helping the rich at the expense of the poor. He also faltered on women's rights, arms control, and Social Security. All of these issues haunted the Reagan campaign during the fall. The problem for Mondale was that campaigns do not occur in a vacuum. Each attack produces a counterattack. The Reagan campaign responded to all of the charges with speeches or television commercials. Further, Mondale's image as a weak leader acted as a screen against the issues. Even when he made inroads against Reagan on specific policies, the voters doubted Mondale's ability to do any better.

In truth, any Democrat would have entered the campaign with the odds against victory. Republicans had won five of the last eight presidential campaigns, three of the last four. Part of the Democrats' problem rests on the decline of the New Deal coalition. Democrats no longer can count on Catholics, blue-collar workers, southern conservatives, and political moderates. Although at least a plurality of the voters in these groups are still registered as Democrats, they have not been as willing to cast actual

Democratic ballots for president in recent elections. And while the Democrats used to have a commanding lead in party identification in the electorate as a whole, they have seen their advantage decline with the growth of independents and the resurgence of the Republicans.

Part of the Democratic problem rests on the dissatisfaction of the post-World War II baby-boom generation with both parties. Born between 1946 and the early 1960s, the generation remains a huge unclaimed political resource. Once drifting toward the Democratic party, the baby boomers recently have become disillusioned with the Democrats' domestic agenda and now seem reluctant to commit to either party. Although they generally support the Democrats' foreign policy—particularly on arms control—baby boomers like the Republican view of the economy and recently have voted on the basis of pocketbook issues.

These problems with the voters are accentuated by the Democrats' failure to keep pace with the Republicans in modern campaign techniques. While the Republicans spent the late 1970s rebuilding their fundraising apparatus and recruiting younger leaders, the Democrats basked in the post-Watergate euphoria, thinking, perhaps, that another Republican could never be elected again. Then came Reagan. Caught behind in basic tools, outmaneuvered in local organizing and fund raising, any Democratic nominee would have found it difficult to mount a strong challenge to a Republican incumbent.

On top of these challenges, Mondale brought his own troubles to the fall campaign. To be sure it is difficult to imagine any scenario in which a Democrat could have won. Nevertheless, four of Mondale's own weaknesses worked to enhance Reagan's strengths: 1) he was nominated only after a brutal primary struggle; 2) he was clearly tied to the Carter presidency; 3) he picked hard issues for his campaign agenda; and 4) he suffered from a very poor image as a leader.

Primary Bruises. It would be difficult to overestimate just how much the bitter primary campaign cost Mondale in the fall. It slowed his momentum and surely left an unflattering portrait in voters' minds. Mondale had been attacked as a tool of special interests, a product of the past, and a supporter of old ideas. Both Sen. John Glenn, Mondale's leading opponent in 1983, and Hart, who turned out to be his main rival in the primaries and caucuses, had campaigned as candidates of the future, painting Mondale as a party hack. Although Mondale eventually adopted the future as a theme for his campaign against Reagan, the primary attacks made it and some of Mondale's own themes less believable to the voters. Ironically, the charges against Mondale lodged by fellow Democrats also gave Reagan plenty of material for his fall attack.

Moreover, the primary contests sapped Mondale and his staff of needed time and energy. Given the hard nature of Mondale's campaign issues, he needed time to educate the public on things such as why deficits matter. Mondale had begun that process early in the nomination campaign, believing that the Democratic mantle was all but his. But Hart's effective challenge forced Mondale to campaign for the nomination, which cost precious time for public education. By the end of the primaries, Mondale and his staff were exhausted.

The Carter Connection. Mondale was clearly linked to the unpopular Carter presidency. As Carter's vice president, Mondale had been an effective adviser and a highly visible campaigner. During the primaries against Hart, he made much of his experience, implying that his opponent could not be trusted to answer the ringing red hotline in a nuclear crisis. In the general election, however, Mondale had to downplay any Carter connection. Even in 1984, memories of the Iranian hostage crisis and double-digit inflation were fresh. And if the voters should forget, Reagan would remind them.

The problem for vice presidents who serve with unpopular presidents is that they carry much of the blame for the administration's troubles but get little of the credit for its successes. Further, for Mondale in particular, it was difficult to attack Reagan for problems that also had existed during the Carter years. Was the American economy in a long-term decline? If so, why didn't Carter and Mondale stop it?

Mondale's predicament was that his term in office was so recent that he could not address the causes of national problems without indicting himself to some extent. What was once the Carter administration was now the Carter-Mondale administration. In that respect, it was almost impossible for Mondale to shed the past and its failures. Voters did not necessarily blame Mondale for the Carter years, but they linked him to the same failed leadership. The Carter connection made it almost impossible for Mondale to improve his poor leadership image, but he continued to try to do so.

Hard Issues. As noted earlier, Mondale adopted a series of hard issues for his campaign agenda, issues that were difficult to explain to voters or to translate into simple images. Budget deficits, international trade, coming crises in Medicare, and foreign policy are usually too remote and complex for the public to understand. Public opinion polls, for example, show that people do not follow foreign affairs closely and often do not know enough about the specifics of a particular issue to form opinions. Although Mondale did support the simple notion of a mutual freeze on nuclear weapons by the United States and the Soviet Union, even that issue was clouded by questions of verifiability—that is, the ability to detect violations.

Perhaps the most difficult of all Mondale's issues was space weapons. Mondale argued that Reagan's so-called Strategic Defense Initiative, or "Star Wars" plan, would destabilize the nuclear balance between the two superpowers, thereby increasing the likelihood of war. Whatever the merits of the argument, it was exceedingly difficult to project. Mondale was asking voters to reject an intuitively appealing idea: a defense against nuclear weapons. Moreover, he faced overwhelming public support for the basic idea of peace through strength.

Ultimately, Mondale's list of issues may have played into Reagan's strength. By fostering the image of an uncertain future, Mondale may have reinforced the public's yearning for presidential assertiveness. By prophesying a "coming collapse," Mondale may have prompted voters to turn to the familiar and keep Reagan—the same, known quantity—in office. At the same time, Reagan worked effectively to soothe voters' concerns about his foreign policy and the economic future. His counterattacks reassured them that it was safe to choose him over Mondale.

Leadership. Along with his efforts to create a sense of imminent crisis, Mondale asked voters to accept his leadership. Unfortunately for Mondale, when asked by the *Washington Post*/ABC News poll whether Mondale had "strong leadership qualities," 43 percent said no, almost 20 percent and more than said that of Reagan. Moreover, when asked by the Harris poll whether Mondale "tends to be too cautious and vague about what he really stands for on the important issues," 60 percent said yes. Mondale's continuing problems with his leadership image led to his celebrated statement at the Democratic convention that he would raise taxes if elected. That tactic was designed to demonstrate his ability both to make tough choices and to level with the American people about those choices. His decision to put Rep. Geraldine A. Ferraro of New York on the ticket as his vice presidential running mate, while reflecting an honest commitment to her candidacy, also was designed partly to demonstrate his willingness to lead boldly. Still, entering the fall campaign, Mondale clearly suffered by comparison with Reagan on the leadership issues. It became an enduring problem for the campaign.

The Campaign

August-September

Coming into August Mondale had some reason for optimism. At the Democratic national convention in San Francisco, his party had seemed genuinely united, and Mondale's choice of Ferraro was widely hailed as evidence of his leadership. Even his promise to raise taxes was well received for its honesty, at least by the delegates and most political commentators. The convention seemed to give Mondale a clean break from the primary battles and his past leadership problems. The Gallup poll even found Mondale pulling to within two points of Reagan, although its result was not confirmed by other surveys. Mondale had taken his best shot at establishing a positive rapport with voters and uniting the Democratic coalition. And at first, his campaign seemed to be working.

Yet, just as quickly as Mondale drew closer to Reagan, he fell back. The Democratic convention was only the first of the two national political conventions in 1984. The Republican gathering in August was equally well orchestrated. Whatever gains Mondale made in July were quickly cancelled a month later. In fact, Mondale's standing slipped even in anticipation of Reagan's nomination—he fell five percentage points before the Republican convention was called to order in Dallas.

In addition, Mondale's vice presidential nominee quickly was engulfed in a major political controversy, sapping much of the initial enthusiasm for her candidacy. Immediately after the convention, she promised to release both her own and her husband's tax returns for public inspection. But a few days later she backed off, saying that her husband objected to the publicity as an invasion of privacy.

Unfortunately for Ferraro, the controversy soon expanded to include her first congressional campaign in 1978. During that campaign, she had received some questionable, perhaps illegal, financing from her husband. By the time the air was finally cleared in a 90-minute press conference on August 21, Ferraro's candidacy had lost much of its luster. Although she was to remain more appealing to women, independents, and young voters than Mondale, her ability to help the ticket was now limited.

Whatever their early troubles, Mondale and Ferraro increasingly ran as a team. Ferraro's growing identification with Mondale, however, reduced her appeal to independent voters. In the final analysis, although her candidacy sparked interest in the ticket during the summer, some voters worried about her lack of experience and her stand on abortion, but most concentrated on the top of the ticket. There is a limit to how much any vice presidential nominee can do, particularly when paired with a weak presidential candidate.

The campaign began in earnest on Labor Day, when Mondale attacked Reagan on the issue of church and state in an effort to take advantage of substantial public worries about Reagan's link to the religious right in general and Falwell in particular. According to a September *New York Times*/CBS News poll, more than three-quarters of the voters opposed the idea of clergy endorsing presidential candidates. But although voters sided with Mondale and Ferraro on the separation of church and state, it was difficult after four years of comfortable experience with Reagan to raise anxieties about religion in politics or to use those issues in competition with the Reagan message of peace, prosperity, and leadership. In addition, the statements by Reagan that prompted the Democrats' attack also had solidified his support among evangelical Christians.

Mondale's most important theme during the first two months of the campaign was the budget deficit. Having raised the issue all year long, Mondale was now forced to offer a deficit-reduction plan. It was not enough simply to argue that deficits were bad; Mondale had to give his own answers. After investing weeks of staff time and energy on the issue, he finally unveiled his budget package. It included a substantial tax increase, a "pay-as-you-go" approach to funding new programs, defense cuts, and limited domestic trimming. The plan was not well understood by voters; in particular, it did not convince independents that Mondale would keep the lid on government costs.

Moreover, although the public believed that a tax increase was inevitable in the near future, many wanted Reagan to inflict the pain because they felt that he would hold the line on the amount. The deficit and tax issue clearly was not working for Mondale, but, having cast his die, he stayed with it anyway. The issue continued to pull the campaign away from other, more attractive themes. Mondale was stuck in a quagmire and continued to thrash through the deficits long past the point of political return.

As summer turned to early fall, Mondale found few signs for optimism. The president stayed inside the White House, venturing out only for highly orchestrated campaign appearances. Reagan was not holding press conferences nor was he taking impromptu questions of any other kind. His was a heavily scripted campaign, with little reason for taking risks. The best Mondale could hope for was to force some kind of mistake. As his campaign manager Robert Beckel noted, Reagan was "a safe candidate when he's kept in his photo-opportunity campaign style." The hope was to draw him out.

By September, however, Reagan had built his overall job rating to 61 percent, according to a *Washington Post*/ABC News poll. This was a remarkable improvement over 1982-1983 and was higher than comparable first-term ratings for any of the four previous presidents. Why should he leave the Rose Garden or, when campaigning, depart from the script? Even when Reagan did make mistakes, they did not appear to stick.

His ability to dodge self-inflicted wounds had earned him the label of the "Teflon president." Never was the title more appropriate than after the third Beirut bombing on September 20. It was just the sort of event that can change a campaign, rocking an incumbent back on his heels. In this case, terrorists had penetrated embassy defenses and had killed two Marines in a suicide bombing.

As the third successful terrorist attack in two years, the September 20 bombing could have reminded voters of Reagan's uncertain Lebanon policy. It could have rekindled memories of the October 1983 bombing, in which 241 Marines were slaughtered in a dawn attack. Moreover, it appeared that Reagan did not appear to take the issue seriously. Only days after the third bombing, he compared the unfinished security defenses to an unfinished kitchen remodeling at home. Delays in building the barriers could be appreciated by "anyone that's ever had their kitchen redone," the president remarked.

Nevertheless, the issue did not stick. "The public sees Ronald Reagan as a very strong, solid leader, as opposed to Walter Mondale as a weak leader prone to flip-flops," a Reagan campaign aide remarked. The voters generally disapproved of Reagan's policies in Lebanon but accepted his argument that the United States simply cannot defend against every terrorist attack. More important, they accepted Reagan himself as a leader, in contrast to evidence that they questioned Mondale's abilities in similar situations. Reagan reminded the public of the Iranian hostage crisis whenever possible and reinforced public concerns about Mondale's indecisiveness.

Reagan made other mistakes in September, but none seemed to matter either individually or as part of a pattern. He inaccurately accused the Carter administration of cutting back on the CIA, then tied those alleged cuts to the Beirut bombing. After being corrected by his own staff, he telephoned Carter to apologize. The incident had no measurable effect on Reagan's standing. The continuing challenge was to keep those kinds of blunders to a minimum and to defuse those that did occur immediately, in order to prevent any Mondale momentum from developing. Voters would not acknowledge Reagan's mistakes until they first came to regard Mondale as a reasonable alternative; as long as they believed that Mondale lacked presidential qualities, particularly strong leadership, that would block their response to his overtures. With the campaign settled into a pattern of attack and counterattack, Mondale's unfavorable ratings continued to rise. By mid-September, 41 percent of the voters had an unfavorable view of Mondale, with 27 percent favorable. (In contrast, 56 percent felt favorably toward Reagan.) Indeed, Mondale's unfavorable rating had jumped seven points in the first weeks of September. Less than half of Democrats felt favorably toward him, which undermined any plans to build a solid electoral base on party identification. Worse, a dramatic and fatal weakness with independents was beginning to emerge—55 percent had a favorable view of Reagan, but only 19 percent felt favorably toward Mondale.

The worst news came at the end of the month in the form of growing evidence that long presidential coattails, even party realignment, were developing. Republican party identification began to increase among voters during the last weeks of September—the first time in history that such a trend had preceded, rather than followed, an election. The *New York Times*/CBS News poll reported that for the first time a majority of likely voters thought the Republican party would do a better job handling the problems they considered most important. The possibility of a major landslide for Reagan and substantial gains in Congress took shape.

Mondale's only hope now lay in televised debates with Reagan. He had asked for six—each one on a major policy topic. Debates could give him an opportunity to turn around the leadership issue and to convince the public that he was not the cold, aloof, despairing politician that the president said he was. In mid-September, Mondale finally received word that Reagan would debate. In part, Reagan's decision reflected his love of political debate. He had won the 1980 debate with Carter and had a reputation as an effective verbal contestant. In part, too, Reagan's acceptance reflected his view of what is fair play in politics. Even though Mondale's attacks were not eroding his support among voters, Reagan wanted a chance to answer. The debates were scheduled for two Sundays, October 7 and October 21, both to begin at 9:00 p.m. Eastern time. The first would cover domestic and economic policy, the second foreign affairs. And there would be a vice presidential debate in between, a chance to showcase Ferraro against Bush.

In preparation for the debate, Mondale made his strongest attack yet on Reagan. Appearing at George Washington University in late September, Mondale set the context for the first debate and tried again to bring defecting Democrats back to the fold. He returned to the issues of foreign policy and fairness—caring for others, the average person, and the middle class. He talked about restoring student loans, protecting Social Security (the miracle issue for Democrats in the 1982 elections), and opening the doors of opportunity for all Americans. Mondale also restated the themes of his candidacy and talked of two Reagans: one who cuts social spending, opposes civil rights, and threatens world peace; the other who says the opposite during the campaign. "For four years, they failed to reach a single arms control agreement with the Soviets," Mondale said. "They proposed to extend the arms race into the heavens. But now, six weeks before the election, they talk of arms control; they dust off the conference table—and they brag about blunting an issue." Moving forward in a classic stemwinder, Mondale rallied the crowd to compare the new and old Reagan: "The new Reagan talks about peace in Central America. The old Reagan said it was none of our business, and opened the sluicegates on material to make the bomb." The speech was a rousing success and led both campaigns to wonder about Mondale's candidacy. Could he generate new support? Could he close the gap? Hubert Humphrey had nearly engineered a miracle in 1968. Could his Minnesota protegé do it in 1984? Entering the debates, the Mondale campaign had new life.

Unfortunately for Mondale, the public did not respond. Throughout the campaign, voters had believed that Mondale would be better for the disadvantaged but not for themselves. Mondale was the altruistic candidate who asked voters to ignore their own interests for others. Reagan's policies may have been of greatest benefit to the rich, but most voters believed that the policies had helped them, too. Although Reagan's policies may have ignored the poor and even hurt the middle class somewhat, voters believed that the president cared about them, and they liked him for it. They seemed to be distinguishing between political involvement and personal sympathy. In a Gallup survey conducted toward the end of September, Reagan was given positive marks by at least 43 percent of the public for his concern for the "average citizen." Mondale scored only nine points higher.

October

Mondale and Reagan entered the stretch run to the election with remarkably distinct issue positions. Yet polls suggested that the election was being decided by voters much more on candidate images than issues. The candidates were partly responsible. Reagan painted Mondale's platform as a vision of "dreary mediocrity" and talked about his own America as an "opportunity society." "I think there's a new feeling of patriotism in our land, a recognition that by any standard America is a decent and generous place, a force for good in the world," Reagan said in his standard speech. "And I don't know about you, but I'm a little tired of hearing people run her down." Mondale's basic speech countered that the "election is about values. I refuse to cut loose from my history and desert the beliefs I have always fought for. I would rather lose a race about decency than win one about self-interest." (The implication, of course, was that decency and self-interest are incompatible, a difficult position to advance among middle-class voters.)

Once the debates were announced, doubtful voters suspended judgment. The debates almost certainly would elevate Mondale, if only because he would appear on an equal footing with the president of the United States. They could give him a needed boost, even offer a new chance for his campaign. Bargaining over the details of the debates had been intense. Mondale had asked for more debates, Reagan for fewer. In the end, Reagan accepted two presidential debates, each 90 minutes long. There would be no stools for the candidates to sit on and no risers to even their height, but Reagan would get a special podium for his hearing problem. After wrangling over the format and the panel of questioners, Mondale and Reagan finally met in Louisville, Kentucky, on October 7.

There is little doubt that Mondale won the first debate. The president seemed tired and confused. His rambling closing statement was cut short by the moderator, Edwin Newman. His answers were poorly focused; he looked and sounded old and often seemed hesitant when asked a question. Later, some of Reagan's supporters would blame David Stockman, the director of the Office of Management and Budget, for overcoaching him. In contrast, Mondale looked vigorous, refreshed. He was on the attack from the opening bell. He openly admitted that he liked the president and asked voters who also liked Reagan but not his policies to separate their personal feelings from the issues. And when Reagan offered a reprise of his 1980 debate statement "There you go again," Mondale was ready with an answer. Confronting Reagan directly, Mondale reminded his opponent that the 1980 remark was in response to Carter's warning that Reagan would cut the Medicare program. Yet, Mondale continued, "you went right out and tried to cut $20 billion out of Medicare."

Every candidate enters a debate facing doubts that voters want to see answered. In 1980, for example, Reagan won his debate with Carter by convincing voters that he was not a trigger-happy nuclear warrior. In 1984 Mondale had three such objectives: 1) to demonstrate his leadership, thereby addressing the voters' lack of confidence in his abilities; 2) to attack Reagan's policies without attacking him personally; and 3) to show his own sense of humor and human qualities.

Thus, Mondale prepared to win the first debate on style more than substance. And that is just what he did. His victory was all the more potent because three of four voters had expected Reagan to win. Moreover, Mondale's achievement was magnified as voters responded to next-day interpretations. The *New York Times*/CBS News poll showed that right after the debate 9 percent more voters thought Mondale had won than Reagan. The victory margin spread to 49 points two days later, reflecting the power of the press to influence such judgments. The more the press talked about Mondale's victory, the more the voters said he had won. More important, on virtually all measures, the debate made Mondale more acceptable to voters. For the first time in the fall campaign, more voters felt favorable toward Mondale than unfavorable. He scored points on both his personal leadership qualities and his campaign issues: Social Security, Medicare, and deficits. And, again for the first time, voters sensed that Mondale did, indeed, have a vision of the future.

Some commentators said that Reagan lost the debate because it was so long and so late—90 minutes takes its toll, particularly at 10:30 in the evening. Whatever the explanation, Reagan appeared exhausted by the end. The *New York Times*/CBS News poll reported that half the voters thought Reagan was not as sharp as he was four years ago. Others said that Reagan lost simply by appearing on the same stage as Mondale. He gave his challenger credibility. Mondale looked decent, had a good sense of humor, was not hostile, and was almost as tall as the incumbent. And, although Reagan was president, he did not stand behind the presidential seal. He looked like just another contender.

Most important, of course, the debate closed the gap between Mondale and Reagan. Before the debate, Reagan's lead had been as high as 26 points in the *Los Angeles Times*/NBC and Gannett polls. Ten days later, it was cut in half. Major shifts came among young voters and independents. Even Democrats whose party loyalty was weak were impressed. The landslide was off—at least for the moment.

The Reagan campaign responded swiftly with a massive media campaign. In his television commercials, Reagan was pictured as strong and knowledgeable. In person, Reagan travelled to college campuses to appear with the young and to answer questions from the floor. He attacked Mondale's tax increase and promised never to cut Social Security. He even suggested that the only difference between the candidates' performances in the first debate was makeup: Mondale's was better. The movement toward Mondale in the polls stalled as voters waited to see how the president would perform in the second debate on October 21.

The second debate was obviously crucial for the Mondale campaign. Reagan needed only to win, tie, or even lose narrowly. Mondale had to win by a knockout. It was clear that Reagan's poor first debate performance had created doubts for many voters. Now he needed to show that he wasn't too old for the job, that he understood the facts. Like the election, the debate was Reagan's to lose.

Within minutes of the opening question, the outcome was settled. Reagan looked refreshed and was ready with his answers. Although he was in trouble on some specific foreign policy issues, his style of presentation was sharp. In the debate's most memorable moment, Reagan tried to deflate the age issue. Asked if he would be able to function during a crisis, Reagan quipped, "I will not make age an issue of this campaign. I am not going to exploit, for political purposes, my opponent's youth and inexperience." That was it. With that one joke and his general demeanor, Reagan had reassured the voters. Mondale continued to hammer away on space weapons and nuclear arms, but Reagan seemed a source of quiet confidence and strength.

As noted above, in an uncertain world, the voters crave security. Firm toward the Soviets, conciliatory toward arms talks, and concerned about human rights, Reagan offered that sense of security to the public. (Two thirds of the voters believed he would work for arms negotiations in a second term.) With that image established and even though he made several mistakes on specific questions—particularly regarding the CIA's publication of an assassination manual for Nicaraguan rebels— he did not lose the debate. Not losing was all that mattered. On virtually all measures, Reagan was now firmly ahead. Independents swiftly returned to the Reagan-Bush column. Ironically, virtually assured of defeat, Mondale responded with some of his best speeches of the campaign.

Meanwhile, Ferraro and Bush had also squared off in debate, on October 11 in Philadelphia. The vice presidential debate, however, was basically considered a draw by the voters. Women were much more likely to think that Ferraro had won; men more likely to pick Bush. Both candidates reassured many voters who previously had doubts about them. According to the *New York Times*/CBS News poll, Bush scored most of his points on foreign policy. Ferraro scored on presentation, competence, composure, and her closing statement. Young voters and women in particular also agreed with her characterization of a remark by Bush regarding her knowledge on foreign policy as "patronizing." But in both the debate and the general campaign, Ferraro was on the defensive on the abortion issue, particularly after Catholic bishops criticized her stance of personal opposition to abortion but legal tolerance. It diverted attention from other, more attractive issues.

Decisions

Although Mondale clearly realized he would lose well before election day, nothing prepared him for the extent of his defeat. He lost everywhere but the District of Columbia and his home state of Minnesota, and he received only 41 percent of the popular vote (*Table 3.1*). The electoral vote tally was 525 to 13, the second largest margin in American history, trailing only Franklin Roosevelt's 1936 victory over Alf Landon. In popular votes, it was the fifth only to Johnson's victory in 1964, Roosevelt's in 1936, Nixon's in 1972, and Warren Hardings's in 1902.

Table 3.1 Official 1984 Presidential Election Results

	Ronald Reagan (R)		Walter F. Mondale (D)		Electoral Votes	
	Votes	%	Votes	%	Reagan	Mondale
Ala.	872,849	61	551,899	38	9	
Alaska	138,392	67	62,018	30	3	
Ariz.	681,416	66	333,854	33	7	
Ark.	534,774	60	338,646	38	6	
Calif.	5,467,009	58	3,922,519	41	47	
Colo.	821,817	63	454,975	35	8	
Conn.	890,877	61	569,597	39	8	
Del.	152,119	60	101,627	40	3	
D.C.	29,009	14	180,408	85		3
Fla.	2,730,350	65	1,448,816	35	21	
Ga.	1,068,722	60	706,628	40	12	
Hawaii	185,050	55	147,154	44	4	
Idaho	297,523	72	108,510	26	4	
Ill.	2,707,103	56	2,086,499	43	24	
Ind.	1,377,230	62	841,481	38	12	
Iowa	703,088	53	605,620	46	8	
Kan.	677,296	66	333,149	33	7	
Ky.	821,702	60	539,539	40	9	
La.	1,037,299	61	651,586	38	10	
Maine	336,500	61	214,515	39	4	
Md.	879,918	53	787,935	47	10	
Mass.	1,310,936	51	1,239,606	48	13	
Mich.	2,251,571	59	1,529,638	40	20	
Minn.	1,032,603	50	1,036,364	50		10
Miss.	582,377	62	352,192	37	7	
Mo.	1,274,188	60	848,583	40	11	
Mont.	232,450	60	146,742	38	4	
Neb.	460,054	71	187,866	29	5	
Nev.	188,770	66	91,655	32	4	
N.H.	267,050	69	120,347	31	4	
N.J.	1,933,630	60	1,261,323	39	16	
N.M.	307,101	60	201,769	39	5	
N.Y.	3,664,763	54	3,119,609	46	36	
N.C.	1,346,481	62	824,287	38	13	
N.D.	200,336	65	104,429	34	3	
Ohio	2,678,559	59	1,825,440	40	23	
Okla.	861,530	69	385,080	31	8	
Ore.	685,700	56	536,479	44	7	
Pa.	2,584,323	53	2,228,131	46	25	
R.I.	208,513	52	194,292	48	4	
S.C.	615,539	64	344,459	36	8	
S.D.	200,267	63	116,113	37	3	
Tenn.	990,212	58	711,714	42	11	
Texas	3,433,428	64	1,949,276	36	29	
Utah	469,105	75	155,369	25	5	
Vt.	135,865	58	95,730	41	3	
Va.	1,337,078	62	796,250	37	12	
Wash.	1,051,670	56	807,352	43	10	
W.Va.	405,483	55	328,125	45	6	
Wis.	1,198,584	54	995,740	45	11	
Wyo.	133,241	71	53,370	28	3	
Total	54,451,450	59	37,574,305	41	525	13

Source: Secretaries of state for the 50 states and the District of Columbia; compiled by Congressional Quarterly.

According to the *Washington Post*/ABC News exit poll, Reagan ran well for a Republican with every demographic group but blacks, voters with incomes under $10,000, and liberals. Mondale gained 65 percent of the Hispanic vote and 69 percent of Jews but won only small majorities among traditional elements of the Democratic coalition—Catholics and union members. Independents went two to one for Reagan, up 10 percentage points from 1980. A quarter of Democrats defected to Reagan, but only 6 percent of Republicans went for Mondale. Reagan made significant inroads among Catholics, high-income blue-collar workers, and southern whites (*Table 3.2*).

Although Reagan did well among almost all groups, there were several "gaps" or would-be "gaps" among voters. One was the "senior gap." Initially, at least, voters over 65 years old were much less favorable toward Reagan than younger voters. They were frightened about cuts in Social Security and Medicare and felt less economically secure than other age groups. But the senior gap, which existed early in the 1984 campaign, disappeared in the last weeks of the election. Senior citizens gave Reagan their solid support on election day. Another gap was expected between men and women. There was an 8 percent "gender gap" in the final results of the election, although both men and women supported Reagan over Mondale. With Ferraro on the ticket and many women's persistent dislike of Reagan's policies, the gap turned out to be less than had been expected. In a landslide, it was too small to make much difference anyway.

Despite labor endorsements, union households went for Mondale only by a bare majority. Reagan actually increased his support by 5 percentage points over 1980. So-called "Yuppies" (Young Urban Professionals) supported Reagan overwhelmingly, reflecting their affluence and lack of partisan attachment. In fact, one-third of Hart's supporters in the Democratic nominating contest went for Reagan, despite Hart's strenuous campaigning for Mondale. Finally, Reagan ran particularly well among white-collar voters and evangelical Christians.

Reagan carried every region, but some important geographical patterns emerged in the election. The Democrats had nominated a ticket designed to unite the East, the liberal Pacific West, and the hard-hit farm belt and industrial Midwest. The Republicans had renominated a ticket whose main appeal was to the West and South. During the campaign these lines were somewhat blurred, however, because Mondale and Ferraro spent a large amount of time campaigning in the South without solidifying their base in the North, while Reagan spent much of the last month in the East and Midwest. Among voters, the East was the weakest region for Reagan but he carried every state. The South and the Rocky Mountain West were the best Reagan areas, and unlike the East and

Table 3.2 ABC News Exit Poll, Voting for President

	% Reagan	% Mondale	Reagan-Carter-Anderson in 1980
Democrats	24	76	25 - 67 - 7
Independents	61	38	52 - 30 - 15
Republicans	94	6	87 - 6 - 5
Men	62	38	54 - 35 - 9
Women	54	46	47 - 42 - 9
Whites	63	37	55 - 34 - 9
Blacks	11	89	13 - 82 - 4
Union household	45	54	41 - 49 - 8
Nonunion household	64	36	55 - 33 - 9
Protestant	66	33	59 - 33 - 6
Catholic	56	44	46 - 42 - 9
Jewish	31	69	35 - 42 - 21
No religion	44	55	38 - 40 - 18
Some high school or less	48	51	45 - 50 - 3
High school graduate	56	44	52 - 40 - 6
Some college	62	38	52 - 36 - 10
College graduate	63	37	52 - 34 - 11
Some postgraduate	52	48	48 - 38 - 14
Conservative	81	18	72 - 22 - 4
In between	50	49	47 - 42 - 9
Liberal	25	74	23 - 58 - 16
German/Austrian	67	32	57 - 32 - 9
English/Scottish/Welsh	70	29	59 - 31 - 8
Hispanic	44	56	37 - 55 - 7
Irish	59	40	52 - 39 - 7
Scandinavian	62	38	53 - 32 - 12
Polish/Slavic	51	49	39 - 43 - 15
Chief wage earner in household			
Hourly	51	48	44 - 47 - 8
Salary	62	38	52 - 35 - 10
Self employed	68	31	62 - 27 - 8
Unemployed	35	64	43 - 50 - 6
18-24	59	40	43 - 42 - 11
25-29	56	44	44 - 42 - 12
30-39	56	44	50 - 38 - 9
40-49	61	39	57 - 34 - 7
50-59	58	42	55 - 37 - 6
60 and older	57	42	55 - 38 - 5

Source: Based on the 1984 and 1980 ABC News exit polls.

Midwest, the states were not close. Mondale and Ferraro suffered in the Pacific West from lower support among Hispanics and the Reagan sweep of independents. Similarly, the Democratic ticket was hurt in the Midwest by the defections of blue-collar workers and farmers.

The election was marked by racial polarization, particularly in the South where 80 percent of the white voters went for Reagan while 88 percent of black voters were going for Mondale. Reagan coattails appeared in the South where a surprising number of the Democratic congressional seats were lost, most of them in North Carolina and Texas. In part, these coattails reflected racial voting—in Mississippi, for example, only 15 percent of the white vote went to Mondale and only 9 percent of the black vote went to Reagan—but they did not extend very far in the rest of the country. Voters supported incumbents at all levels of government. More than 90 percent of the House incumbents who sought reelection were successful, leaving Republicans with a net gain of only 14 seats, 12 fewer than they needed to make up for their 26-seat loss in 1982. Republicans suffered a net loss of 2 seats in the Senate, where reelection-seeking incumbents also had an unusually good year: 27 of 30, or 90 percent, were successful. At the state level, Republicans gained only one governor but won approximately 300 additional seats in the state legislatures.

Within those boundaries, the election was clearly a referendum on the state of the economy. Exit polls found that 76 percent of those who expected their economic situation to improve voted for Reagan, while 84 percent of those who thought that they were both worse off today and would be in the near future voted for Mondale. In addition voters had significant concerns about how a Mondale presidency would affect existing economic good times. Half the voters thought the economy would get worse in the future if Mondale were elected, while only a quarter thought it would get worse if Reagan were reelected.

Voters who went for Reagan most often mentioned the good economy and a strong defense as the issues that motivated their vote. Mondale voters were most concerned about the threat of nuclear war and the fairness issue. Voters mentioned military spending as the issue that most disposed them to vote *against* Reagan, and the tax increase as the issue that worked *against* Mondale. Leadership clearly emerged as the dominant voter concern about the candidates themselves, and Reagan was overwhelmingly favored. As to the future, 63 percent of Reagan voters thought it would be a good one for the next generation, while 70 percent of Mondale voters thought that future generations would be bogged down in problems left behind for them.

Although Ferraro's presence on the ticket had little measurable effect on the final vote, it was an important part of the campaign and probably will be remembered as Mondale's most significant contribution to American politics. Ultimately, her selection probably made more difference in tearing down barriers for future women candidates than it did in the Democratic vote in 1984. Expectations and promises were too high in the beginning; few vice presidential candidates have ever had more than a 5 percent effect on the final vote. Vice presidential candidates can communicate a sensitivity to issues and groups by their selection and can bring a great deal of excitement to a party's ticket. But they are hardly the major force in a campaign.

Still, Ferraro's influence on the voting has yet to be fully analyzed. From the beginning, it was clear that she made some groups, particularly the young, women, and independents, more likely to support the ticket, mostly because of her sex. Older white male Democrats were particularly unhappy with her choice, but among the 10 percent of all voters who said that they decided on the basis of vice presidential candidates, 54 percent went for Mondale and Ferraro.

For some time to come, observers and partisans will try to guess the enduring meaning of the 1984 election. Republicans must try to sort out how much it was a policy mandate for the party and its highly conservative platform and how much it was a referendum on current good times and a personal victory for Reagan. They have put together a temporary coalition at the national level that may be difficult to hold together. It is hard to imagine libertarian Yuppies and moralistic evangelical Christians holding together if abortion and other social issues ever dominate an election, or bankers and steel workers again voting alike if unemployment starts to rise. For their part, Democrats must ask how much their defeat was the result of Reagan's incumbency and other short-term forces and how much was a rejection of what voters regard as outdated ideas. This soul-searching is made all the more acute by 32 years of both sweeping Republican victories at the presidential level and Democratic dominance at the congressional, state, and local level.

Most important, both parties must wonder about lasting party realignment, particularly among southern whites and the young. There has been a clear drift to the Republican party in the South, caused by its distinct identity as the conservative party, vigorous new Republican party machinery, and population movement from the North. Among young voters who are still in their formative political years and whose first strong political memory will be eight years of Reagan, there may also be some long-term change. At this point, their Republican leanings reflect their support for Reagan, but this certainly could develop into a more deeply rooted psychological attachment to his party if Republicans continue to nominate appealing candidates. Realignment will depend very much on events of the next few years—what crises emerge, how the parties respond to them, and what alternatives come to the forefront.

Conclusion

Looking back over the 1984 election, it is difficult to imagine any winning strategy for Mondale. Although he did make mistakes—staying with the deficit and tax issues long after their value was exhausted, for example—no Democrat could have done much better against such a strong opponent as Reagan.

On virtually all of the issues that matter to voters, Reagan had substantial support. Just as voters had punished Reagan's party for skyrocketing unemployment in 1982, they rewarded the president for economic recovery in 1984. Despite continuing problems in Lebanon and elsewhere, voters did not seem particularly troubled by the lack of a consistent foreign policy. To the extent that they worried about nuclear arms, Reagan was either reassuring or on the attack against Mondale. If there was an area in which Mondale's own image cost him votes, it was in concerns about his leadership. Hart or Glenn may not have suffered on that issue but may have had liabilities of their own and still would have faced a remarkably strong incumbent in any event.

In many respects, Reagan peaked at the right moment. The economy was weak in the middle of his term, not at the end. Each year of peace refuted Mondale's message that Reagan was unreliable and trigger-happy. Voters clearly believed that the nation was better off at the end of Reagan's term than at the beginning and that problems that remained were directly traceable to the administration in which Mondale had served as vice president. Because voters decide on the basis of recent events and use retrospective judgments in making their choices, Reagan's timing was perfect. Unlike Carter, who peaked in his first year and slid downhill from then on, Reagan peaked in his third and fourth years.

In choosing to run on a retrospective theme, Reagan foreclosed the possibility of winning a clear mandate for specific policies. The postelection choice of Republican moderate Robert Dole as the new Senate majority leader and the lack of substantial Republican gains in the House also augured stalemate rather than consensus. Dole immediately signalled his independence from the White House by rejecting parts of the administration's tax simplification proposal. Considering the natural second-term cycle of decreasing influence and the 22d Amendment limitation on a third term, Reagan became a lame-duck very early in his new administration. His own party already was fighting over his successor within weeks of his reelection. If there was one area left for presidential leadership, it was foreign policy. Reagan would have a chance on nuclear arms control. Whether he could achieve a breakthrough with the Soviets on the scale of Richard Nixon's détente with China would depend on his own dedication and energy.

Such postelection speculation, of course, is very much in the nature of American politics. The system appears well designed for stalemate and frustration. The Founding Fathers intended to protect the public against rapid change and built a government that would move slowly. The problem with the ever-lengthening electoral season, however, is that it makes action even more difficult. Although Reagan had substantial success in the first months of 1981, he was stalemated for the next three years. At least on domestic policy, he was given even less time in his second term. Certainly Reagan's inability or unwillingness to address future issues in the campaign only made the impasse worse.

Notes

1. This original model was laid out in Angus Campbell et al., *The American Voter* (New York: John Wiley and Sons, 1960).
2. Arthur H. Miller and Martin P. Wattenberg, "Throwing the Rascals Out: Policy and Performance Evaluations of Presidential Candidates, 1952-1980" (An unpublished paper).
3. Donald R. Kinder and D. Roderick Kiewiet, "Economic Discontent and Political Behavior: The Role of Personal Grievances and Collective Economic Judgments in Congressional Voting," vol. 23, no. 3 *Journal of Political Science* (August 1979), 495-527.
4. Donald R. Kinder, "Presidential Character Revisited" (An unpublished paper delivered at the 19th Annual Carnegie Symposium on Cognitive and Political Behavior, Carnegie-Mellon University, Pittsburgh, Pa., May 18-20, 1984).

4. THE MEDIA CAMPAIGN: STRUGGLE FOR THE AGENDA

Thomas E. Patterson and Richard Davis

Political campaigns are essentially struggles to control the election agenda. Opposing candidates seek to wage the campaign on battlefields of their own choosing, believing that how voters perceive the particular choices at stake in an election may affect its outcome. The candidates, however, are not the only ones at work on the agenda. Members of the news media, although they serve in part as carriers of the candidates' messages, also contribute their own ideas about the nature of the campaign. In their traditional position as public trustee, journalists question, refute, or support the claims the candidates themselves are making. More fundamentally, journalists affect the election agenda simply by selecting from an election's many aspects those few that will become part of each day's news. Because of the media's space and time constraints, a campaign is much larger than the news about it can possibly be.

National elections in all Western democracies are media-centered in the sense that candidates depend primarily on mass communication to reach the voters. Only the United States, however, has developed a national election system that relies so heavily upon journalists to organize the choices facing the voters. Although journalists in other democracies are active participants in campaigns, their efforts are largely subordinate to the campaign structure that is established by the political parties and the electoral laws that support the parties' claim to be the principal intermediary between candidates and voters. In the United States, parties play a secondary role. Presidential elections have become plebiscites in which candidates stand alone before the electorate and must depend upon the press to mediate their appeals.

The media's influence is not prescribed by law but is the result of the void that was created when America's political parties surrendered control of the nominating process. Through the 1968 elections, nominations still were decided mostly by party leaders. Primary elections were held in several states, but they were not decisive in the selection of nominees. In 1952, for example, Sen. Estes Kefauver defeated President Harry S. Truman by a 55-45 margin in New Hampshire's opening primary, went on to win all but one of the other 12 primaries he contested, and was the clear preference of rank-and-file Democrats in the final Gallup poll before the national convention. Yet, Democratic party leaders rejected Kefauver, choosing instead Illinois governor Adlai Stevenson, who, they felt, was more representative of the party's traditions. On the other hand, Sen. John F. Kennedy in 1960 used a primary victory in West Virginia to demonstrate that a Catholic candidate could attract voters of all religions, which helped persuade party leaders to support his nomination.

The nominating system, however, changed fundamentally following the bitter Democratic campaign of 1968. After setbacks in the early primaries, President Lyndon B. Johnson was forced from the race, leaving senators Eugene McCarthy and Robert F. Kennedy to contest the remaining states. But Kennedy was assassinated on the night of the California primary, and McCarthy's strident opposition to Johnson's Vietnam policy made him unacceptable to Democratic leaders. They chose instead Vice President Hubert Humphrey on the first ballot. Humphrey had not contested the primaries, and his nomination split the party. After his general election defeat, the Democrats undertook reforms that shifted control of the nominating process from the party's leadership to its rank-and-file voters. Beginning in 1972, national convention delegates were chosen either through state primaries or open caucuses. Serious presidential contenders then had to appeal directly to the voters.

As a result, the media's influence in the nominating process greatly increased. No amount of support from party leaders can substitute for support among millions of ordinary voters. Consequently, candidates are forced to work through the news media. Jimmy Carter's efforts in the year preceding his 1976 presidential nomination exemplify the new, expanded role of the media. Instead of making the traditional rounds among party leaders, Carter traveled about the country meeting journalists.

Changes in the mass media during the past 25 years also have contributed to reporters' growing influence. Just before President John F. Kennedy was assassinated in 1963, the CBS and NBC television networks extended their nightly newscasts from 15 minutes to a half hour. Kennedy had been nearly the ideal president for television. He was witty, charming, handsome, dignified, and bright, and the television networks had become convinced that viewers' interest in national news broadcasts had grown. Since 1963 the networks have continued to expand their news coverage, and most television stations now provide from three to five hours of news programming every weekday.

Although broadcast technology now allows rapid, even instantaneous, communication with many parts of the nation and world, network newscasts concentrate particularly on developments in Washington. The president, as the most visible national leader, receives more attention than any other person or institution. Would-be presidents are also a natural subject for the networks. During a presidential election year, each network features campaign stories nearly every day, a practice also followed by the wire services and by prestigious newspapers such as the *New York Times, Los Angeles Times,* and *Washington Post.*

News versus Politics

Despite their growing importance in American electoral politics, the news media are poorly suited to their role as the principal intermediary between candidates and voters. Although the media are neither as obsessed with trivia nor as self-interested as some critics suggest, they are unable to organize the election's agenda in a meaningful way. The media are in the news business, and their inadequacy as a linking mechanism for candidates and voters becomes obvious once the difference between news values and political values is understood. Election news conveys scenes of political actions, not the values represented by those scenes. Election news emphasizes what is different about the events of the previous 24 hours, not enduring political concerns. Election news concentrates on competition and controversy, not basic questions of policy and leadership.[1]

In part, the nature of election news reflects the tradition in American journalism that news is to be found in activity rather than in the causes of that activity. The function of news, said Walter Lippmann in 1922, is not to explain events but "to signalize events." Lippmann gave several explanations for why reporters concentrate on the surface aspects of life: insufficient space in which to deal with the more complicated causes of events, the need to report events in terms that are familiar to their audience, and the natural tendency to note the most immediate aspects of events when meeting daily deadlines. In all, said Lippmann, reporters prefer "the indisputable fact and the easy interest." [2]

The media's orientation also is rooted in their conception of politics as a "game." Paul Weaver suggests that the news media do not regard elections primarily as struggles over the direction of national policy and leadership. Instead, a campaign is seen mainly as a contest between the candidates for personal success and power. "The game," says Weaver, "takes place against a backdrop of governmental institutions, public problems, policy debates, and the like, but these are noteworthy only insofar as they affect, or are used by, players in pursuit of the game's rewards." [3]

No one would argue that the role of the media should be simply to convey what the contenders in an election are saying in undiluted form. That would be to transform newspapers, news magazines, and television news programs into collections of free commercials for the candidates. But what is noteworthy in modern campaigns is that the candidates' agendas are not readily evident in election coverage, as a look at five "cases" from the 1984 presidential election will show.

Case 1. Quest for Recognition

Russell Baker of the *New York Times* aptly calls the news media the "Great Mentioner." The nominating campaign of a candidate who is largely ignored by the media almost certainly is futile, while the campaign of one who receives heavy coverage gets an important boost. Before the campaign officially begins, the news media essentially screen the contenders, deciding which ones are worthy of serious consideration by the electorate and which ones are also-rans. It is a role once exercised by party leaders.

Eight Democrats contested for their party's 1984 presidential nomination. Their early efforts were designed primarily to win support from constituent groups in the party and to generate news coverage. Although all the Democratic challengers worked to gain the press's attention, they were not equally successful. A content analysis of newspaper coverage in January and February 1984 reveals that Walter F. Mondale received substantially more coverage than his Democratic opponents.[4] He received, for example, twice as much coverage as Sen. Gary Hart and five times as much as another opponent, Sen. Alan Cranston *(Table 4.1)*.

No period of the campaign offers the news media as much freedom as the weeks immediately preceding the first nominating contests in Iowa

Table 4.1 News References to Mondale, Hart, and Cranston, January and February 1984

Candidate	Number of References in			
	New York Times *(92 articles)*		Syracuse Post-Standard *(22 articles)*	
Mondale	370	(59%)	110	(58%)
Hart	186	(29%)	56	(30%)
Cranston	76	(12%)	22	(12%)
Total	632	(100%)	188	(100%)

and New Hampshire. The formulas of "objective journalism" lead the press in the fall general election campaign to distribute its coverage rather evenly between the two major party nominees. But before the campaign officially begins, there are no clear journalistic guidelines. As Michael Robinson and Margaret Sheehan have noted, "Polls, punditry, and seat of the pants assessment" determine coverage before the first balloting.[5]

Journalists do not use the same criteria to evaluate would-be nominees as party leaders once did. Those leaders' judgments were based on several considerations, including the contenders' experience, allegiance to party interests and principles, and electability in the fall campaign. Journalists, however, appear to base their judgments on only one standard: the candidates' chances of emerging victorious from the nominating campaign. Thus, Mondale, as the early favorite in the polls, "deserved" more attention in the news than any of his Democratic challengers.

The tendency for news coverage to follow the likely "winner" reaches its peak with the first primary in New Hampshire. In an abstract sense, a narrow victory or defeat or even a landslide in the New Hampshire primary is not all that important. It is but one indicator of the candidates' popularity in a system of 50 state contests, almost all of which involve more convention delegates than New Hampshire does. It lacks, moreover, the finality of a general election. The primary produces no officeholder, but it does distribute delegates and measure the candidates' relative support among the state's voters.

The media's interpretation of the New Hampshire primary, however, rests on entirely different principles. Reporters tend to project New Hampshire's results onto the nation as a whole, and something close to a "winner-take-all" rule applies to subsequent coverage. Hart placed first in New Hampshire with 37 percent of the vote to Mondale's 28 percent and Sen. John Glenn's 12 percent, but Hart was essentially the only candidate of interest to the media. He was in the headlines, at the top of newscasts, and on the front cover of national magazines. The media's message was clear: Hart was the Democratic front-runner. In a front-page *New York Times* article after his New Hampshire victory, references to Hart accounted for more than 60 percent of the story; his seven Democratic rivals combined received less than 40 percent of the space.[6]

In the journalistic tradition of which Lippmann wrote, the concentration on New Hampshire's winner meets almost every criterion for good news. Reporters were careful not to submerge the results in explanations of the intricacies of the presidential nominating system, for to do so would have ignored the limited news space available and the need to capture what Lippmann called the "easy interest." The extraordinary emphasis on only the most salient fact about New Hampshire—Hart's victory—also was rooted in the media's perspective on the campaign as a game. Although New Hampshire voters are not representative of the national electorate, the candidates' tasks there were not much different from their tasks elsewhere: raise money, mold an organization, gain press coverage, make speeches, build momentum. Since the press regards the candidates' ability to do these things as the keys to their success, it treats New Hampshire as a valid indicator of their national standing.

Case 2. Creating an Agenda

The media's concern with the election game makes it difficult for candidates to communicate their ideas, despite the great efforts they make to do so. Throughout their campaigns, candidates spend much of their time discussing national problems, policy goals, issues, and government performance. Although much of this speechmaking may appear perfunctory, it has a definite purpose—to establish the candidates' agendas in the voters' minds. The candidates necessarily look to the press for help in getting their messages across to the public. The news media, however, are not a reliable transmitter of the candidates' agendas.

Perhaps the best single indicator of the candidates' policy goals is the standard speeches they deliver again and again with only slight variations.[7] A content analysis of Mondale's stump speech reveals two themes: economic fairness and world tensions. The fairness issue was developed primarily through Mondale's criticism of Ronald Reagan's policies on tax reduction, social welfare assistance, affirmative action, and related matters; the "safer world" argument was carried mainly by reference to arms control and negotiation. Hart's theme was "a new generation of leadership," reflected in a variety of specific proposals relating particularly to economic development, energy, and defense.

In the two months preceding the first balloting in Iowa and New Hampshire, Hart's and Mondale's themes were not featured prominently in news coverage of the Democratic race *(Table 4.2)*. With the exception of Hart's "new leadership" agenda, neither candidate's themes even appeared in more than a tenth of the articles. Moreover, these themes were almost never the basis for a news story, being mentioned instead in only a sentence or two.

Nor were the specific issues that contributed to Hart's and Mondale's themes singled out for heavy coverage. In 114 articles about the Democratic campaign, Mondale's charge that Reagan's tax cuts benefited the rich was mentioned only four times; his "progressive tax plan" was not mentioned once. Hart's specific proposals fared no better. His idea of new job and training programs received the heaviest coverage of any of his

Table 4.2 News Coverage of Hart's and Mondale's Themes and Issues, January and February 1984

| | Number of References in | |
| | New York Times | Syracuse Post-Standard |
Candidate	(92 articles)	(22 articles)
Mondale		
Themes		
Economic fairness	9	2
World tension	5	4
Example Issues		
Tax cuts	5	0
Medicare	5	2
Reaganomics	2	0
Social Security	1	0
Progressive taxes	0	0
Arms negotiation	0	0
Hart		
Theme		
"New leadership"	15	2
Example Issues		
New jobs	3	0
Economic infrastructure	3	2
Energy	0	0
Military reform	2	1
Leadership style	0	0

Note: Candidates' themes and issues are taken from their stump speeches. Any mention of a theme or issue in a news story, regardless of how brief, was counted as a reference.

proposals; it was mentioned three times in the 114 articles. Among the ideas contained in his stump speech that received no mention at all in the news were world economic change, synthetic fuels, and energy conservation.

The news media, then, made no significant attempt to define Hart and Mondale in the ways that the candidates themselves wanted to be seen. The apparent reason is that the candidates' standard political appeals are not considered very newsworthy. Such appeals are predictable, routine, and uncontroversial. Although the messages of stump speeches are finely tuned by the candidates and their staffs to embody their positions and are repeated at nearly every campaign stop and before every audience, the media seem to think that these messages are largely meaningless, at least by journalistic standards. "When candidates say the same things over and over," said television correspondent Judy Woodruff, "it is not news." The news, instead, is about novel developments, a point evident in this Knight-Ridder wire story of February 26, 1984:

> Fritz, John, Jesse, Gary and the other Democratic munchkins for president spent 90 minutes on television in Manchester, N.H., Thursday night with Barbara Walters.
>
> It was about 80 minutes too much. . . . This seemingly 10,000th debate proved that the White House hopefuls have nothing new left to say. They're even starting to bore one another.
>
> They're like the dogs in Pavlov's experiment. Ring a bell and they make stump speeches. . . . Walters tried but failed to inject life into Thursday night's ritual.

News about Hart and Mondale, however, was not completely issueless. After the first balloting in Iowa and New Hampshire, the two candidates were saddled by the media with corrupted versions of their themes. Mondale was portrayed as the "captive of special interests" and Hart as the candidate of unhatched new ideas. These portrayals only partly originated with the press. It was Mondale, for example, who crystallized doubts about the substance of Hart's new ideas by asking, "Where's the beef?" But they came to be used heavily by reporters, who gave them far more prominence than the themes the candidates were trying to develop for themselves. This turnabout was perhaps predictable. The press, as Colin Seymour-Ure notes, has a liking for issues that neatly divide the candidates, generate controversy, rest on principle rather than on complex relationships, and can be stated in simple terms, usually by reference to shorthand labels.[8] "Where's the beef?" and "captive of special interests" fit journalistic needs much better than did the themes of new leadership and economic fairness.

Case 3. The Ferraro "Campaign Issue"

The news media's lack of interest in normal election discourse stands in stark contrast to the extraordinary news coverage that occurs when the unexpected happens. When a candidate says or does something completely out of character during the campaign, usually because of an error in judgment, it becomes major news. All recent elections have had such "campaign issues"—issues that are born of, and eventually die in, the events of the campaign itself. Carter's *Playboy* interview in 1976 is one example; Reagan's 1980 remark about the supposed birth of the Ku Klux Klan in Tuscumbia, Alabama, is another.

When campaign issues first break, they make the headlines and the top of television newscasts. For a week or more, they are likely to remain major news stories. This was true of several campaign issues in 1984, among them Jesse Jackson's reference to Jews as "Hymies" and his association with Muslim leader Louis Farrakhan. When Jackson appeared on NBC's "Meet the Press" in April, he was asked nine straight questions about Farrakhan. Jackson protested: "I want to talk, if I might, about industrial policies to put people back to work, or about African policy, which most of you tend to ignore, or South African oppression. I think that continuing to raise this [Farrakhan] issue, frankly, is overspending my time." [9]

No campaign issue of 1984, however, received more attention from the media than did Democratic vice presidential candidate Geraldine A. Ferraro's tax problems. From the time she announced that she would not release her husband's tax returns until her exculpatory news conference eight days later, the issue was rarely out of the news. It topped the nightly newscasts and, the day before Ferraro's news conference, the *New York Times* devoted four news stories to the issue. The following front-page headlines appeared in the *Times* during the eight-day period:

- *G.O.P. Seizes Genderless Issue of Tax Returns to Attack Ferraro*
- *Finances of Ferraro and Husband Are Interwoven*
- *Zaccaro: Competitive, Private Man*
- *Husband Plans Tax Disclosure with Ferraro*
- *Ferraro Is Termed Surprised by Loan Taken by Husband*
- *Ferraro Reveals Her Tax Figures and Husband's*
- *Ferraro Denies Any Wrongdoing; 2d Loan by Zaccaro from Estate*

No policy issue during the entire campaign commanded this level of news attention. Indeed, policy issues usually were not mentioned in the headlines or covered for more than a day or two consecutively.

Campaign issues have a special appeal to the press, in part because they conform with traditional news values—they are unexpected, colorful, and unique. Who could possibly have predicted that, with all the emphasis in recent years on full financial disclosure by politicians, Ferraro would decide to withhold her husband's tax returns? Campaign issues, moreover, usually build upon themselves, creating suspense and heightened expectation as they unfold. They involve what James David Barber identifies as the most common type of developing news story, that of "action-reaction." [10] Where there is error there is potential for dramatic resolution, as when Ferraro finally changed her mind about releasing the tax information.

Campaign issues usually have no relevance to national policy. For example, Gerald R. Ford's statement in a 1976 presidential debate that Eastern Europe was free from Soviet domination was understood by the press to be a misstatement, not a deeply held belief. Similarly, Ferraro's refusal to release her tax data was regarded mainly as a tactical error in campaign politics. It is, in fact, the electoral effects of campaign issues that fuel news about them. There was the suggestion in the Ferraro story that she was hiding illegal financial activities, but the news theme was the damaging effects of her action on the momentum the Democratic campaign had gathered during the party's national convention.

Christopher Arterton suggests that the appeal of campaign issues to the press also lies in the control they provide reporters. Arterton conceives of candidate-press interactions as constituting a power relationship in which each side has a major source of influence—the media through their gatekeeping role of deciding what to report and the candidates through their ability to decide what and how much they will say. When an incident becomes a campaign issue, however, the candidate's power is greatly reduced; there is little choice but to face the issue because the media refuse to let it die. [11]

Case 4. The Debates: Creating Expectations

The news media do not inject partisan values into their evaluation of election activities. Instead, they have developed the practice of creating "expectations" for events and then assessing them in light of those expectations. A celebrated example is the 1972 Democratic primary in New Hampshire. The media determined on the basis of polls and predictions by the campaign staff of Sen. Edmund Muskie that Muskie would have to get 60 percent or more of the vote there if he was to be judged the winner. He failed to do so, and the mantle of victory was placed by reporters upon Sen. George McGovern, even though he placed behind Muskie in the popular voting. In 1984 Glenn failed to live up to the media's expectations in the Iowa caucuses, where he finished seventh. On the next morning's CBS newscast, a reporter said that the New Hampshire primary would be Glenn's "last chance to prove that he deserves to be counted in the race."

In general, the media's emphasis on predicting the outcomes of events limits the way these events later are interpreted. The 1984 presidential debates provide an example. Mondale's chances of victory in November were said to hinge on a "knockout" of Reagan in the debates. Few journalists, however, felt this would happen. The "Great Communicator," as Reagan was labeled by the press, was expected to dominate Mondale easily. This expectation was built partly on the course of the campaign to that point. As a general rule, the media develop their image of presidential candidates by assessing their standing with the electorate, rather than their record of public service or their intrinsic personal qualities.[12] According to the media's conception of politics as a game, the true test of a leader is the ability to attract votes. The leading candidate is portrayed in the news as abundantly appealing, while a candidate who trails badly in the polls normally is presented as lacking essential leadership and personal qualities. A *Washington Post* writer, two days before the October 7 first debate, said Mondale appears "shrill, harsh—sometimes even menacing. Yet, at the same time—primarily because of his voice—he comes off as somehow 'weak' and a 'wimp.' "

The first presidential debate did not unfold as the media had predicted. Reagan was hesitant in his delivery and unsure of his facts, while Mondale gave the more confident and commanding performance. In explaining this surprising outcome, the media were confined by the standards they themselves had created. There was no suggestion that their prediction of a Reagan victory was based on faulty assumptions. Although Reagan's age as a possible explanation for his performance surfaced momentarily ("Had he tired during the debate's last half-hour?"), the general view quickly emerged that he simply had had an off night. Said a *Washington Post* reporter on October 12:

> If Reagan is slowing down, if at 73 he's slipping off to senility, is occasionally befuddled, unable to come up with the precise word and verbally treads water by repeating himself, it's indeed a cause for concern and should be discussed. He is, after all, the president, and the job calls for mental acuity.... [But] we all have our off nights. Maybe Reagan did not sleep well. Maybe he ate something that disagreed with him. Maybe, for some unexplainable reason, he simply was not himself.

The doubts raised by the first debate increased the political significance of the second debate on October 21, which would decide whether a major reassessment of the candidates was necessary. The interim news theme became "Will Reagan repeat his performance?" Reagan did perform somewhat better, providing the press with an answer to its question. "There certainly was no 'knockout,' " said a network commentator, voicing the general conclusion reached by reporters. Meanwhile, throughout the whole period of the debates, little attention was given in the news to the candidates' policy differences or knowledge of national issues. Less than a fourth of *Time* magazine's lead story on the first debate, for example, dealt with the issues discussed by the candidates.[13] The debates initially were framed in the context of the election game, and by this standard they were judged.

Case 5. Predicting the Reagan Landslide

In their coverage of a presidential campaign, the media concentrate on the strategic games played by the candidates in their pursuit of the presidency, thereby de-emphasizing questions of national policy and leadership. This partly reflects the tradition in journalism that news is to be found in activity. The candidates' campaign appearances constitute the most visible aspects of the campaign and therefore are most likely to be treated by the media as election news. Heavy emphasis is given to the simple mechanics of campaigning—the candidates' travels here and there, their organizational efforts and their strategies, as well as voting projections and poll results. The press does not stress the candidates' policy positions, personal and leadership characteristics, and private and public histories; nor does it produce much background information on the issues or on group endorsements of candidates or their backing of specific groups.

Consequently, most election coverage is devoted to the campaign contest itself rather than to what the choice of one candidate or the other may mean to the nation. Studies of presidential elections have thoroughly documented this "horse race" emphasis by the media. In the 1976 campaign, for instance, about twice as much news coverage was devoted to the election's competition as to its substance.[14]

A presidential campaign is, of course, a game of strategy as well as a time for the candidates to offer the voters a choice about national policy and leadership. One naturally would expect to see both aspects presented in the news. What is surprising is the recent growth in the media's concern with the game at the expense of the choice. During the 1940s, Paul Lazarsfeld and Bernard Berelson found that about 35 percent of election news dealt with the fight to gain the presidency; 50 percent concerned subjects related to policy and leadership.[15]

A number of causes appear to underlie the change. For one, strategy and maneuver play a larger and more visible role in modern campaigns. Candidates now organize earlier and more thoroughly than in the past. The increase in the number of primaries is another reason that substance has been upstaged by the game. Primaries now consume nearly half the campaign year, and it is during the primaries that the game aspect of the election is emphasized most heavily. Finally, modern campaigns, because of their length, give journalists more time (and thus more freedom) to pursue their game conception of politics. Candidates can expect their major policy statements to be reported, but once they make their views known, further statements on these issues decline in news value. Until recently, general election campaigns did not really begin until Labor Day, and the candidates could fill much of the two-month news period before the November election with their policy speeches. Now, however, more than ten months pass between the beginning and end of the campaign year, and candidates cannot offer enough fresh issues to control the flow of information for this long period. On most campaign days, reporters have great freedom in their choice of news material. Given their general view of election politics, they tend to use this freedom to offer updates on the players' strategies and standings, rather than reruns of the candidates' policy statements, records, backgrounds, and qualifications.

Sometimes journalists themselves recognize this tendency, as did Charles Peters, editor of the *Washington Monthly,* when he attempted to explain the media's coverage of Hart's candidacy:

> ... I believe that the most important reason for the tilt against Mr. Hart is that his best side, his leadership on national defense and economic-growth issues, is something that most political reporters don't understand or care very much about—or can't fit into the newspaper or the evening news because of everyone's preoccupation with the horse race.
>
> For them, "issues" are the start of boring position papers, the kinds of things that are discussed at seminars held by worthy, dull institutions. Reporters love to do stories about momentum and opinion polls, about gaffes and details from the candidates' personal lives, like Mr. Hart's birth date. But even the best of them tend to avoid the issues. In his now famous television interview with Mr. Hart, Roger Mudd—one of the most intelligent political reporters—addressed 18 questions or comments to the candidate. Only one was the subject of Mr. Hart's stand on an issue.[16]

In the final stages of the 1976 and 1980 election campaigns, the news media adjusted their coverage somewhat by placing greater emphasis on the substantive differences between the candidates.[17] The media seemed to be signaling to voters, even if belatedly, that the direction of national policy and leadership hinged on their choice. Most of the major news outlets ran lengthy stories, often a series of reports, on the implications of selecting one candidate or the other. Of course, this more issue-oriented reporting stood side by side with stories about the candidates' final appeals for support, poll results, and other "election game" news. Nevertheless, in many news outlets, coverage of the election's substance equaled or exceeded reports on the "horse race."

This shift in the agenda of media coverage did not occur in the final two weeks of the 1984 campaign. Instead, one question overshadowed all others: Will Reagan win in a landslide? It was not the substantive significance of the election outcome but the size of Reagan's pending victory that dominated election eve reporting. Perhaps the debate scenario developed by the media explains this preoccupation. Since reporters assumed that Mondale had to score a knockout in the debates to have any chance of being elected, his failure to do so signaled the end of the election to them.

Another possibility, and one with more significant implications for future elections, is that reporters' growing use of polls concentrated their attention on the election's likely outcome. In the last week of the campaign, the *New York Times* ran 15 stories based wholly or in significant part on polls, nearly a third of its election coverage in this period. Another fourth of its stories made at least some mention of poll results *(Table 4.3)*. The increasing availability of polls—many of them conducted by news organizations themselves—has elevated the probable outcome of the election to an everyday news subject, and thus this speculation has become a constant competitor with the election's substance for space in newspapers and time on television.

A Concluding Note: Disorganized Politics

Although America's news media now exercise many of the functions previously conducted by political parties, these two institutions are not equivalent. The parties have an incentive to identify and represent organized interests that are making demands for symbolic and policy representation. Parties are in the business of developing coherent political agendas and organizing majorities. The press is not designed to play this

Table 4.3 News Stories Involving Polls in the *New York Times,* October 31-November 6, 1984

Type of Story	Number of Stories	Percentage of Stories
Poll results as major emphasis	7	14%
Poll results as important aspect (several paragraphs)	8	16
Poll results mentioned in a paragraph or sentence	13	27
Poll results not mentioned	21	43
Total	49	100%

role. Although reporters often claim that they can organize the public's choices in meaningful ways, the truth is that they cannot. The problem is not that the media are lacking in public spiritedness, but that they have no incentive to build political coalitions and to establish a policy agenda. The media are guided by news values, and properly so. The news business is not the same as the business of politics. As Lippmann observed, "The press is no substitute for institutions. It is like the beam of a searchlight that moves restlessly about, bringing one episode and then another out of darkness into vision. Men cannot do the work of the world by this light alone. They cannot govern society by episodes, incidents, and interruptions." [18]

The United States has developed the world's longest and most disorganized system of choosing national leaders. Whether they like it or not, the media have the burden of guiding the electorate through this process. But the press has not the means to bring order to this chaos. The media, said Lippmann, "necessarily and inevitably reflect, and therefore, in greater or lesser measure, intensify, the defective organization of public opinion." [19] The presidential nominating process, for instance, naturally gives added emphasis to states that hold early contests, a bias that is magnified by the press's extraordinary buildup of these contests and its determination to call and cover the winners.

The nature of election coverage by the media also combines with the length and structure of modern campaigns to make the "game" the election's agenda. It is easier to concentrate on questions of national policy and leadership when the campaign is a few months long and waged primarily between the parties than it is today when the campaign lasts a year and centers mostly on intraparty conflict. By finding significance primarily in the campaign's contests, activities, and episodes, the news media contribute to an election that de-emphasizes issues. Increasingly, election news has come to reflect journalistic rather than political values.

Finally, the press's added influence on the election agenda has increased the probability that "natural" political forces will be diverted. As Seymour-Ure has noted, the press's biases introduce into the campaign an element of "random partisanship" in the sense that prevailing news subjects coincidentally may favor one candidate or another. The publicity advantage that accompanies the winning of an opening contest, the adverse news that follows a campaign blunder, or the emphasis that is placed on poll results can influence the candidates' chances of winning nomination or election. [20]

For the most part, however, the problem of modern campaigns lies deeper than the media's reporting biases. To be sure, the press could recognize more fully how it exaggerates the system's weaknesses. Must the importance of the New Hampshire primary be magnified beyond all reasonable proportion? Must the candidates' small mistakes be among the major news stories of the campaign? Must their participation in presidential debates be judged almost solely on how they say what they say rather than on what is said? No. But the press is necessarily guided by its own values, conventions, and organizational imperatives, and these are certain to dominate its news decisions. The ills of the modern system of presidential selection will not be cured by getting the news media to behave as if they were political parties. Indeed, the real weakness of the modern system is that it was built upon the dismantling of the political party—in Everett Carll Ladd's words, the one "institution able to practice political planning." [21]

Notes

1. The ideas of this essay owe substantially to Thomas E. Patterson's previous work, especially *The Mass Media Election* (New York: Praeger, 1980).
2. Walter Lippmann, *Public Opinion* (1922; reprint, New York: Free Press, 1965), 221-226.
3. Paul Weaver, "Is Television News Biased?" *Public Interest* (Spring 1972): 69.
4. The content analysis in this and the following section is based on reporting in the *New York Times* and the *Syracuse Post-Standard* (New York). The *Times* represents an elite newspaper with its own staff to cover the campaign. The *Post-Standard* is an example of a daily newspaper that depends upon wire services for national election coverage. None of the articles about the Democratic candidates in the *Post-Standard* originated with its reporting staff. Only articles about the Democratic candidates in January and February 1984 were coded. Other campaign-related stories (such as those on the Republican campaign or the nature of the electorate) were excluded. The content analysis also was limited to news stories. Editorials and letters to the editor were not included.
5. Michael Robinson and Margaret Sheehan, *Over the Wire and on TV* (New York: Russell Sage, 1983), 85.
6. *New York Times,* March 2, 1984, 1.
7. Each candidate's stump speech was printed once in the *New York Times* in late February.
8. Colin Seymour-Ure, *The Political Impact of Mass Media* (Beverly Hills, Calif.: Sage, 1974), 223.
9. Morton Kondracke, "The Jacksonian Persuasion," *New Republic,* April 30, 1984, 13.

10. James David Barber, "Characters in the Campaign: The Literary Problem," in *Race for the Presidency*, ed. James David Barber (Englewood Cliffs, N.J.: Prentice-Hall, 1978), 117.

11. F. Christopher Arterton, "The Media Politics of Presidential Campaigns," in *Race for the Presidency*, 48-51.

12. Patterson, *Mass Media Election*, Chapter 5.

13. "Getting a Second Look," *Time*, October 22, 1984, 24-28.

14. Patterson, *Mass Media Election*, 22-25.

15. Paul Lazarsfeld, Bernard Berelson, and Hazel Gaudet, *The People's Choice*, 3d ed. (New York: Columbia University Press, 1968), 115-119; Bernard Berelson, Paul Lazarsfeld, and William McPhee, *Voting* (Chicago: University of Chicago Press, 1954), 248.

16. *New York Times*, April 6, 1984, A20.

17. Patterson, *Mass Media Election*, 29; Robinson and Sheehan, *Over the Wire and on TV*.

18. Lippmann, *Public Opinion*, 228.

19. Ibid., 19.

20. Seymour-Ure, *Political Impact of Mass Media*, Chapter 8.

21. Everett Carll Ladd, *American Political Parties* (New York: Norton, 1970), 2.

5. FOREIGN POLICY: DOMINANCE AND DECISIVENESS IN PRESIDENTIAL ELECTIONS

Stephen Hess and Michael Nelson

"You can say all you want about foreign affairs," said the Republican governor of Illinois, William G. Stratton, "but what is really important is the price of hogs in Chicago and St. Louis."

The setting for the governor's remark was a post-midnight meeting in Vice President Richard Nixon's suite at the Sheraton-Blackstone Hotel in Chicago. Only hours before, the delegates to the 1960 Republican National Convention had chosen Nixon unanimously as their party's nominee for president, and the candidate now had summoned 36 party elders to advise him on choosing a vice presidential running mate.

Ultimately, Nixon rejected Stratton's advice and picked Henry Cabot Lodge, whose face was known to millions of American television viewers as their country's chief spokesman at the United Nations for nearly all of the previous eight years. Later, explaining his decision, Nixon said: "If you ever let them [the Democrats] campaign only on domestic issues, they'll beat us—our hope is to keep it on foreign policy." [1]

In 1960 Stratton was right, but then so was Nixon. A close look at the eight presidential elections that took place prior to 1984 generates two main propositions whose basis and explanation make up the greater part of this essay and, taken together, set the stage for our discussion of the 1984 election. Stated baldly, the two propositions are:

1. Foreign policy usually plays a *dominant* role in the campaigns waged by candidates for the presidency. It did so in six of the eight elections that took place from 1952 to 1980.

2. Nonetheless, foreign policy generally is not *decisive* in determining the results of presidential elections. (These results are listed in Table 5.1.) There is a corollary to this proposition: to the extent that international issues benefit one or the other major party candidates, it usually is the Republican.

Foreign Policy Dominance in Presidential Campaigns

The best evidence for the proposition that foreign policy issues usually play a dominant role in the presidential campaigns of the major party candidates can be found in a review of the record.

1952: Eisenhower vs. Stevenson

The Republicans, with Dwight D. Eisenhower, the supreme Allied commander during World War II, as their candidate, ran a sort of "three Cs" campaign: "Korea, Communism, and Corruption." Poll data showed the Korean War steadily rising in its share of prime voter concern, from one-fourth (January) to one-third (September) to more than one-half (late October).[2] On October 24 in Detroit, just two weeks before the election, Eisenhower delivered the most politically skillful foreign policy pronouncement in recent history. "Where will a new Administration begin?" he asked, then answered:

> It will begin with its president taking a simple firm resolution. That resolution will be: to forego the diversions of politics and concentrate on the job of ending the Korean war—until that job is honorably done.
> That job requires a personal trip to Korea.
> I shall make that trip. Only in that way could I learn how best to serve the American people in the cause of peace.
> I shall go to Korea.

The origin of the speech was simple, wrote Emmet John Hughes, its draftsman. "It rose from the need to say something affirmative on the sharpest issue of the day—without engaging in frivolous assurances and without binding a future administration to policies or actions fashioned in mid-campaign by any distorting temptations of domestic politics."[3] Interestingly, Gov. Adlai Stevenson, the Democratic nominee for president, earlier had decided that he would go to Korea if elected, but kept the idea to himself for fear that he would be accused of making a grandstand play.[4]

1956: Stevenson vs. Eisenhower

In the rematch between Eisenhower and Stevenson, the Republicans changed their alliterative slogan to "Peace, Prosperity, and Progress." If Eisenhower's most important statement in 1952 had been "I shall go to Korea," four years later it was "Ladies and gentlemen, I feel fine." The state of Ike's health had been in question after his heart attack the previous year and a major ileitis operation in June, and Stevenson tried to

Table 5.1   Presidential Election Returns, 1952-1984

Year	Candidates	Percent of popular vote	Number of electoral votes*
1952	*Dwight D. Eisenhower (R)*	*55.1*	*442*
	Adlai E. Stevenson (D)	44.4	89
1956	*Dwight D. Eisenhower (R)*	*57.4*	*457*
	Adlai E. Stevenson (D)	42.0	73
1960	*John F. Kennedy (D)*	*49.7*	*303*
	Richard Nixon (R)	49.6	219
1964	*Lyndon B. Johnson (D)*	*61.1*	*486*
	Barry M. Goldwater (R)	38.5	52
1968	*Richard Nixon (R)*	*43.4*	*301*
	Hubert H. Humphrey (D)	42.7	191
	George C. Wallace (Am-Ind[1])	13.5	46
1972	*Richard Nixon (R)*	*60.7*	*520*
	George S. McGovern (D)	37.5	17
1976	*Jimmy Carter (D)*	*50.1*	*297*
	Gerald R. Ford (R)	48.0	240
1980	*Ronald Reagan (R)*	*50.7*	*489*
	Jimmy Carter (D)	41.0	49
	John B. Anderson (Ind[2])	6.6	0
1984	*Ronald Reagan (R)*	*58.7*	*525*
	Walter F. Mondale (D)	40.5	13

[1] American Independent
[2] Independent
* The total number of electoral votes has been 538 since 1964; in 1952 and 1956 there were 531 and in 1960, 537.

Source: Congressional Quarterly, *Elections '84* (Washington, D.C.: Congressional Quarterly, 1984); *Congressional Quarterly Weekly Report,* November 10, 1984; Congressional Quarterly, *Guide to U.S. Elections* (Washington, D.C.: Congressional Quarterly, 1975); secretaries of state of the 50 states.

connect lingering public doubts to deeper issues of foreign policy. As Theodore H. White observes, Stevenson "made the axis of his final thrust the fact that Eisenhower (then 66) was too old to be a good president; that he lacked the vigor to master foreign affairs." [5] Besides the president's health, the issue of sharpest disagreement in 1956 was the testing of nuclear weapons.

The campaign was complicated during its final days by an uprising of Hungarian "freedom fighters" against their nation's domination by Soviet troops, and by violence in the Middle East. Egyptian president Gamal Abdel Nasser had seized the Suez Canal in July, jeopardizing Europe's oil lifeline and prompting Israel, France, and Great Britain to try to win it back a week before the American election. Eisenhower's response in a nationally televised address was to denounce both invaders equally—the Soviets in Hungary and the Israeli-French-British coalition in the Suez. The speech preempted the moral high ground of international law and fair play on this potentially explosive election-eve issue, even at the price of treating American allies no better than the Soviets and their friends. It also allowed Vice President Nixon to make the case for his party's ticket in national security terms: "This is not the moment to replace the greatest commander-in-chief America has ever had."

1960: Kennedy vs. Nixon

Although foreign affairs were discussed in 1960—the desired U.S. response to Cuba's recent takeover by Fidel Castro and to a possible Chinese invasion of the offshore islands of Quemoy and Matsu, the alleged missile gap between the United States and the Soviet Union, and American prestige abroad—the campaign revolved around religion and mood. "I have premised my campaign for the presidency," said Democratic nominee John F. Kennedy, a Roman Catholic, "on the simple assumption that the American people are uneasy at the present drift in our national course . . . and that they have the will and the strength to start the United States moving again." Nixon, the Republican candidate, "pointed with pride to an eight-year record of unparalleled national growth. . . . But at the same time . . . warned against smugness or complacency." In sum, wrote White in the first of his series of books called *The Making of a President*, "specifics and issues had all but ceased to matter; only 'style' was important." [6]

1964: Goldwater vs. Johnson

The tone of the 1964 campaign was set by a television commercial, aired only once but imbedded forever in political lore, in which a little girl plucks daisy petals while a doomsday voice begins a countdown, followed by a mushroom cloud and the voice of President Lyndon B. Johnson reminding viewers that "these are the stakes. . . ." The world view of Republican candidate Barry Goldwater had been expressed in his book *The Conscience of a Conservative:* "The communists' aim is to conquer the world. . . . Unless you contemplate treason, your objective . . . will be victory. Not 'peace,' but victory." [7] After years of musing aloud about using nuclear weapons to defoliate forests in Southeast Asia and delegating authority to fire tactical nuclear weapons to North Atlantic Treaty Organization (NATO) field commanders, Goldwater found himself entwined in a tangle of statements. These were used against him with brutal effectiveness by governors Nelson Rockefeller and William Scranton during the battle for the Republican nomination and by Johnson in the fall campaign. Even when a personal scandal occurred in October that involved one of Johnson's closest aides, the news was driven off the front page by two international events—Soviet premier Nikita Khrushchev's forced resignation and China's first explosion of an atomic device—whose main effect was to remind voters of the importance of responsible leadership in a dangerous age. As election day approached, Johnson rephrased the question that was on voters' minds: "Who do you want to be sittin' beside that hot line when the telephone goes ting-a-ling and the voice on the other end says 'Moscow calling'?"

1968: Nixon vs. Humphrey

Vietnam dominated the election year, beginning with the nomination campaign. North Vietnam's Tet offensive in January set the stage for antiwar senator Eugene McCarthy's stunning near-victory over Johnson in the New Hampshire primary, which prompted the president to withdraw as a candidate for reelection. On the day of Johnson's withdrawal, Republican contender Nixon had been set to go on radio with his own Vietnam plan. It called for pressure on Moscow: "Without Soviet military assistance, the North Vietnamese war machine would grind to a halt. . . . If the Soviets were disposed to see the war ended and a compromise settlement negotiated, they have the means to move Ho Chi Minh to the conference table." The speech never was delivered. Instead Nixon backed off from specifics, declaring that once a presidential candidate "makes a statement indicating what he would settle for he pulls the rug out from under the negotiators."[8] His television spot ads stressed hopeful generalizations:

Video:	*Audio:*
Proud faces of Vietnamese peasants ending in CU [a close-up] of the word "Love" scrawled on the helmet of American G.I. and pull back to reveal his face.	Nixon: I pledge to you we will have an honorable end to the war in Vietnam. *Music up and out*

As *New York Times* columnist James Reston wrote of the Vietnam issue: "Mr. Nixon is exploiting it very shrewdly. He is simply saying it's a mess, which it obviously is, and holding . . . the Democrats responsible for it."[9]

After a bitter split over the Vietnam platform plank at their convention, the Democrats chose Vice President Hubert Humphrey as the party's nominee. Some of his advisers recommended an open break with Johnson's policy on Vietnam, but in his Salt Lake City speech of September 30 Humphrey would go only so far as to announce his willingness "to stop the bombing of North Vietnam as an acceptable risk for peace." The president declared a bombing halt on October 31, six days before the election. But the immediate refusal of the South Vietnamese to join peace talks left the American people confused, which minimized any potential benefit to the Democrats. Pressing his advantage, Nixon reminded campaign workers in the closing minutes of the campaign, "As we come down to the wire, I think the major issue in your final telephone calls that you should emphasize is the issue of peace."

1972: McGovern vs. Nixon

For a time the 1972 election came as close to a single-issue campaign as there ever has been, a result guaranteed by the nomination of Democratic senator George McGovern, whose rise from obscurity was based almost entirely on his passionate opposition to the Vietnam War. But, as Nelson Polsby and Aaron Wildavsky note:

> Once he faced President Nixon in the general election, McGovern's avowed willingness to sponsor a quick withdrawal of American troops, to cut defense spending, to "beg" Hanoi for the release of American prisoners, and to refuse future military aid to South Vietnam all were seen in a context in which voters were used to trusting Republicans, not Democrats. Thus the issue that may have been McGovern's trump card in winning the nomination could only do him harm [when] it remained salient in the general election.[10]

In contrast, seeking "peace with honor," President Nixon had mined Haiphong's harbors, bombed Hanoi, and invaded Cambodia. Yet Nixon also had been the first American president ever to visit China, negotiated the Strategic Arms Limitation Treaty (SALT) with the Soviets, made some progress in the Middle East, and withdrawn more than 400,000 American soldiers from Vietnam. Spurred perhaps by McGovern's fumbles in selecting a vice presidential candidate and in sending (or not sending—it never was clear) Pierre Salinger to meet with North Vietnamese delegates to the Paris peace talks, the voters' verdict was to approve overwhelmingly Nixon's handling of foreign affairs.

1976: Carter vs. Ford

The 1976 campaign revolved around controversies more than issues. Among the controversies were Democratic candidate Jimmy Carter's offhand remarks in a *Playboy* interview and a racial joke by Republican secretary of agriculture Earl Butz. The burden of Watergate proved too great for President Gerald R. Ford, and the voters narrowly chose former Georgia governor Carter, whose principal campaign theme was that he never had been a part of Washington "politics-as-usual."

One of the campaign's minor (in hindsight) controversies did concern foreign relations: Ford's statement in the second televised debate that "I don't believe that the Poles consider themselves dominated by the Soviet Union." The seemingly trivial blooper generated the most publicized foreign policy discussion of the campaign.

Interestingly, writes Frederick Steeper of the Market Research Corporation, which the President Ford Committee had commissioned to conduct several national surveys on the debate, "the general public did *not* know that Ford had made an error until they were told by the media the next day." Some 44 percent of the voters interviewed right after the debate thought Ford had done a "better job" than Carter (35 percent). The next morning, however, Ford's 9-point lead became a 13-point disadvantage— probably the result of the emphasis placed on the gaffe in the morning newspapers and television news programs. The gap widened to 26 points during the afternoon and to more than 40 points by evening.

Ford's blunder had a major effect on his campaign. The Republican nominee was put on the defensive, and, Steeper concludes, "the two-month trend toward Ford ... in the public polls came to a halt." [11]

1980: Reagan vs. Carter

The seizure and "embassy arrest" of several dozen American hostages by Iranian radicals on November 4, 1979, dominated the election year, both as a problem in its own right and a metaphor for other foreign policy concerns. For President Carter, the short-term political effects were favorable; his Gallup approval rating soared from 32 percent on the eve of the hostage crisis to 61 percent one month later.[12] For Sen. Edward Kennedy, who was challenging Carter for the Democratic nomination, the result was correspondingly disastrous: he went from a 23-point lead over Carter to a 34-point deficit in almost as short a period.[13] Carter locked up the nomination in the early primaries and caucuses while remaining cloistered inside the White House, attending to the crisis.

Ronald Reagan, the leading candidate for the Republican nomination, rarely talked about Iran. His main foreign policy concern during the preconvention period was to repudiate the Nixon-Ford-Carter policy of détente with the Soviet Union and substitute one of increased defense spending and American interventionism abroad—"peace through strength." Reagan continued this theme into the fall campaign, and, in the context of his constant hammering at alleged American impotence in international politics, the continuing crisis in Iran came to be seen as a living symbol and constant reminder of all that Reagan had been saying. Carter's approval rating skidded down to new lows (21 percent in July); his attacks on Reagan as a dangerous warmonger backfired by feeding the voters' impression that their president was "mean," something he apologized for in an interview with Barbara Walters on "20/20," a television program. Reagan's closing remarks in his debate with Carter convey the mixture of economic and foreign policy appeals that led to his landslide victory:

> Are you better off than you were four years ago? . . . Is America respected throughout the world as it was? Do you feel that our security is as safe, that we're as strong as we were four years ago? And if you answer all of these questions "yes," why then, I think your choice is very obvious as to whom you will vote for. If you don't agree . . . then I could suggest another choice that you have.

The Anomaly of Foreign Policy Dominance

Considering three factors that have worked powerfully to keep foreign policy discussions out of election-year politics, the quantity, if not always the quality, of these debates is noteworthy.

First, there has been the belief that "politics stops at the water's edge," the widespread notion that political conflict is not only out of place in foreign affairs but almost unpatriotic. Americans have put partisanship aside and at least temporarily "rallied-'round-the-flag" (in the form of the president) in all sorts of international circumstances, especially wars, military crises, summit meetings, and sometimes even foreign policy disasters like the hostage seizure or the Bay of Pigs fiasco.[14] (For example, President Kennedy's popularity jumped 11 points in the aftermath of the aborted invasion of Cuba in 1961.) Massive disillusionment with U.S. involvement in Vietnam eroded this feeling somewhat, but candidates still find it necessary to tread carefully. Senator Kennedy found out the costs of doing otherwise when, early in his campaign for the 1980 Democratic nomination, he criticized the Carter administration's generous treatment of the Shah of Iran shortly after the hostages were seized. Although the Shah was not popular with the American public, Kennedy was roundly chastised for injecting political controversy into a foreign policy crisis.

Second, issues tend to surface in American politics because of strong prompting from interest groups, which traditionally are organized along occupational lines. Labor unions, professional associations, and farm groups may have positions on international relations, but they generally are not central to their being. Thus, American policy on issues of great importance, such as African famines or the world monetary situation, may affect almost no votes at all.

Yet, American policy toward some countries has become so important politically that both parties must play special themes on them at all times. The "three-I" circuit—Italy, Ireland, and Israel—remains a potent force in American politics, as McGovern learned during the 1972 California primary when, to counter charges that he was not sufficiently supportive of Israel, he suddenly had to begin proclaiming that he "would go to Jerusalem" and, if elected, move the American embassy there. McGovern at least won the primary; Carter lost New York's in 1980 when he appeared to flip-flop on a United Nations vote that involved Israel. Other examples of ethnic politics abound: Irish- and German-Americans lobbied to prevent U.S. intervention in both world wars, and predictable pressure continues to come from Eastern European nationalities groups (anti-Soviet), blacks (anti-South African), Cubans (anti-Castro), and Greeks (anti-Turk). Yet on the scale of forces that weigh most heavily in the making of presidential election issues, these are modest.

A third force has worked to minimize the importance of foreign policy in presidential campaigns: historically the American voter has not been as knowledgeable about most international issues as about those that hit closer to home. Indeed, the ignorance of the electorate about specific items of foreign policy is probably the most thoroughly documented tenet of voting research. A University of Michigan survey of voters in 1964 found that 28 percent did not know there was a communist regime in China. A majority (three out of five) of those who voted for McCarthy in the 1968 New Hampshire primary probably did not know that the Minnesota senator was a dove, since their main complaint about the Johnson administration was that it was not hawkish enough in Vietnam. In 1979 only 23 percent could name the two nations involved in the SALT talks. More recently only 25 percent knew that the U.S. government was backing the rebels in Nicaragua (fewer than those who thought we were supporting the Sandinista government there).[15]

Still, as V. O. Key points out, "voters are not fools."[16] Specific issues aside, one can find tides in public opinion that are both internally coherent and politically influential. During the last decade, for example, the public mood shifted from post-Vietnam neo-isolationism to militant internationalism. Only 40 percent in a 1974 survey were willing to use American troops to defend Western Europe from a Soviet invasion, and only 43 percent thought the Central Intelligence Agency should work inside other countries to strengthen pro-American elements. In 1980 both these figures had risen to 73 percent.[17] "By the time of the 1980 election . . ," note pollsters Daniel Yankelovich and Larry Kaagan, "voters were more than ready to exorcise the ghost of Vietnam and replace it with a new posture of American assertiveness." [18]

Explaining Foreign Policy Dominance

Why has foreign policy played the dominant role it has in the great majority of recent presidential campaigns? The answer comes from two sources: the voters and the candidates.

First, it is clear that on the international issues the voters do care about, they care very deeply. This rule tends to apply when foreign policy begins to reach deeply into daily life in the manner of a domestic policy issue. "Vietnam was precisely such an issue," write Charles Kegley and Eugene Wittkopf. "Mothers and wives, fathers and sons, taxpayers and draftees—all were intimately touched by Vietnam." [19] Vietnam, of course, was a war, a fact that distinguishes it from most matters of foreign policy. More significant in the long run may be the rise of "intermestic" issues, that is, issues that include both *inter*national and do*mestic* components. [20] In truth, the foreign-domestic distinction always has oversimplified reality, but historically, as long as the United States was able to seal off its economy from extensive international influences, the oversimplification was not serious. That situation is changing, as any trip to an appliance store, gas station, or abandoned steel mill will make clear. Already, traditional occupational interest groups are increasing their involvement in foreign policy issues. Their organizational purpose has stayed the same— to enhance their members' economic well-being—but in the new international economy new political strategies for achieving this goal are necessary.

A second, perhaps no less important reason that foreign policy frequently has become an issue in presidential campaigns is that the candidates have wished it to be, sometimes because it was the area in which they were most interested.

Many have noted the abrupt post-World War II switch from Statehouse to Capitol Hill in producing most of our presidential contenders, those who vie for the party nominations and often those who win them. Numerous reasons are cited: the flow of power to Washington; the problems of governors in performing their duties without incurring serious political bruises, while the less-vulnerable legislators do not have to share equally in government failures; and the ability of senators and some representatives to dominate the media, in part because Washington is where political-governmental news is written. All true, yet equally important may be the simple predominance of international relations in national life—the great stakes of nuclear war and peace, the heightened role in the world that the United States has assumed for itself since World

War II, and the rise of intermestic issues, all of which are outside the purview and expertise of the politicians in the states.

What makes these developments significant in any explanation of the prominence of foreign policy in presidential politics is that the process has most engaged those who through some mysterious mechanism have become labeled in the press as "presidential timber." More of this breed has served on the Foreign Relations Committee than on any other single Senate committee.[21] Many exceptions actually help to demonstrate the rule. For example, Johnson, Goldwater, and Henry Jackson (a strong contender for the Democratic nomination in 1972 and 1976) were members of the Senate Armed Services Committee; Eisenhower served in military assignments that heavily involved international diplomacy; Nixon's foreign relations experience went back to 1947 and his membership on the Herter Committee of the House of Representatives to investigate the Marshall Plan; McGovern was Food for Peace director; his ultimate running mate, Sargent Shriver, had been Peace Corps director and U.S. ambassador to France; and George Bush served as director of the CIA, ambassador to the United Nations, and U.S. envoy to China. Even many of the governors whose names have been in that magic circle of potential presidents have had foreign policy experience—Stevenson, Rockefeller, Scranton, and Averell Harriman. (Governors who lack a background in foreign affairs usually have tried to simulate such experience through overseas trade commissions and memberships in organizations such as the Trilateral Commission, as did Jimmy Carter.) In view of this record of personal concern by would-be presidents for foreign policy, it is not altogether surprising that they willingly introduce the subject into their campaigns.

Take the case of Stevenson in 1956. Well before his party's convention, Stevenson's advisers had reached the conclusion, based on detailed study of voter attitudes, that the Democratic campaign should be waged on domestic policy. "Concentrating on domestic issues," wrote two of the candidate's braintrust, Arthur Schlesinger, Jr., and Seymour Harris, "would renew the image of the Democratic party as the people's party, leading the nation out of depression and poverty, while too much talk about foreign policy might simply remind people that the nation had been at war several times when Democratic administrations were in power." [22] The Stevenson offensive was to be called "The New America," a phrase he used in accepting the nomination, and would emphasize issues such as education, medical care, civil rights, civil liberties, and the problems of children and the aged.

As the campaign progressed the candidate became increasingly restless with this strategy. The most important decisions facing the nation, he felt, were international, not domestic. By late October he was telling audiences, "I want to talk with you about the most serious failure of the Republican administration. I mean its failure in conducting our foreign policy." And so "The New America" fell into disuse as Stevenson fought his lost cause over terrain on which he knew himself to be at a decided disadvantage when compared with Eisenhower, but to which he seemed to be attracted almost magnetically.

Foreign Policy Decisiveness in Presidential Elections

Although foreign policy issues have tended to dominate the candidates' campaigns for the presidency, they usually have not been decisive in determining the result on election day. The recent record suggests, however, that to the extent that international issues affect the election, they generally provide an advantage for the Republicans.

Foreign Policy and the Presidential Vote, 1952-1980

Beginning in 1952, the Center for Political Studies of the University of Michigan has asked voters the following eight open-ended questions, with minor variations in wording, in each of its election year surveys:

I'd like to ask you what you think are the good points and bad points about the parties. Is there anything in particular that you (like, dislike) about the (Democratic, Republican) parties? What is that?

Now I'd like to ask you about the good and bad points of the two candidates for president. Is there anything in particular about (name of Republican, Democratic candidates) that might make you want to vote (for, against) him? What is that?

Michigan researchers take the many and varied responses to these questions and sort them into categories that appear to be strongly related to "the perceptions and evaluations which orient an individual's behavior in casting a vote, namely, attitudes toward the two candidates, attitudes toward the groups and group interests involved in politics, attitudes toward the two parties' records as managers of government, attitudes toward domestic policy, and attitudes toward foreign policy." [23] These categories are of necessity a bit arbitrary—voters' attitudes toward the candidates, for example, sometimes are hard to separate from their attitudes on policy, and their attitudes on both (and on party management and groups) are very much shaped by their longstanding affiliations, if any, with one or the other political party. Still, taken together the categories of attitudes have proven a useful indicator of each voter's final choice. (Indeed, when first applied before the 1952 and 1956 elections, they were better predictors of the respondents' final votes than their own statements about whom they

Figure 5.1 The Partisan Effects of Voter Attitudes to Presidential Elections, 1952-1980

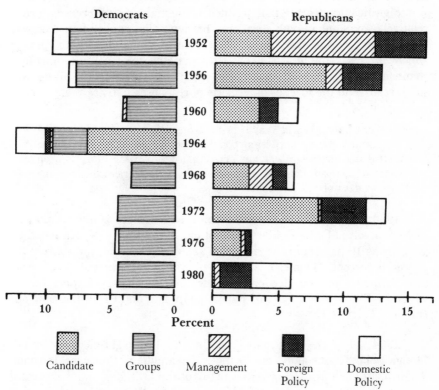

Source: Herbert Asher, *Presidential Elections and American Politics,* 3d ed. (Homewood, Ill.: Dorsey Press, 1984), 119, 123, 130, 137, 143, 156, 164.

planned to vote for.) More important for our purposes, the Michigan categories offer a consistent way of assessing the electoral influence of foreign policy on the eight most recent presidential elections prior to 1984. Figure 5.1 summarizes the net advantage each cluster of attitudes gave to either the Republican or Democratic candidate in each of those elections.

1952 and 1956. A quick glance at Figure 5.1 shows that of "Corruption, Korea, and Communism," the first two clearly made a difference in the Republican presidential election victory of 1952—both the party and candidate Eisenhower, who was substantially more popular than his opponent, scored high in competence to manage government and foreign policy. In 1956 foreign policy again fueled the Republican advantage, but a fourth "C," candidates, towered above all else—the force of Eisenhower's appeal in his reelection bid was of paramount importance. The best thing going for the Democrats was voter attitudes about how the election might affect the interests of various groups.

Significantly, foreign policy issues, while making a difference, made a relatively small one in both elections—foreign policy ranked fourth among the five categories of attitudes in 1952, third in 1956. The authors of *The American Voter* found it "noteworthy that the total volume of [voter] comment about war and peace and other issues of foreign affairs was small relative to the level of other sorts of responses in these years." They concluded:

> Neither conflict [World War II or the Korean War] seems to have had a great and lasting impact on popular political attitudes. It could be argued that a foreign war has not supplied a partisan dimension on which American political attitudes have been reoriented since the earliest days of the Republic.[24]

1960.   Four of the five issues identified by voters as most important in 1960 involved foreign policy, but not one of the four was mentioned by as many as 10 percent of the electorate and added together they barely engaged 20 percent. "Domestic and foreign policy issues exercised relatively little influence on the election outcome, . . ." concludes Herbert Asher, which "reflected the impact of partisanship as modified by the religious issue." [25]

1964.   For the first and only time in this eight-election period, foreign policy issues aided the Democratic candidate, President Johnson. Angus Campbell also reports that many of the attitudes voters expressed toward Republican candidate Goldwater involved personal qualities that they regarded as dangerous in a commander in chief, including impulsiveness, fanaticism, and instability.[26] Still, as Figure 5.1 shows, in an election in which everything went Johnson's way, the contribution to his victory made by foreign policy was negligible.

1968.   The war in Vietnam was the critical issue of the 1968 election—on the list of national problems identified by voters as most important, more than twice as many rated it first than the next four issues combined.[27] Nonetheless, voter attitudes on foreign policy again ranked fourth among the five categories in their effect on the election outcome, providing a small advantage to the Republicans. The reason, according to Gerald Pomper and Susan Lederman, is that voters

> showed the human tendency "to see what you want to see." Advocates of withdrawal who liked Humphrey, for whatever reason, thought he favored withdrawal, while pro-Humphrey advocates of more military

involvement thought he was a "hawk." The same pattern was evident among Nixon voters. The election was not an example of issue voting, but of widespread projection and rationalization.[28]

1972. The Vietnam War still ranked first in the minds of voters, and again foreign policy provided an advantage to the Republicans. Indeed, next to the edge Nixon gained from voters' attitudes toward the two candidates, foreign policy was second in contributing to his landslide reelection victory. The explanation, Pomper and Lederman show, is that this time voters knew not just where they stood on the war but also where the candidates stood. (This time, too, the candidates' stands were much more distinct.) Of Democrats who favored American withdrawal from Vietnam, 76 percent voted for McGovern; of those who wanted to use all force necessary to win the war, only 30 percent did. (The McGovern vote among Democrats who took a moderate position on Vietnam was 46 percent.) Republicans favoring withdrawal voted 15 percent for McGovern, those for force, 1 percent, and moderates, 6 percent. Independents who favored withdrawal gave McGovern 54 percent of their votes, those favoring force, 13 percent, and moderate independents, 24 percent.[29]

1976. Not one of the five most important issues in the minds of voters in 1976 involved foreign policy, and the partisan advantage that Ford gained over Carter was the smallest ever for a Republican.[30]

1980. Right up until election day, polls indicated that the 1980 election probably would be one of the closest in American history. But election day that year fell on November 4, the anniversary of the Iranian hostage seizure, and numerous media retrospectives on the year's frustrations, combined with the failure of Carter's last-minute attempts to secure the hostages' release, may account for the landslide Reagan victory that actually occurred. Next to the economy, Iran was the issue voters cared about most in 1980 (national defense was fourth), and Reagan reaped a distinct electoral advantage from the voters' attitudes about foreign policy.[31]

Conclusion. The decisiveness of any single element in a presidential election is always hard to calibrate, but by any reckoning foreign policy would disqualify as decisive. In none of the eight elections that took place from 1952 to 1980 did foreign policy rank first or even second among the categories of voter attitudes that are closely related to the vote. Only in three elections (1952, 1972, and 1980) did it play even a significant role in the electorate's decision process. But since all three of those elections were landslides, it seems clear that other forces also were at work.

The Republican Advantage

One other aspect of foreign policy as an element in voters' decisions cries out for attention: in seven of the last eight presidential elections, public attitudes on foreign policy provided the Republican candidate with an advantage.

From 1952 to 1972 the explanation for Republican success seemed obvious: voters regarded the Republican party as the party of peace, perhaps because the presidency had been occupied by a Democrat at the beginning of each of this century's wars.[32] (In a similar manner, voters regarded the Democrats as the party of prosperity during this period, probably remembering that a Republican presided over the start of the

Figure 5.2 Public Opinion on Political Parties and Peace, 1952-1980

Question: "Which political party do you think would be more likely to keep the United States out of World War III—the Republican or Democratic Party?"

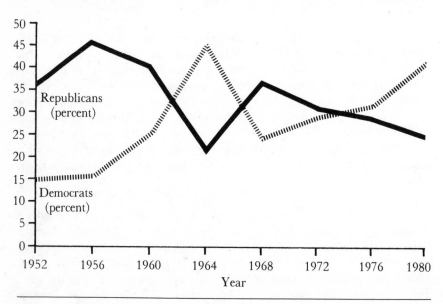

Source: "Party Best for Peace," *Gallup Report* (April 1984): 19.

Great Depression.[33] Evidence for this explanation can be found in the Gallup poll's quadrennial rendering of the question: "Which political party do you think would be more likely to keep the United States out of World War III—the Republican or the Democratic party?" Through 1972 voters answered "Republican" in every election year but one, often decisively *(Figure 5.2)*. The exception, 1964, seemed to affirm the rule that a reputation as the party of peace prompts a foreign policy edge on election day. In 1976 and 1980, however, while the Republican nominees continued to enjoy the foreign policy advantage in the voting, the Democrats won the mantle of the peace party.

The Election of 1984

The experience of presidential elections since 1952 probably would have led one to predict that foreign policy would play a dominant role in the candidates' 1984 campaigns, that it would not be decisive in determining the election's outcome, and that the Republican nominee would derive whatever advantage there was to be had.

Still, there also was reason to suppose that each of these expectations might be violated. Foreign policy is not always dominant, after all. (In 1960 and 1976 it was not.) More significantly, foreign policy need not always be indecisive—two of the three elections in which it played a larger than usual role happen to have been two of the last three elections (1972 and 1980). This may not be surprising, considering the rise of intermestic issues and the growing share of the public that takes an interest in international affairs. Finally, there was reason to doubt the staying power of the Republican edge in foreign affairs. To the extent that this advantage was rooted in the public's perception of the Republicans as the party of peace, that perception was reversed more than a decade ago.

Democratic Nomination

The campaign year began with a prediction by a senior aide to the front-runner, Walter Mondale, that "foreign policy is going to be extremely important in this campaign, perhaps even more important than is normal for a presidential election." [34] Mondale laid plans to highlight his unique experience as vice president in waging his foreign policy campaign, but few of his rivals could be called neophytes either. Alan Cranston, John Glenn, and George McGovern had experience on the Senate Foreign Relations Committee; Sen. Gary Hart was a member of the Armed Services Committee; and Reubin Askew was a recent U.S. Trade Representative. Only Sen. Ernest Hollings and Jesse Jackson were unable to claim special credentials in foreign policy.

The eight candidates did not differ greatly on the war-and-peace issues of defense and diplomacy. All of them had to deal somehow with the great foreign policy schism in the Democratic party: on the one hand, the "peace bloc," consisting mainly of activists from the Vietnam generation who made support for a mutual and verifiable freeze on nuclear weapons and opposition to American military involvement in El Salvador, Honduras, and Nicaragua litmus tests for the candidates; on the other hand, grass-roots public opinion, reinforced in the party by the AFL-CIO, in favor of a strong national defense. The candidates tried to bridge this divide in generally similar ways: all eight endorsed the freeze; all, with the exception of Askew, promised to reduce the American presence in Central America; and all but McGovern and Jackson proposed increases in real defense spending. Of the three contenders who survived the early caucuses and primaries—Mondale, Hart, and Jackson—Mondale took a slightly less dovish position on Central America. ("I don't like commies any more than I like right-wingers," he curtly told aides who were trying to move him to the left.) But for the most part the candidates' similarities outweighed their differences.

Still, Hart gained a clear electoral edge on the security issues. Both Hart's youthful personal style and his record as McGovern's campaign manager in 1972 certified him to the generation that dominated the freeze movement, as did his undiluted opposition to the U.S. military role in Central America. But Hart was able to balance this appeal with strong credentials on the defense issue. He often pointed to his record as founder of the bipartisan Military Reform Caucus in Congress, naval reserve officer, and advocate of "new ideas" on defense strategy that would substitute smaller, more numerous, and more flexible weapons for the larger and less mobile ones that currently dominate the nation's defense arsenal. In the New Hampshire primary, which propelled Hart's candidacy from obscurity to front-runner status with Mondale, voters mentioned nuclear arms control and military spending as the two issues that most influenced their choice. These issues also led the list 14 weeks later in the California primary, Hart's final victory.[35]

Mondale was far more successful in winning votes on the only ethnic foreign policy issue to take hold in the nomination campaign: the Israeli proposal, which he consistently endorsed, that the United States move its embassy from Tel Aviv to Jerusalem. (A backhanded tribute to Mondale's success on this issue is that Jackson and Hart tried, albeit unsuccessfully, to make the American role in South Africa and Northern Ireland, respectively, the main ethnic issues.) Jackson, who had enough problems with Jewish voters because he favored statehood for Palestinian Arabs, triggered angry charges of anti-Semitism when he referred to Jews as

"Hymies" and New York as "Hymietown." Hart, for his part, could not win on this issue either and only complicated his problems when he tried. Having earlier said that he would move the embassy only after consulting with Israel's Arab neighbors, Hart endorsed the Israeli proposal during the New York primary campaign, which left him wide open to Mondale's charges of "flip-flops" and "politics-as-usual," thus tarnishing Hart's image as a new style of politician.

Intermestic issues divided the candidates more sharply than any others. The most prominent ones were the Carter administration's bailout of the Chrysler Corporation and proposed "domestic content" legislation to require that cars sold in the United States contain a specified proportion of parts made in the United States. Mondale was a leading proponent and Hart an outspoken opponent of both, which helps to explain the labor unions' enthusiasm for Mondale and animosity toward Hart during the campaign. Mondale certainly benefited from labor's organizational support, but Hart portrayed the unions' opposition as evidence of his independence and freshness.

Security, ethnic, and intermestic issues—all played a part in the nomination contest. So did the voters' perceptions of candidate qualities that they related to competence in foreign policy. Mondale asserted with some accuracy that as Carter's vice president, he had been involved in policy making to a degree matched only by the president. He had felt the burden, he frequently said, of being told on the eve of his inauguration that "any time, night or day, I might be called upon to make the most fateful decision on earth; whether to fire these atomic weapons that could destroy the human species." (Mondale also noted that, his public speeches of support notwithstanding, he had privately advised against Carter's decisions to impose a grain embargo on the Soviet Union and to sell AWACS surveillance aircraft to Saudi Arabia.) In virtually all the caucuses and primaries, polls showed that Mondale's experience counted more heavily in his favor with the voters than anything else.

The perceived inexperience of Jackson and Hart in the international arena was, conversely, a great political liability to their candidacies. Jackson won a certain measure of respect when he went to Syria at New Year's and secured the release of Navy Lieutenant Robert Goodman, whose plane had been shot down there in December. But this isolated accomplishment was far outweighed by Jackson's complete lack of service in government, much less foreign policy, and his later efforts to repeat the Goodman episode with personal visits to Nicaragua and Cuba were widely regarded as unsophisticated toadying to communist regimes. Similarly, inexperience in the foreign policy-making process was the flip side of Hart's freshness and outsider status. Much was made of his offhandedness when he was asked at a March candidate debate what he would do if, say, a Czechoslovak passenger plane headed toward an American air base ignored warnings to turn back. Hart replied, "If the people they looked in and saw had uniforms on, I would shoot the aircraft down. If they were civilians, I would just let them keep going." Had voters felt more confidence in Hart, they probably would not have made so much of this gaffe. A Mondale commercial reinforced their doubts: it showed a red telephone blinking ominously while a somber voice warned of the dangers of having an "unsure . . . unsteady . . . untested" president on the receiving end of the call.

Mondale won the Democratic nomination in July, and all his opponents endorsed and later campaigned for him. Still, it is clear that he carried some scars into the fall campaign that originated in foreign policy. Over a period of several months, Hart had attacked Mondale relentlessly for being a captive of special interest groups (as evidenced by his stands on the intermestic issues), tied him to the frustrating "Carter-Mondale" policy in Iran, and suggested that his public support for policies he had disagreed with as vice president was hypocritical. Jackson's severe unpopularity with Jews over Israel and his controversial trip to Nicaragua and Cuba caused Mondale other difficulties: not only did he constantly have to negotiate a no-man's-land between two vital but now antagonistic Democratic groups, he had to stand silently when Reagan taunted him for not denouncing Jackson for praising Fidel Castro and the Sandinistas. Thus, when the battle between Mondale and Reagan began, the president was well stocked with ammunition supplied by the challenger's fellow Democrats.

General Election: Mondale vs. Reagan

The most important foreign policy events of the campaign of 1984 took place within two days of each other in October of 1983. On the 23d a terrorist bomb killed more than 200 American soldiers in Beirut, Lebanon; on the 25th President Reagan announced that he had ordered U.S. soldiers to invade the Caribbean island of Grenada, overthrow its government, drive out Cuban soldiers, and rescue American medical students. In traditional fashion, voters "rallied 'round the flag" in support of the president. Reagan's Gallup approval rating rose above 50 percent for the first time since 1981, and he took the lead from Mondale in trial-heat polls on the presidential election.[36] In the months that followed, the president kept his role as commander in chief and chief diplomat prominently before the voters, traveling to the Korean border to stare fiercely into North Korea, meeting with fellow heads of state in Japan and China, and presiding over the 40th anniversary commemoration of the D-Day invasion in France.

The Grenada victory, more than any other event of his presidency, laid the foundation for Reagan's basic campaign theme, namely, that his leadership had made America strong and proud again, in stark contrast with the condition it was in when he assumed office. By itself Grenada seemed to offer a day-and-night comparison with the Iranian hostage crisis: in Grenada the United States moved quickly, the rescue attempt worked, and the Americans there were brought home right away. More generally, Reagan used Grenada as a metaphor for his broader theme that through his actions as president, America had regained its spirit and self-confidence. This theme shone through in his acceptance speech at the Republican convention:

> In four years before we took office, country after country fell under the Soviet yoke. Since January 20, 1981, not one inch of soil has fallen to the communists.
>
> But worst of all, Americans were losing the confidence and optimism about the future that had made us unique in the world. Parents were beginning to doubt that their children would have the better life that has been the dream of every American generation.
>
> We can all be proud that pessimism is ended.
>
> America is coming back and is more confident than ever about the future.

Patriotism and prosperity were the keynotes of Reagan's candidacy for reelection, but two other "Ps"—peace and preparedness—also figured prominently. The campaign's most memorable television commercial showed a bear lumbering menacingly through the forest, then halting and stepping back when it confronts a silent hunter with a rifle. In a confident, reassuring voice a narrator asks, "Isn't it smart to be as strong as the bear?" and the commercial fades out with the words "President Reagan— Prepared for Peace" printed on the screen.

Reagan had certain political liabilities in foreign policy, but he effectively used the power of the presidency to minimize them. At the start of the year, Lebanon and Central America seemed like time bombs ready to explode at any moment. The president defused them by removing the marines from Lebanon, downplaying his active support for the contra rebels in Nicaragua, and scaling back the American military presence in Honduras. In September Reagan reinforced his faltering image as a peacemaker by giving a conciliatory speech to the United Nations and meeting with Soviet foreign minister Andrei Gromyko.

Despite all this, foreign policy remained Reagan's achilles heel going into the fall campaign. An early gaffe did not help matters any: during a voice check prior to the airing of his weekly radio address on August 11, Reagan said, "My fellow Americans, I am pleased to tell you today that I've signed legislation that will outlaw Russia forever. We begin bombing in five minutes." But polls showed that all through his term the public had rated Reagan far lower on Central America, arms control, relations with the Russians, and foreign policy in general than it had on domestic matters and overall peformance. In a September Harris survey, voters ranked Reagan above Mondale on four of the six domestic issues they were asked about, but not on the two foreign policy issues.[37]

Mondale did his best to capitalize on Reagan's vulnerability. One line of attack took the president's simple competence as its target. In almost every speech, Mondale said:

> I don't doubt that the president is for peace. But he has not mastered what he must know to command his own government and to lead. . . . When a president is not vigorously involved, things just don't happen, and they're not. In Central America, there are no talks. In the Middle East, there is no policy. In Lebanon, there was no protection. And on earth, there is no arms control.

Mondale's main indictment of Reagan involved nuclear arms. He argued with passion in his acceptance speech to the Democratic convention that

> Every president since the bomb went off . . . [has] talked with the Soviets and negotiated arms control. Why has this administration failed? Why haven't they tried? Why can't they understand the cry of Americans and human beings for sense and sanity in control of these God awful weapons? Why, why?

The most widely telecast Mondale commercial reinforced this theme, with specific reference to the administration's "star wars" proposal to develop weapons that could shoot down Soviet missiles from space. The ad showed a picture of Earth on a television monitor in the middle of what one soon realizes is an empty war room. In the foreground a blinking red telephone goes unanswered. An alarm buzzer sounds and a computer clicks on, its program running in graphic and relentless motion. Through all this a narrator says: "Ronald Reagan is determined to put killer weapons in space . . . with a response time so short there'll be no time to wake a president. Computers will take control. On November 6, you can take control"—on screen, the computer stops—"No weapons in space by either side. Draw the line at the heavens, with Mondale."

On October 7 Mondale scored a surprise victory in the first debate between the candidates. This energized both him and his supporters, and in the eyes of many voters Mondale went from wimpish loser to fighting underdog. What's more, even though the topic of the debate had been domestic policy, Reagan's tired, sometimes disoriented performance seemed to underscore the issue of competence that Mondale had been raising in connection with foreign affairs. It also resurrected a question in many people's minds about the 73-year-old Reagan's stamina and alertness in the event of an international crisis.

Mondale approached the second debate on October 21 with considerable confidence. Its topic was foreign policy, his strong suit with the voters. A *New York Times*/CBS News poll showed that many voters were undecided and willing to be persuaded. Unlike those who had made up their minds, the undecideds took a dim view of how Reagan had handled foreign policy and a favorable one of Mondale's leadership qualities. Mondale's pollster, Peter Hart, said that his data showed that in addition to the undecideds, large numbers of Reagan supporters could be won over as well. "We've analyzed every question and every attitude and we find them as shaky as Jello," he said. "They're very sensitive on the whole arms control issue, foreign policy, the war-and-peace issue." [38]

Reagan, however, was able to take advantage of these expectations on the night of the debate. From the beginning he was energetic and forceful, disposing of the age question with a quip and the competence issue with a firm manner. On arms control Reagan took what seemed to be a dramatically dovish position, saying that as soon as the United States developed its own antimissile defense, he would tell the Russians: "We'll even give it to you. Now, will you sit down with us and, once and for all, get rid, all of us, of those nuclear weapons and free mankind from that threat?" By any standard Mondale held his own in the debate, but it did not matter. He had made Reagan the issue, and, when Reagan did well, that issue was settled.

A final contribution to the Reagan cause was made by Vice President George Bush, who consistently was rated more highly in the polls than Mondale's running mate, Rep. Geraldine Ferraro. In the best-remembered moment of their debate on October 11, Ferraro responded with quiet fury to Bush's condescending attempt to "help you with the difference, Mrs. Ferraro, between Iran and the embassy in Iran." She said, "Let me just say, first of all, that I almost resent, Vice President Bush, your patronizing attitude that you have to teach me about foreign policy." But increasingly since the advent of atomic weaponry, voters have insisted that candidates for vice president be almost as qualified in foreign policy as presidential candidates. To many, Bush's record as ambassador, CIA director, and vice president seemed superior than that of the three-term representative from Queens, New York.

Conclusion

Was foreign policy dominant in the 1984 campaign? Was it decisive in the voting? Did it gain Republicans an advantage? Of these questions only the third can be answered readily. Reagan's victory was so overwhelming that even though postelection polls showed arms control to be Mondale's most effective issue, the president still came out on top in foreign policy voting. The Republicans also closed the 11-year gap on the question of which political party would best be able to keep the nation out of World War III by a margin of 39 to 38.[39]

Questions of foreign policy dominance and decisiveness are harder to settle. If foreign policy is defined narrowly, the answer is that the 1984 election was atypical in that it was not dominant and typical in that it was not decisive. Voters did rank foreign relations third and nuclear arms control fourth on their list of issue concerns, but taken together the various economic issues that filled out the rest of the top seven slots far outnumbered them.[40] Exit polls on election day suggested that the economy underlay voters' decisions far more than anything else.[41]

But in 1984 and in future elections a narrow definition of foreign policy dominance and decisiveness may cloud more than it illuminates. The foreign policy positions of Mondale, Hart, and Jackson seem to have figured little in the voters' choices; their assessment of candidate qualities that they related to competence in foreign policy, such as Mondale's experience and Hart's new ideas, mattered greatly. Grenada had only a minor place in the actual fall campaign and election, but it went a long way toward establishing the context in which that campaign and election took place. Similarly, the second debate changed few minds, which is exactly the point: Mondale's only opportunity to close the gap with Reagan was lost. There also is the complex influence of Mondale's vice presidential selection to consider. Because no Democratic women have served in the Senate or in prominent foreign policy-making positions, Mondale had less to choose from when he decided to make the historic breakthrough and name a female. As much as voters may have been sympathetic to the idea and to Ferraro herself, they held that lack of international experience against her. Finally, the continued rise in the significance of intermestic issues, such as domestic content legislation, complicates any easy assessment of the role of foreign policy in the 1984 election.

So as the lines between foreign policy and other issues become even more murky, the difficulty of assessing foreign policy's place in presidential politics will grow in direct proportion to the importance of our understanding it.

Notes

1. This chapter draws in part on two earlier essays by Stephen Hess: "Foreign Policy and Presidential Campaigns," *Foreign Policy* (Fall 1972): 3-22 and "Does Foreign Policy Really Matter?" *Wilson Quarterly* (Winter 1980): 96-111.

2. Stanley Kelley, Jr., *Professional Public Relations and Political Power* (Baltimore: Johns Hopkins University Press, 1956), 200.

3. Emmet John Hughes, *The Ordeal of Power* (New York: Atheneum, 1956), 33.

4. Stephen E. Ambrose, *Eisenhower*, vol. 1 (New York: Simon and Schuster, 1983), 569.

5. Theodore H. White, *America in Search of Itself* (New York: Harper and Row, 1982), 89.

6. Theodore H. White, *The Making of a President, 1960* (New York: Pocket Books, 1962), 390.

7. Barry Goldwater, *The Conscience of a Conservative* (Shepherdsville, Ky.: Victor Publishing, 1960), 89.

8. See Richard J. Whalen, *Catch the Falling Flag* (Boston: Houghton Mifflin, 1972), 293-294; Earl Mazo and Stephen Hess, *Nixon* (New York: Harper and Row, 1968), 310.

9. James Reston, "Mr. Nixon and the Arts of Evasion," *New York Times*, October 2, 1968.

10. Nelson W. Polsby and Aaron Wildavsky, *Presidential Elections*, 6th ed. (New York: Charles Scribner's Sons, 1984), 179.

11. "The Repercussions of a Blooper," *Wilson Quarterly* (Winter 1980): 107.

12. *The Gallup Poll, 1980* (Wilmington, Del.: Scholarly Resources, 1981), 159.

13. "Democratic Showdown," *Gallup Opinion Index* (December 1980): 51.

14. Jong R. Lee, "Rally Round the Flag: Foreign Policy Events and Presidential Popularity," *Presidential Studies Quarterly* (Fall 1977): 252-256.

15. Charles W. Kegley, Jr., and Eugene R. Wittkopf, *American Foreign Policy*, 2d ed. (New York: St. Martin's Press, 1982), 272; Philip E. Converse, et al., "Continuity and Change in American Politics: Parties and Issues in the 1968 Election," *American Political Science Review* (December 1969): 1083-1105; "National Security: The Public's View on War and Peace," *National Journal*, July 28, 1984, 1450.

16. V. O. Key, Jr., *The Responsible Electorate* (New York: Vintage Books, 1966), 7.

17. Michael A. Maggioto and Eugene R. Wittkopf, "American Public Attitudes toward Foreign Policy," *International Studies Quarterly* (December 1981): 601-631; Kegley and Wittkopf, *American Foreign Policy*, 275.

18. Daniel Yankelovich and Larry Kaagan, "Assertive America," *Foreign Affairs* (Special Issue, 1981): 696-713.

19. Kegley and Wittkopf, *American Foreign Policy*, 298.

20. Coining of the term "intermestic" generally is attributed to Bayless Manning, former president of the Council on Foreign Relations.

21. For example, Hubert Humphrey, John Kennedy, Eugene McCarthy, Howard Baker (a candidate for the Republican nomination in 1980 and probably 1988), Alben Barkley (the Democratic nominee for vice president in 1948), Frank Church (a Democratic contender in 1976), Edmund Muskie (a Democratic candidate in 1972 and 1976, after being the party's vice presidential nominee in 1968), and Stuart Symington (a candidate for the Democratic nomination in 1960).
22. Adlai E. Stevenson, *The New America* (New York: Harper and Row, 1957), xiv-xvi.
23. The questions and categories are described in Donald E. Stokes, Angus Campbell, and Warren E. Miller, "Components of Electoral Decision," *American Political Science Review* (June 1958): 367-387.
24. Angus Campbell, et al., *The American Voter* (New York: John Wiley and Sons, 1960), 50.
25. Herbert B. Asher, *Presidential Elections and American Politics,* 3d ed. (Homewood, Ill.: Dorsey Press, 1984), 125, 126
26. Angus Campbell, "Interpreting the Presidential Victory," in *The National Election of 1964,* ed. Milton C. Cummings, Jr. (Washington: Brookings Institution, 1966), 256-281.
27. Asher, *Presidential Elections,* 141.
28. Gerald M. Pomper and Susan S. Lederman, *Elections in America,* 2d ed. (New York: Longman, 1980), 62.
29. Asher, *Presidential Elections,* 146; Pomper and Lederman, *Elections in America,* 71.
30. Asher, *Presidential Elections,* 155.
31. Ibid., 164.
32. This is the argument of Polsby and Wildavsky, *Presidential Elections,* 177.
33. "Party Best for Peace," *Gallup Report* (April 1984): 19.
34. Bernard Weinraub, "Mondale May Shift Attention to War and Peace," *New York Times,* December 12, 1983.
35. Hedrick Smith, "Polls Outline Bases of Hart's Victory," *New York Times,* March 1, 1984; Hedrick Smith, "Mondale, Hart and Democrats Who Make Their Decisions Late," *New York Times,* June 6, 1984.
36. "Reagan Popularity," *Gallup Report* (December 1983): 18; "Reagan vs. Mondale Trial Heats," *Gallup Report* (April 1984): 26.
37. "Presidential Performance: The Public's View of Ronald Reagan," *National Journal,* September 29, 1984, 1844.
38. David E. Rosenbaum, "On Debate Eve, Foreign Policy Divides the Voters," *New York Times,* October 20, 1984; Howell Raines, "Democrats Focus upon the Wavering," *New York Times,* October 19, 1984.
39. David Treadwell, "Confidence in Economy Aided Reagan," *Los Angeles Times,* November 7, 1984; "National Security: The Public's Views on War and Peace," *National Journal,* October 20, 1984, 2006.
40. Treadwell, "Confidence."
41. Hedrick Smith, "The Economy: Still the Key for Reagan," *New York Times,* November 7, 1984.

6. THE ECONOMY: ECONOMISTS, ELECTORAL POLITICS, AND REAGAN ECONOMICS

Paul J. Quirk

"Myopic policies for myopic voters"—so a prominent political scientist once described how American presidents manage the economy. In a 1980 book, *Political Control of the Economy,* Edward R. Tufte argued that presidents often try to ensure that the economy is booming, with high employment and rising personal income, during election years.[1] This political manipulation of the economy causes prosperity in the short run, at least until the election, but it may undermine price stability and economic growth in the long run. Hence, "myopic policies." Presidents do this because the electorate will appreciate the booming economy, fail to realize the future costs, and reward the manipulation at the polls. Hence also, "myopic voters."

As a matter of fact, further research has shown, such presidential manipulation is by no means obviously common. Yet the events of economic management in President Ronald Reagan's first term and of the subsequent election in 1984 bear a definite resemblance, at least on the surface, to the pattern Tufte described. Reagan ran for reelection during a period of exceptionally strong expansion, with a rate of economic growth of more than 6 percent in 1984, for which he naturally claimed the credit. At the same time his economic policies implied widely recognized long-term risks. Mainly because of Reagan's large tax cuts and increases in defense spending, the federal deficit had soared to about $180 billion a year, with even larger figures likely in the future—and with ominous implications, nearly all economists agreed, for the health of the economy. The Committee for Economic Development, a leading business group, judged that in 40 years "few developments have posed such serious problems for our economy and its prospects as the huge and growing federal budget deficits that loom in the years ahead."[2] True to form, the voters seem to have been impressed by the good current performance and unconcerned about the long-term problem. In fact, as typical commentary on the election pointed out, the economy was probably the most important single reason that the president was so easily reelected.[3]

This chapter will examine two broad questions that these observations suggest. How, if at all, did electoral politics affect economic policy in Reagan's first term? That is, did his administration manipulate the economy for short-term electoral purposes or respond to electoral influences in other ways? And, in turn, what effect did the administration's economic policies and performance have, and why, on the 1984 presidential election? In particular, why did the huge federal budget deficit not become a damaging issue for the Republican presidential ticket, despite sustained effort by the Democratic candidates to make it one?

Aside from their current interest, these issues have broad significance for the respective roles of economic expertise and electoral politics in shaping economic policy. The Reagan administration departed from past practice in the use of economic advice. And the election posed a test, under especially revealing circumstances, of the voters' response to economic conditions and campaign debate about the economy.

Presidents, Voters, and Economists

Public policy making, to be successful in a complex democratic society, must respond to the principal forces of democratic politics—that is, to interest group demands and public opinion. Policy makers are induced to respond to these forces by several means but above all through elections. At the same time, policy making must also take advantage of the available expertise—whatever scientific, analytical, or specialized knowledge bears importantly on the policies at stake. To meet both requirements is often difficult, because democratic political forces and expert advice may push policy makers in opposite directions. It is sometimes especially difficult for presidents and their advisers in making policy to manage the economy. Expert advice on economic policy is often conflicting and, even when not, is never wholly reliable. Compounding the difficulty, the public attaches great importance to the president's management of the economy but uses very simple—and potentially very misleading—methods to judge it.

Economics has the reputation of being the most advanced of the social sciences, with a powerful, tested, and generally agreed upon body of theory. That reputation comes primarily from microeconomics, the study of individual markets. Macroeconomics, the study of price levels, employment, growth, and other aspects of the economy as a whole, is the branch of economics most pertinent to the president's responsibility to manage the economy. Compared with microeconomics, it is in theoretical disarray.[4] Even so it is a useful, indeed indispensable, source of guidance.

Mainstream macroeconomists—those to be found in large numbers in universities and other institutions that employ economists—are mostly divided between two loosely defined schools of thought. Many of them are monetarists, who assert the central if not exclusive importance of monetary policy (the control of the money supply by the Federal Reserve Board). The other and still the larger group are Keynesians, who emphasize fiscal policy (taxing and spending), or more often neo-Keynesians—a term for those who also accept some of the monetarists' claims. Blending and cross-cutting the two major schools, there are various additional tendencies and theoretical positions, and the views of individual economists are quite diverse. The differences among macroeconomists exist, fundamentally, because of genuine ambiguities in theory and research findings, but they also have a political dimension. Monetarists, who are most concerned with controlling inflation, tend to be political conservatives, while neo-Keynesians, much more concerned with unemployment, tend to be liberals.[5]

Although they disagree on a number of basic issues, there is also much on which mainstream macroeconomists generally agree. Acting as a coherent scientific community whose members seek to persuade mainly each other rather than laymen, they uphold common standards of argument and evidence. They recognize a common body of research findings. And since not every economic relationship and magnitude is controversial, they often agree within broad limits in their advice on policy. None, for example, would want government to increase the rate of growth of the money supply or run a large budget deficit in a full-employment economy.

There are also certain fringe groups within economics, such as Marxists, long a small minority of the profession, and more recently "supply-side" economists; such groups hold unconventional views and may make little effort to meet the profession's standards of argument and evidence. Insulated from other economists, fringe-group economists often find their audience primarily outside the profession, among lay readers, journalists, political activists, and in rare instances leading politicians. Nothing rules out the possibility that, in the end, a fringe group could prove correct and the mainstream wrong. But, given the predominance of informed opinion to the contrary, presidents and other policy makers are seldom inclined to gamble that this will happen.

In shaping economic policy, the advice of economists often must compete with powerful influences based in the electoral process. First, and most obvious, presidents tend to use macroeconomic policy to bestow the fruits of political victory on their partisan constituencies. Democrats, allied mainly with labor and lower-income groups, act more firmly against

157

unemployment and less firmly against inflation than do Republicans, allied mainly with upper-income groups who are rarely unemployed.[6] Practiced within limits, this partisan economic policy poses no threat to expert influence, and in fact represents merely what competing political parties are supposed to do in a democracy. But it sometimes gets out of hand: most major mistakes in economic policy, wrote economist Arthur Okun, have involved Democrats overstimulating the economy to reduce unemployment, or Republicans understimulating it to reduce inflation.[7]

Second, any president of either party would like the economy to be in an expanding phase of the business cycle—the natural rise and decline of economic activity—at the time of an election, especially one in which the president himself seeks reelection. Understandably, presidents would prefer to ask the voters for a second term in a period of high employment and rising personal income rather than during a recession. Indeed Tufte, as we have mentioned, and other scholars were arguing a few years ago that presidents regularly manipulate the timing of the business cycle for electoral ends.[8] One economist even hypothesized that presidents try to cause recessions early in their terms so that the economy will be rebounding again when they seek reelection.[9] Whatever the means, presidents were said to create a "political business cycle" in which the economy's natural ups and downs are brought into line with the schedule of elections—booms at election times, busts between them—all at a cost to the long-run health of the economy. As more recent research has shown, these allegations were wildly exaggerated.[10] Neither macroeconomic policy instruments (such as monetary policy and the federal budget deficit) nor actual economic activity (such as employment) fluctuate in a systematic and reliable way with the electoral cycle. But at least an occasional president—such as Richard Nixon, who pumped up personal income mainly through increased spending in a number of transfer programs before the 1972 election—attempts to manipulate the economy for electoral purposes and succeeds in doing so.

Third, and finally, presidential economic management is influenced by the electoral politics of taxing and spending. Apart from any macroeconomic purposes or effects, voters and affected interest groups generally want the benefits of government programs. In opinion polls many say they want less spending, but only when the issue is posed in the abstract; when asked about spending for nearly any specific program, large majorities express support. Yet, at the same time, majorities of the voters consistently oppose higher taxes.[11] Because these attitudes may be strong and the issues of taxing and spending highly salient, the president and Congress may feel intense pressure to subordinate considerations of fiscal policy in order to give the public or particular interest groups what they want. To some extent, they usually do.

The politics of taxing and spending have a biased effect on macroeconomic policy. Because programs are popular and the taxes to pay for them are not, the main pressures tend to encourage large federal budget deficits.[12] In doing so they also favor stimulative policy to reduce unemployment and disfavor restrictive policy to reduce inflation. As a result, moreover, they also have a biased political effect on the two parties. Democrats, who are put at an advantage, often have the best of all possible political worlds—the opportunity to cut taxes and increase spending while serving the party's core constituency by attacking unemployment. Less fortunate in this respect, Republicans, to serve their core constituency by attacking inflation, must keep spending down and sometimes (despite their preference for less government) keep taxes up: they tend to be the party of austerity.[13] This bias did not apply, however, in the late 1970s or in President Reagan's first term, because many Republicans and especially Reagan rebelled against it.

All of the electoral pressures and incentives that affect economic policy are exaggerated by the peculiar character of popular concern with the economy. The public attaches vast importance to the president's management of the economy but uses very simple information relative to the complexity of the subject to judge it. Most people probably obtain their information about the economy, without making a special effort, in the course of holding a job, making consumer purchases, or watching network news.[14] Paying only casual attention, the public judges presidential performance mainly by highly visible current indicators, such as the level of unemployment. It is easily seduced by promises of rapid and painless economic progress. And, in assessing political debate about the economy, it is limited in its comprehension and critical capacity by the fragmentary and nonjudgmental treatment the media provide. Biases and misperceptions in the public's response to the economy tend to distort the policies that politicians adopt.

It is thus easy to see how economic policy can be shaped by electoral politics, but perhaps harder to see how it can be shaped by professional economic analysis, giving serious attention to long-term stability and economic health. Although economic analysis lacks self-evident political weight (economists do not, for example, contribute notable amounts of money to election campaigns), presidents have a number of reasons to respond to it. The most straightforward reason is that presidents, like most educated people, credit economists with having real expertise—a distinctive and useful, even if manifestly imperfect, understanding of the economy. Since presidents want their policies to work, partly but not only for electoral reasons, they tend to prefer policies that economists support.

Presidential deference to economists is reinforced by pressures from what may be called the political elite, including prominent reporters, interest group representatives, executive branch officials, and congressional leaders. An important constituency for the president, this political elite also tends to credit economists, and a president whose policies are out of line with economists' advice risks a loss of reputation within it. To some degree, elite criticism of such a president may filter down to a larger public and thus may also have costs for him in voter support, creating electoral incentives that would reinforce economists' advice instead of competing with it. Indeed, part of the importance of the 1984 election was as a test of this effect.

Pressured, so to speak, in two directions, presidents in the post-New Deal era generally have sought to reconcile the demands of electoral politics with the requirements for responsible management of the economy as defined by mainstream economists. Economic policy has not been, nor could it be, apolitical. As part of the exercise of political leadership, presidents have chosen economic advisers to reflect the views within the economics profession that were most compatible with their political objectives.[15] Dwight D. Eisenhower had traditionalists who emphasized balancing the budget and controlling inflation. The Kennedy-Johnson years saw the rise to power of a new generation of economists, committed to ambitious use of Keynesian fiscal policy to ensure high employment and economic growth. Later, in the Republican administrations of Nixon and Ford, conservative economic advisers reemerged with a monetarist tendency, to be supplanted again when liberal neo-Keynesians returned under Carter.

Never alone in having influence on economic policy, the leading economists in each administration have had to struggle to advance their views. They have not always succeeded; but when they have clearly failed, and had their advice ignored on a basic issue, it usually has been caused by especially threatening economic circumstances or especially severe political pressure. President Lyndon B. Johnson set aside the advice of his economists in refusing to ask Congress for a tax increase to pay the cost of the Vietnam War. Both the war and his Great Society program were facing serious political challenges, and Johnson feared that opponents in Congress would seize on a tax increase proposal as an opportunity to cut domestic programs or rally additional opposition to the war. Nixon, against the advice of his economists (and very much against his own instincts), instituted wage and price controls to fight rapidly rising inflation in 1971. Nixon's decision was a response to heavy pressure for such controls from the Democratic Congress and also, with polls showing massive popular support, from the general public. Both of these decisions were isolated cases; and, although they had unfortunate consequences, both were reversed before long.[16]

On the whole, presidents have taken their bearings in economic management quite consistently from some segment of mainstream economics, whether liberal or conservative, Keynesian or monetarist. When they have departed from that course, generally under severe pressure, they have considered it risky and have felt constrained to limit the magnitude and duration of the departure. In his first term and especially his first year, however, President Reagan was an exception to the rule.

Electoral Politics and Reagan Economics

Any of the leading candidates for president in 1980—from Sen. Edward Kennedy to Ronald Reagan—would have adopted a conservative agenda for economic policy, argues a prominent conservative economist, Herbert Stein.[17] The liberal policies that were pursued through most of the two preceding decades had put too much emphasis on reducing unemployment, instead of controlling inflation, and on redistributing wealth, instead of creating more wealth by economic growth. Made worse by drastic increases in world energy prices and other uncontrollable shocks to the economy, the result was "stagflation," the new and distinctly unwelcome condition of high inflation and high unemployment at the same time.

The conservative agenda in 1980 as outlined by Stein had several elements:

1. Slower, more stable and more predictable monetary growth.
2. Reduction of federal deficits.
3. Slowing down the growth of federal spending.
4. Reducing some federal tax rates, especially those bearing on investment and saving.
5. Reducing the burden of federal regulation.

Even liberal economists had come to agree, in large part, with this agenda, and there had been a corresponding conservative trend in public opinion. Before the election, in fact, the conservative agenda already had emerged as an influence in policy, in the Carter administration's relatively austere fiscal 1980 and fiscal 1981 budgets and the restrictive monetary policy that the Federal Reserve Board adopted with Carter's support in 1979.

President Reagan's economic program was in many ways indeed conservative. Nevertheless it was not a program that conservative economists or any other mainstream economists either had devised or, without serious reservations, could endorse. The Economic Recovery Program, as it was called, departed from the practice established by previous presidents of running economic policy, by and large, based on guidelines derived from mainstream economics. In certain respects the program took its guidelines instead from electoral politics. The influence of electoral politics worked in several ways, involving the consequences of the 1980 campaign even more than the anticipation of campaigns in 1982 or 1984; and it depended very much on the personality and style of decision making of Ronald Reagan.

The Development of Reagan Economics

President Reagan's economic program consisted of a number of very large policy changes, which rested on claims that were equally large.[18] Embodied mainly in the tax and budget proposals that he sent to Congress in the spring of 1981, the program included a plan to raise spending for defense by 8.6 percent in real terms each year until 1986, for an overall increase of more than 50 percent. For most of two decades, defense spending had been receiving a dwindling share of the federal budget, and Reagan, intent on asserting American power in the world, was determined to reverse sharply the downward trend. Spending for nondefense programs was to be reduced by $40 billion in fiscal 1982, an amount rising to $100 billion in 1986, with most of the reductions coming in grants to state and local governments and benefit programs for low-income people. The proposed domestic cuts were ambitious, especially considering that they were concentrated in a relatively small part of the budget, but their effect on overall spending was offset by the increases of roughly similar size proposed for defense.

The main item of the program, the one most relied upon to invigorate the economy, was an impressively large reduction in both personal and corporate taxes. As originally proposed, the Reagan tax cuts would have reduced personal income tax rates by 10 percent in each of three successive years, and then beginning in 1985 indexed the tax brackets to price levels so taxes no longer would rise automatically as a result of inflation. These cuts were delayed and reduced to a modest extent in the administration's final bill. But, added to a variety of corporate and other tax measures that the administration also supported, they still would reduce federal revenues by roughly $100 billion, about 2 percent of the gross national product (GNP), by 1986. Finally, the administration called upon the Federal Reserve Board to continue the tight monetary policy it was already following to bring down rapidly the rate of inflation.

By any straightforward calculation of its effect, the program turned upside-down one of the main elements of the conservative economic agenda, the reduction of budget deficits. With massive tax cuts, and expenditures increasing on balance because of the defense buildup, the deficit seemed bound to rise dramatically instead of decreasing. To defend the program, the administration offered an unconventional and exceedingly optimistic economic forecast. It argued that the tax cuts—by increasing the incentives of individuals and businesses to work, save, and invest—would so stimulate economic growth that even with much lower tax rates, tax revenues would actually increase, the deficit would narrow, and thus by 1986 a balanced budget would be reached.

The problem with the administration's forecast, roundly criticized by economists, was that there was neither any theoretical reason nor any empirical evidence to indicate that the tax cut actually would stimulate even remotely the amount of economic growth the forecast required. The forecast "strained credulity," according to Stein, who served the administration as an occasional adviser. "It showed from the beginning a willingness to take great risks with balancing the budget in order to push the tax cut and the increase of defense spending." [19] As another conservative economist assessed the forecast, the projected rates of economic growth "were totally unreasonable given the monetary policy advocated by the administration, unless the amount of economic activity that could be financed by a given money supply grew at a rate far higher than anything experienced in past history." [20]

The Reagan administration had not invented its ideas about the tax cut out of thin air; it had gotten them from a small fringe group of economists and publicists, called supply-side economists. Founded primarily by Arthur Laffer, an economist at the University of Southern California, supply-side economics moved from a demonstration that revenue increases from tax cuts are logically conceivable, the significance of the famous Laffer curve, to the conclusion that they would actually occur. Supply-siders thus advocated very large tax cuts as a painless way to eliminate budget deficits and achieve prosperity. [21]

To account for the Reagan tax proposals, one must explain why the administration adopted supply-side economics as the basis of its program. One thing is clear: its adoption cannot be explained by the scientific persuasiveness of the evidence or arguments for the supply-side claims or by the credence granted them in professional economics. There was "absolutely no empirical evidence in scholarly studies," [22] and the arguments were purely speculative. Few economists paid any attention. "Supply-side economics," remark Hugh Heclo and Rudolph Penner, "was a peculiar addition to the economic scene of the 1970's in that it grew up outside mainstream economics and its propositions were debated in the popular press rather than in economic journals." [23]

At bottom the main explanation for the adoption of supply-side economics was its potency for electoral use: the obvious, powerful appeal of large tax cuts (without guilt about budget deficits) to the voters.[24] The utility of supply-side economics as a basis for campaign rhetoric was first discovered by congressional Republicans, who used it, and the Kemp-Roth tax bill that embodied its principles, to run against the Carter administration and the Democratic Congress in the 1978 midterm elections. Through all of his political career, Ronald Reagan had advocated conventional, austere Republican economics. But, stumping in 1978, he joined the new strategy and asked voters to support Republican congressional candidates for the sake of Kemp-Roth.

As he sought the Republican presidential nomination in 1980, Reagan for a time resisted renewing his commitment to supply-side economics, but, in the heat of the hard-fought campaign, he finally did. Although a panel of economic advisers to the campaign generally did not endorse the supply-side proposals, Reagan's political advisers urged him to use them, and the political advisers ultimately won. They did so only after Reagan suffered an upset defeat by George Bush in the Iowa caucuses. The defeat demonstrated that Reagan needed to generate new enthusiasm for his candidacy, and, despite Bush's colorful protest about "voodoo economics," supply-side tax cuts were a natural vehicle by which to do so.[25] After winning the nomination, Reagan stuck with the radical tax cut proposal in the general election campaign against Jimmy Carter. And after winning the election he carried the supply-side rhetoric and commitments with him into office.

It perhaps does not require a great deal of explanation to understand why many Republican congressional candidates chose to campaign on a platform of radical tax cuts and supply-side economics, or even why a leading Republican presidential candidate, whose base was the party's extreme conservative wing, chose to join them in doing so. Members of Congress of the minority party and persons aspiring to the presidency can afford to indulge in a certain amount of flamboyant rhetoric. What requires more explanation is why Reagan, having acquired responsibility for governing as president, still went ahead with a supply-side plan. Presidents often can modify or quietly drop some of their campaign promises without too great a political cost. In fact one high-level White House official, Deputy Assistant to the President Richard G. Darman, argued in a February 1981 memo that the administration's budget program, then nearing completion, not only was based on economic assumptions that could not stand scrutiny, but, because it would be perceived as inequitable, was also politically risky.[26]

Despite such advice, no fundamental changes in the budget proposals were seriously entertained. Once the administration was in office, its adherence to the supply-side program no longer represented, in any simple way, electoral calculation. More important to its commitment were the president's personality and methods of decision making. As a close observer of his presidency, Laurence I. Barrett, has pointed out, Reagan has a strong desire to be consistent, especially when he feels he has taken a clear position in public.[27] He has a deeply ingrained, almost boundless optimism, which at times can make him all but oblivious to bad news. And in making decisions, including important ones, he neither takes much interest in reviewing lengthy analyses nor defers consistently to judgments by experts. Instead, Reagan uses a more thematic and ideological mode of thinking, refined by an implicit sense of what will be persuasive to the general public, to reach judgments of his own. Quite distinctive among contemporary American political leaders, the combination of these traits apparently allowed supply-side notions that Reagan originally had adopted primarily for electoral advantage to become, before long, determined beliefs—which he thus insisted on carrying out. With Reagan himself firmly committed, most dissent was suppressed within the administration, as skeptical aides feared alienating the president or appearing disloyal.

Dissent was also suppressed among Republicans and even many Democrats in Congress, enough to pass the president's program despite widespread doubt that it could work. Reagan's landslide victory in the election—which, as polls showed, was primarily a landslide rejection of President Carter—was nevertheless interpreted by politicians and the public as a mandate for Reagan's policies, and thus became one after the fact. Reagan bolstered the mandates by masterful performances in television addresses that helped establish a prevalent opinion among the voters that his policies deserved a chance.[28] Perhaps crucial, Reagan's popularity increased in the aftermath of an attempted assassination. Deluged by constituent mail supporting the president, Congress on the whole chose to comply with his demands. Majority Leader Howard H. Baker, Jr., called the tax cuts "a riverboat gamble" but nonetheless helped push the president's program through the Republican Senate. Even the House of Representatives, with a Democratic majority, went along, and Congress passed most of the president's proposals with remarkably little modification, including essentially the entire supply-side tax program.[29] The passage of the economic program was hailed as an extraordinary legislative victory for the president, which indeed it was.

The resulting mood of exultation, however, was short-lived. A major recession, an effect of the administration's tight monetary policy that its forecasts had entirely ignored, began almost immediately—"as the ink was still drying" on the tax and spending bills.[30] According to some economists, though by no means all, the administration's fiscal policy not only failed to prevent the recession, which lasted from mid-1981 to nearly the end of 1982, but actually made it worse. It was in any case extremely severe. The recession brought unemployment to a level, almost 11 percent by mid-1982, that was unprecedented since the Great Depression.

One effect of the recession, which became apparent only later, was to create the depressed conditions out of which came the rebounding economy in 1983 and 1984 that vastly improved Reagan's prospects for reelection. From the bare facts one might suspect that the administration, in a case of drastic and successful political manipulation of the economy, caused the recession intentionally for that purpose. But no evidence that it did so has come to light. To all appearances the administration's economic strategy for reelection was not to cause a well-timed recession but, quite the contrary, to unleash the private sector and bring about permanent prosperity.

More immediately, the recession aggravated the huge shortfall already built into the administration's budgets and pushed federal deficits to levels that were unprecedented in peacetime. Carter had been excoriated for permitting a deficit of $60 billion; projected deficits under the Reagan administration quickly soared to $100 billion, and before long to $180 billion. The political context for economic policy making was transformed. By the end of 1981, how to deal with the deficits had become the preeminent issue in economic policy, and how to avoid a substantial reversal of Reagan's policies had become the major preoccupation of the administration.

Since Congress already had cut domestic spending quite severely and was not disposed to cut it much more, deficit reduction came to mean in politically realistic terms primarily increasing taxes and slowing the growth of defense spending. Pressure for such action during the remainder of Reagan's term came from several quarters, including certain parts of the administration itself. Senate Republican leaders, especially Finance Committee chairman Robert Dole and Budget Committee chairman Pete V. Domenici, took the lead in directing governmental attention to the deficit. In developing the fiscal 1983 budget, they went so far as to set aside the president's budget virtually without discussion and to substitute a more austere plan of their own. A sense of urgency surrounded the issue in financial circles, where a bipartisan committee was formed to press for action. Including business leaders and several recent secretaries of the Treasury from both parties, the committee warned that the deficits being projected would undermine the health of the economy for years to come.[31]

Two of the three principal economic advisory bodies in the executive branch itself, the Office of Management and Budget (OMB) and the Council of Economic Advisers (CEA), entirely concurred—leaving the Treasury Department as the lone supporter of large deficits. OMB director David Stockman (who very briefly had been a supply-sider himself) and CEA chairman Martin Feldstein (long a leading conservative economist) both argued within the administration for remedial action on the deficit. Feldstein also argued for it vigorously in public. In early 1984 he was so insistent about the need for a tax increase to reduce the deficit that the White House staff became distinctly irritated, causing speculation (as it happened, incorrect speculation) that he would leave the administration earlier than he originally planned.[32] (Apparently fed up with criticism of his policies from the CEA, Reagan later considered trying to abolish it.)

The administration yielded to these pressures only to a slight extent, permitting the adoption between 1982 and 1984 of some modest tax increases (styled "revenue enhancements") and cuts in defense and other spending—making what administration and congressional leaders were pleased to call "a down payment on the deficit." Aptly described as such, the down payment left deficits for 1985 and beyond still in the range of $175 billion by the administration's own estimates.[33]

Despite all the criticism and Reagan's 1980 promise to achieve a balanced budget by 1984, the administration was willing to tolerate enormous deficits "as far as the eye can see" (in Stockman's phrase) for a number of reasons, both economic and political. In the first place, the administration tolerated the deficits partly because Congress would not cooperate in reducing them the way Reagan wanted to, that is, by further reductions in domestic spending. Deficit politics from 1982 to 1984 were in some ways a classic case of institutional deadlock. Neither the president nor Congress liked big deficits, but each preferred them at least in the short run to what the other proposed as a solution.[34]

Besides institutional conflict over how to reduce the deficit, there were also important considerations of timing. Secretary of the Treasury Donald Regan was the main defender of deficits among the president's economic advisers. ("We call him 'Deficit Don,'" Senator Dole said of Regan in an after-dinner speech.) Presenting the administration's budget proposals in 1983 congressional hearings, Regan argued that the deficits, although potentially a serious problem in the long run, would strengthen the recovery in 1983 and 1984. He concluded that significant budgetary action to reduce them should be postponed until 1985.[35] With regard to 1983 and 1984, Regan's argument was nothing more than a return to conventional Keynesian deficit spending to end a recession. What caused many to be concerned was mainly the significance of the administration position for 1985 and beyond—when, with no action having been taken beforehand, the deficit easily could get out of control.

Conventional economics only for the short run, the administration position was even more clearly conventional politics. Despite long-run risks to the health of the economy, it used massive fiscal stimulus to ensure a vigorous recovery that would continue through the coming presidential election year. And it prudently put off discussion of tax increases and reductions in defense spending—potentially embarrassing and politically costly reversals for the administration—until after the election. That Regan, a highly political Treasury secretary, wanted action on the deficit only after the election, while less political officials such as Stockman and Feldstein wanted it sooner, was probably not coincidental; nor is it surprising that Regan's position won.

Economic Consequences

To assess the economic consequences of the first four years of Reagan economics is an uncertain exercise, requiring judgments about what would have happened under different policies and what is likely to happen in the future; and there is at least some disagreement on any aspect of the subject. Nevertheless, several pertinent observations can be made.[36] The Reagan administration can claim at least one genuine achievement—a very substantial reduction in inflation, from almost 12 percent in 1980 to about 4 percent in 1984. Much of this reduction, and by one estimate the largest part of it, was caused not by government policy but rather by good fortune, declining world energy prices, and other favorable economic developments. But much of the reduction, too, was caused by the Federal Reserve Board's tight monetary policy, which would have been difficult to maintain without support from the administration.

The reduction in inflation was gained, however, at an enormous cost—a nearly two-year-long recession, with a record number of bankruptcies, and unemployment that approached 11 percent of the work force. The recession cost the average family roughly $3,000 in lost income between 1981 and 1983 (in addition to long-run costs from lost growth of productive capacity). Instead of being widely shared, this burden was concentrated on lower-income groups, especially blacks, who were far more likely to be unemployed. Whether the decline in inflation was worth the price is debatable, partly because economists disagree about the basic question of how much harm inflation does. There is also disagreement among economists about whether, through a different mix of policies, the reduction in inflation that occurred under Reagan could have been achieved with less misery.[37]

Through energetic Keynesian stimulation of the economy, the Reagan administration also produced an extraordinarily strong recovery, with two successive years of 6 to 7 percent real growth in the GNP while inflation remained under control. Industrial investment, although financed in large part by a temporary influx of foreign funds, was at record levels, and unemployment fell to about 7 percent. As we will see below, it was primarily this recovery that voters remembered in the 1984 election. But, taking the four years of Reagan's first term together, economic performance was by no means unusually strong. The growth of real family income, a modest 3 to 4 percent for the entire period, was more than Carter achieved but less than the average rate of the 1970s and, given the boost provided by declining energy prices, hardly impressive.

The most important issue, perhaps, is the effect of Reagan's policies on the prospects for the long-term growth of the economy. The administration's supply-side tax cuts and reductions in benefit programs certainly have not had the dramatic effects on savings, investment, and work effort that the administration originally predicted. Even if not so dramatic, some administration policies, such as the tax cuts directly aimed at saving and investment, do appear likely to have positive effects. On the other hand, however, by all accounts the darkest cloud hanging over the economy is the enormous annual federal budget deficit and rapidly accumulating national debt, which may prove to be the principal legacy of Reagan economics.[38] Projected to approach 6 percent of GNP by 1988, the deficits threaten to absorb by government borrowing more than half of all domestic saving and thus to crowd out much of the business investment, necessary for economic growth, that those savings would otherwise permit.[39]

By one set of estimates, which are necessarily imprecise, the overall effect of Reagan's first-term policies on GNP in 1990 could range from an increase of 4.4 percent (in addition to the growth that would have occurred under the previous policies) to a decrease of 3.4 percent. The estimates assume, generously, that about half of the potential crowding-out effect of the deficit on business investment will be avoided through increased private saving, foreign investment, and congressional action to reduce the deficit.[40] Based on the midpoint of the range, the analysis would suggest a 0.5 percent addition to GNP by 1990 as the most plausible single estimate of the administration's overall effect—a modest accomplishment, one would think, for an administration that stressed increasing economic growth as its first priority and defended benefit cuts and a general redistribution of income toward the well off as necessary means to that end. But the actual effect on growth, as the analysts point out, will depend on whether and how much the president and Congress actually manage to reduce the deficit in years to come. The presidential campaign and election of 1984 had much to do with the prospects for that.

Reagan Economics and the 1984 Presidential Campaign

Based on an even moderately thorough evaluation of Reagan's economic performance, taking into account not only economic activity in 1984 but the administration's entire four-year record and the evidence then available about the future, one could plausibly have supposed that the voters' response would be divided or ambivalent. Indeed, the administration's first CEA chairman, Murray Weidenbaum, who resigned in frustration with its policies in 1982, totaled up Reagan's economic successes and failures and assigned a middling overall grade of C+.[41] Yet on election day, in sharp contrast, the voters assigned a grade of A. Their view that his economic program had been an outstanding success was, without doubt, one of the principal reasons for Reagan's easy victory over Democratic candidate Walter F. Mondale.

From one perspective this was no anomaly but merely the predictable result of a robustly prosperous election-year economy, what any shrewd observer would have predicted. But, from a broader perspective, the result was not so obvious except in hindsight. As we will see, the debate on the economy in the 1984 election amounted to a highly significant test of the character of the voters' response—determining whether, under almost ideally favorable conditions for it, they would take more than just recent economic conditions into account in assessing a president's performance. The result of the test was important both for its immediate electoral consequences and for its bearing on the incentives of economic policy makers in the future.

The Political Effects of the 1983-1984 Expansion

Voters in presidential elections, any self-respecting pundit will feel obliged to point out, "vote their pocketbooks." Like much of what pundits say, this maxim admits of several meanings. It has been clarified by a large body of political science research, however, and the findings of this research were most auspicious for the reelection prospects of President Reagan.

What the maxim means primarily is that the voters treat presidential elections as referendums on the incumbent administration's management of the economy. They reward what they see as success by returning to office the incumbent president or a successor from his party and punish what they see as failure by replacing him. What they see as success and failure depends above all on the current and very recent state of the economy at the time of the election.[42]

This habit of the voters is apparent in the relationship over time between national economic indicators, such as the growth of GNP or the rate of unemployment, and the popular vote in presidential elections. In one analysis of this relationship, using evidence from presidential elections from 1916 to 1976, it was estimated that, for each percentage point of growth in real per capita GNP in the election year, the presidential candidate of the incumbent party gained an additional 1.2 percent of the popular vote.[43] Since real growth in GNP in the post-World War II era has fluctuated by roughly 6 or 7 percentage points, this would account for swings of up to 7 to 8 points in the popular vote of the incumbent party's candidate—14 to 16 points if one looks at the margin between him and an opponent in a two-candidate race. The same effect appears in the fluctuations of presidential popularity in public opinion polls; support for the president tends to wax and wane in tandem with the economy.[44] The voters' reactions appear to be shaped mainly by quite recent economic conditions, and there is little evidence to suggest that they try to evaluate the administration's policies apart from their apparent results, or take note of the future economic conditions expected to result from current policies.[45]

The public's enthusiasm for Ronald Reagan was as dependent on the current state of the economy as it generally had been for other presidents. Early in Reagan's administration, this dependence worked against him. As the economy sank into a deep recession, his popularity sank in proportion, plunging two years into his term to the lowest point reached so early in any presidential administration since Truman's, 35 percent approval in the Gallup poll. In the summer of 1982, according to the Harris survey, more than 60 percent of the public judged Reagan's economic program a failure while less than 30 percent judged it a success.[46] In the 1982 midterm elections, Reagan's unpopularity contributed to the loss of 26 Republican seats in the House of Representatives, a substantial loss even though, as Gary Jacobson has shown, it was limited by effective, well-financed Republican campaigns.[47] If Reagan had been required to run for reelection in 1982, in all likelihood he would have lost. Matched against Mondale in the Gallup poll's presidential preference trial heats, Reagan trailed consistently by margins of up to 12 percent from June 1982 to June 1983.

As the economy eventually recovered from the recession—which, given the dynamics of the business cycle, was all but inevitable—Reagan's popularity recovered with it. In fact, because the recovery and expansion were long and vigorous (representing largely the resumption of activity that had been lost during the recession), his popularity soared. The economy bottomed out and began to rise again in late 1982, and Reagan's approval ratings followed with a few months' lag, picking up about five points in the Gallup poll by February and March of 1983 and climbing more or less steadily the rest of the year.

Thus by late 1983 the handwriting on the wall pointed to the reelection of President Reagan. He was again winning the trial heats against the leading candidates for the Democratic nomination, at that time Mondale and Sen. John Glenn. More important, the recovery, stimulated by the budget deficits, seemed likely to continue through 1984 and perhaps into 1985. A year after the Republican defeat in the midterm congressional elections, Reagan's political aides were becoming increasingly confident—almost too confident, some of them feared—of victory in the presidential election a year later.

Throughout the election year the economic recovery supplied the main claims of achievement, as well as the main basis for the symbolic themes, of the Reagan campaign. In his acceptance speech after receiving the Republican nomination, Reagan could boast: "Today, of all the major industrial nations of the world, America has the strongest economic growth; one of the lowest inflation rates; the fastest rate of job creation, six-and-a-half million jobs in the last year-and-a-half; and the largest increase in real after-tax personal income since World War II. We're enjoying the highest level of business investment in history." Reagan drew larger implications of the recovery in the campaign's main themes of general optimism and good feeling. Added to the new assertiveness of U.S. foreign policy, the recovery meant, in the words of the campaign slogan, "America is back."

As election day approached the economy continued to cooperate for Reagan, with generally good economic news lasting into the fall. A few days before the election an economic forecasting company, Wharton Econometrics, made the prediction (by then hardly a venturesome one) that Reagan would win. It pointed out that no incumbent president running for reelection had been defeated when economic growth in the election year had exceeded 3.8 percent. In 1984 economic growth exceeded 6 percent.[48] Based on standard expectations about the electoral effects of economic conditions, in other words, the 1984 presidential election should not have been close. Even Reagan's 18 percentage point margin of victory in the popular vote, though very large, was not altogether unexpected.

The Failure of the Democratic Challenge

A booming election-year economy bestowed victory on the incumbent president. This was as usual. Still, it was hardly evident as the campaign began that the standard electoral advantage of such an economy would apply, and apply fully, in the quite unusual circumstances of 1984.

Although the economy performed splendidly in 1983 and 1984, there was, as we have seen, a vast discrepancy between that performance and both the economy's performance earlier in the administration and that expected of it, weakened by federal deficits, in the future. However heedless of past and future they may be in most elections, one could have thought that the voters would notice a discrepancy of such magnitude and hold the incumbent to account for it.

The Democrats recognized this possibility and, by using an attack on Reagan's management of the economy as a major element of their campaign, made it a premise of their strategy. Because it violated standard political practice when the economy is currently in good shape, such an attack seemed unpromising to many Democrats. (Liberal economist Lester Thurow, for example, warned against it.) But the strategy also had some intellectual support; indeed it had been recommended, in effect, four years earlier by Tufte in the book mentioned at the beginning of this essay. Worried about how presidents could be deterred from manipulating the economy for short-term electoral ends, Tufte held that it was the responsibility of the out-party to expose the shortsighted policies of the incumbent.[49] They were to do so, one presumes, even if those policies seemed to be working in the election year.

Thus the effect of the economic issue in the 1984 campaign was not entirely a foregone conclusion; in fact it would pose some important questions that previously had not been posed in a comparable way. To what extent was the voters' preoccupation with the current state of the economy a fixed attribute, and to what extent susceptible to change? Specifically, as they assessed a president's economic management, would voters respond to the economy's performance earlier in his term or to information about the future consequences of current policies if either were unusually problematic? And could voters' attention to these things be heightened appreciably by a challenger's campaign that set out to do so? The answers to these questions, at least those that emerge from the 1984 presidential campaign, do not suggest much potential for change in the nature of voters' attention to the economy. Indeed, the events of the campaign help to explain why the potential for such change may be very limited.

The Democratic Strategy. .Speaking before a large national television audience, as he accepted his party's nomination at its convention in July, Mondale sought to define the deficit issue and establish its central role in his campaign. He addressed his attack on Reagan's conduct of office to those who had voted for him in 1980. "You did not vote for $200 billion deficits," he said in the first item of his indictment. Very explicitly, he tried to draw voters' attention to the consequences of the deficits for the future: "We are living on borrowed money and borrowed time. These deficits hike interest rates, clobber exports, stunt investment, kill jobs, undermine growth, cheat our kids and shrink our future." The deficits, he went on to say, in clipped, emphatic phrasing, also had a further consequence: "Let's tell the truth. Mr. Reagan will raise taxes, and so will I. He won't tell you. I just did." Mondale promised that, by the end of his first term, he would reduce the deficit by two-thirds from the size it would reach under Reagan's current policies.

Immediately after the convention Mondale and vice presidential candidate Geraldine A. Ferraro began working to reinforce and elaborate their attack on Reagan economics; they occasionally reminded audiences of the recession, but most of the emphasis was on the deficits. Mondale stressed the deficits in the first of a series of weekly radio broadcasts, and he followed up with a number of rallies in which he attempted to show specific groups—farmers, educators, and so on—how the problem was hurting them. In September, Mondale outlined his plan for reducing the deficit, including spending cuts in some domestic programs, a slowdown in the growth of defense spending, and a tax increase of $85 billion by 1989.[50]

As the campaign wore on, with no evidence that the deficit issue was helping Mondale's candidacy and some evidence it was hurting, some of his advisers urged him to abandon it. During brief periods, he appeared to do so, but the issue kept reemerging. Asked to appraise Reagan's leadership in the first televised debate in early October, Mondale used Reagan's position on the deficit to illustrate what he called poor leadership.

The Defects of the Strategy. The deficit was a very serious matter to economists, business leaders, and other elites, but, as rapidly became evident, it was not an effective campaign issue for the Democratic ticket. The deficit and Reagan's responsibility for it proved to have at least three serious weaknesses as a campaign issue.

The first was a more or less apparent tendency of the public to be bored with it. The undesirability of large budget deficits was not seriously in dispute between the candidates, and, according to polls, most of the public agreed (at least verbally) that the deficit was a serious problem.[51] Nevertheless, few of the voters appeared to be very interested in it. The budget deficit is an abstract condition (an arithmetical relation between taxing and spending), with effects that are remote in time and somewhat indefinite. Low-level partisan controversy over the years about deficits that were tiny compared with Reagan's may have anesthetized the public to the entire subject.

Mondale, whom many found boring most times he spoke, was especially boring when he spoke about deficits. Part of the problem arose from his effort to overcome the public's initial indifference by educating it about the issue. Giving classroom-style performances, with charts, blackboards, and a lot of numbers, Mondale succeeded only in appearing ridiculous—at least to the reporters covering the campaign. Thus the deficit issue worked poorly for Mondale in meeting the first requirement for an effective campaign issue, to get and hold the public's attention.

A second weakness was that, when the deficit issue did get attention, it did not automatically benefit the Democratic side. Conscientiousness about deficits was a new and not altogether convincing posture for a Democratic candidate to assume; conversely, irresponsibility about deficits was hard to pin convincingly on a Republican. Both notions conflicted with the longstanding public images of the two parties.[52] Taking advantage of those images, Reagan blamed the deficits on Democrats in Congress and pointed out that Mondale, as a senator, had been a habitual supporter of deficit spending. On balance, some commentators felt, all the attention Mondale drew to the subject of deficits may have harmed his party's prospects—reminding voters of a problem for whose responsible handling they did not primarily look to Democrats.

Finally, and most damaging to Mondale's chances, the deficit issue made him, in an exceptionally clear and pronounced way, the candidate of austerity. It led him to promise, at considerable political cost, increased taxes but did not force Reagan either to promise them himself or to offer the voters any comparable bad news. One reason for Mondale's unconventional pronouncement on taxes, one of his aides later said, was that he was concerned that the public doubted his capacity for leadership and, to remove that doubt, wanted to take actions that would be perceived as conspicuously bold. Perhaps so; but in any case Mondale could hardly have campaigned on the deficit, emphasizing its dangers and portraying Reagan as ignoring them, without at some point saying what he himself proposed to do about it. If that included raising taxes or cutting support for popular programs, as it inevitably would, there would be unavoidable political costs.

Mondale's strategy was to persuade the voters that Reagan not only was responsible for the deficit, but that he would have to do the same kinds of unpleasant things as Mondale to get rid of them and would do them in a way that was less fair. Straining to get the point across, Mondale, without producing concrete evidence, accused Reagan of having a "secret plan" to raise taxes after the election. In choosing this strategy, Mondale undoubtedly calculated that during the campaign Reagan either would have to admit the need for a tax increase or else would lose credibility with the voters. That calculation proved erroneous.

For a brief time the issue of taxes and the deficit caused the Republican ticket some embarrassment. In his initial response, Reagan flatly denied that he planned to raise taxes. But, in earlier long-range budget discussions between the administration and congressional leaders, the likelihood that significant tax increases would be needed some time after the election had in fact been generally assumed. On a day when Reagan reiterated his denial that he would increase taxes in his second term, Vice President Bush, reflecting the general assumption, as much as admitted that he might. This gave Mondale and Ferraro a few days of fun at the Republicans' expense, telling audiences that Reagan and Bush should debate each other. According to a *New York Times*/CBS News poll in August, the public by a 52 to 38 percent majority agreed with Mondale that a tax increase would be needed.[53]

In the end Reagan himself was forced to waffle, but a revised and mildly qualified position on taxes held up through the rest of the campaign. Undoubtedly urged by aides to preserve the possibility of a tax increase as an option, Reagan said he would increase taxes only as "a last resort," predicting that economic growth and further, mainly unspecified, cuts in domestic spending would reduce the deficit enough to avoid it. The amended position still enabled Reagan to maintain a sharp distinction between himself and Mondale, who, according to Reagan's aides, would increase taxes "as a first resort." [54]

One reason that Reagan's position on the deficit held up and was effective, it is important to note, is that economic reality as understood by the preponderance of economists exercised no significant constraint on the ensuing debate. Reagan's contention that most of the deficit would disappear through economic growth, which was the main basis of his rebuttal to Mondale, was without support in any conventional forecast of the economy, just as the claims for the original economic program had been four years earlier. The Congressional Budget Office (CBO) was projecting that, under existing policies, deficits, instead of shrinking, would increase through the rest of the 1980s, reaching $263 billion by 1989. To shrink the deficit would have required that at least 5 to 6 percent growth in GNP, a rate that had been achieved in 1983 and 1984 only as the economy rose out of a recession, be sustained indefinitely. Among nine major private forecasting companies surveyed by the *New York Times,* none expected that much growth; on average they expected about 3 percent.[55] Even experts associated with Reagan rejected the claim. Feldstein, who had returned to academe from Reagan's CEA, wrote after the election: "An absolutely unprecedented 5 percent rate of real GNP growth for the remainder of the decade would still leave a deficit of more than $150 billion in 1989. There is just no basis in experience for the suggestion we can grow our way out of these deficits." [56]

However implausible it was as economics, the shrinking-deficit scenario was serviceable for Reagan as campaign rhetoric, and Mondale sought in vain to refute it convincingly to the voters. In the televised debate on domestic policy, he tried to refute it by invoking the authority of recognized experts. When a panelist asked Reagan about the deficit and referred to the projections by the CBO, Reagan said he did not take the CBO's forecasts seriously, because "they have been wrong on almost all of them." In rebuttal, Mondale asserted that Reagan's projection of a shrinking deficit was rejected in "virtually every economic analysis that I've heard of," including that of "the distinguished Congressional Budget Office, which is respected by ... almost everyone." The exchange probably gave Reagan a bad moment in the debate (one of several in a subpar performance that evening)—but certainly not a terrible one. An attentive viewer, especially one with some awareness of the CBO, probably would have found Reagan's dismissal of the agency's projections a bit suspicious. Most viewers, one imagines, would not have noticed it.

There were, aside from the debates, many other opportunities for the voters to assess the candidates' respective claims about the deficit, especially in the day-to-day news coverage of the campaign. But most such coverage gave the voters little more in the way of pointed, usable information than accounts of the trading of assertions by the candidates— the kind of account the media define as evenhanded. Journalists rarely assessed the evidence themselves or even described the preponderance of professional opinion, although the latter, at least, is not especially hard to do.

Thus the voters' assessment of the deficit debate probably was shaped above all by the simple, though nearly irrelevant, fact that the economy was indeed growing at the time. In September, a poll showed, a 51 to 33 percent majority of the public believed that Reagan would do a better job than Mondale of balancing the federal budget—a striking finding in that Mondale and not Reagan was proposing drastic action to do so. On election day, the *New York Times*/CBS News exit poll showed that 60 percent of the voters (and 72 percent of Reagan's supporters) believed the deficit could be substantially reduced without a tax increase.[57]

The Effect of the Deficit Debate. The debate on taxes and the deficit, although only one of several debates on issues during the campaign, in all likelihood had the most important effect on the outcome. If Reagan had not been able to sidestep the deficit problem by claiming that economic growth would take care of it, it may have been a much different campaign. He would have been forced either to promise the unpleasant medicine of major spending cuts and tax increases (hence losing the advantage he gained over Mondale by refusing to do so) or else to accept as permanent huge deficits and a rapidly escalating national debt (hence appearing irresponsible). Either way it would have been obvious to the voters, as it was to economists, that Reagan's economic program had not worked according to plan, and that its legacy was problematic.

Instead, Reagan and Republican congressional candidates were able to use Mondale's tax increase proposal as a powerful weapon against him and other Democrats, featuring it prominently in their campaign advertising. Seeing the obvious political costs, Democratic congressional candidates refused to endorse the proposal in their own campaigns, and Mondale himself conceded after the election that making it had been a mistake. It was, he said, a "political disaster." [58]

With the effects of the tax increase issue added to the ordinary effects of an economic boom, voters who considered that they were "voting their pocketbooks"—that is, who were concerned primarily with the economy—voted overwhelmingly for Reagan. "It comes down to cash," said one Reagan voter in explaining his choice to a reporter. As a variety of poll evidence showed and postelection commentators agreed, Reagan benefited enormously from the public's perception that his management of the economy had been a success.[59]

Within days after the election, the Office of Management and Budget revised its estimate of the fiscal 1985 deficit upward by more than $30 billion, to $210 billion, and an administration budget group set as a goal the reduction of deficits to less than $150 billion by 1988, urging consideration of massive cuts in domestic spending to do so. At the same time, evidence of a possible new recession was beginning to accumulate; the two-year period of rapid economic growth that had so impressed the voters and boosted President Reagan to an easy reelection appeared to be coming to an end.

Democracy and Economic Policy

The period of Reagan economics, up to and including the election of 1984, was a distinctive and highly significant one for the making of economic policy. Modern presidents before Reagan generally felt obliged to avoid drastic departures from the path (although neither straight nor narrow) of mainstream economics—even when, as occasionally occurred, strong electoral pressures seemed to call for such departures. Reagan economics, in important respects, represented a very pronounced subordination of economic expertise to electoral politics and to policies shaped by political campaigns. Supply-side economics, the foundation of the administration's 1981 economic recovery program, could claim little attention from politicians on the strength of its arguments and evidence or based on its standing among professional economists. It claimed attention and support from a number of Republicans—including Ronald Reagan in 1980—because of its appeal as a platform on which to conduct an electoral campaign. The enactment of supply-side economics in 1981 represented the carrying forward into actual policy of commitments that had been shaped by the exigencies of that campaign.

From 1982 to 1984, still ignoring the advice of most economists (including its own), the Reagan administration resisted proposing substantial tax increases or cuts in defense spending that would staunch the flow of red ink in the federal budget. Its inaction was partly the result of policy deadlock with Congress, especially the Democratic House of Representatives, but it also had an electoral basis. Cognizant of the short-term stimulative effects of the deficit and of the potential political costs of reversing its position on taxes, the administration openly postponed consideration of deficit-reducing tax increases until after the 1984 election.

The period shows not only that electoral influence on economic policy can take several forms, but that the form it takes and the strength of the effect depend heavily on each president's political strategy, personality, and style of decision making. In his responsiveness to one sort of electoral influence, Ronald Reagan was perhaps the limiting case. This is not because he was especially cynical; it is hard to find any evidence of cynicism in him. It is because, in his own thinking about economic policy, Reagan apparently made little distinction between electoral politics and substantive conviction. Instead, to an extraordinary degree, he adopted as firm and genuine belief economic views that although lacking professional support would powerfully appeal to the general public, especially but not only to conservatives. His deeply ingrained, reflexive optimism overrode professional opinion, including that of his own economic advisers, when that opinion suggested that policies to which he felt committed would not work.

The consequences of this episode of electorally driven economic policy were vast. Some important and potentially lasting gains from the conservative standpoint were made under Reagan—especially cuts in domestic spending and a sharp decline in the rate of inflation. But the federal deficit approached 5 to 6 percent of GNP, a level previously unprecedented except in wartime; and it threatened, among other harmful effects, to absorb more than half of the domestic savings on which most business investment, and hence vigorous economic growth, crucially depends.

The presidential campaign and election of 1984 clearly and generously rewarded those policies. Of course one cannot object, on the basis of the evidence and analysis of this chapter, to the outcome of the election. There were other issues at stake besides the economy, and other considerations—such as personality and leadership—besides issues. Even on the economy, a well-informed conservative voter may have doubted that a Mondale administration (subject to the constituency pressures of the Democratic party) would be so responsible about the deficit, or a second Reagan administration so irresponsible, as their respective campaigns implied—and so quite reasonably voted for Reagan. But one can and should be concerned, regardless of one's partisan preference, about some aspects of how the outcome was reached.

The campaign and election failed markedly to perform the functions they would have to perform to support and encourage economic policy that is both responsible and genuinely responsive to the public's wishes. One of these functions is in some loose way to accomplish the expression, recording, and eventual implementation of those wishes. But it is very doubtful that the public, in endorsing Reagan's management of the economy and choosing to have more of it, understood in any realistic sense what it was endorsing and choosing. The public's appraisal of Reagan's economic performance swung wildly: sharply downward during the recession, even though a case could be made that a recession was necessary to cure inflation; and sharply upward during the recovery, even though some kind of recovery was almost inevitable, and even though this recovery was accompanied by abundant warnings of dire prospects in years to come. In the end voters responded at the polls as if Reagan's economic program were an unambiguous, resounding success, when its success in fact was much in doubt.

The other function that elections would have to perform to encourage responsible, responsive policies is—by the behavior of the electorate and the commitments elicited from candidates—to create incentives for incumbent administrations to pursue such policies. Instead, the election of 1984 created or strongly reinforced perverse incentives in regard to economic management, both for the Reagan administration in its second term and for administrations of either party in the future. For Reagan's second term, the campaign made action to reduce the deficit even more difficult than it would have been in any event, and perhaps impossible. Pressed by Mondale's charges, yet acknowledging no effective discipline of economic reality, Reagan promised not to raise taxes and also in emphatic terms not to cut benefits for Social Security, in addition to reiterating promises to increase spending for national defense. In practical effect, given the limited potential for cuts in other areas of the budget, he thus promised not to do anything significant about the deficit.

For future presidents, the 1984 election demonstrated, more impressively than ever before, the electoral benefits to be obtained by skillful political manipulation of the business cycle—that is, by making periods of expansion coincide with elections—if such manipulation can be achieved. It demonstrated what previously had not been known for sure, that an election-year boom will bear the customary electoral reward even it it results partly from a deep recession, if it is produced with the help of policies (such as enormous deficits) that entail very serious long-term costs, and if the candidate of the out-party makes every attempt to challenge the incumbent's economic management on both of these counts. The Reagan administration did not intentionally create the recession early in its first term, but a later administration, acting on the lessons of 1984, may well do so.[60] And a later administration, acting on both the lessons of 1984 and Reagan's example, may decide to set almost no limit on the amount of fiscal stimulation it would use to ensure a vigorous economy in a presidential election year.

The events recounted here raise a broader concern about the relation between democratic politics and economic policy: whether the demands of electoral politics are compatible with the making of responsible economic policy. Elections, it seems, tend to encourage irresponsibility and penalize attempts to be responsible. One is led to speculate, therefore, about the conditions that could support responsible economic policy under American democracy in the future.

Just possibly, the electorate could become more discriminating in assessing the economic proposals and promises of candidates for president and in evaluating the economic record of incumbents. It may learn to reject and penalize unrealistic scenarios or, if not that, at least to confer on unrealism a smaller reward. In judging performance, it might take into account the cyclical character of the economy. Unfortunately, at least one route to such improvement, although logically conceivable, is more or less clearly foreclosed: voters will not devote much more time than they do now to evaluating presidential candidates or, even less appealing, learning economics. Considering the many legitimate prior claims on their attention—those of work, family, community, and so on—it is hard to argue that they even should.

The voters' awareness and discrimination can improve, it seems, only if election campaigns and public policy debate somehow become more useful to them as sources of information. As of now, it is not hard for voters to find out the presidential candidates' positions on issues (although it is much easier to find out who is leading); but it is very hard for them to make informed judgments about the merits of those positions. They certainly cannot do so on the basis of televised presidential debates in their current form. Amounting to a series of brief comments and set speeches by each candidate, with little direct confrontation of any kind, such debates test if anything the candidates' ability to memorize and their quickness on their feet—marginally useful traits for presidents.

Coverage of campaigns and policy debate in the media, of which network television is most important, gives surprisingly little additional help. Reporting on policy debate is dominated by the twin motifs of "the two sides of the issue" (notably, it is almost always *two*) and public opinion. Rarely do the news media attempt to report the state of the evidence or even the weight of informed opinion on a matter of partisan dispute. Covering presidential campaign debate, therefore, the media will eagerly tell what percentage of the public believes that budget deficits will shrink through economic growth. But it will omit to tell, clearly, explicitly, and alongside the candidates' statements, how much evidence supports that view or what percentage of economists believe it. To report on such matters of complex fact would not always be easy or without risks for the media: audiences could be bored or alienated by the coverage, and politicians could be induced even more than now to attempt to shape it by exerting pressure. But, in the absence of such reporting from some nonpartisan, highly salient source that is perceived as reliable, candidates can claim almost whatever they like about their policies, and voters, except through heroic efforts, can hardly even attempt to sort out the claims.

With respect, specifically, to the issue of the deficit, an increase in voter awareness and discrimination is all but inevitable. By the next presidential election, in 1988, the issue of the deficit—deciding what to do about it and assigning the blame—almost certainly will have dominated domestic policy debate throughout Reagan's second term. In all probability, very large deficits will not have been eliminated, even if perhaps significantly reduced. And if the preponderance of economists are correct, the country will have had painful experience of the consequences—slow economic growth, a budget overwhelmed by interest payments on the national debt, and possibly high interest rates and a return of inflation. All this is bound to make an impression on the American public.

Notes

A number of people provided very helpful comments on earlier drafts of this chapter: Art Frank, Jack Nagel, and several students in the senior seminar in American politics at the University of Pennsylvania.

1. Edward R. Tufte, *Political Control of the Economy* (Princeton: Princeton University Press, 1980). The phrase quoted appears on p. 143.
2. Timothy B. Clark, "All Talk, No Action?" *National Journal,* October 6, 1984, 1880.
3. See, for example, William Schneider, "An Uncertain Consensus," *National Journal,* November 11, 1984, 2130-2132.
4. An overview of the main theoretical positions in contemporary macroeconomics is in James E. Alt and K. Alec Chrystal, *Political Economics* (Berkeley: University of California Press, 1983), Chapter 3.
5. Milton Friedman and Walter W. Heller, *Monetary vs. Fiscal Policy: A Dialogue* (New York: Norton, 1969).
6. Douglas Hibbs, "Political Parties and Macroeconomic Policy, *American Political Science Review* 71 (1977): 1467-1487; Alt and Chrystal, *Political Economics,* 112-118; Tufte, *Political Control of the Economy,* Chapter 4.
7. Arthur M. Okun, "Comments on Stigler's Paper," *American Economic Review* 63 (1973): 172-177, cited in D. Roderick Kiewiet, *Macroeconomics and Micropolitics: The Electoral Effects of Economic Issues* (Chicago: University of Chicago Press, 1983), 14.
8. See also G. D. MacRae, "A Political Model of the Business Cycle," *Journal of Political Economy* 85 (1977): 236-263.
9. William Nordhaus, "The Political Business Cycle," *Review of Economic Studies* 41 (1975): 169-190.
10. For an excellent review, see Alt and Chrystal, *Political Economics,* Chapter 5; on policy instruments, see Nathaniel Beck, "Presidential Influence on the Federal Reserve in the 1970s," *American Journal of Political Science* 26 (August 1982): 415-455; John T. Woolley, *Monetary Politics: The Federal Reserve and the Politics of Monetary Policy* (New York: Cambridge University Press, 1984), Chapter 6; B. S. Frey and F. Schneider, "An Empirical Study of Politico-Economic Interaction in the United States," *Review of Economics and Statistics* 60 (1978): 243-253; and David Lowrey, "The Keynesian and Political Determinants of Unbalanced Budgets: U.S. Fiscal Policy from Eisenhower to Reagan" (Paper presented at the annual meeting of the Midwest Political Science Association, April 1984).
11. As Seymour Martin Lipset describes this pattern, Americans are ideologically conservative but programmatically liberal. See Lipset, "The Economy, Elections, and Public Opinion" (Working Papers in Political Science No. P-83-1, Hoover Institution, Stanford University, July 1983).
12. J. M. Buchanan and R. Wagner, *Democracy in Deficit* (New York: Academic Press, 1977).

13. Traditional Republican economics, Herbert Stein observes, have been referred to as "castor-oil economics." See Stein, *Presidential Economics: The Making of Economic Policy from Truman to Reagan* (New York: Simon and Schuster, 1984), 236.

14. Samuel Popkin et al., "Comment: What Have You Done for Me Lately? Toward an Investment Theory of Voting," *American Political Science Review* 70 (1976): 779-805; Kiewiet, *Macroeconomics and Micropolitics,* Chapter 2. The importance of economic management to voters is apparent in data reported by Kiewiet: in the five national election surveys by the Center for Political Studies from 1972 to 1980, proportions of respondents ranging from 26 to 62 percent cited an economic problem, either inflation or unemployment, as the main national problem; the most frequent response apart from these two categories ranged from 9 to 43 percent.

15. Stein's *Presidential Economics* is an excellent historical account of the relation between presidential politics and economic advice.

16. See Stein, *Presidential Economics,* chapters 4 and 5.

17. Ibid., 235.

18. The following summary of Reagan's 1981 proposals is based primarily on Gregory B. Mills and John L. Palmer, *The Deficit Dilemma: Budget Policy in the Reagan Era* (Washington, D.C.: Urban Institute Press, 1983), chapters 2 and 3; and Hugh Heclo and Rudolph G. Penner, "Fiscal and Political Strategy in the Reagan Administration," in *The Reagan Presidency: An Early Assessment,* ed. Fred I. Greenstein (Baltimore: Johns Hopkins University Press, 1983), Chapter 2.

19. Stein, *Presidential Economics,* 270.

20. Heclo and Penner, "Fiscal and Political Strategy," 26. (Penner is the conservative economist; Heclo is a political scientist.)

21. For a statement of the theory, see Jude Wanniski, *The Way the World Works* (New York: Simon and Schuster, 1979). Laffer and his followers could properly be called *radical* supply-side economists to distinguish them from many mainstream economists in recent years who have become concerned with the supply-side consequences of government policy, that is, its effects on savings, investment, and work effort. Such economists have used careful empirical research to estimate such effects, arriving at far more modest conclusions about their magnitude.

22. Heclo and Penner, "Fiscal and Political Strategy," 26.

23. Ibid. For a critique of the theory, pointing out its lack of any substantial basis, see Stephen Rousseas, *The Political Economy of Reaganomics* (New York: M. E. Sharpe, 1982); and Stein, *Presidential Economics,* 237-249. The title of one essay conveys something of the doctrine's professional standing: Martin Gardiner, "Mathematical Games: The Laffer Curve and Other Laughs in Current Economics," *Scientific American,* December 1981, 18-31.

24. On Reagan's adoption of supply-side economics, see Stein, *Presidential Economics,* Chapter 7 (subtitled "The Economics of Joy"), especially 254-261; a very similar account is given in Laurence I. Barrett, *Gambling with*

History (New York: Penguin Books, 1984), 131-133.

25. Stein, *Presidential Economics,* 257-258.

26. Barrett, *Gambling with History,* 143.

27. Barrett gives a balanced and perceptive account of Reagan's personality and style of decision making, *Gambling with History,* Chapter 2. As the White House correspondent for *Time* magazine, he had exceptional access for a reporter, including considerable personal contact with Reagan. See also Paul J. Quirk, "Presidential Competence," in *The Presidency and the Political System,* ed. Michael Nelson (Washington, D.C.: CQ Press, 1984), 133-153.

28. See Samuel Kernell, "The Presidency and the People," in *The Presidency and the Political System,* 233-265.

29. The administration managed to win congressional approval of only about half of its proposed cuts in domestic spending, but to do even this well was more than most observers had expected. If all of the cuts had been adopted, the deficit would still have been about two-thirds as large as it ultimately was. John L. Palmer and Isabel V. Sawhill, "Overview," in *The Reagan Record,* ed. Palmer and Sawhill (Washington, D.C.: Urban Institute Press, 1984), 9.

30. Isabel V. Sawhill and Charles F. Stone, "The Economy: The Key to Success," in *The Reagan Record,* 70.

31. Clark, "All Talk, No Action?"

32. Feldstein left the CEA in July, roughly when he had planned, to resume teaching at Harvard in the fall.

33. For this period, see Barrett, *Gambling with History,* chapters 11 and 12.

34. On the negotiations between the administration and Congress, see Barrett, *Gambling with History,* Chapter 20.

35. U.S. Senate, *Administration's Fiscal Year 1984 Budget Proposals,* Hearing before the Committee on Finance, 98th Cong., 1st Sess., February 3, 1983, 57-65.

36. Except as otherwise indicated, the following discussion of the effects of Reagan's policies is derived from Sawhill and Stone's, "The Key to Success," in John L. Palmer and Isabel V. Sawhill, eds., *The Reagan Record* (Washington, D.C.: Urban Institute Press, 1984). Sawhill and Stone estimated the short-term effects of Reagan's policies, compared with pre-Reagan policies and three alternative policy mixes, based on a simulation using the Data Resources Inc. econometric model of the American economy. Their estimates of long-term effects are based on an extensive survey of research on the administration's specific policies; they reflect uncertainty that arises from disagreements among, and ambiguities in, those studies. A more detailed discussion is provided in Sawhill and Stone, *Economic Policy in the Reagan Years* (Washington, D.C.: Urban Institute Press, 1984).

37. Sawhill and Stone point out: "Notwithstanding the widespread belief that inflation is a major problem, there is remarkably little analytical evidence on the costs of inflation" ("Key to Success," 89). Based on available estimates of these costs, they doubt that Reagan's reduction of inflation will have benefits

sufficient to outweigh the costs of the recession. They also argue, like many economists, that inflation could have been reduced with a less severe recession through a policy of more moderate monetary restraint and smaller budget deficits, "Key to Success," 86-88. Stein, on the other hand, disputes that view, concluding that a severe recession was an inevitable result of the monetary policies needed to bring down the rate of inflation, *Presidential Economics,* 299.

38. See Charles R. Hulten and Isabel V. Sawhill, eds., *The Legacy of Reaganomics: Prospects for Long-term Growth* (Washington, D.C.: Urban Institute Press, 1984).

39. See Mills and Palmer, *The Deficit Dilemma,* Chapter 4.

40. Sawhill and Stone, "Key to Success," 98.

41. *New York Times,* October 24, 1984.

42. For a careful specification and testing of several models of economic voting, see Kiewiet, *Macroeconomics and Micropolitics.*

43. R. Fair, "The Effect of Economic Events on Votes for President," *Review of Economics and Statistics* 60 (1978): 159-173, summarized in Alt and Chrystal, *Political Economics,* 149-150.

44. Samuel Kernell, "Explaining Presidential Popularity," *American Political Science Review* 72 (June 1978): 506-522.

45. Some statistical studies have estimated the rate at which the effect of economic events on incumbent popularity dissipates with time. By such estimates, some effect of economic conditions in a given year remains for four or five years afterward, but most of it occurs earlier, with roughly half of the total effect occurring in the first year. See the summary and literature cited in Alt and Chrystal, *Political Economics,* 164-165. On voters' disinclination to assess policies directly, see Morris P. Fiorina, *Retrospective Voting in American National Elections* (New Haven: Yale University Press, 1981), 8-9. This argument would seem to apply only to the macroeconomic rationale for those policies; as we have argued, voters sometimes have strong attitudes about taxing and spending that do not depend on observing their effects.

46. The poll evidence cited in this and the following two paragraphs is from compilations in *Public Opinion* (April-May 1984): 39; (February-March 1984): 35-38.

47. Gary C. Jacobson, "Reagan, Reaganomics, and Strategic Politics in 1982: A Test of Alternative Theories of Midterm Congressional Elections" (Paper presented at the annual meeting of the American Political Science Association, September 1983).

48. *New York Times,* November 5, 1984.

49. Tufte, *Political Control of the Economy,* 154.

50. *Washington Post National Weekly Edition,* September 24, 1984.

51. Clark, "All Talk, No Action?"

52. See Kiewiet, *Macroeconomics and Micropolitics,* 111-116.

53. *New York Times,* September 9, 1984.

54. *New York Times,* August 13, 1984.

55. This is the annual prediction of real growth in GNP averaged over the nine forecasts and the three years from 1985 to 1987. The forecasts were reported in the *New York Times,* November 18, 1984.
56. *New York Times,* November 18, 1984.
57. Clark, "All Talk, No Action?"; *New York Times,* November 11, 1984. (Additional data obtained by telephone from CBS News.)
58. *New York Times,* November 8, 1984.
59. Based on a late October poll, the *Times* concluded that the economy was "by far the most important issue during the election," with 55 percent of the voters saying it was more important than anything else, and that it worked "very strongly" for Reagan. *New York Times,* October 28, 1984.
60. At the beginning of the Carter administration, OMB director Bert Lance advised the president against stimulating the economy to avert a recession, as suggested by other advisers, partly on the grounds that it was a good time, politically, for one to occur. Erwin C. Hargrove, *Fidelity to Style: A Study of Jimmy Carter* (draft manuscript, 1984), Chapter 3.

7. THE PRESIDENCY: REAGAN AND THE CYCLE OF POLITICS AND POLICY

Erwin C. Hargrove and Michael Nelson

As recently as inauguration day 1981 the prevailing wisdom among pundits, politicians, and political scientists was that the presidency was a weak, even endangered, institution. Former president Gerald R. Ford wrote an essay for *Time* magazine whose title referred to the office as "Imperiled, Not Imperial." Others used more vivid imagery—the "tethered presidency," "revolving-door presidency," and "no-win presidency." [1] Whatever the term, the agreed-upon explanation for presidential weakness was that public expectations of the office were rising precipitously even as its institutional capacity to meet them was declining. A series of one-term presidents, worn down inexorably by the hopelessness of their situation, was the consensus forecast for the future.

Four years later things could not have been more different. Both in anticipation of and soon after President Ronald Reagan's landslide reelection victory on November 6, 1984, one heard a different tune from the chorus of experts: the presidency is strong again. Some found this cause for celebration, others for lamentation. Harvard professor and former Reagan aide David Gergen represented the first group when he trumpeted that Reagan had "restor[ed] the strength of the institutionalized presidency." In stark contrast *New York Times* columnist Anthony Lewis warned, "The imperial presidency is on the rise again." [2]

Such wild oscillations of opinion are all too common among presidency watchers—they result from widespread overreactions to the nation's experience with whoever has just been president. (During the administrations of Lyndon B. Johnson and Richard Nixon, a different kind of swing took place, from a judgment that the presidency was a benign institution to a sense that it was dangerous.) In truth the presidency is best regarded as neither strong nor weak, good nor bad, but rather as, on the one hand, empowered for different purposes at different times by the nation's political culture and electoral voice and, on the other, shaped by the varying skills and purposes of individual presidents. Viewed this way, the recent history of the presidency, far from being unusual, fits comfortably into a pattern that pervades the entire twentieth century.

Cycles of Politics and Policy

The history of American politics and domestic public policy in this century can be told in terms of a recurring cycle of electoral politics and governmental response whose focus has been the presidency. Here we present the cycle theory and treat the first three runs of the cycle, covering the period 1901-1974.[3] In the next section we turn to the current era.

Presidency of Achievement

At the heart of each cycle is a presidency of achievement, during which great bursts of legislative activity occur that significantly alter the role of government in society. These changes are grounded in American political culture, the nation's widespread and deeply rooted beliefs about how the political system ought to work and the ends it ought to serve. Presidencies of achievement manifest new, intensely felt definitions of liberty and equality, which are the culture's two main values concerning the ultimate purposes of government. Optimism runs high, providing a sense that it is within our power to solve any problem. The usual ambivalence toward political authority resolves temporarily into faith in government, especially the president, to act as the embodiment of national purpose.

Woodrow Wilson was the president of achievement in the century's first cycle of politics and policy. His New Freedom program inaugurated a role for the federal government as an umpire that would regulate the excesses of private corporate power in defense of individual liberty. The public philosophy of Franklin D. Roosevelt's New Deal, also grounded in libertarian values, was that within the bounds of capitalism and private property, the federal government is ultimately responsible for securing the foundations of the people's liberty: employment, security, and welfare. The legislation of the fabled "first 100 days" of Roosevelt's presidency in 1933 was designed mainly to salvage the depression-battered economy; the Second New Deal, which followed the 1934 congressional elections, aimed more directly at economic reform and redistribution of income to the working class. Johnson, the third president of achievement, extended the helping hand of government to economically deprived minorities and addressed quality-of-life concerns like education and the environment in pursuit of his Great Society agenda.

Quite clearly, presidencies of achievement are relative rarities in American politics. They occur only when three conditions are met: an empowering election, a politically skillful president, and suitable policy ideas.

Election. A president is empowered for achievement if he campaigns with promises, however general, of significant reform, is elected by a landslide majority, and sees large gains for his party in the accompanying congressional elections. It is the size of the gains more than the size of his party's contingent in Congress that makes the difference, because the gains invariably are attributed to the president-elect's coattails or to a mandate that he and Congress share. Either way the election heightens the disposition of legislators in both parties to support the president's postelection legislative initiatives: fellow partisans because they want to ride his bandwagon, members of the opposition who represent districts the president strongly carried because they want to avoid being flattened by it. A president whose election is not accompanied by large gains in Congress is less likely to be effective because he will be seen by legislators as tangential to their own political standing with the voters.

Skill. The presidency requires above all a strategic sense of the grain of history—an ability to understand the public mood and to shape and fulfill the historical possibilities of the time. Presidents also must be able to present themselves and their policies to the general public through rhetoric and symbolic action and to deal in a tactically skillful way with other Washington politicians through negotiation, persuasion, and other kinds of political gamesmanship. Finally, presidents need skills of management, both of lieutenants in the administration who can help them form their policy proposals and of large organizations in the bureaucracy that are charged to implement policies that already are on the books. Presidents at different stages of the cycle need these abilities in different combinations, but for presidents of achievement all but the implementation skills are important.

Ideas. The rhetoric of dramatic change may be enough to get a president elected if that is what the public wants to hear, but once in office it must be translated into specific ideas for legislation. Successful ideas are characterized not just by their grounding in expert knowledge but also by their fit with culturally rooted moral sentiment and the public expectations of the day. Such a rigorous definition raises the possibility that ideas may not always be available even if the other conditions for a presidency of achievement are met. Historically, they always have been, however, partly because ideas go through long periods of incubation during the other two stages of the cycle and partly because virtually everyone in politics has a stake in developing them. The main challenge for most presidents is to recognize which policy ideas best suit their purposes and the times.

The Postachievement Phase of a Presidency of Achievement. Presidencies of achievement only constitute a part of the cycle, and the period of achievement in such a presidency only constitutes a part of it, usually the first two to four years. Achievement ends when administrative difficulties arise from the attempt to attain social change through governmental action so quickly, when older meanings of cultural values are reasserted, and when the antigovernment strain in the public's ambivalence toward authority reemerges. This presents a problem. The grateful citizenry, voting "retrospectively," [4] is likely to reward the president with reelection, but it may no longer support his basic temperamental and philosophical ambition, which is to continue to make his mark on government through legislative action.

For the president of achievement, who is unlikely to change his spots even if the voters change theirs, two strategies present themselves. The first is to throw caution to the winds and seek another achievement-style election victory—either a landslide for him and gains for his congressional party in response to a reelection campaign that promises more dramatic changes to come or (a variation) a reversal of the pattern of losses for the incumbent party in a midterm congressional election that the president has transformed into a referendum on his agenda for change. Historically, however, the first variation of this strategy has never worked, and the second only once, in 1934. In terms of legislation, the postachievement phase almost always is one of domestic-policy stalemate.

The second strategy for a president who wants to keep on achieving is to emphasize foreign policy. On the world stage, the constraints that ended the brief period of domestic legislative success are weaker: the public is more consistent in its support of strong presidential leadership in foreign policy and the problems of administration are less severe. One cannot help but note the coincidence of presidencies of achievement and war: Wilson and World War I, Roosevelt and World War II, Johnson and Vietnam. In each case, these were wars that the United States, led by a president who appealed to the culture's highest ideals, chose to enter. One need not draw a deterministic connection between domestic achievement and war: what is common to both is a high tide of cultural optimism, the belief that Americans have the power to remake the system, at home or abroad, in conformance with their notions of right. Thus, one might just as logically expect a president of achievement to try to forge some other kind of dramatic foreign policy success, such as disarmament.

Presidency of Consolidation

Each presidency of achievement has been followed by a presidency of consolidation, in which the reforms of the achievement stage were not rejected but woven into the administrative fabric of government, made more efficient and economical, and retired from the roster of divisive political issues. The presidencies of Warren G. Harding, Calvin Coolidge, and Herbert Hoover during the 1920s were of this kind: for all Harding's talk about a return to the "normalcy" of the McKinley administration, neither he nor his successors did much to roll back Wilson's New Freedom reforms. Similarly, Dwight D. Eisenhower confined his efforts to bringing fiscal and administrative order to the New Deal, and Nixon concentrated not on repealing the Great Society but on devolving responsibility to administer its programs to state and local governments.

Presidents of consolidation often come to power through elections that meet two of the three conditions for achievement-style empowerment: a landslide victory for the president and significant gains for his party in Congress. Such victories can be misinterpreted: Eisenhower, a landslide winner whose party seized control of both houses of Congress in 1952, frequently was criticized by both liberals and conservatives for not using his popularity to move government in the manner of a president of achievement. In truth, the mandate of a president of consolidation comes from his promise *not* to push for substantial policy changes. Eisenhower's realization of this was born of a political skill that presidents of consolidation, like all other presidents, need: a strategic sense of the historical possibilities of their time. The other skill that presidents of consolidation must have, to a greater degree than others, involves the management of authority for policy implementation.

A presidency of consolidation ends a cycle, but it also overlaps with the period in which the seeds of the next cycle are planted. New social discontents arise—as they inevitably do in a dynamic society—and intellectuals in the universities and think-tanks, interest group leaders, journalists, legislators, bureaucrats, and others on the fringes of power begin developing policy ideas to meet them. The president of consolidation, empowered only with an electoral mandate not to push aggressively for change and preoccupied in any event with the reforms of his own cycle, is likely to be inattentive or unresponsive to these new forces.

Presidency of Preparation

Eventually, some of the social discontents that develop during the latter stages of a presidency of consolidation become strong enough to dominate presidential politics. A new president is elected because of his

193

ability to articulate the new problems and offer new ideas to meet them, but the victory is far from overwhelming. Thus, the president's main task during the preparation stage of the cycle is to lay the political groundwork for the presidency of achievement that will follow. To do this successfully requires a mix of leadership skills: a well-developed strategic sense, an ability to move the public through rhetoric and dramatic action, and a capacity to manage authority for policy formation.

Theodore Roosevelt, a Republican but one out of step with most of his party, was the president of preparation for Democrat Wilson's New Freedom, and John F. Kennedy prepared the way for Johnson's Great Society. In truth, there is no reason why a president of preparation could not become a president of achievement through an empowering reelection victory, thus reaping the harvest of his own labors. But Roosevelt chose not to run for a second term, and Kennedy, who planned to do so, was assassinated.

Conclusion

Although the cycle of preparation, achievement, and consolidation is rooted in American political culture, we derive it more from historical observation than from any theory of historical determinism. It is recurring but not inevitable. A severe national crisis can break the cyclic flow: the abruptness of the depression catapulted Franklin Roosevelt's New Deal into existence without any preceding presidency of preparation. So can a mismatch between presidential purpose and public mood. The presidency of William Howard Taft foundered because Taft, who had been handpicked by Theodore Roosevelt and elected by the people to carry on Roosevelt's agenda of reform, turned out to be temperamentally and philosophically unsuited to the task. Taft's was a presidency of stalemate, one in which the president's purposes bear little resemblance to what the public is willing to accept. The presidency of Harry S. Truman also fits into this category, although Truman, unlike Taft, was trying to set off a new round of achievement in the face of a strong public disposition for consolidation. As we have seen, similar periods of domestic stalemate also have occurred within each presidency of achievement, usually with consequences for foreign policy. (Truman, the would-be president of achievement, entered the United States into the war between North and South Korea.)

Similarly, although each of the first three runs of the cycle that have taken place in this century moved public policy in a liberal direction, there is nothing inevitable about that either. What characterizes a cycle is that after the dust has settled, the role of government in society has been altered in some significant way, liberal, conservative, or otherwise. Indeed, in the mid-1970s American social, economic, and, consequently, political life began to change in ways that turned the cycle in a conservative direction.

Ford, Carter, Reagan, and the Cycle

The turn from liberal to conservative in the cycle of politics and policy was neither accidental nor easy. Its origins lay in the last years of the Nixon presidency. These were unusual for all sorts of reasons, including one that sometimes is overlooked: the nature of intellectual ferment and social discontent that was occurring outside government. New problems seemed less tractable than older ones had been: in the economy, "stagflation," a condition of simultaneous high inflation and unemployment; in social policy, the development of a seemingly permanent underclass; in foreign policy, disorientation about the post-Vietnam American role in world affairs. Many liberals lost confidence in their ability to define the direction of policy change and to develop appropriate programs to achieve it. Some of them joined ranks with ideologically aggressive neoconservatives and New Right intellectuals, whose ideas on supply-side economics, deregulation, administrative decentralization, moral conservatism, nuclear strategy, and a hawkish foreign policy were percolating in conservative think-tanks like the Heritage Foundation, Hoover Institute, and American Enterprise Institute; in journals of opinion (*The Public Interest* and *Commentary,* among them); and in groups of legislators led by Rep. Jack F. Kemp of New York, Rep. David Stockman of Michigan, and others.

The Ford presidency, nominally a continuation of the Nixon administration, inherited the intellectual and social confusion that accompanied this shift from left to right. Ford's was a presidency of stasis. The basic problem in such a presidency is not that the public and its president want different things, as in a presidency of stalemate, but rather that confusion about how government can attain even widely shared goals prevents their accomplishment. In Ford's case, neither he nor his opponents had sure answers to the new problems or to the challenge of energy production and conservation posed by the cartel policies of the Organization of Petroleum Exporting Countries (OPEC). The intellectual uncertainty of the times was especially apparent in the ad hoc twisting and turning of Ford's economic policy: "Whip Inflation Now" was followed by the largest public employment program and budget deficits in peacetime history. The cycle simply stalled, and as the 1976 election approached, many experts wondered whether American politics had entered a period of long-term instability.

195

The Carter Presidency

The results of the 1976 election allowed for virtually no claim of a mandate from the voters: Jimmy Carter's margin of victory over Ford was tiny and his party gained only one additional seat in Congress. Worse, Carter was the first Democratic president in this century to be forced to confront policy problems that were not amenable to the traditional programmatic impulses of his party's coalition. Stagflation seemed chronic, with the "misery index" of unemployment plus inflation at 12 percent in January 1977; the federal budget deficit was growing precipitately, largely because of rapid increases in the costs of Great Society entitlement programs such as Medicare, Medicaid, and food stamps; industrial productivity was declining; and the continuing rise in OPEC oil prices seemed to require severe conservation measures. To complicate matters, Carter had played to the public's disenchantment with government in his campaign, with special attention to bureaucratic inefficiency and the moral laxity of Watergate. This was not a good platform from which to launch an activist reform administration.[5]

Carter came to the presidency with a coherent philosophy about domestic policy, one grounded in an approach of comprehensive solutions based on sound and dispassionate analysis. He was a fiscal conservative and social liberal who thought it was possible to pursue humane social goals through restrained budgetary policies and efficient management. Conservative but tolerant on moral issues, Carter preached conscience and traditional values while eschewing the demands of the religious right to write into law its positions on school prayer and abortion. In general, he tried to articulate the ideal of a national community in contrast to the claims of special interest groups, even those of his own party.[6]

Carter's appeals to morality, fiscal restraint, and national unity, all in the context of traditional liberal ideals, were quite effective during his campaign for the 1976 Democratic nomination, which was decided directly by voters in the caucuses and primaries. But after the convention he was uncomfortable with his responsibility as the party's candidate for president to lead a coalition of unions, minorities, women, farmers, and other organized groups, and most of these traditional Democratic constituencies were uncomfortable with him. His search for a new synthesis of liberalism and conservatism that would broaden the popular appeal of the Democratic party antagonized those groups, which insisted on trying to move the party further to the left. Once in the presidency, Carter found that his social policy initiatives did not bear fruit because there was no organized political constituency for his centrist approach. For example, his welfare reform proposal, which sought to provide greater security for the poor at no additional cost through more efficient design and administration, incurred the opposition of liberals because it was fiscally austere and conservatives because it did not carry austerity to the point of spending reductions. Similarly, Carter vacillated for three years on national health insurance because he could not persuade Sen. Edward Kennedy, the unions, and other liberals to accept what he thought was an economically sound proposal. Kennedy's more comprehensive bill could not pass Congress, but without the liberal senator's support Carter's more modest plan could not pass either. Ultimately, the public became convinced that a president who could not lead his own party must be ineffectual, and Carter lost his original base of support among ordinary voters.[7]

Economic policy provides further illustrations of Carter's predicament. After initial steps in 1977 to reduce unemployment through a stimulus package, the standard Democratic approach, Carter decided that the nation's main economic nemesis was inflation. Returning to a major theme of his campaign, he presented himself to his party's congressional leaders and the groups of the Democratic coalition as a budget balancer, something they associated with conservative Republicanism. Yet Carter's concern for fiscal restraint grew during his term. Indeed, when inflation reached double-digit levels he was willing to risk an election-year recession as a necessary antidote. Ultimately Carter got—and was blamed for—inflation and recession both. More generally, on matters of microeconomic policy, the administration carefully tried to balance the president's fiscal caution with Democratic coalition politics, also at great cost to Carter. On issues such as the minimum wage and farm price subsidies, he usually ended up splitting the difference between his own standards and group demands, which made no one happy. Carter's conservative advisers in the Office of Management and Budget (OMB) urged him to reach past his party to the voters. Liberals in his administration, including Vice President Walter F. Mondale and most of the Domestic Policy Staff, argued with equal persuasiveness that he could not govern without the support of the Democratic coalition. In truth, neither strategy by itself could yield enough returns from one constituency to replace what was lost by neglecting the other.[8]

Like Theodore Roosevelt, Carter was a president whose orientation to change placed him at odds with much of his own party. Unlike the vastly talented Roosevelt, Carter's problems were complicated by his limited repertoire of political skills. As one who felt that, once elected, his main task was to make "correct" decisions and simply explain them, he gave little attention to the persuasive presentation of his policies and himself to the nation. In dealing with other Washington politicians, he showed even less interest in appealing to their political incentives as a means of tactical leadership. As for Carter's management of authority for policy formation, it oscillated between drowning himself in the technical details of some policies, often losing sight of the larger political realities in the process, and freely delegating responsibility for remaining issues to others, usually with little guidance about what he desired. Finally, Carter's strategic sense of the historical possibilities of his admittedly unusual time was limited. The contrast with Kennedy, another president of preparation, is instructive. Kennedy was consciously preparing the way for a presidency of achievement in his second term. He was working with a rising tide, both in his party and among the voters. Carter did not see the need for a preparation stage in which he would select a few crucial goals, nurture political support for them, and tie their enactment to a clear sense of policy direction. Bucking the tide in his party and with no other base of support to substitute for it, Carter tried to be a president of achievement.

Still, despite his woes in office and his humiliating defeat in the 1980 election, Carter served as a president of preparation for Reagan and his policies. The themes of Carter's administration, the most conservative of any twentieth century Democrat, foreshadowed Reagan: moral conservatism, by example and exhortation if not by legislation; fiscal conservatism in the realm of social policy; a preoccupation with inflation, growth, and deregulation in economic policy (Carter's success in securing legislative deregulation of the airline, trucking, and banking industries was unparalleled); and an antibureaucracy, anti-Washington-politics-as-usual posture that more than anything else accounted for his rise from the obscure status of a former southern governor to the presidential nomination of the Democratic party.

In foreign policy, too, Carter prepared the way for Reagan. Although he campaigned in 1976 with a call for defense spending reductions, even beyond the decreases that had occurred under Nixon and Ford, Carter reversed course in office and increased spending every year. Equally important, he altered the basis of the U.S. stance toward the Soviet Union and other nations from Nixon and Ford's style of pragmatism to judgmental moralism in the service of human rights.

The Reagan Presidency: First Term

Carter's actions as president reflected his rhetoric but were unable to fulfill it. In 1980 voters' concerns about inflation, high taxes, slow growth, excessive regulation, big government, and the decline of American power in international politics and economics, although not moving them squarely into the conservative camp, did create a climate in which a candidate who promised great and sudden policy change could thrive. Reagan's election was clearly in the achievement mode: he pledged enormous tax cuts, serious reductions in social spending, and an unprecedented peacetime defense buildup; won by the largest electoral vote margin against an incumbent president in history; and secured substantial gains for his party in Congress—33 seats in the House (the highest increase in a presidential election year since Johnson in 1964) and 12 seats in the Senate, which gave the Republicans control for the first time since 1955.

Seizing the moment, Reagan moved on almost all fronts during his first months in office. For domestic policy ideas, he drew from the ranks of supply-side economists and other conservative intellectuals in the universities and think-tanks and from Stockman's draconian "Dunkirk memorandum" on the federal budget. His initial budget included 84 proposals to reduce or eliminate federal programs. A *New York Times* survey later found that he had won on 60 percent of them, including assaults on political "untouchables" such as housing assistance, public service employment, food stamps, child nutrition, and aid to working welfare mothers. (Most important, these victories involved "85 to 90 percent of the dollar savings he wanted in 1981.")[9] Reagan also was able to reduce the number of federal categorical grant programs to state and local governments to 259 from 361 by eliminating some and consolidating others into block grants, which gave the states and localities more discretion about how the money would be spent. (At the same time, that money was substantially reduced.)[10] His Task Force on Regulatory Relief, with Vice President George Bush as its chairman, checked the historical increase in new federal regulations, and his reductions in the enforcement divisions of agencies such as the Federal Trade Commission and the Occupational Safety and Health Administration diminished the effectiveness of existing ones. Reagan secured the enactment of a three-year, 25-percent cut in the federal income tax on individuals, with indexing of the tax brackets to changes in the cost of living to start soon after. (Corporations and the wealthy received additional tax relief.) On August 13, 1981, a denim- and cowboy-boot-clad president was able to stand before reporters at a bill-signing ceremony at his California ranch and proclaim with little fear of contradiction that he had achieved "the biggest tax cut and the greatest reduction in federal spending in our nation's history."

Congress's acquiescence in all this was nearly complete. House Republicans supported the president on the two most important budget votes by margins of 190-0 and 190-1, respectively. Republicans in the Senate voted 51-1 with Reagan on the budget and 80 percent of the time with him overall in 1981, the highest index of loyalty since Congressional Quarterly began making measurements in 1953.[11] The conservative coalition also had its best year ever, winning 92 percent of the votes on which it was active, as Republicans were joined by conservative "Boll Weevil" Democrats, who represented districts in which Reagan and his policies were especially popular.[12] Even the House Democratic leadership bowed to Reagan's power in 1981, offering an alternative plan of budget and tax cuts that was very similar to the president's and, more important, handing over virtual control of the legislative agenda to the Republicans. An aide to Speaker Thomas P. O'Neill, Jr., said:

> What the Democrats did, in extraordinary fashion, was to recognize the cataclysmic nature of the 1980 election results. The American public wanted this new president to be given a chance to try out his programs. We weren't going to come across as being obstructionists.

Reagan's mark on security policy was equally distinct. Matching his own convictions to the new strategic thinking of conservative intellectuals in the Heritage Foundation, the Committee on the Present Danger, and certain universities, Reagan had argued throughout the 1980 campaign that Carter's increases in defense spending were inadequate to match the supposed speed of the Soviet arms buildup and that the United States soon would face a "window of vulnerability" to Russian nuclear superiority. Once in office, again drawing on conservative intellectual capital and again with Congress's eager complicity, he massively increased defense spending in general and weapons procurement in particular, downplayed strategic arms negotiations with the Soviet Union pending the "restoration" of American military might, and let it be known that his administration would resist communist advances throughout the world, especially in nations of the Western Hemisphere such as El Salvador, Nicaragua, and, as it turned out, Grenada. Like Carter, he viewed foreign policy in moral terms; unlike Carter, he defined anticommunism rather than human rights as the paramount moral tenet that the United States should try to fulfill. At his first news conference, Reagan said that the Russians "reserve unto themselves the right to commit any crime, to lie, to cheat"; later he described the Soviet Union as "the evil empire."

Reagan saw himself from the start as a president in the mold of Franklin Roosevelt. Like his Democratic predecessor, Reagan wished to bring a new deal to the nation that would form the basis for a new political era, a Republican one. He had all the rhetorical skills required of a president of achievement: having spent most of his adult life either as a public speaker or before the camera as an actor, he was particularly adept at clarifying complex issues through a simple, straightforward, smoothly delivered message. Reagan's presentational skills supplemented his sense that voters wanted root-and-branch solutions to the problems that concerned them. Traditional "stop-go" Republican policies, with moderate economic stimulus followed by belt-tightening response, would have been no more popular for Reagan than they had been for Ford. Similarly, the "realism" of the Nixon-Ford foreign policy of détente and restraint would not have revived the politically appealing idea of national power and prestige. Reagan also realized that both as an overall strategy and as a tactical ploy with members of Congress and other Washington politicians he should set his policy course and stay with it, even in the face of short-term adversity, such as the recession of 1981-1982, thus conveying a strong sense of purpose and self-confidence that reinforced the perception of him as a leader. This belief carried over into his management of authority within the executive branch; there he reserved fundamental choices to himself and delegated almost everything else to lieutenants who had been appointed to the White House staff, Office of Management and Budget, the departments and agencies primarily because of their political loyalty and ideological purity. Sometimes this created a buffer that detached the president from unpleasant but important realities, which his more politically attuned advisers knew he needed—but did not want—to hear, but it made persistence in policy easier for him to maintain.

By the end of Reagan's first term, a welter of numbers testified to the new directions he had imposed on government, both in foreign and domestic affairs. Spending on Aid to Families with Dependent Children was down 13 percent ($1.3 billion) from what it would have been if the nation had simply continued the budget policies that were in place when Reagan became president. Spending on food stamps was down 13 percent ($2 billion). Medicaid spending was 6 percent lower; housing assistance, 4 percent; compensatory education, 17 percent; child nutrition, 28 percent. Public service employment, a $4.5 billion program, had been eliminated. In all, spending on the nondefense activities of the federal government other than Social Security and Medicare was 12.5 percent less in real dollars than when Reagan took office, and the proportion of the total economy devoted to social programs was rapidly descending to the level that existed prior to the passage of Johnson's Great Society. Meanwhile, defense spending was up 48.7 percent in real dollars, and the federal work force, which had been reduced by 10 percent in the domestic bureaucracies, had risen in the defense department.[13]

Not all of Reagan's proposals for policy change were adopted, but even the failures are illuminated by the cycle theory. His efforts to turn the nation's environmental policies in a conservative direction provoked a hostile and politically overwhelming response, as did his attempts to remove civil rights landmarks such as the Voting Rights Act and the Internal Revenue Service policy of denying tax-exempt status to racially segregated schools. Unlike those policies with which Reagan was successful, these were areas in which no period of public education had occurred through a presidency of preparation. (Indeed, Carter strongly supported environmental and civil rights efforts.) Reagan's stance on moral issues was shrewder, if no more successful. Although his electoral debt to the religious right meant that he could not adopt Carter's position of personal moral conservatism but official tolerance, Reagan did downplay the proposed constitutional amendments on school prayer and abortion for the sake of pursuing his economic and defense policies. At the same time, he frequently invoked traditional American values in more general and less controversial terms, to good effect. Finally, there was Reagan's greatest failure, which eventually became his greatest political problem: four years of unprecedented 12-figure budget deficits that, taken together, almost doubled the national debt. Reagan's policies helped to achieve certain macroeconomic wonders—a decline in inflation from 12 percent to 4 percent chief among them—but the budgetary effects of his defense increases and tax cuts simply overwhelmed those of his domestic spending cuts. (The unemployment rate for his first term ended up where it began, at 7 percent, but only after rising to a 40-year high of more than 10 percent in 1982, which cost the Republicans dearly in the midterm congressional elections and consequently brought the achievement phase of the first term almost to an end.)

Reagan's status as a president of achievement rests on a firmer foundation than any tally sheet of particular successes and failures. His policies, in addition to being dramatic, involved a sufficiently clear change in the direction of federal activity as to make them heroically incremental in the tradition of other presidents of achievement. Although conservative in substance, they were imbued with familiar cultural optimism about the capacity of political engineering to bring about desired change: prosperity through tax cuts, the defeat of leftist revolutionaries abroad through American military aid and advice, and so on. Finally, more than anything, Reagan transformed the agenda of political discussion, including the liberal Democratic component of it. He "redefined the terms of the national debate," lamented historian Arthur M. Schlesinger, Jr., a longtime adviser to Democratic politicians and presidents. "In domestic affairs, he placed a stigma on 'big government' and exalted the capacity of the unregulated marketplace to solve all our problems. In foreign affairs, he placed a stigma on détente and exalted large military budgets and an indefinitely escalating arms race." [14] Sen. Ernest Hollings of South Carolina, a candidate for the Democratic presidential nomination in 1984, echoed Schlesinger: "Reagan has changed the political dialogue in this country so that instead of thinking about how to spend money, all we can do is think about how to cut." (This was true except in defense, where even liberals called for real increases of 3 percent per year.) That Democrats selected as their main point of attack on Reagan the great unmet pledge of his 1980 campaign for a balanced budget was the highest tribute of all, albeit a backhanded one, to his political prowess. The assumption on the eve of the 1984 campaign seemed to be that Reagan's transformation of the national agenda had been so complete that the only politically effective argument against him was a traditional conservative one.

The Democrats in 1984

Nomination. Since the death in 1945 of Franklin Roosevelt, the tapestry that is the Democratic party's New Deal coalition—labor and southerners; blacks, Jews, and ethnics; union workers, government employees, and intellectuals—has been slowly unraveling. The status of the party in 1984 aggravated this condition: for the first time, the Democrats were the out-party during a presidency of achievement, compelled to react to a changed national agenda rather than write the agenda themselves. The three candidates for the party's presidential nomination who remained serious contenders after the sound and fury of the Iowa caucus and New Hampshire primary—Mondale, Jesse Jackson, and Sen. Gary Hart—each represented a theory about how the Democratic party should cope with the new political reality.

Mondale grounded his campaign in the belief that political majorities are constructed group by group. He had risen in politics through the Democratic-Farmer-Labor party in Minnesota, whose very name reflects this understanding, and as Carter's vice president he had represented the demands of unions, teachers' organizations, women's groups, and other party constituency groups in a generally unsympathetic administration. Fortunately for Mondale, these groups, determined not to be left on the periphery of another Democratic administration, had decided to make early candidate endorsements in order to influence the party's presidential nomination. Mondale won the support of the AFL-CIO, the National Education Association (NEA), the National Organization for Women (NOW), and others before the primaries and caucuses began. This gave him an electoral base and made clear to voters who he was. But it also left him vulnerable to the charge that he was a "captive of the special interests." Mondale's problems on this point were dramatized as early as the caucus-eve debate in Iowa, when he refused to respond to Hart's request that he name a single issue on which he differed with organized labor.

As a preacher and civil rights activist with no governmental experience, Jackson never was regarded as a serious contender for the presidency. Nevertheless, his vote-getting ability in the primaries made him a leader in the battle for the soul of the Democratic party. If Mondale's roots were in the New Deal, Jackson's were in the Great Society and the poor and minority groups it had helped to politicize. His proposals for a massive public employment program, renewed federal spending on social service agencies, and a foreign policy centered on the Third World were efforts to forge a "Rainbow Coalition" of blacks, Hispanics, Indians, and other minorities. He also reached out to those whites whose political orientations had been formed by the antiwar movement of the late 1960s with a plan to reduce defense spending dramatically. Jackson's campaign really took off, however, only when he decided to concentrate his appeals on blacks, articulating their demand for a larger voice in the party that they regularly provided with one-fourth to one-third of its electoral support.

Hart's rise to front-runner status with Mondale after his smashing victory in the New Hampshire primary was the greatest political surprise of 1984. Hart directly challenged Mondale's understanding of the Democratic party as a congeries of groups and tried instead to define a party identity that transcended narrow political interests and adapted traditional liberal values to contemporary social and economic conditions. In that sense he was carrying on Carter's work, extending it beyond a simple stance of fiscal conservatism and social liberalism with more tangible ideas. It is hardly accidental that, although Carter loyally endorsed his former vice president, Hart won the support of Patrick Caddell, Carter's pollster and political strategist. Caddell had been searching for a candidate who could do more skillfully what he constantly had urged Carter to do: appeal over the heads of the entrenched party leadership and coalition to a new generation of voters by offering a sense of youth, daring, and vision.[15]

Caddell's concern was for style and strategy: Hart supplied the substance by drawing ideas from young Democratic intellectuals like economists Lester Thurow and Robert Reich and a group of innovative defense strategists he met through Congress's Military Reform Caucus, which he had founded. The central theme of Hart's economic appeal was the need for government to stimulate growth by promoting high-tech industries without undue intervention or regulation. Wage increases were to be tied to improvements in productivity, and social programs would be streamlined. Economic protectionism was to be avoided, as was government support for failing firms. (Hart opposed domestic content legislation and had voted against the bailout of the Chrysler Corporation.) Defense spending would be more discriminating, eschewing large and technologically complex weapons in favor of smaller, simpler, and more mobile ones.[16]

Hart's ideas appealed to the young, educated professionals whom Democrats had lost to Reagan in 1980 and who were hostile to the more traditional Mondale. But he had little to say to blacks, workers, and other mainstream Democratic voters. This was painfully apparent in the Pennsylvania primary, which ended Hart's realistic chances of winning the nomination. Mondale trumpeted Hart's vote against Chrysler to workers in the ailing steel industry and promised immediate protection from foreign competition. Hart's vision of future productivity through new technology seemed remote to people who were out of work.

Mondale, Jackson, Hart—the limitation of all three contenders was that the strategies that animated their candidacies were incomplete. The pieces of a healthy electoral coalition existed, but the common beliefs that could forge them together were lacking. A healthy Democratic party would include each of the three candidates' supporters bound together by shared ideals and agreed-upon policy ideas that transcend but satisfy group demands. Hart came closest to a successful strategy with his realization that a liberal party cannot be competitive in presidential elections without broad support from the middle and professional classes. It is perhaps no surprise that Hart and Carter were outsiders in the Democratic party. Such outsiders often appear at crucial transition periods in presidential politics. In that sense Carter and Hart were cut from the same cloth as Wendell Willkie, Adlai Stevenson, and George Wallace.

General Election. In the campaign against Reagan, Mondale tried to break free of his identity as the candidate of the Democratic party's past in order to broaden his appeal to voters who had supported Hart. He chose Rep. Geraldine Ferraro of New York as his vice presidential running mate, a decision his staff portrayed as bold and path breaking, even as critics charged that it was simply the latest example of Mondale caving in to the special interest groups, this time to NOW. More significantly, Mondale accepted most of the achievements of Reagan's first term and campaigned as a would-be president of consolidation who not only would make Reagan's policies fairer but would complete the agenda of the 1980 campaign and balance the budget. Specifically, Mondale pledged to continue increasing defense spending, although at a slower rate than Reagan; leave most but not all of the domestic budget reductions intact; and preserve the 1981 tax cut and the plan to start indexing in 1985, except for those in the higher tax brackets. In foreign policy he belatedly endorsed the Grenada invasion, said he might "quarantine" Nicaragua, and oscillated between accenting his commitment to arms control and his toughness as a prospective commander in chief. (In the foreign policy debate, Mondale used the word "strength" 39 times; he said "peace" twice.)

These were shrewd decisions on Mondale's part, but to no avail: he never really had a chance. Mondale simply could not dent the public's satisfaction with a president who, it was felt, had brought peace, prosperity, and, as Mondale himself conceded, renewed feelings of patriotic pride to most Americans. Historically, voters always have rewarded presidents of achievement with reelection. But even if they had decided to vote in 1984 for a president who would move the cycle on to its consolidation stage, they would have had no more plausible choice than Reagan, who campaigned entirely on the record of his first term and promised no new policy innovations in the second.

Prospects for Reagan's Second Term

All reelected presidents share a common condition, namely, that having served a first term, they are beginning their last term. Presumably, four years of on-the-job training have taught the president and his team a great deal about governing that they could have learned no other way. Presumably, too, the administration will start to benefit from the absence of reelection distractions. But the burdens that accrue to a second-term president may be greater than the benefits. In the first two years, he will suffer the absence of the automatic honeymoon period that newly elected (but not reelected) presidents enjoy, as well as the presence of politically intractable problems that may have been postponed from the first term until after the election. In the latter two years, the president probably will face his most hostile Congress ever, given the historical pattern of disastrous second-term congressional elections. Worst of all, he will become a lame duck, increasingly uninteresting and unimportant as all eyes turn to the selection of his successor.

For a president of consolidation, the liabilities of second-term status will be less than for others—his modest policy purposes can be accomplished largely through the inherent constitutional and administrative powers of the office. But for a president of preparation or achievement who by definition wants change, the only real vaccine against domestic policy stalemate in the second term is that it be ushered in by an achievement-style reelection—a landslide victory for the president and large gains for his congressional party in response to a campaign whose theme is dramatic policy innovation.

A Continued Presidency of Achievement?

Reagan did not wage the kind of reelection campaign that could have empowered him for another round of domestic policy achievement. His speeches stressed the record of the past four years, not the promise of the next four, and only sporadically did he offer his coattails to Republican candidates for Congress. The result was an enormous personal victory for Reagan but little else. Not having asked for a mandate, the president could hardly claim to have one. Nor did he try—in a postelection news conference he refused even to use the word.

It seems unlikely, then, that Reagan will push for domestic policy changes on the order of those achieved in his first term. An occasional fiery speech to the religious right aside, he probably will soft-pedal moral issues like school prayer and abortion because they are so unpopular with young professionals who like his other policies and whose support he would like to keep. The same will be true of environmental deregulation. Another favored Reagan theme—the decentralization of federal power to the state and localities—also will get only lip service from the president because it generates so little of the public excitement needed to overcome the power of the entrenched interests that favor the status quo.

What, then, will be the central questions that are taken up by the second Reagan administration? The budget deficit must be faced one way or another because it may threaten the economic recovery that assured Reagan's reelection. In addition, the reduction of nuclear arms through a negotiated agreement with the Soviet Union may need to be pursued because defense spending is so destructive of any deficit-reduction effort. These issues, usually regarded as separate, are more likely to be regarded as interrelated during the next four years, and the strategies developed for their resolution will be tests of presidential resilience and creativity.

The difficulties that face the president if he simply continues the policy of inaction on the budget that he followed in the first term may be enormous. If annual deficits stay in the $200-billion range for several years, financial pressures, especially from foreign investors concerned about the overvalued dollar and from the continued high interest rates the government must pay to attract private capital to finance its borrowing, could move the economy gradually into a state of decline in which growth would cease. In such an instance, unemployment would rise and recession reappear in short order. Reagan's popularity probably would plummet in response, as it did in 1982. Congress, for its part, would look for ways to pump federal money into the economy rather than cut domestic spending. As for arms reduction, continued intransigence by the administration will make it ever more difficult to achieve much, for two reasons. First, the increasing technological sophistication of weapons systems is aggravating the problem of monitoring compliance and therefore is reducing confidence on both sides that any verifiable agreement can be reached. Second, mutual distrust and misunderstanding between the United States and the Soviet

207

Union, which certainly antedates Reagan, will continue to worsen the longer it lasts.

Despite the high risks of failure that would attend continued presidential inaction on the deficits and arms control, such a course would be consistent with Reagan's political style and beliefs. His style is to set a general policy direction, rouse public support for it through speechmaking, and delegate the development of specific programs to subordinates. This works well when there is strong political support for the direction he wants to take and when the lieutenants charged with policy formation are in general agreement with him and with each other. These conditions existed in the first term and made possible the tax cuts, domestic spending reductions, and defense buildup. Although they may no longer exist, especially with regard to the budget and arms control issues, the president will be loathe to abandon a style that has worked so well in the past and that suits his preference for "rhetoric" over "homework." [17] And style aside, Reagan really seems to believe, perhaps beyond all possibility of persuasion to the contrary, that the supply-side tax cuts of the first term will stimulate business activity and economic growth to such a degree that the deficit will shrink. He also may think that through continued weapons buildups, he can force the Soviets to negotiate an arms control agreement that is highly favorable to the United States.

President Reagan may be right in each of these beliefs. But if, as seems quite possible, the deficits do not go away and Reagan does not alter his leadership style or philosophy to meet them, domestic policy stalemate seems the likely fate of the second term. This being the case, Reagan may do what other second-term presidents of achievement have done and turn to foreign affairs as an arena for dramatic accomplishment. At various times, he has spoken longingly of his desire to break free of the pattern of earlier incremental arms control agreements and negotiate a sweeping nuclear disarmament treaty with the Soviet Union. Such an achievement would solve most of Reagan's problems both abroad and at home (through reduced defense spending), but he may not be willing to immerse himself in the details of nuclear weaponry and impose his views on more hawkish and anti-Soviet advisers. In any event, he would need the cooperation of the Soviet Union, whose leaders historically have preferred to move cautiously in this area.

Reagan's foreign policy initiatives may as easily run to war as to peace. Given his hard-line views about communism in Central America and about the Soviet Union as the "evil empire" (with Cuba its minion), Reagan may seize upon some provocation as reason to engage in military action in Cuba or Nicaragua. Polls show the public to be unhappy with the administration's first-term policies in Central America, but its enthusiastic support of the Grenada invasion in October 1983 indicates that it may respond more favorably to an all-out military effort. (After the invasion, Reagan's public approval rating rose—and stayed—above 50 percent for the first time since 1981.) Historically, the only wars Americans have opposed have been halfway efforts, such as Korea and Vietnam, in which no attempt was made by the president to rouse the nationalistic, even messianic, sense of purpose that is so deeply ingrained in American political culture. With Reagan's rhetorical capacity to "make the eagle soar," he may find war a way to continue to shape history while simultaneously diverting attention from the budget deficits.

A Presidency of Consolidation?

The logic of the political situation that was created by Reagan's enormous but coattail- and mandate-less reelection suggests an alternate strategy of presidential politics and policy making during the second term. The president lacks a working majority in Congress, a condition that is likely to worsen after the 1986 midterm elections, in which 22 Republican and only 12 Democratic Senate seats will be at stake and in which the out-party historically has made sweeping gains in the House. Facing this reality, Reagan may decide to rest on the achievements of his first term and work to consolidate them into the fabric of government. The best way to accomplish this would be to reach out for a bipartisan coalition in Congress and the country in support of a compromise package of spending reductions, including both defense and domestic programs, and a tax increase combined with tax reform. Similarly, he could offer concessions to the Soviet Union that would make it possible for the two nations to negotiate the sort of incremental arms control agreement that came out of the Strategic Arms Limitation Talks (SALT) in the Nixon, Ford, and Carter administrations.

There also are administrative questions from the first term to be dealt with, the inevitable aftermath of a presidency of achievement. The speed of rearmament meant little attention was given to economy or efficiency, thus calling many of the Pentagon's procurement procedures into question. The successive fiascos in Lebanon suggest a need for better management of the nation's military field operations. And it is not at all clear that the Reagan administration has found an effective way to institutionalize the newly active role of OMB in program analysis.

To be sure there would be drawbacks to a strategy of consolidation. Any effort by Reagan to join with Democrats to create a majority coalition for deficit reduction and arms control will generate deep conflicts in the Republican party, both within the administration and in Congress, especially the House. Republican archconservatives like representatives

Jack Kemp and Newt Gingrich would fight tax increases bitterly because they have staked their political careers on the populist appeal of supply-side economics. Similarly, a strong presidential initiative for an incremental arms control agreement would trigger opposition not only among congressional Republicans but in Reagan's own Department of Defense.

Still, a concentration on second-term consolidation offers Reagan certain advantages. More than anything else it would acknowledge the limited possibilities of second-term presidencies that are not ushered in by achievement-style reelections. It also would implicate congressional Democrats in the president's policies, thereby making Republican dissenters seem almost unpatriotic. Finally, consolidation having been the traditional domain of conservative presidents, it would not be that far out of character for a president of achievement who happens to be conservative to seek consolidation. Reagan himself worked closely with the Democratic legislature during his second term as governor of California and, even in his first term as president, showed a willingness to accommodate the opposition when all else failed through bipartisan commissions on subjects such as Social Security, Central America, and the MX missile system.

A Presidency of Stasis?

There is a third possibility for the second term, that of a tired president who lets things drift into stasis by failing to choose between the achievement and consolidation strategies and who offers instead symbolic leadership without decisive purpose of any kind. When Eisenhower left office he said that no one older than he should serve in the presidency. Eisenhower was 70; Reagan turned 74 two weeks after inauguration day and will be almost 78 at the end of his term. He is an unusually youthful and vigorous man, but one cannot be certain that he will remain so.

The policy effects of a tired presidency of stasis in the second term are hard to ascertain—it all depends on who or what would fill the void. But a near-certain political result would be strong factional struggles within the Republican party on economic and defense policies—worse than those one would expect if Reagan were to set a clear course of any kind and heightened by the battle for the 1988 party presidential nomination. The strength of the Republican party and the Reagan administration has been its high degree of presidentially forged unity. A tired president would not be able to maintain that.

Conclusion

The cyclic theory of politics and policy is an analytic, not a predictive, tool; it can help to predict the resources for and limits on action within a period, but presidents have styles and purposes of their own. Acknowledging this and barring war, disarmament, or other dramatic foreign policy developments whose political effects are impossible to know, it seems likely that for some time economic policy will have a much stronger influence on presidential politics than foreign or social policy. If that is the case, three scenarios seem plausible.

1. Supply-side economics, however it may be redefined or revised, will be pursued by the Reagan administration and will produce continued economic prosperity, with deficits shrinking to a smaller share of the Gross National Product or coming to be regarded as unimportant to the economy. Should this happen, the conservative hold on the Republican party will be strengthened, and voters likely will choose a succession of Republican presidents, perhaps after an intervening Democratic presidency of consolidation. Party realignment, with Republicans replacing Democrats as the nation's majority party, probably would occur.

2. The president's economic policies will embody a compromise that blurs the partisan advantage of economic success (or the disadvantage of failure). Such an outcome probably would not affect the existing balance between the parties in any serious way.

3. Supply-side economics will be tried, as in the first scenario, but will fail, prompting large Democratic gains in the midterm congressional elections of 1986 and the election of a Democrat as president in 1988. In such an instance, of course, the new president will face the enormously difficult task of simultaneously closing the budget deficit and bringing the economy out of recession.

The third scenario is in some ways the most complex of the three. If Democrats were to misread the meaning of their election victories in 1986 and 1988 and revert to old policies and programs, a period of stasis would ensue. Problems would remain unsolved, with frequent alternations in power by the parties as they struggled with economic problems that neither could solve. This is a real danger, in view of the Democrats' experience during Reagan's first term. In the wake of the 1980 election, even traditional Democrats like Mondale began an active search for new liberal economic ideas to replace the no-longer-effective theories of the past. But the party's rebound in the 1982 midterm elections, which occurred in the midst of the recession, deluded them into thinking that the old New Deal coalition would simply knit itself back together again in 1984, wanting the same old policies.

Party leaders were wrong in 1984, and regardless of what happens in the elections of 1986 and 1988 they will be wrong again if they fail to recognize that traditional New Deal and Great Society policies will not restore them to dominance. No doubt the power of the party's organized constituencies will ensure that Democratic policies promote a concern for social justice and economic opportunity. But to build a national coalition, these policies also must make the economy work for the middle class. Fortunately, from the party's standpoint, a new generation of Democratic presidential politicians will be on center stage in 1988—Hart will be joined by senators like Bill Bradley, Sam Nunn, Dale Bumpers, Jay Rockefeller, and Joseph Biden and governors like Mario Cuomo, Michael Dukakis, and Bruce Babbitt. These are leaders who came of age in the idealism of the New Frontier and Great Society but who first cut their teeth in politics on the failure in Vietnam and the economic troubles of the 1970s. Their formative years have been spent trying to invent new strategies and ideas that can be harnessed to their personal ambitions. Unless Reagan's economic policies succeed in a way that sweeps all before them, these Democrats may be able to forge a new coalition from new ideas that will prepare the way for a fifth cycle of politics and policy.

Notes

1. Gerald Ford, "Imperiled, Not Imperial," *Time,* November 10, 1980, 30-31; Thomas Franck, ed., *The Tethered Presidency* (New York: New York University Press, 1981); Michael Nelson, "The Revolving-Door Presidency," *Miami Herald,* November 9, 1980; and Paul C. Light, *The President's Agenda* (Baltimore: Johns Hopkins University Press, 1982).
2. Lou Cannon, "Reagan Looks Ahead to Unfinished Business," *Washington Post National Weekly Edition,* February 6, 1984, 11; Anthony Lewis, "Imperial Presidency on the Rise," *Nashville Tennessean,* January 10, 1984.
3. A fuller treatment of the theory of cycles can be found in Erwin C. Hargrove and Michael Nelson, *Presidents, Politics, and Policy* (Baltimore: Johns Hopkins University Press, 1984), especially chapters 3, 4, 6, 7, and 8. The theory applies to the twentieth century because only then did the federal government, in particular the presidency, become the main object of the public's political demands.
4. Morris Fiorina, *Retrospective Voting in National Elections* (New Haven: Yale University Press, 1981).
5. Herbert Stein, *Presidential Economics* (New York: Simon and Schuster, 1984), Chapter 6.
6. Jimmy Carter, *Why Not the Best?* (New York: Bantam Books, 1975), Chapter 16.
7. Laurence E. Lynn, Jr., and David deF. Whitman, *The President as Policymaker* (Philadelphia: Temple University Press, 1981); Joseph Califano, *Governing America* (New York: Simon and Schuster, 1981), Chapter 3.

8. "Oral History Interview with Charles Schultze," in *The President and Economic Policy Formation,* ed. by Erwin C. Hargrove and Samuel Morley (Boulder, Colo.: Westview Press, 1984), 463-501.
9. Robert Pear, "The Reagan Revolution," *New York Times,* January 31, 1984.
10. John L. Palmer and Isabel V. Sawhill, "Overview," in *The Reagan Revolution,* ed. by John L. Palmer and Isabel V. Sawhill (Cambridge, Mass.: Ballinger, 1984), 17.
11. Bill Keller, "Voting Record of '81 Shows the Romance and Fidelity of Reagan Honeymoon on Hill," *Congressional Quarterly Weekly Report,* January 2, 1982, 19.
12. Irwin B. Arieff, "Conservatives Hit New High in Showdown Vote Victories," *Congressional Quarterly Weekly Report,* January 9, 1982, 50.
13. These figures are drawn from Nicholas Lemann, "The Culture of Poverty," *Atlantic* (September 1984): 26; David Gergen, "Is Ronald Reagan Really Ready for the Future?" *Washington Post National Weekly Edition,* March 5, 1984, 23; and Nicholas Lemann, "The Peacetime War," *Atlantic* (October 1984): 71.
14. Arthur M. Schlesinger, Jr., "The Democratic Party after Ted Kennedy," *Wall Street Journal,* December 7, 1982.
15. Martin Schramm, "A Memo to Someone Who Isn't Running Helped Hart Take Off," *Washington Post National Weekly Edition,* March 19, 1984, 10.
16. Gary Hart, *A New Democracy* (New York: William Morrow, 1983).
17. James David Barber, "Classifying and Predicting Presidential Style: Two 'Weak' Presidents," *Journal of Social Issues* (July 1968): 51-80.

8. CONGRESS: POLITICS AFTER A LANDSLIDE WITHOUT COATTAILS

Gary C. Jacobson

Ronald Reagan's landslide victory over Walter F. Mondale in 1984 could hardly have been more decisive, yet its full meaning and consequences remain elusive. Was it purely a personal victory, as Democrats would like to believe? Was it a mandate for a conservative policy agenda, as some Republicans claim? Did it signal the long-awaited partisan realignment, the final breakup of the New Deal coalition and the emergence of a new Republican majority?

The answers to these questions remain obscure because the Republican sweep was confined to the top of the ticket; Reagan's landslide was without coattails in the popular meaning of the term. Republicans picked up only 14 additional seats in the House of Representatives, well short of the 24 seats they needed to match the 192 seats they held after the 1980 election; this left the Democrats with a 253-182 House majority for the 99th Congress. Republicans suffered a net loss of two Senate seats, reducing their majority in that body to 53-47. Despite evidence that Reagan's victory entailed far more than a ratification of his personal leadership, Republicans were unable to achieve significant gains in Congress. My purpose in this essay is to explain why and to examine what this failure portends for national politics in the second Reagan administration.

A Landslide without Coattails

Election outcomes like that of 1984—landslides without coattails—are by no means unprecedented. In the last 30 years four other presidential candidates have won more than 55 percent of the two-party presidential vote; they are listed in Table 8.1. In two of these elections—1964, when President Lyndon B. Johnson defeated Sen. Barry Goldwater, and 1980, when Reagan defeated President Jimmy Carter—the winner's party also enjoyed major congressional gains. In the other two—

1956, when President Dwight D. Eisenhower beat Gov. Adlai Stevenson, and 1972, when President Richard Nixon defeated Sen. George McGovern—it did not. Reagan's 1984 reelection clearly fits into the second pattern. Why? The explanation, which applies mainly to the House elections—I will deal with the more idiosyncratic Senate contests later—has two basic parts. One, which is best understood by comparing 1984 with the other four landslide elections, lies in specific qualities of the presidential campaign itself. The other lies in the kinds of individual congressional campaigns waged across the nation by the hundreds of candidates of the two parties. The defining characteristic of present-day congressional elections is that they are predominantly local affairs.[1] Indeed, the electoral effects of national political phenomena of any kind, including issues, party labels, and presidential candidates, depend on how they are incorporated into local congressional campaigns.

In a candidate-centered system of electoral politics, the relative quality of the individual candidates and the resources they have to expend on the campaign are naturally crucial. Because the great majority of congressional incumbents are effective candidates, benefit from generous perquisites of office, and can raise as much money as they need to finance a full-scale campaign, most of what varies from election to election concerns differences in the quality and resources of challengers and the number of districts that lack an incumbent. This means that to take away any significant number of congressional seats from the opposition, a party must field a formidable, well-financed group of challengers to incumbents and candidates for seats that have become open because the incumbent has retired, lost a primary, or decided to run for another office.

Most of the time, members of Congress who seek reelection do not face very serious challengers and so win by default. Normally, the odds on

Table 8.1 Coattails in Landslide Elections, 1956-1984

Year	Winning Presidential Candidate	Party	Percentage of the Two-Party Vote	Net Congressional Seat Shift House	Senate
1956	Dwight D. Eisenhower	R	58%	2 D	1 D
1964	Lyndon B. Johnson	D	61	37 D	1 D
1972	Richard Nixon	R	62	12 R	2 D
1980	Ronald Reagan	R	55	34 R	12 R
1984	Ronald Reagan	R	59	14 R	2 D

defeating an incumbent are so long that the best potential candidates—ambitious professional politicians with experience in elective office—refuse to risk their political careers and reputations. They are fully aware that a great deal of money is needed to mount a serious campaign; they also know that campaign contributors are less than generous to candidates who cannot demonstrate a plausible chance of winning. Thus, unless for some reason the chances of defeating the incumbent in a particular district seem unusually favorable, a formidable challenger is unlikely to emerge. Typically, the nomination goes by default to some underfinanced amateur who poses no threat to the incumbent.

When the chances of winning do seem unusually favorable, stronger challengers enter the fray, and campaign contributors are more easily persuaded to invest in their campaigns. Since attractive and experienced candidates with money to advertise their virtues do well in candidate-centered electoral contests, an element of self-fulfilling prophecy is at work. Challenges are more likely to be successful when potential candidates and potential donors anticipate success and act accordingly.

How well a party does collectively in an election thus depends to an important degree on the number of strong challenges it mounts locally. This in turn depends on how its potential candidates and contributors assess the party's chances on election day. Although a final decision about whether or not to run can be delayed until the early months of the election year, a full-scale campaign must begin at least a year in advance of the election. This means that potential candidates are forced to guess how national tides are likely to be moving long before this can be estimated with much certainty. Campaign contributors can delay their decisions until political trends are clearer; still, the money can be used most effectively by challengers if it arrives early in the campaign. And contributors are limited to a choice among the candidates who finally do emerge.

One necessary condition for long presidential coattails, then, is that serious congressional candidates of the president-elect's party anticipate a good year well in advance and so position themselves to take advantage of the electoral benefits that later flow from the top of the ticket. This was clearly true of Republican congressional candidates in 1980. Some, particularly in Senate contests, no doubt were helped by Reagan's victory; but they, and especially Republican challengers in House elections, had to realize vote increases far larger than the national party average in order to win. Only six House seats would have shifted to the Republicans in 1980 if every Republican had enjoyed merely the average vote swing from 1978 to 1980 of 3 percentage points in their favor. Actually, Republicans picked up 34 seats, with victorious Republican challengers enjoying an average increase of 13 percentage points over the vote that candidates of their party received in 1978. Strong individual candidacies were a crucial source of Reagan's coattails in 1980.[2]

This suggests one reason for the absence of coattails four years later: too few Republican challengers were positioned to benefit from Reagan's sweep. Campaign professionals in both parties concurred that Republicans "didn't field a good enough group of candidates to take advantage of the political climate out there." [3] Why did so few strong Republican candidates emerge to exploit such a golden opportunity? There is no single answer; several circumstances conspired to limit the number of strong Republican candidacies.

First, the electoral strategies of political elites are conditioned by what happens in the previous election. Politicians, like generals, prepare for the last war. Easy reelection in 1978 lulled many House Democrats into a false sense of security in 1980, and a number lost. The survivors ran scared in 1982, absorbing so much of the campaign money available to Democrats that their party was unable to take full advantage of the deep recession and Reagan's low approval ratings, because many otherwise serious and attractive Democratic challengers remained underfunded.[4] Republican successes in 1980 led to another major assault on Democratic incumbents in 1982; but in the face of recession and fully mobilized Democratic incumbents, their failure was nearly total. Thus "a lingering bad memory of the 1982 elections [persuaded] many Republicans to bypass House campaigns" in 1984.[5]

The lagged influence of the last election is compounded by the need to make essential decisions regarding candidacy a year or more before the next election. One reason Republicans were able to field so many good candidates in 1982 was that most of the National Republican Congressional Committee's recruiting took place in 1981, in the warm afterglow of the 1980 elections and at a time when the Reagan administration was racking up impressive budget and tax-cut victories in Congress.[6] In that setting, ambitious, career-minded Republican politicians could be persuaded that taking on a sitting Democrat was not a hopeless enterprise. Recruiting was, by the same token, slow throughout 1983, not only because of the apparent lessons of 1982, but also because the strength of the economic revival was still uncertain and Reagan was running behind potential Democratic presidential contenders more often than not in straw polls.[7] Certainly there were no signs of a major ideological shift or party realignment.[8] Not until well into 1984 was it clear that the economic upturn would continue through election day and that Reagan had forged a wide lead over every Democratic hopeful. By then it was too late for potential candidates for Congress to decide to run.

In some states, Republican party leaders actually discouraged Republican challengers. In Florida and Texas, party officials blamed defeats in local and statewide contests on vigorous 1982 Republican House challenges that stimulated Democratic incumbents to mobilize supporters who otherwise would have stayed home on election day. They did not want the same thing to happen in 1984, when their main concerns were to reelect Reagan and to use his name at the top of the ticket to help local candidates.[9] Ironically, Texas is where congressional Republicans made their biggest gains in 1984, picking up four House seats. Nationally, whether by decisions of potential candidates or party leaders, more Democratic incumbents were allowed to run without Republican opposition in 1984 (53) than in 1980 (41) or 1982 (41).

Another reason that Republicans were unable to exploit Reagan's triumph more fully was the dearth of open Democratic House seats. Normally, it is much easier to take a seat from the other party when it is not defended by an incumbent; House incumbents typically win more than 90 percent of contests they enter. In 1980 there were 27 open seats that had been held by Democrats; Republicans won 10 of them. In 1984 there were only 13; Republicans took 5. The Republican success rate was the same in both years, but the party enjoyed twice as many opportunities in 1980. Republican gains were smaller in 1984 in part simply because there were fewer of these easier targets.

The pattern of campaign contributions to Republican House candidates in 1984 reflected the relatively small number of competitive challengers and candidates for open seats. Data on fund raising through September 30 showed that Republican incumbents received an average of $253,500 from contributors, compared with $88,300 for Republican challengers.[10] This gap was much greater than in 1980 or even 1982. Business political action committees (PACs), something of a bellwether in this regard, were notably reluctant to invest in the campaigns of most Republican challengers. Unlike 1980, when they helped a number of the longshots who sent surprised incumbent Democrats into involuntary retirement, business PACs took few chances in 1984. Incumbents and a few "blue chip" challengers were the main beneficiaries of their largess. "The challengers this year don't measure up," one PAC official simply explained.[11]

For good reasons, business PACs carefully calculate the electoral odds before deciding who to fund. They normally prefer Republicans on ideological grounds. Yet because Democrats control the House and the committees and subcommittees where decisions of crucial importance to the business community are made, many business PACs are reluctant to contribute to opponents of Democratic incumbents unless chances of success are high. (For example, they were far more generous to Republican challengers in 1980 than they were in 1982.[12]) In 1984 the chairman of the Democratic Congressional Campaign Committee, Rep. Tony Coelho of California, explicitly warned PACs that support for the opponents of incumbent Democrats would not be forgotten.[13]

On the financial side, Republicans were clearly not as well positioned to exploit Reagan's victory in 1984 as they had been in 1980. Republican party money (direct and coordinated contributions from national party committees) was just as available as it had been four years before, but the party, like the PACs, found fewer promising races in which to spend it. Even though they contemplated a Reagan sweep of historic proportions, Republican party officials could not imagine doing much better than regaining the ground they had lost in 1982.[14] The potential for additional gains was just not there on a district-by-district, candidate-by-candidate basis.

The National Campaigns

Fielding a large number of attractive, well-funded challengers is a necessary condition for major gains in the House, but it is not sufficient, as the 1982 election made clear. Although an unusual number of formidable Republican challengers ran, only one incumbent Democrat lost. Upsets proved to be nearly impossible in the face of well-prepared Democrats and the worst economic slump since the depression.

Even the most polished and lavishly financed challenger needs to give voters clear reasons to abandon the incumbent. Survey data indicate that challengers must accomplish two principal tasks to win: they must apprise voters of their own virtues and qualifications, and they must persuade voters that the incumbent's recognized strengths and accomplishments are outweighed by other, stronger, considerations.[15] Unless the incumbent has made major political blunders or been caught in egregious moral lapses, this can be remarkably difficult; most members of Congress are masters of defensive political maneuver. But salient national political issues can sometimes provide the kind of weapon needed to break through the incumbent's defenses and persuade voters to shift their allegiance to the challenger.

This is what happens in a landslide with coattails. The substance of the presidential campaigns offers congressional candidates a way to tie the local vote to the national vote. In the 1980 campaign, for example, Reagan promised major, rather explicit, policy changes: tax cuts, budget cuts, sharply increased defense spending, a full-scale assault on inflation. The broader campaign theme of "vote Republican, for a change" was designed to tap the public's deep discontent with the entire drift of American political life, not merely with Carter. The substance of the national campaign was readily adapted to the needs of Republican congressional challengers. The logic of "throwing the rascals out" extended downward to other Democrats in federal office. Many voters evidently listened. It is no coincidence that the House Majority Whip and five committee chairmen were among the Democratic losers.

In the other recent landslide with coattails, the 1964 election, President Johnson's winning campaign also promised new policy directions, primarily the completion of the New Deal agenda and its "Great Society" extensions. Democrats argued that the administration's program—largely a continuation of the agenda of his assassinated predecessor in office, John F. Kennedy—had suffered at the hands of a recalcitrant Congress (Republicans had picked up 22 House seats and 2 Senate seats in 1960) and could benefit from additional Democratic votes. More importantly, the Goldwater campaign, which promised radical—and unpopular—departures in the opposite direction, gave Democratic congressional candidates something to use against those Republican incumbents who could be linked to the Goldwater candidacy. As a consequence, Democratic challengers were most successful against Republican House members who had allied themselves publicly with Goldwater.[16]

In contrast, landslides without coattails take place when congressional candidates are unable to give voters much reason to connect the presidential and congressional vote. The winning presidential campaigns for a second term in 1956, 1972, and 1984 share two related qualities: they occurred at times of rising prosperity and improvements in foreign policy, and they were campaigns in which voters were asked simply to ratify what had been done in the first term. Continuity, not change, was the theme. The campaigns emphasized how much better things were than they had been four years earlier but were vague about future intentions. Each exploited the aura of the presidency and stressed the personal leadership qualities of the president. This has proved to be a sound strategy for presidents, but it does nothing at all to help congressional challengers of the president's party.

No matter how popular a president, a backward-looking, defensive national campaign that offers voters continuity but few specific changes for the future gives the party's other candidates little rhetorical leverage. If continuity is the goal, why replace the incumbents of either party? If times are good, if peace and prosperity are on the way, incumbents of the opposition party can hardly be blamed for obstructing progress; indeed, they may plausibly claim a share of the credit for what has gone right. Unless an incumbent representative has stubbornly resisted presidential initiatives that are popular in the district or identifies too strongly with the party's locally unpopular presidential candidate, the party's national campaign, however successful, will offer a challenger little ammunition to persuade voters to turn the incumbent out of office.

The essence of the Reagan campaign in 1984 became evident in the first debate, when the president refused to specify any concrete plans for the second term and instead rested his case for reelection entirely on his administration's past performance. Reagan carefully avoided the trap (set by the Mondale campaign) of disclosing just who would bear the costs of dealing with the nation's central economic problem, the massive federal budget deficits. But Reagan's vague assurances that economic growth would take care of the deficits without additional action by government gave Republican challengers no help in convincing voters that more Republicans in Congress were needed for the president to reach his second-term objectives. Their problem was compounded when Reagan, pursuing an all-embracing personal victory, claimed for his own Democratic heroes such as Franklin D. Roosevelt, Harry S. Truman, and Kennedy. Why vote against congressional Democrats if your favorite Republican campaigns from the rear platform of Truman's train?

The first debate helped congressional Democrats in another way. Mondale's surprisingly effective performance and Reagan's equally surprising inept one abruptly halted the Reagan juggernaut, at least for a while. The Reagan campaign spent the next two weeks trying to control the damage and prepare for the rematch. Crucial time that Reagan might have spent campaigning for Republican congressional candidates was devoted instead to shoring up his own candidacy. The first debate also took some of the sting out of being on the Mondale ticket in districts where Reagan was very popular. A Democratic House candidate noted this difference: "Mondale is now a respectable candidate, even among people who are not going to vote for him. In the eyes of people who have decided to vote for Reagan, I am not automatically disqualified as a congressional candidate just because I support the nominee of my party for president." [17] This effect of the debate, if widespread, certainly should have helped incumbent Democrats; many were vulnerable to association with the top of the ticket because three-quarters of them had been convention delegates, most as Mondale supporters.

Whether because of the first debate or because popular presidents seeking reelection cannot resist the temptation to maximize their personal triumph (think of Nixon in 1972), the national campaign did less than it could have to help Republican candidates lower on the ticket. Reagan's final-hour campaign in Mondale's home state of Minnesota was symptomatic; he was after that 50th state, even if it meant ignoring congressional districts where Republicans in close contests were desperately trying to cling to his coattails. At least this is what some disappointed Republicans, notably House Minority Leader Robert Michel, were saying after the election.[18] (For a summary of the House election results, see Table 8.2.)

The experience of Norm Murdock captures the congressional party's disappointment. Murdock, a Republican county commissioner from the Cincinnati area, was giving incumbent Democrat Thomas Luken a stiff challenge. Murdock had been an early Reagan supporter, cochairing his 1980 campaign in Ohio and voting for him at the 1980 Republican convention. In 1984 the president visited the district on Truman's campaign train:

> Reagan, speaking to more than 10,000 flag-waving supporters in the nation's third most Republican city, pledged not to raise taxes, extolled the importance of family and religion—and had even gone so far as to praise Democratic Sen. John Glenn of Ohio as "an authentic American hero." But he did not say a word about Murdock, who was sitting expectantly on the platform near him.[19]

The Republican national party apparatus did mount a coordinated nationwide campaign to help the entire ticket during the last week before the election. In that sense, 1984 was no mere repeat of 1972, when the

Table 8.2 House Elections, 1984

98th Congress		*99th Congress*	
Democrats	267	Democrats	253
Republicans	168	Republicans	182

Democrats	
Net loss	14
Freshmen	12
Incumbents reelected	241
Incumbents defeated	13
Open seats retained	8
Open seats lost	5

Republicans	
Net gain	14
Freshmen	31
Incumbents reelected	151
Incumbents defeated	3
Open seats retained	13
Open seats lost	1

party organization was much smaller. But even so, Republicans in 1984 ran neither the kind of congressional candidates nor the sort of national campaign that could have produced a landslide with coattails.

Despite a much larger Reagan victory in 1984 than in 1980, the Republican party's strength in the House declined. Ironically, support for the party apparently increased between 1980 and 1984; exit polls and other preliminary survey data from 1984 suggest that the proportion of voters who call themselves Republicans had increased about 5 percentage points over 1980, with the proportion of Democratic identifiers falling by a similar amount. On election day, at least, Republicans were approaching parity with the Democrats.[20] Voters' expressions of party identification are subject to the short-term influences of election-year politics.[21] Nevertheless, the argument that a partisan realignment is taking place is much stronger after 1984 than it was after 1980. Yet the results of the House elections seriously undermine it because Republicans collectively were unprepared to take advantage of their historic opportunity.

Senate Results

Senate elections are far more idiosyncratic than House elections. Systematic patterns, such as coattail effects, are more difficult to detect and measure. In five of the last ten presidential elections, the winner's party has lost Senate seats, which suggests that coattail effects in Senate elections are minor. But this is not necessarily true. To be sure, presidential coattails in postwar elections have never been worth more than a few percentage points to congressional candidates.[22] But Senate contests tend to be closer than House elections—competition is generally stiffer, challengers are usually more experienced and better funded, states are harder to represent without making enemies as well as friends[23]—and the opportunity for coattails to make a difference is thus greater.

The 1980 Senate elections show what can happen. Republicans defeated 9 incumbent Democrats and won 3 previously Democratic open seats, which gave them a majority in the Senate for the first time since the 1952 election. Many of these contests were remarkably close; 14 were won with 52.1 percent or less of the vote, 11 of them by Republicans. Thus if Reagan's coattails were worth only 2 or 3 percent of the vote, they still had a major effect on the aggregate results. Idiosyncrasy played into Republican hands in 1980; 22 of the 34 seats that were up for election were held by Democrats, many clearly vulnerable. (Only Watergate had kept several of them in office in 1974.)

Republican opportunities were much more limited in 1984. Democrats had only 14 seats to defend, and most of the vulnerable incumbents were Republicans. Two of them, Charles Percy of Illinois and Roger

Jepsen of Iowa, were defeated, and Democrats picked up one open seat (in Tennessee) while losing one incumbent (Walter Huddleston of Kentucky), for a net Democratic gain of two. But Republicans won in five other states where Democrats at one time had plausible hopes of taking over. Four of these contests (in Mississippi, New Hampshire, Texas, and Minnesota) were not even close; the fifth was Sen. Jesse Helms's narrow victory over Gov. James B. Hunt in North Carolina. The Helms-Hunt race was astonishingly expensive; it cost more than $20 million. Spending in at least one other race (in Texas) surpassed $10 million. Senate contests as vigorous and intensive as these may well produce reverse coattails, with the local race affecting the presidential vote rather than the opposite. Certainly massive efforts to get out the vote for Helms and Hunt may have affected the presidential vote, not to mention the House vote; credit for the three House seats taken by Republicans in North Carolina may be more due Helms's campaign than Reagan's. (For a listing of Senate election results by state, see Table 8.3.)

Aside from North Carolina, the only Republican Senate victory that was close enough to be attributed directly to Reagan's coattails was Mitch McConnell's upset of Huddleston in Kentucky. Still, in the face of very limited opportunities and potentially serious threats, Republicans came out of the 1984 Senate elections in good shape. It is entirely possible that Reagan helped Republican Senate candidates just as much in 1984 as he did in 1980, but that local circumstances were so different that his coattails had little effect on the outcome as measured by the number of seats changing hands, which in the final analysis is what matters.

Interpreting the Election

Throughout this essay I have treated the notion of "coattails" informally, implicitly following its popular definition: a president has coattails when his party adds a large number of seats to its congressional contingent. This has been deliberate. The more carefully analytic and nuanced definitions of political scientists[24] are appropriate to the study of electoral behavior but less helpful in exploring the political meaning of an election. For example, research keeps turning up evidence that Nixon's coattails in 1972 were, in fact, quite strong.[25] This is important for our theoretical models of U.S. elections but of little relevance for understanding the political context that was shaped by that election. The critical data are the raw numbers of seats gained or lost in the House and Senate, and by this measure Nixon's coattails were short.

Raw numbers matter for two principal reasons. The first is simple: seats translate into legislative votes. The more seats a president's party holds, the more a president can get Congress to do. Beyond that, major

Table 8.3 Senate Election Results by State, 1984

	Vote Total	Percent
Alabama		
Howell Heflin (D)*	860,535	63
Albert Lee Smith, Jr. (R)	498,508	36
Alaska		
Ted Stevens (R)*	121,879	71
John E. Havelock (D)	49,237	29
Arkansas		
David Pryor (D)*	481,943	58
Ed Bethune (R)	354,147	42
Colorado		
William L. Armstrong (R)*	833,821	64
Nancy Dick (D)	449,327	35
Delaware		
Joseph R. Biden, Jr. (D)*	147,056	60
John M. Burris (R)	97,903	40
Georgia		
Sam Nunn (D)*	1,316,545	80
Jon Michael Hicks (R)	327,695	20
Idaho		
James A. McClure (R)*	293,416	72
Peter M. Busch (D)	105,487	26
Illinois		
Paul Simon (D)	2,397,165	51
Charles H. Percy (R)*	2,308,039	49
Iowa		
Tom Harkin (D)	713,286	56
Roger W. Jepsen (R)*	559,176	44
Kansas		
Nancy Landon Kassebaum (R)*	735,080	77
James R. Maher (D)	206,187	22
Kentucky		
Mitch McConnell (R)	638,816	50
Walter D. Huddleston (D)*	635,441	50
Louisiana		
J. Bennett Johnston (D)*	X	X
Maine		
William S. Cohen (R)*	400,953	74
Elizabeth H. Mitchell (D)	142,312	26
Massachusetts		
John F. Kerry (D)	1,393,150	55
Raymond Shamie (R)	1,136,913	45
Michigan		
Carl Levin (D)*	1,915,831	52
Jack Lousma (R)	1,745,302	47
Minnesota		
Rudy Boschwitz (I-R)*	1,199,926	58
Joan Anderson Growe (DFL)	852,844	41
Mississippi		
Thad Cochran (R)*	580,314	61
William F. Winter (D)	371,926	39

	Vote Total	Percent
Montana		
Max Baucus (D)*	215,704	57
Chuck Cozzens (R)	154,308	41
Nebraska		
J. James Exon (D)*	334,278	53
Nancy Hoch (R)	299,787	47
New Hampshire		
Gordon J. Humphrey (R)*	225,828	59
Norman E. D'Amours (D)	157,447	41
New Jersey		
Bill Bradley (D)*	1,986,644	64
Mary V. Mochary (R)	1,080,096	35
New Mexico		
Pete V. Domenici (R)*	357,987	72
Judith A. Pratt (D)	140,252	28
North Carolina		
Jesse Helms (R)*	1,156,768	52
James B. Hunt, Jr. (D)	1,070,488	48
Oklahoma		
David L. Boren (D)*	906,131	76
Will E. Crozier (R)	280,638	23
Oregon		
Mark O. Hatfield (R)*	748,952	66
Margie Hendriksen (D)	382,121	34
Rhode Island		
Claiborne Pell (D)*	277,022	73
Barbara Leonard (R)	104,074	27
South Carolina		
Strom Thurmond (R)*	644,815	67
Melvin Purvis, Jr. (D)	306,982	32
South Dakota		
Larry Pressler (R)*	235,176	74
George V. Cunningham (D)	80,537	26
Tennessee		
Albert Gore, Jr. (D)	991,212	61
Victor Ashe (R)	553,331	34
Texas		
Phil Gramm (R)	2,988,346	59
Lloyd Doggett (D)	2,110,834	41
Virginia		
John W. Warner (R)*	1,406,194	70
Edythe C. Harrison (D)	601,142	30
Wyoming		
Alan K. Simpson (R)*	146,373	78
Victor A. Ryan (D)	40,525	22

*	indicates incumbents	DFL	Democratic-Farmer-Labor Party
X	denotes candidate without major-party opposition	I-R	Independent-Republican Party

Note: As of January 8, 1985, Alaska, Ark., Del., Ga., Idaho, Iowa, Kan., Ky., La., Maine, Neb., N.M., Ore., R.I., Tenn., and Texas had not submitted official returns to Congressional Quarterly; unofficial returns compiled by Congressional Quarterly from various sources, including the News Election Service, were used.

policy innovations usually require a large influx of new members. The best historical examples are Woodrow Wilson's New Freedom, Roosevelt's New Deal, Johnson's Great Society, and Reagan's tax and budget cuts in 1981; all were contingent on large swings to their party in Congress. More generally, newcomers who have taken seats from the other party provide a disproportionate share of votes for new policy initiatives.[26]

The second reason why raw numbers matter is more subtle. A partisan sweep that extends to Congress does more than replace members; it also sends a potent message to the incumbents who survived (and to other Washington politicians). If the electorate seems to have spoken clearly and decisively, political wisdom dictates that its message be heeded, at least for a while. The resistance of recalcitrant senior Democrats to the Kennedy-Johnson programs collapsed for a time after 1964. Republican gains in 1980 transformed congressional Democrats into tax and budget cutters; the only issues were where to cut and how deep to go.

Long coattails clearly improve prospects for passing the president's legislative agenda. A decisive partisan shift in Congress alters both the political arithmetic and the bounds of politically conceivable policy alternatives. The psychological effect of a sweeping victory is no less important than its numerical consequences. Winning presidential candidates and their supporters routinely claim a mandate from voters, but without major congressional gains those claims lack substance.

A landslide without coattails leaves the claim of a mandate (again, as perceived by other politicians rather than as by students of voting behavior, which is quite another matter) open to serious doubt. The 1984 elections were immediately followed by claims and counterclaims about just what the electorate had meant by reelecting Reagan overwhelmingly while leaving Congress only slightly changed. The point of this postelection analysis was not to discover the real intentions of voters, of course; it was to establish the political context for the next session of Congress. Republicans hailed the president's 49-state sweep as evidence that his policies were extraordinarily popular and that Congress should fall in line behind them. Democrats denied that anything more than Reagan's personal popularity had been established because other Republicans did not do particularly well.[27] Democrats also could deny that Reagan's reelection had any explicit policy implications because of the nature of his winning campaign. By extolling the past and leaving plans for the future vague, Reagan, they felt, was in no position to argue that voters had ratified any specific second-term policy initiatives.

The very fact that Democrats could comfortably refuse to recognize a mandate means that they will feel little psychological or political pressure to cooperate with the president on his own terms. For practical purposes, mandates are in politicians' minds. In 1984 members of Congress ran their own campaigns, and they will read their own messages from their victories. Insofar as these mesh with the administration's proposals—few Democrats supported Mondale's proposed tax increase, for example—a basis for cooperation with the president exists. But nothing like the post-1980 political climate emerged from 1984.

Prospects for the 99th Congress

What kind of politics will follow this landslide without coattails? Consider the partisan makeup of the House and Senate in the 99th Congress. The 1984 congressional election results fell far short of Republican hopes and potential. The House remains firmly in Democratic hands; the Republicans' gain of 14 seats was too few to resurrect the coalition of Republicans and conservative Democrats that dominated the House in 1981 and 1982. And small as it was, the partisan shift in Congress was greater than the ideological shift; almost half the Republican gains were in seats formerly held by Democrats who were friendly to the administration. The Senate in the 99th Congress is also less Republican—and less conservative—than it was during the first Reagan administration. On the surface, this would appear to spell trouble for Reagan's second term. Certainly this is not a Congress that will respond readily to new conservative policy initiatives from the White House. But it is plausible that the long-term interests of both the president and his party will be better served by the *absence* of any Republican congressional surge in 1984. Ironically, Reagan may well have been helped by his own lack of coattails.

To understand how this could be so, it is important to remember how much Reagan has won already. The agenda remains as it was after 1980. Congressional Democrats did not win reelection in 1984 by proposing large new social programs, income redistribution schemes, affirmative action, or major cuts in defense spending. Such notions were confined to the party's fringe (for example, Jesse Jackson's campaign). Rather, they won by adapting their positions to the mood of an electorate that generally approved of the changes made during the first Reagan administration. Democrats are not about to mount a counterrevolution. The range of politically conceivable policy alternatives will be biased strongly in the president's favor. And of course he can wield the veto if necessary; he has the numbers in Congress to sustain it.

Reagan may not have any grand new plans for his second term. The tenor of his 1984 campaign may reflect more than a cautious electoral strategy; it may indicate that the administration's second-term goals have yet to be resolved and that, if only by default, Reagan will end up working mainly for marginal policy changes that are designed to consolidate victories won in the first administration. If so, the absence of sizable Republican congressional gains will be much less of a hindrance than would be the case if major new policy initiatives were at the heart of the president's agenda. Because the agenda is still so vague, projections about politics in the 99th Congress remain highly speculative; thus the following comments on major policy issues are offered with a good deal of trepidation.

The central domestic issue for the 99th Congress is what to do about the budget deficits. Mondale tried, and failed, to make the deficit a major campaign issue. He recommended increasing taxes for those in higher income brackets and demanded, unsuccessfully, that Reagan tell what his solution to the problem would be—and who would bear the cost. Reagan avoided the trap by claiming that robust economic growth plus unspecified savings from greater government efficiency would solve the problem painlessly.

This pipe dream was quickly abandoned after the election. But Reagan's promise not to raise taxes, except perhaps as a "last resort," was not so readily forgotten, particularly by Democrats who intend to make sure that Reagan and his party pay dearly for their handling of the issue during the campaign. Any serious attack on the deficits will probably require substantial tax increases, large programmatic cuts, or some combination of the two. Democrats plan to force the administration to take the blame for whatever pain ensues. "If there is going to be a tax bill, it is going to be Ronald Reagan's tax bill," said House Speaker Thomas P. O'Neill on election night. "If there is going to be cutting of [cost-of-living increases] for veterans or Social Security benefits or anything of that nature, it's going to be the program of the president." [28]

Statements like O'Neill's suggest that limited congressional gains promise extra headaches for the White House on the deficit issue. But not necessarily. If Reagan is eventually persuaded that he must resort to the "last resort" and raise taxes—a very strong possibility—it will be easier to negotiate tax increases with the current Congress than it would be with one that contained a larger contingent of enthusiastically conservative Republican freshmen who thought they had won because they promised not to raise taxes. Reagan would have to take responsibility for a tax increase in either case. With the current Congress, blame is more likely to be shared with the Democrats regardless of their party's intentions. If huge and growing deficits are, in fact, economically destructive and nothing serious were done to reduce them by the administration and a Congress filled with fresh Republican troops, then Reagan's historical reputation, the ideas he stands for, and his party would probably suffer major damage. Any chances for an era of Republican dominance would fade. With the current balance in Washington, such an outcome is less likely because effective bipartisan action is more likely, although by no means guaranteed.

As of early January 1985, the administration had considered only a "revenue neutral" tax reform package. Of course, if it is really revenue neutral—that is, keeps the total tax collection the same—it will do nothing to help the deficits in the lifetime of this administration. (In the long run, it may help by raising the growth rate by eliminating inefficient incentives.) On the other hand, it will be almost as controversial as a tax increase because the taxes of millions of people will rise even if the net revenues remain the same. It is hard to see the wisdom of paying the political price for tax reform without making any headway against the deficit. It makes more sense to regard tax reform as a Republican strategy to lay the groundwork for tax increases by rendering the tax system simpler, less progressive, and less riddled with unproductive incentives. Ironically, the principal losers under the Treasury Department's reform proposal would seem to be business corporations, prime constituents of this administration. The most favorable reactions have come from tax specialists on the Democratic side. A reform proposal that shifts the tax burden from individuals to business corporations probably has a better chance in a more Democratic Congress.

Thus far, Reagan has made no concrete proposals for dealing with the deficit. When he does, he will have to cut a deal with an unfriendly House and a Senate already looking forward to the 1986 midterm election, and even then he will have to absorb the blame for the pain they inflict. But assuming a deal can be worked out, it is more likely to benefit the president and his party in the long run than would either blind faith in the capacity of supply-side economics to stimulate historically unprecedented growth rates or drastic cuts in social programs that benefit middle-class voters.

Similarly, the 99th Congress may be more supportive of Reagan's second-term foreign policy initiatives than would be a more Republican and conservative one—assuming that his main objective is to improve relations with the Soviet Union and negotiate arms controls. Any move in this direction is likely to have Democratic support; opposition will come from the Republican right. With the Republican right weakened in the Senate, arms control treaties should be easier to push through, especially since Senator Helms chose to keep faith with North Carolina's voters and take the chair of the Agriculture Committee rather than Foreign Relations.

The greatest potential for conflict between the president and Congress is over U.S. policy toward Central America. The administration clearly finds the Sandinista government in Nicaragua intolerable and is prepared to take drastic steps to depose it. Whether direct military intervention is a step it would take is uncertain, but it would certainly like to do more than Democrats in Congress are willing to allow; bipartisan consensus is nowhere in sight. Divisions in Congress reflect those in the public at large. When asked during the campaign whether they were more concerned about American involvement in a Central American war or a communist takeover in the region, a sample of voters split 50-40, albeit with the majority more worried about the communist takeover.[29]

Certainly the 99th Congress will resist a hard-line policy more stubbornly than would a more conservative and Republican Congress, but lacking a consensus supporting U.S. military intervention in Central America among either political elites or the general public, the Reagan administration is well served by a congressional brake. If the Vietnam experience offers one clear lesson for domestic politics, it is the destructive potential of foreign military adventures that lack broad elite and public support. A Congress that keeps the administration from ignoring that lesson is doing it a favor regardless of the inherent wisdom or folly of the policy itself.

On the related issue of defense spending, expect no enthusiasm on Capitol Hill for increases as large as those requested by the administration or passed by recent Congresses. The budget deficits dictate much smaller requests for increases in any case, and there is no widespread congressional sentiment for major defense cuts. The fate of the Reagan-backed MX missile is still in doubt, but it is threatened more by its intrinsic liabilities than by general opposition to expanded strategic weapons systems. The administration's proposal for a "Star Wars" defense against a nuclear attack will be hard to sell, but as long as only relatively small sums for research and development are requested, congressional resistance is likely to be limited. That defense spending probably will not be at the center of controversy in this Congress despite further real increases (on the order of 4 percent per year) is yet another quiet sign of the Reagan agenda's ascendancy.

The Reagan administration is least likely to get its way from the 99th Congress on the "social agenda," which includes abortion, private school tuition tax credits, and school prayer. Social conservatives in the Republican coalition face another four years of neglect and disappointment. The more moderate new Senate, although Republican, will be at least as big an obstacle as the Democratic House. Democrats and moderate Republicans in both houses will do their best to bury these divisive, emotionally charged issues.

Again, this "failure" may be to the long-run benefit of Reagan's historical reputation and the Republican party. With the possible exception of school prayer (and even on that issue, consensus dissipates once discussion gets down to specific proposals), the conservative social agenda lacks broad public support. To enact it would require imposing the values of an intense minority on a less adamant, but still larger, majority. If the administration felt obligated to push hard for the New Right's programs, it could easily waste its limited political resources, generating only resentment and disenchantment in the process. It could also alienate most of the younger college-educated voters who were first brought into the Republican coalition in 1984, thereby reducing the chances for an eventual Republican majority. Low taxes and growth-oriented economic policies appeal to this group; government imposition of conservative social norms does not. On the other hand, Republicans do not want to alienate the evangelicals, the source of so much of the party's energy during the 1984 campaign. Insufficient support in Congress offers the administration an easy way out; it can say, in effect, "We'd love to enact your social agenda, but we just don't have the votes, and if we waste our resources trying, other conservative policies will suffer." Instead the New Right can be paid off with acceptable appointments to the Supreme Court and to the Department of Education and other social agencies.

Because Republicans are far more united on economic than on social values, the prospects for their coalition are better when the former are emphasized and the latter ignored. Anything that permits Republican leaders to avoid the social agenda—without taking blame for its neglect—contributes to their long-term party-building strategy. This includes the landslide without coattails of 1984, which protects Reagan from the temptation to join battle on divisive emotional issues that are bound to cost him dearly in public support and affection no matter how they come out.

The 99th Congress will not readily do the president's bidding. The alternatives are hard bargaining followed by compromise, or stalemate. Stalemate, especially on the deficit-budget-taxes complex of issues, is a real possibility. But a stalemate that leaves serious problems festering would be politically costly all around, so both administration and congressional leaders have reason to deal. The president is hardly without resources for this sort of politicking; the White House has played its hand with Congress skillfully in the past, and Reagan's talent for going public seems undiminished. The 1984 congressional elections make the prognosis for radical policy departures of the kind that were achieved in 1981 bleak; but they do not preclude a successful period of consolidation. Indeed, they may contribute to it and so to the long-run success of the president and his party.

1986 and Beyond

The 1984 votes had scarcely been counted when speculation began about the 1986 elections. As the midterm election draws nearer, members of Congress will increasingly calculate how their voting decisions will affect their electoral fortunes. Democrats look forward to 1986 with undisguised delight. In recent decades the biggest losses to the administration's party in Congress have come at its second midterm: Republicans lost 49 House seats in 1958 and 1974, Democrats lost 71 seats in 1938 and 47 seats in 1966. Many ambitious Democratic career politicians deliberately sat out the 1984 election in the expectation that 1986 would be a much better year to take on Republican incumbents.[30] (As a result, the 1984 Democratic challengers were the least politically experienced group the party had fielded in 30 years.) Should many of them run as planned in 1986, the Democratic party will be able to mount the large number of strong House challenges that are necessary for sizable congressional gains. The Senate looks even more promising to Democrats, as the Republican victors of 1980 come up for reelection without Reagan to head the ticket. Democrats see in the preponderance of Republican seats up for reelection in 1986 (22 of 34) an excellent opportunity to retake the Senate.

Soon 1986 will replace 1984 as the election that shapes congressional politics. This will certainly strain Republican loyalties if the administration asks for harsh medicine—large cuts in middle-class benefits, for example—to stem the flow of red ink or if it solicits support for controversial foreign policy decisions. Republican senators elected in 1980 will be especially skittish and reluctant to back a lame-duck president at significant political cost to themselves. Congressional Republicans will have a powerful incentive to do what they can to keep the economy healthy through 1986 and to avoid policies that trigger zealous opposition in their states and districts. Again, the most likely consequence will be pressure on the White House for caution, moderation, and consolidation rather than bold new steps of the kind pushed by New Right enthusiasts.[31]

Democrats, who are freer to enjoy the pleasures of opposition, may be sorely tempted to let the administration take all the political heat in proposing painful solutions to serious national problems—a sure path to stalemate—while biding their own time until 1986. But the message of 1984 speaks forcefully against such a course. Reagan, after all, was given an enormous vote of confidence, and intransigent opposition from Democrats in Congress would give Republicans a fine target for 1986. The old

Democratic coalition lies in ruins; its traditional approaches to policy are widely regarded as moribund and unmarketable. Many Democrats have hung on in Congress by catering to the same public sentiments that put Reagan in the White House, and few of those who attack the president offer any coherent policy alternatives. Even if the economy slips once more into recession, traditional Democratic spending programs to stimulate recovery are inconceivable in light of the budget deficit, and raising taxes to reduce the deficit would only worsen the recession.

Without an alternative program of their own, Democrats are in no position to take more than temporary advantage of Republican policy failures. Although they have little reason to extend themselves to make the president look good, neither have they much to gain in the long run, either individually or as a party, from blind opposition. Until they come up with plausible alternatives that are popular with the public, Democrats are better off trying to moderate Republican proposals in ways that protect their core constituencies without alienating a middle-class majority that is generally pleased with administration policy.

Looking behind 1986, Republicans have good reason for optimism—and for the sense of responsibility that befits a governing party. Despite the Republican party's weaker performance in the congressional elections, more signs of a realignment emerged from 1984 than from 1980. Both the scope of Reagan's victory across regions and social categories—with most notable gains over 1980 coming from young voters—and polling data on party identification indicate that the Republican party is more popular today than it has been in years. Republican candidates actually won about half the vote in contested House elections. And although Republican House gains were still limited, their location is significant. Eight seats were added in the South, including four in Texas and three in North Carolina; Republicans also took three seats in heavily blue-collar northern districts and came close in several others.[32] Republican strength should continue to grow in the South. If the party can continue to make inroads into the white working class in the East and Midwest, it could be well on its way to firm majority status.

Whether or not this happens hinges on what occurs during the next four years. Massive deficits, negative trade balances, overexposed banks, and high interest rates hold some serious risks for the economy (although economists do not agree on how serious they are or what should be done to improve them). Another major recession under Reagan, while not necessarily reuniting the old Democratic majority, would probably abort a new Republican one. A divisive foreign adventure opposed by a substantial segment of the public would also damage the Republicans' chances of becoming "America's party." So would intense national conflict over social values that divide important segments of the Reagan coalition. If Reagan's short coattails have created political conditions that compel him to pursue policies through public persuasion and compromise with Congress, it is more likely that some of these problems will be avoided. The landslide without coattails may well turn out for the best for the president and his party—and, not incidentally, for the country.

Notes

1. The evidence for this is summarized in Gary C. Jacobson, *The Politics of Congressional Elections* (Boston: Little, Brown, 1983).
2. Gary C. Jacobson and Samuel Kernell, *Strategy and Choice in Congressional Elections,* 2d ed. (New Haven: Yale University Press, 1983), 72-84.
3. Benjamin Shore, "How Will the Race Change Congress? Not Much," *San Diego Union,* October 28, 1984, C5. See also Alan Ehrenhalt, "GOP Challengers Find PACs Wary This Year," *Congressional Quarterly Weekly Report,* October 20, 1984, 2763.
4. Gary C. Jacobson, "Party Organization and the Efficient Distribution of Campaign Resources: Republicans and Democrats in 1982," *Political Science Quarterly,* forthcoming, 1985.
5. Phil Duncan, "House Campaigns Quiet as Few Seek to Run," *Congressional Quarterly Weekly Report,* March 24, 1984, 657.
6. Jacobson and Kernell, *Strategy and Choice,* 96-99.
7. "Trial Heats," *Public Opinion* (February/March 1984): 35.
8. Duncan, "House Campaigns Quiet," 659.
9. Ibid., 657-658.
10. Paul Houston, "Money for House Candidates Levels Off," *Los Angeles Times,* October 27, 1984, Part I, 24.
11. Ehrenhalt, "PACs Wary This Year," 2763.
12. See Michael J. Malbin, ed., *Money and Politics in the United States: Financing Elections in the 1980s* (Washington, D.C.: American Enterprise Institute for Public Policy Research, 1984), tables A18 and A19.
13. Ehrenhalt, "PACs Wary This Year," 2763.
14. Karen Tumulty and Paul Houston, "GOP Sees Less Chance for Key Gains in House," *Los Angeles Times,* October 28, 1984, Part I, 1, 7-8.
15. Jacobson, *Politics of Congressional Elections,* 114-118.
16. Robert A. Schoenberger, "Campaign Strategy and Party Loyalty: The Electoral Relevance of Candidate Decision Making in the 1964 Congressional Elections," *American Political Science Review* (June 1969): 515-520.
17. Tumulty and Houston, "GOP Sees Less Chance for Gains," 7.
18. Rob Gurwitt, "GOP Disappointed with Gains in the House," *Congressional Quarterly Weekly Report,* November 10, 1984, 2898.

19. Tumulty and Houston, "GOP Sees Less Chance for Gains," 8.
20. Averaged across four national exit polls, 36 percent of the voters called themselves Democrats, 32 percent, Republicans. See William Schneider, "Incumbency Saved the Democrats This Time, But What about Next?" *Los Angeles Times,* November 11, 1984, Part V, 1.
21. John E. Jackson, "Issues, Party Choices, and Presidential Votes," *American Journal of Political Science* (February 1975): 161-180; Morris P. Fiorina, *Retrospective Voting in American National Elections* (New Haven: Yale University Press, 1981), Chapter 5.
22. Randall L. Calvert and John A. Ferejohn, "Coattail Voting in Recent Presidential Elections," *American Political Science Review* (June 1983): 413-416.
23. Jacobson, *Politics of Congressional Elections,* 72-74.
24. Calvert and Ferejohn, "Coattail Voting," 407-409; Warren E. Miller, "Presidential Coattails," *Public Opinion Quarterly* (Winter 1955-1956): 353-358.
25. Gary C. Jacobson, "Presidential Coattails in 1972," *Public Opinion Quarterly* (Spring 1976): 194-200; Calvert and Ferejohn, "Coattail Voting," 415.
26. David W. Brady and Naomi B. Lynn, "Switched-Seat Congressional Districts: Their Effect on Party Voting and Public Policy," *American Journal of Political Science* (August 1973): 528-543.
27. George E. Condon, "Democrats Challenge President's Mandate," *San Diego Union,* November 8, 1984, A1.
28. Richard E. Cohen, "Republican Leaders in Congress Are Less Than Happy with Gains," *Los Angeles Times,* November 11, 1984, Part V, 1.
29. Samuel L. Popkin, "The Donkey's Dilemma: White Men Don't Vote Democratic," *Washington Post,* November 11, 1984, D2.
30. Duncan, "House Campaigns Quiet," 659.
31. Leaders of the New Right are convinced that a new Republican majority can be built only through an all-out assault on the "Liberal Welfare State" and reliance on radical supply-side economic policies. See, for example, Newt Gingrich's open letter to David Stockman in the *Washington Post* (national weekly edition), November 26, 1984, 6-7. It is always possible that they are right, but their views are currently based far more on faith than on analysis or evidence. Most of what is known about American politics suggests that this would be an extremely risky strategy; the present makeup of Congress probably renders it moot in any case.
32. Gurwitt, "GOP Disappointed with Gains," 2898-2899.

9. THE COURTS: 40 MORE YEARS?

Robert H. Birkby

The subtitle of this chapter expresses the hopes of the Republicans and the fears of the Democrats in the wake of the 1984 election. Presidents do, of course, influence the federal judiciary by their appointments to the bench, and Ronald Reagan has an unusual opportunity in his second term to affect the composition and attitudes of the U.S. Supreme Court if not for 40 years, then for 20 or more. The Court's membership has been relatively stable in recent years: Lyndon B. Johnson made two appointments, Richard Nixon four, Gerald R. Ford one, and Jimmy Carter none. Reagan already has made one appointment (Sandra Day O'Connor) and may have the opportunity to make several more. Five of the current justices were 76 years old or older on inauguration day 1985—Warren Burger (77), William Brennan (78), Thurgood Marshall (76), Harry Blackmun (76), and Lewis Powell (77). Byron White, although only 67, has 22 years of service on the Court and could choose to retire. Thus it is possible that Reagan will have six appointments to make in his second term. Added to the O'Connor appointment, that would give him more opportunities than any president except George Washington and Franklin D. Roosevelt.

The Court and the Campaign

Although the Court was not a major issue during the campaign, there were comments that made it clear the candidates were mindful of the age of the justices. Gov. Mario Cuomo, keynote speaker at the Democratic convention, asked "what kind of Supreme Court will we have" if Reagan serves four more years? Gary Hart drew a loud "no" when he asked the delegates, "Do you want Ronald Reagan to appoint the next Supreme Court?" And in his acceptance speech, Walter F. Mondale said that "by the start of the next decade I want to point to the Supreme Court and say 'justice is in good hands!' " The Democrats clearly understood what could happen to the Court's decisions if the power to replace five or six justices were given into the hands of a conservative Republican administration.

At their own convention, the Republicans were more restrained about the Court. Keynoter Katherine Ortega and nominee Ronald Reagan did not mention it in their speeches. In his vice presidential acceptance speech George Bush opined that "the Supreme Court should not be all caught up and involved in the political system" but should merely "interpret the Constitution and not legislate." The Republican platform said only that the party supports the appointment of judges "who represent traditional family values and the sanctity of human life." This plank led the Reverend Jerry Falwell of the Moral Majority to assert that "this gives us two or three judges of the Supreme Court." [1]

Out on the campaign trail there were some efforts by the Democrats to make an issue of the possibility that Reagan would make a large number of appointments to the Court if reelected. In a late September speech at George Washington University, Mondale asserted, "This election is about Jerry Falwell picking justices for the Supreme Court." In the first debate in Louisville, Kentucky, Mondale charged that a religious test would be used by the Reagan administration to select new justices. A few newspaper columnists, notably Anthony Lewis and Tom Wicker, joined in asking what type of person would be appointed and what a few new justices could do to the pattern of Court decisions. *Newsweek, Time, Readers' Digest,* and other periodicals presented more or less balanced articles on the age of the justices and the opportunity open to the next president. Nevertheless, there is no indication that the Court and the possible vacancies on it ever became salient issues for the general public. The candidates' comments were aimed at specific groups, most notably those concerned with abortion and with civil rights. The larger question of how much the president should influence Court decisions by appointments did not become a major issue because (1) the subject is too complex for capsule treatment in a campaign speech; (2) the issue does not touch closely the lives of most members of the voting public; (3) Mondale was as open as Reagan to the charge of intending to manipulate the Court; and (4) the public still wants to believe that judges are above politics.

The Court and the President

The relative silence about the Court in 1984 did not mean that the candidates had no quarrel with the federal judiciary or that the courts are now less important to presidents than in the past. No president with a policy agenda can afford to underestimate the significance of the courts. Courts, especially the Supreme Court, make public policy, and some of that policy making may run counter to the president's preferences and may even invalidate those preferences. In addition, presidents need the Court to legitimize the executive and legislative policies they develop.

Three recent examples illustrate the president's dependence on the Court. In his first term Reagan ordered the Internal Revenue Service (IRS) to restore tax-exempt status to educational institutions that discriminate on the basis of race. After a series of maneuvers, which included the appointment by the Court of special counsel to argue the IRS position, the justices struck down the president's order by an 8-to-1 vote.[2] In a different case, however, the administration's wish to limit the effect of the anti-sex discrimination provisions of the Civil Rights Act of 1964 was approved 6 to 3 by the Court in *Grove City College v. Bell*.[3] And in a third case, the Court upheld by 6 to 3 the legality of worker layoffs under a nondiscriminatory seniority system that affected more blacks than whites.[4] The blacks had been hired under the terms of a district court order to integrate the Memphis, Tennessee, fire department. Although the suit did not directly involve the national government, it was argued by Solicitor General Rex Lee as a friend of the court, supporting the city and the seniority system. Within a week of the decision, the Justice Department moved to review and challenge all antidiscrimination agreements to which the government is a party. Administration policy preferences again had been legitimized by the Court and, therefore, could be implemented.

There are many other possible illustrations of the relationship between the president and the Court. Presidents must keep the Court in mind as they shape their domestic policy agendas because the justices can legitimize or reject those policies. Generally, this relationship is not one of major conflict; during its entire history the Court has invalidated only 122 federal statutes and, through 1975, 24 executive orders. Although those laws can be said in some degree to have embodied the policies of the presidents who signed them, they are a small part of the total statutory output of the legislative process, and the decisions to invalidate them constitute only a slightly larger part of the output of the judicial process. The Court is often with the president simply because both are a part of what Robert A. Dahl called "a national policy-making majority," the president through election and the justices through selection by an elected president and Senate.[5] Conflict between president and Court tends to arise only when the chief executive represents an emerging and dramatically new set of policies—a realignment—and the Court, with its longer-term membership, is still more representative of the older, disappearing era.[6] In those circumstances, the Court, by trying to hold back change, as it did in the years 1934-1937, will come into sharp conflict with the president, Congress, or both. Occasionally, the Court will try to move faster than the other branches.[7]

None of this means that presidents can do no more than trim their sails to the prevailing winds that blow from the Supreme Court building. They do have constitutional means to check the Court and to moderate the potential for conflict between themselves and the justices. A president firmly in control of both houses of Congress could try to impeach and remove one or more of the justices. Thomas Jefferson tried this with Justice Samuel Chase in 1803 but failed to get a conviction in the Senate. Since then impeachment has not been seriously considered by Congress, and it is unlikely that an attempt based on disagreement over a policy would succeed. The president and Congress together could withdraw certain subjects from the Court's appellate jurisdiction,[8] as they have done on a few occasions.[9] Congress and the president together can increase the size of the Court, presumably to add "right-minded" justices. Roosevelt's abortive attempt to "pack" the Court in 1937 was more dramatic than earlier efforts and may have diminished the legitimacy of this tactic. Finally, the president can urge Congress to recommend the adoption of an amendment to the Constitution to overturn a disliked decision of the Court. Four such amendments have been adopted (the 11th, 14th, 16th, and 26th), but getting a two-thirds vote in each house of Congress and then a favorable vote in three-fourths of the state legislatures is an undertaking more likely to fail than succeed.[10] President Reagan is on record favoring amendments to overturn the Court's school prayer and abortion decisions, but he has not been able to get them through Congress.

Impeachment, alteration of appellate jurisdiction, court packing, and constitutional amendment—it is not often that the president and Congress can collaborate on any of the four because a concerted attack on the Court would appear too blatantly political. However, executive options go beyond these improbable tactics. The president can appoint new Supreme Court justices as vacancies arise, appoint lower court judges to vacant or new positions, and decide, with the solicitor general, which issues the government will litigate, either as a party or as an *amicus curiae* (friend of the court). How these three tactics will be used by Reagan to influence the courts will be the main concern of the rest of this chapter.

Supreme Court Appointments

The president's power to appoint members of the federal judiciary, subject to confirmation by the Senate, is the most direct and certain means of influencing court decisions. There is no mandatory retirement age for members of the Supreme Court, and most twentieth century justices have remained active as long as possible. Therefore, we can only speculate about what may happen during the next few years. We know that Justices Marshall and Brennan are the only sure liberals on the Court and that they may want to remain rather than be replaced by more conservative justices. And we know that they vote with each other more regularly than either votes with any other member of the Court.

We know that Burger, Blackman, and Powell were appointed by a Republican president (Nixon), and they may find the prospect of being replaced by a Republican president and Senate appealing. And we know that Burger and Powell are among the more conservative members of the Court and probably want a conservative president to name their successors. We know that Blackmun, now 76, once suggested that age 75 was a good age to begin thinking about retirement.[11] Blackmun can be described as centrist; he has said that he shifted somewhat to the liberal side in his voting behavior to balance the addition of O'Connor to the conservative bloc. Unlike his fellow Nixon appointees, Blackmun may not want his replacement to be named by a conservative president.

Justice White is more problematic. He is only 67, but his years of service and age together qualify him for full retirement benefits. He is a Democrat who was appointed by a Democrat (Kennedy), but he has been voting recently with the conservative bloc and may find the prospect of being replaced by a Reagan appointee attractive. Finally, it should be noted that surprise resignations or retirements are always possible. Ill health, opportunities to enter elective politics, or job frustration could produce an unanticipated vacancy.

Criteria for Appointment

With the justices' intentions unclear, one can talk only in terms of what could happen should one or more of them decide to leave. If a vacancy develops, President Reagan's course of action and the constraints on his freedom are fairly clear. In finding a nominee he very likely will follow the practice of other presidents and show concern for "(1) objective merit; (2) personal and political friendship; (3) balancing 'representation' on the Court; and (4) 'real' political and ideological compatibility." [12]

Objective merit, or professional qualification, is the baseline requirement for a justice. Without it no nominee can withstand scrutiny by the American Bar Association Committee on the Federal Judiciary, which usually is asked to rate the professional qualifications of potential nominees.[13] Nor would an unqualified nominee survive the Senate Committee on the Judiciary, which conducts hearings on the appropriateness of all nominations. For the sake of the party, a Republican-controlled committee would not want an unqualified person to be recommended even if the Democratic minority would permit it.

Objective merit is not easy to define and ascertain. But it would include an assessment of the potential nominee's educational background, performance as a lawyer and, if appropriate, as a judge, and the judgments of peers (as ascertained by the ABA committee). Republican presidents to a greater degree than Democrats tend to look at judges of other courts in seeking nominees because there is a clearer record to examine in assessing both objective merit and what is called judicial temperament. But presently sitting judges would not be the only persons considered, even by a Republican president.

Personal and political friendship plays an indeterminate role in Supreme Court appointments. President Washington knew personally every man he named to the Court; subsequent presidents have known an average of 60 percent of their nominees. The desire for personal knowledge of would-be justices helps to explain the presidential propensity to appoint from the top positions in the Department of Justice. Three of the present members of the Court—White, Marshall, and William H. Rehnquist—were serving or had served in the appointing president's Justice Department before going to the Court. Bearing in mind that even friends must be objectively qualified for the position, it is more pleasant to reward one's friends than strangers.[14] Also, considering the importance of ideological compatibility (our fourth factor) in Court appointments, that presidents turn to friends should not be surprising.

In the context of Supreme Court appointments, "representation" is a slippery term. Clearly the nine-member Court cannot be representative of the nation as a whole in the same sense that the House of Representatives with its 435 members is. But presidents do try to keep in mind several forms of representation in making their appointments. Geography is always a consideration; no section of the nation can be left without a justice for a long period of time, and no section should have a disproportionate number of members sitting on the same Court. On the present Court the Deep South and New England are unrepresented, while the upper Midwest (Burger, Blackmun, and John Paul Stevens) and the West (White, Rehnquist, and O'Connor) are overrepresented. It is likely that the president will be under pressure from the unrepresented sections to give them the first vacancies. The Deep South, especially, may expect a reward for its support in the election.

In this century the idea of representativeness has taken on an additional meaning. There have been references to the "Jewish" seat and the "Catholic" seat since the 1930s and 1940s, but the Jewish seat was filled with a Protestant after the resignation of Justice Abe Fortas in 1969, and no Catholic was on the bench between Frank Murphy's death in 1949 and William Brennan's appointment in 1956. That Reagan probably perceives a political obligation to Catholics but not Jews may determine how effective demands for religious representation turn out to be. Justices Marshall and O'Connor present another facet of representativeness. Their appointments may have created expectations of race and gender that no president can safely ignore.

One last aspect of representation is party affiliation. While presidents overwhelmingly have appointed justices of their own party,[15] the present Court may present a special problem. The party lineup is currently five Republicans and four Democrats, but three of the Democrats (Powell, Marshall, and Brennan) are among the potential retirees. Should all three retire, it may be politically wise to appoint another Democrat so that the party would have two seats; the Roosevelt Court of seven Democrats and two Republicans was as lopsided as any Court has been in this century and may represent the acceptable extreme.[16]

None of these representation elements of geography, special interests, and party affiliation is an absolute. Each has been ignored for what an appointing president has considered good reason, and Reagan, in his second term, secure in his position, and with a superb nominee, may be able to ignore them again. But he will be under pressure from organized groups and from senators of his own party not to do so. Thus, in the initial stages of considering replacements, the president undoubtedly will consider representativeness and then search for an explanation if he wishes to depart from it.

We come finally to the ultimate touchstone of judicial acceptability—political and ideological compatibility with the views of the president. In an unusually candid statement, Theodore Roosevelt explained to Sen. Henry Cabot Lodge why he was considering appointing Horace Lurton, a Democrat serving on the Court of Appeals for the Sixth Circuit, to the Court:

> Nothing has been so strongly borne in on me concerning lawyers on the bench as that the nominal politics of the man has nothing to do with his actions on the bench. His real politics are all important. In Lurton's case . . . he is right on the Negro question; he is right on the power of the federal government; he is right on the Insular business; he is right about corporations; he is right about labor. On every question that could come befjre the bench, he has so far shown himself to be in much closer touch with the policies in which you and I believe than even [Edward Douglass] White because he has been right about corporations where White has been wrong.[17]

Despite all this compatibility, Lurton did not get the appointment. Lodge wrote back wondering "why Republicans cannot be found who hold those opinions as well as Democrats."[18] Finding a person who is objectively qualified and thinks "right" is every president's chief concern. If several such persons are found, then representativeness and party loyalty can be taken into consideration in choosing among them. Ideological purity itself may be downplayed a little if the Court already has a solid majority that thinks as the president does, but even then a little insurance is comforting to the chief executive.

Ideological compatability can be inferred from a number of indicators. That a candidate is of the same political party as the president is a good hint but no more than that. The type of law practice engaged in may hold a clue—criminal defense lawyers and corporate lawyers are likely to have different value systems. Speeches made on current political issues, especially those made during a political campaign, reveal only a little about a candidate's philosophy. Published books and law review articles reveal a little more. Service in the administration gives an indication of both ideological bent and loyalty to the president's views. Those candidates who already are serving as judges have a record of decisions and written opinions that may give the clearest possible view of their philosophy. (This helps explain why almost 60 percent of the justices have had some prior judicial experience.[19]) And, of course, the candidates can be asked about their views on current issues that may come before the Court. These questions cannot be too direct, nor can they be phrased so that they seem to be asking for a promise to vote in a specific way. Dennis Mullins, a Reagan Justice Department official, indicated how the questions are put to potential judges: instead of asking whether they approve of abortion, "we would ask them whether they thought Justice Blackmun's analysis was sound [in *Roe v. Wade*]. . . . If they said yes, that would give us real concern about their judicial philosophy." [20]

Application of Criteria

Generally speaking, presidents and those who help them in their search for Supreme Court nominees have done a good job of identifying the "real" politics of their justices: only about one appointee out of every five has displeased the nominating president.[21] But some of the mistakes have been major ones. Wilson's appointment of his own attorney general, James Clark McReynolds, put on the Court a man who voted against everything Wilson stood for. Dwight D. Eisenhower has been quoted as saying that naming California governor Earl Warren to the Court "was one of the two biggest mistakes I made in my administration." [22] And that appointment was made after the president and his attorney general, Herbert Brownell, had talked with Warren at length.

One can only guess how objective merit, political and personal friendship, representativeness, and ideology will operate in Reagan's Court appointments, if any, during the next four years, but it is certain that all four factors will play some role. The methods used in identifying and nominating Justice O'Connor may well be the methods the president will employ as vacancies occur in his second term. The attorney general was the point man in the search, but he worked within Reagan's guidelines. He was instructed to find a woman with a conservative judicial philosophy who possessed high qualifications for the position. Suggestions came to the attorney general from a variety of sources—state party officials, senators, other government officials, and private citizens associated with the Republican party, among others. As the list was narrowed, the FBI conducted a background check on O'Connor; the attorney general's staff scrutinized her record as a state legislator and a state judge; and the ABA Committee on the Federal Judiciary assessed her qualifications. That she was cochairman of the Arizona Committee to Re-Elect the President in 1972 and supported Reagan's campaign for the Republican nomination against Ford in 1976 did not harm her case. Early on she had the support of Republican senator Barry Goldwater of Arizona, a Senate power with impeccable conservative credentials.

The Role of the Senate

Once the president sends a name to the Senate, the Judiciary Committee holds hearings to give both supporters and opponents of the nomination a chance to express their views. This committee, currently chaired by Republican senator Strom Thurmond of South Carolina, has members from all segments of the political spectrum and can be expected to examine the nominee's credentials and philosophy very closely. Some 15 of the 26 Court nominations that have failed have been stopped in this committee by an adverse vote (followed by the president's withdrawal of the nomination) or by failure of the committee to take any action at all near the end of the president's term. Barring either of these eventualities, the Judiciary Committee makes a recommendation to the whole Senate, which then debates the wisdom of the nomination for as long as it deems necessary before voting. Historically, the Senate has formally rejected only 11 nominations of the 115 that reached the floor. This includes only 3 of the 53 persons nominated in this century—John J. Parker, Clement F. Haynsworth, and G. Harrold Carswell. (Two more of the 53 nominations did not reach the floor at all, those of Abe Fortas as chief justice and Homer Thornberry). It seems likely that nominations will be contested more hotly than usual in the Senate that took office in January 1985 because the Republican majority is slim (53 to 47), the Democrats expect to be able to control the Senate after the 1986 elections, and the president is a lame duck. One way of defusing heightened partisanship in the Senate would be for the president to nominate conservatives who are politically "untouchable" on other grounds—women, blacks, or sitting senators, for example. But whatever Reagan does, the lesson of this century is that any nominee will be confirmed unless that person has some particularly noisy skeletons in his closet (Haynsworth), is patently unqualified (Carswell), or is opposed by an unusually powerful coalition of interest groups that make the nomination a major issue (Parker).

It is, of course, impossible to specify the names of the persons Reagan may select, but we can construct a general profile of the type of person he will be looking for. The typical nominee will be objectively qualified by virtue of a better-than-average undergraduate and legal education; will have some judicial experience, probably on a state supreme court or the federal court of appeals; will have the endorsement of the ABA committee; will be Republican with some prior involvement in partisan politics; and will be "representative" in some way, perhaps geographically. Another woman is a possibility, but the O'Connor appointment may have done all that Reagan thinks is needed at the Supreme Court level. The nominee probably will be white unless the vacancy is caused by the retirement of Justice Marshall, in which case Reagan may feel it necessary to appoint a black even though that group gave him little electoral support in November 1984. Most important, the nominee will be someone who seems to share the president's views on major domestic issues.

Assessment

Every president has tried to ensure that his views would be represented on the Court long after he left office; the only thing unusual about the next four years is the number of possible appointments. If all six possible vacancies develop, if Reagan does a careful job of selecting nominees, and if he has a great deal of luck, he will be able to pack the Court in a way unmatched since Franklin Roosevelt. Those who do not share Reagan's philosophy should not instantly conclude, however, that the Republic is in danger or that what they want is unattainable. As we already have mentioned, the overall performance of one justice out of every five has been unsatisfactory to the appointing president, and every justice has voted occasionally against the president's views.[23] This is partly because the times change and new issues arise that neither the president nor the nominee could have foreseen. When Franklin Roosevelt was considering potential nominees in the late 1930s, civil rights attitudes were not thought important enough to investigate, yet they became important within a decade.[24] As Yale law professor Alexander M. Bickel observed: "You shoot an arrow into the far distant future when you appoint a Justice and not the man himself can tell you what he will think about some of the problems that he will face." [25] Harry S. Truman had a terser comment: "Packing the Supreme Court simply can't be done. . . . I've tried it and it won't work. . . . Whenever you put a man on the Supreme Court he ceases to be your friend. I'm sure of that." [26] Times change, people change, and the process of change is protected and fostered on the Court by the independence justices have by virtue of their tenure during "good behavior," which means for life in practical terms. Change occurs also by virtue of the opportunity for intellectual persuasion that exists in any collegial decision-making group. Indeed, it is for this last reason that some significant differences in outlook among the justices are desirable.

Beyond these there is a more important reason why Reagan's opponents should not be dismayed. The Court is one part of a tripartite system of government. Each branch was intended by the Founding Fathers to check and balance the other two. The Court's check on Congress and the chief executive through the use of judicial review and statutory interpretation is obvious and is generally accepted as legitimate. Why then should we not accept as legitimate the president's appointment power as a check on the judiciary, especially when there are so few other effective checks on the courts? [27] Judges do not make their decisions uninfluenced by what Justice Oliver Wendell Holmes called "the felt necessities of the times," [28] but they occasionally need new colleagues to help them determine what those felt necessities are. As Dahl put it in a now classic article, the appointment power helps to ensure that "the policy views dominant on the Court are never for long out of line with the policy views among the lawmaking majorities of the United States. Consequently, it would be most unrealistic to suppose that the Court would, for more than a few years at most, stand against any major alternatives sought by a lawmaking majority." [29]

Dahl was writing at a time when the Court generally exercised only negative power—saying to Congress or the president "you can't do that." The Court was exercising a check on elected officials, but the appointment of a new Supreme Court justice once every 22 months—the historical average—was a good check on the Court by the president and Senate. Since that time the Court has expanded its role to include affirmative policy making.[30] Courts in the past three decades have "embarked upon the imposition of large-scale affirmative obligations, some as remedies for past violations of the Constitution but others as interpretations of what the Constitution itself requires." [31] It makes little difference whether this changed role or its results are good or bad. What is important is that a Court that needed checking by the regular appointment of new justices when it was performing a less obtrusive role in the policy process is, if anything, more in need of it now that it is playing a larger and more important role. Nor does the Court seem likely to give up its activist role. It has been the supposedly conservative Burger Court, after all, that has given us the school bus as an instrument of integration, that has rewritten the death penalty statutes in practically every state, and that has made abortion legal even if not always financially possible.[32] Indeed, the Burger Court has declared more federal statutes unconstitutional than any other Court in our history.[33]

Lower Court Appointments

Supreme Court appointments are the most visible and dramatic presidential activities in relation to the judiciary, but appointments to the other federal courts are just as important because these courts handle more cases. Approximately 80,000 cases are decided in lower courts annually, compared with 150 or so that are decided by the Supreme Court. Also, because it is from the 12 courts of appeals and the 95 district courts below them that the Supreme Court gets most of its business, the president's ability to affect the decisions of the lower courts by the appointment power in turn can affect the issues the Supreme Court decides to tackle. There is no way to predict how many vacancies on the lower federal courts Reagan will fill in his second term. He made 131 such appointments in his first term, and there probably will be no fewer in the second.[34] As with Supreme Court appointments, we may be able to determine what he will do with future lower court appointments by examining what he has done already.

First, however, a brief survey of the appointment process is important. At the district court (trial court) level, the president is constrained by the customary requirement that nominees come from the state in which they are to serve and that they be approved, or at least not opposed, by the senators from that state, especially if they are of the president's party. Senatorial courtesy is not the ultimate weapon that it once was, but it remains true in a broad sense that "the senator nominates and the Senate approves." [35] In 1977 President Carter requested that all senators convene nominating panels within their states to screen possible candidates for these positions. Once such a panel has made a recommendation and the senator has approved it, it is difficult for the president to nominate someone else. These panels were not *required* by Carter, but many senators used them, and a significant number apparently have continued to do so, even though Reagan did not renew his predecessor's request.[36] If the president's choices are limited without the nominating panels, with them the choices are constrained even further because of the apparent elimination of politics from the process.

Presidents possess a major weapon in district court nominations—delay. They can refuse to accept names proposed by senators, thus leaving positions vacant. As the lack of a judge is felt in a district, pressure on the senator will grow to compromise with the president. Of course, if neither senator from the state is of the president's party, the president has greater flexibility, but the state party leaders will play a role by suggesting names and insisting on their preferences. Reagan, in his last term, may believe that he can ignore party leaders since he has nothing to gain from them in the future, but he may have past debts to pay.

At the court of appeals level, senatorial influence wanes. These courts operate in multistate circuits so that a president is not confined to a single state in making selections. (Presidents are, by tradition, confined to the circuit.) They may make nominations from states without troublesome senators, but it is expected that each state in the circuit will be represented on the court of appeals. Carter also created nominating panels at this level to aid in the selection process and to further dilute the influence of the individual senators. These were abolished by Reagan, which placed the selection process more completely back in presidential hands.[37]

In short, presidents must pay a great deal of attention to senators of their party from the affected states in making district court appointments and, in the case of court of appeals nominations, must carefully consider the candidates proposed by senators from the circuit. Because party label is not a clear indicator of ideological preference, the greater influence of senators in these appointments will dilute any presidential effort to create a monolithic lower federal judiciary. Presidents can always have their way if they want it badly enough, but they run the risk of losing support from senators on other, more important, matters.

As in the case of Supreme Court nominees, appointments to the district courts and the courts of appeals are scrutinized by the ABA Committee on the Federal Judiciary. For the Supreme Court the committee uses the ratings "acceptable" and "opposed." For lower court nominees, it uses rankings of "not qualified," "qualified," "well qualified," and "exceptionally well qualified." Presidents and senators must be sensitive to these rankings and, ideally, should avoid too many appointments at even the "qualified" ranking.

With all that in mind, we can assess what Reagan has done with his lower court appointments. A pattern emerged from the nominations he submitted to the 97th Congress during his first two years in office.[38] Reagan has been more partisan in his appointments than any president since Wilson (97.1 percent Republicans to the district courts and 100 percent Republicans to the courts of appeals). His district court appointees were more likely to have been politically active and more likely to be white than Carter, Ford, Nixon, or Johnson appointees. They were more likely to be male than Carter-appointed judges, but less likely than Nixon, Ford, or Johnson appointees. A majority (51 percent) of the district court appointees came from positions in private law practice; another 37 percent were state court judges. At the court of appeals level one major difference is noticeable in Reagan's pattern of appointments: two-thirds have come from the ranks of sitting federal or state judges. This reflects the greater policy-making role of the appeals courts—a prior judicial record offers more evidence about a nominee's philosophy than does a record in private legal practice. Finally, the socio-economic status of Reagan nominees for both kinds of courts was higher than for Carter appointees. One-third of Carter's judges had a net worth of less than $200,000, as compared with 18 percent of Reagan's nominees. At the other end of the scale, 10 percent of Carter's nominees had a net worth of more than $1 million; 22 percent of Reagan's appointees were millionaires.

It is not certain that Reagan will continue the same pattern of lower court appointments in his second term, but there is no reason to think he will not. Regardless of the demographic and socio-economic characteristics of the second-term appointees, it seems certain that a concern for conservative philosophy will continue to be overriding. Jonathan C. Rose, head of the Office of Legal Policy in the Justice Department, said in an interview that "philosophy certainly has been a factor with regard to our appointments." He added that the administration was attempting to correct the imbalance created by Carter's appointment of so many liberals to the lower federal courts.[39] In practical terms this has meant that Reagan has tried to appoint judges "who share his opposition to busing, racial hiring quotas and elaborate procedural protections for criminal defendants, and his disagreement with Supreme Court decisions on the death penalty, abortion, and school prayer."[40] He has done this by having every possible source of information on the nominee's attitudes checked.

Before turning from appointments to other efforts to influence the decisions of courts, we should consider one recent piece of legislation. The Supreme Court and Congress have been trying for some time to restructure the nation's bankruptcy courts in the wake of a Court decision that called into question the powers of these specialized courts. In the early summer of 1984, Congress passed compromise legislation to clarify the power and status of bankruptcy court judges. The statute created positions of 14 years duration for 227 bankruptcy judges. They are to be appointed by the president with the advice and consent of the Senate. While many of the incumbents probably will be reappointed to provide continuity, some new judges also will be named. In addition, the statute provided for 61 new district court judgeships and 24 new court of appeals judgeships, but limited the president to the appointment of only 40 of these in 1984. With 45 remaining lower court appointments to be made early in the second term, Reagan will have a chance to continue shaping the federal courts in his own image.

As with Supreme Court appointments, "real" politics or philosophy plays an important role in the appointment of judges to the district courts and courts of appeals. But again there is no intent to suggest that such considerations are wrong or ignoble. A life-tenured judiciary must absorb periodic infusions of persons who hold views that reflect contemporary attitudes on matters of public policy, lest it get hopelessly out of date. By appointing conservative Republicans to the bench, Reagan will be doing nothing different from what predecessors of a contrasting political philosophy have done.

The Solicitor General

Success in appointing like-minded persons to the federal courts will go a long way toward fulfilling the goal of legitimizing Reagan's policies. But there is one major nonjudicial appointment to be made by the president that also is important to achieving this purpose. The solicitor general of the United States (presently Rex Lee) is the third-ranking official in the Department of Justice and the most important in presenting the administration's point of view to the appellate courts. As the president's lawyer, the solicitor general performs four vital functions: (1) screening cases that were lost by the government in the trial courts for possible appeal;[41] (2) briefing and arguing cases in appellate courts when the United States is a party; (3) filing arguments with the Supreme Court for or against the granting of writs of certiorari (that is, requests that the Court hear an appeal) in cases not involving the United States as a party; and (4) filing *amicus curiae* (friend of the court) briefs with the Supreme Court in cases that are important to the government but to which it is not a party. As an examination of these four functions will show, the president must give careful consideration to the appointment of the person who is to perform them.

When the government has lost a suit at the trial court level, it is the solicitor general who must, with few exceptions, approve taking an appeal to the court of appeals, and, if necessary, to the Supreme Court. In numerical terms the solicitor general authorizes appeal from the district courts to the courts of appeals about 30 to 33 percent of the time. Ten percent of the cases lost in the courts of appeals are submitted to the Supreme Court.[42] And when solicitors general decide to carry cases to the Supreme Court, they are exceptionally effective—between 60 and 80 percent of the government's petitions for certiorari are granted, as compared with about 7 percent of the petitions of other parties. This screening process is important. An astute solicitor general takes the losses in the trial courts when they are deemed unimportant or unwinnable at the appellate level and goes up the judicial ladder only if the decision reached or the precedent set will advance the administration's policy goals. For example, Solicitor General Lee refused to appeal to the Supreme Court any of the 215,000 cases lost by the Social Security Administration in challenges to Reagan's policy of removing persons from disability payment rolls. By doing so, he probably avoided a decision adverse to the government and an opinion giving a clear-cut determination of the meaning of the statute and the methods used to cut off benefits. On the other hand, it was Lee and his staff who briefed, argued, and won the Grove City College case referred to earlier in this chapter.

Once the decision to appeal has been made, the solicitor general either reviews the briefs and arguments to be presented to the appellate court by the government agency that is involved or assists in the preparation of those briefs and arguments. In this fashion, solicitors general act as coordinators for administration policy making as that policy is presented to the judicial branch. They bring to the process a greater degree of objectivity than the original agency lawyers can have, a broader perspective on how the case at issue fits into overall government policy. They generally are better able to articulate to the courts the larger policy implications contained in the litigation.

Over the years solicitors general have been unusually effective in their presentations to the Supreme Court. The government, on average, wins 70 to 75 percent of the cases it takes to the Court and well over half the cases in which the other party has persuaded the Court to review a lower court decision in favor of the United States. In the 1983 Term of Court, Lee and his staff won 85 percent of their cases.[43] We will return to consider the high victory rate for the government after looking at the other two functions of the solicitor general.

When the government is not a party to litigation before the Supreme Court, solicitors general may intervene at either or both of two stages by means of an amicus curiae brief. They may file such a brief either to support or oppose the granting of certiorari or argue the case on the merits once certiorari has been granted. The position they take will depend on their assessment of the appropriateness of the litigation for resolving issues that are important to the administration. When, for example, a private citizen brings suit against an employer for racial or sex discrimination, the solicitor general may want the Court to know the government's position on the findings and the remedy chosen by the lower courts. In recent terms of Court the solicitor general has filed amicus briefs in an average of 20 percent of the cases heard by the Court and has supported the side that ultimately prevailed more than 80 percent of the time.[44] In these instances, policies favored by the administration were advanced or legitimized by the Court's decision.

Solicitors general make a good many decisions by themselves, but there are indications that in major policy areas the attorney general and the president are consulted.[45] There is no solid information on the number or frequency of presidential interventions in the solicitor general's conduct of the office, but the very nature of the presidency precludes regular oversight of all litigation that involves the government or has implications for administration policies. This is why the solicitor general is appointed by the president rather than by the head of the Justice Department, the attorney general: a solicitor general with the proper policy preferences does not have to be supervised closely by the president in order to carry out the administration's policies.

There are at least three reasons for the success rate of the solicitors general, Rex Lee in particular, in dealing with the appellate courts. First, they and their staffs have more experience dealing with these courts than most other lawyers in or out of government. Their own litigation constitutes half of the Supreme Court's docket, and their amicus briefs make up another fifth. Expertise breeds success, so much so that in many instances the solicitor general will predict correctly the outcome of a case before it is argued.[46] Second, solicitors general over the years have built a credible image with the justices. By screening out unimportant cases, by writing excellent briefs and making careful arguments that reflect accurately the administration's position, and by confessing from time to time that the government should not prevail in a particular case, solicitors general have made themselves aides to the Court as well as advocates for the president.[47]

The third reason for the solicitor general's high success rate relates back to our earlier discussion. As we have noted, the Court is not often out of step with the other branches of government, at least not for very long. By presenting the administration's position to a Court that already may be predisposed in its favor, the solicitor general is almost sure to win a substantial share of cases. There is little doubt that Solicitor General Lee's 85-percent success rate in the first term is attributable to all of these factors. Especially important, however, was his acute sense of the Justices' predispositions and ability to present to them only cases they were ready to decide his way. Lee or a successor may have a similar success rate during the next four years unless political pressures from the Far Right force him to appeal cases for which the justices are not ready. And that takes us back to the whole discussion of appointment of justices.

This chapter has been devoted to looking ahead. For that reason it has had to be tentative and to rely on what has happened in the past as a predictor of what may happen in the next four years. We cannot be sure that any justices will leave the Court. If some do, neither the president nor anyone else can be certain that their replacements will behave as predicted and hoped for at the time of appointment. Nor can anyone be too sure of what types of issues will be brought to the courts during the next four years. About all that can be said with certainty is that Reagan *may* have a chance to give the Supreme Court its second major reorientation in this century.

Notes

1. My transcriptions from the television coverage of the two conventions.
2. *Bob Jones University v. United States,* 76 L Ed 2d 157 (1983).
3. *Grove City College v. Bell,* 79 L Ed 2d 516 (1984).
4. *Firefighters Local Union No. 1784 v. Stotts,* 81 L Ed 483 (1984).
5. Robert A. Dahl, "Decision-Making in a Democracy: The Supreme Court as a National Policy-Maker," *Journal of Public Law* 6, no. 1 (1958): 285. A supporting view is offered by Richard Funston, "The Supreme Court and Critical Elections," *American Political Science Review* 69 (September 1975): 795-811. But compare Jonathan Casper, "The Supreme Court and National Policy Making," *American Political Science Review* 70 (March 1976): 50-63.
6. Funston, "Supreme Court and Critical Elections."
7. Of course, the Court has ample room for policy making on its own even when its members are in general agreement with the president. See Casper, "Supreme Court and National Policy Making."
8. Article III, sec. 2, cl. 2, provides that "the Supreme Court shall have appellate jurisdiction . . . with such exceptions, and under such regulations as the Congress shall make."
9. The Habeas Corpus Act of 1868, the Norris-LaGuardia Act of 1932, and the Emergency Price Control Act of 1942 all limited the appellate jurisdiction of the Court. There is increasing doubt that this check upon the Court is as complete as the words of Article III make it appear to be. *Judicature* (October 1981) is devoted entirely to this issue.
10. The proponents of the Equal Rights Amendment discovered how difficult it is to convince three-fourths of the state legislatures.
11. *New York Times Magazine,* February 20, 1983, 66.
12. Henry J. Abraham, *Justices and Presidents* (New York: Oxford University Press, 1974), 54.
13. For a detailed analysis of the ABA Committee, see Joel Grossman, *Lawyers and Judges* (New York: John Wiley, 1965).
14. Maybe even *especially* qualified, to avoid charges of cronyism.

15. The range extends from Taft's 82.2 percent Republicans to Wilson's 98.6 percent Democrats. Abraham, *Justices,* 60.

16. Roosevelt may have aided acceptance of this division by promoting Republican Harlan Fiske Stone from associate justice to chief justice.

17. H. C. Lodge, Jr., *Selections from the Correspondence of Theodore Roosevelt and Henry Cabot Lodge,* vol. 2 (New York: Charles Scribner's Sons, 1925), 228, 230, 231.

18. Ibid., 229.

19. Whether prior judicial service should be a requirement for appointment to the Supreme Court is a regularly debated issue. For a strongly negative view, see Felix Frankfurter, "The Supreme Court in the Mirror of the Justices," *University of Pennsylvania Law Review* (April 1957): 781-796.

20. *New York Times,* April 22, 1984, E5.

21. My tally from the individual discussions in Abraham, *Justices.* Robert Scigliano, *The Supreme Court and the Presidency* (New York: Free Press, 1971), Chapter 5, estimates the failure rate at one of four through the Johnson appointments. On October 19, 1984, Justice William Rehnquist in a speech at the University of Minnesota School of Law said there was nothing wrong with a president trying to appoint to the Court persons sympathetic to his philosophy. But, he added, "history teaches us that ... a number of factors militate against a president having anything more than partial success." Nashville *Tennessean,* October 20, 1984, 1.

22. J. H. Pollack, *Earl Warren: The Judge Who Changed America* (Englewood Cliffs, N.J.: Prentice-Hall, 1979), 200. Some, including Warren, have said that the statement was "my biggest damn-fool mistake," but either way Eisenhower's unhappiness is obvious.

23. Oliver Wendell Holmes disappointed Theodore Roosevelt in the *Northern Securities Co. v. United States,* 193 U.S. 197 (1904), and Richard Nixon must have been chagrined to find Warren Burger leading a unanimous Court in *United States v. Nixon,* 418 U.S. 683 (1974).

24. This is part of the point made by Justice Rehnquist in the speech referred to in note 21.

25. Quoted in *Time,* May 23, 1969, 24.

26. Quoted in Abraham, *Justices,* 63. It should be noted that Truman was singularly inept in selecting justices.

27. Much of this discussion is based on John Agresto, *The Supreme Court and Constitutional Democracy* (Ithaca, N.Y.: Cornell University Press, 1984), which develops the argument fully.

28. *The Common Law* (Boston: Little, Brown, 1881), 1.

29. Dahl, "Decision-Making in a Democracy," 285.

30. See Abram Chayes, "The Role of the Judge in Public Law Litigation," *Harvard Law Review* 89, no. 4 (1976): 1281-1292.

31. Archibald Cox, *The Role of the Supreme Court in American Government* (New York: Oxford University Press, 1976), 101. See also Donald Horowitz, *The Courts and Social Policy* (Washington: Brookings Institution, 1977); and

Robert H. Birkby, *The Court and Public Policy* (Washington, D.C.: CQ Press, 1983).

32. *Swann v. Charlotte-Mecklenburg Board of Education,* 402 U.S. 1 (1971); *Furman v. Georgia,* 401 U.S. 238 (1972); *Roe v. Wade,* 410 U.S. 113 (1973).

33. Henry J. Abraham, *The Judicial Process,* 4th ed. (New York: Oxford University Press, 1980), 305-310. See Vincent Blasi, ed., *The Burger Court: The Counter-Revolution That Wasn't* (New Haven, Conn.: Yale University Press, 1983) for a discussion of the continuity between the Warren and Burger Courts. Agresto, *Supreme Court,* argues that the courts should not give up their more activist role in the policy process.

34. President Carter had by the end of his term appointed 40 percent of the lower federal court judges, in part because of an expansion of the federal judiciary.

35. A casual observation of Sen. James Eastland of Mississippi to the author.

36. Alan Neff, *The United States District Judge Nominating Commissions: Their Members, Procedures and Candidates* (Chicago: American Judicature Society, 1981); W. Gary Fowler, "Judicial Selection under Reagan and Carter: A Comparison of Their Initial Recommendation Procedures," *Judicature* (December/January 1984): 265-283. Senatorial motives for continuing to use these panels are mixed—to protect themselves from pressures, to reduce presidential interference, to advance affirmative action, to improve the quality of nominees, and to "reform" the system.

37. Larry C. Berkson and Susan B. Carbon, *The United States Circuit Judge Nominating Commission: Its Members, Procedures and Candidates* (Chicago: American Judicature Society, 1980).

38. These data are from Sheldon Goldman, "Reagan's Appointments at Midterm: Shaping the Bench in His Own Image," *Judicature* (March 1983): 334-347, and are the most complete available at this time.

39. *Congressional Quarterly Weekly Report,* January 15, 1983, 83-85.

40. *New York Times,* April 22, 1984, E5.

41. The decision to appeal or not is the loser's; the solicitor general has no control when the government wins.

42. Scigliano, *Court and Presidency,* 168-169.

43. *Newsweek,* July 16, 1984, 57.

44. Karen O'Connor, "The Amicus Curiae Role of the United States Solicitor General in Supreme Court Litigation," *Judicature* (December/January 1983): 256-264, 261.

45. Ibid., 261.

46. Ibid.

47. Of course, an inadequate solicitor general could destroy this relationship of trust and confidence in short order.

10. IMPLICATIONS:
WHAT AMERICANS WANTED

Nicholas Lemann

Two months before election day, my first child was born, and as a mental exercise I tried during the campaign to broaden my relentlessly short term journalist's perspective by wondering what I would tell him if in 20 years he were to ask me what the presidential campaign of 1984 had been all about. What was at stake? Where were we as a nation? What were we trying to decide? What difference did it make who won?

The quickest and easiest answer to these questions is that 1984 was a fairly prosperous year, and an incumbent president blessed with prosperity always wins reelection. The historical record of the past 60 years is ironclad on that. That the president is responsible for the rates of inflation, unemployment, interest, and growth in the gross national product is universally assumed, even though the connection isn't direct. The economic recovery of 1983-1984 that helped President Ronald Reagan so much had its clear roots in President Jimmy Carter's appointment of Paul Volcker as head of the Federal Reserve Board in 1979 and Volcker's quick tightening of the money supply, which did much to bring down inflation. But in the world of practical politics, Reagan took the credit, without anyone really challenging him.

The matter need not end there, though. In particular three broad areas of inquiry suggest themselves as ways of understanding what the 1984 election meant: the lines along which the electorate divided; the ways in which the candidates practiced, and perhaps changed, the craft of politics; and the ways government policy was discussed—even determined—during the course of the campaign.

Constituencies

Republicans

Reagan rose as a national politician from the ashes of the 1964 presidential campaign of Sen. Barry Goldwater, which accounts for the

259

difficulty that most contemporary observers have explaining his success. Goldwater's resounding defeat by President Lyndon B. Johnson was seen as a repudiation of conservatism by the voters. In the next few presidential elections, it seemed that the center always beat the left and the right, in both intraparty and interparty politics. (The one exception was Sen. George McGovern's capture of the Democratic nomination in 1972; his resounding defeat in the general election by President Richard Nixon only underscored the overall point.) From late 1964 until early 1980, Reagan was seen nationally as a member of the conservative movement, and it could be argued that no "movement" politician of any sort was ever elected president before 1980. How then could he have won? Who voted for him? What had changed since 1964?

A lot had changed. For one thing, Reagan is not Goldwater, and Jimmy Carter and Walter F. Mondale are not Lyndon B. Johnson. Also, the assassination of President John F. Kennedy was obviously a major factor in the 1964 election that one hopes will never recur. But there must be more to it than personalities and extraordinary events.

Goldwater's strength, such as it was, was in the Sun Belt—the South and West. Since 1964 those parts of the country have grown in population, economic strength, and self-confidence more than anyone would have predicted, and they have remained strongly conservative by, in effect, converting their immigrants to the prevailing faith. Typically, in the booming parts of the Sun Belt, people feel that they have cast off the social and economic straightjacket that one must wear in the older parts of the country and entered a more freewheeling and libertarian society, where risks are greater but so are rewards and where your family name, college diploma, and union card don't matter nearly as much as in other parts of the country. It is a great eastern misconception that only the prosperous hold these views—in booming areas of the West, median income often declines as the broke but hopeful (and conservative) stream in.

The Sun Belt is only one region, but it has cultural, economic, and social-class implications that reach into various groups of voters nationally. The eastern establishment, which grew up in reaction to the late nineteenth century Gilded Age of unbridled business competition and reached its zenith of influence in the Marshall Plan years of internationalism just after World War II, engendered, by virtue of its power, considerable resentment—to a much greater extent than its own members probably suspected. Several trends after 1964 deepened and sharpened this resentment. The sophisticated, rebellious left-of-liberal culture of the late 1960s and early 1970s that was the motive force behind such causes as the antiwar movement, the post-Martin Luther King black movement, and the sexual and drug revolutions was widely despised; although it had little to do with the eastern establishment, the two were linked in most voters' minds. The war in Vietnam made Goldwater's warnings about American military and diplomatic weakness, which seemed nutty in 1964, look sensible to many people—and the establishment, having tightly controlled foreign policy for a generation, naturally got the blame. The economic problems that followed the OPEC oil-price increases of 1973— most importantly, inflation—made the establishment's stewardship of our material well-being look suspect too. So by the late 1970s there was a vast constituency of people wanting, in the manner of westerners, to break free of the shackles of the East. Carter tapped that emotion in 1976, then inexplicably became a dutiful establishmentarian and let Reagan have it all to himself in 1980. Mondale did the same in 1984.

Reagan, while always staunchly conservative, has been brilliant at spotting and at making himself the avatar of new conservative causes that were not a part of his standard repertoire. In 1976, after losing a string of primaries to President Gerald R. Ford, he began to campaign in North Carolina largely by attacking the proposed treaty to give the Panama Canal to Panama—a classic strong-foreign-policy, antiestablishment issue. He won an upset victory in that primary, and he used the theme of American weakness to great advantage thereafter. Similarly, in 1980 he was quick to pick up the themes of the late-1970s grass-roots tax revolt and of supply-side economics. Both of these were politically potent because they were new twists on one of the oldest ideas in politics, namely, that people hate to pay taxes. The emotional content Reagan gave to this issue was, again, pure antiestablishment. Taxes and government were "them," tax cuts were "us." He encouraged middle-class people to think that somehow, in the transaction between themselves and the federal government, they were net losers, being taken advantage of by an odd alliance of poor people on welfare and liberal fat cats.

The Democratic party, for all its rhetoric about the little man, has never won a presidential election simply by getting the dispossessed to vote as a bloc against the moneyed; in fact it lost in 1984 by doing precisely that. Democrats have won the presidency only when they were able to peel off some "haves" from the Republicans—farmers, for instance, or white southerners, or above-median-income skilled workers—to add to their base of "have-nots." Ever since the Republicans became firmly the party of business in the 1870s, it has been theoretically possible for them to line up everyone middle class and above on their side. Reagan in effect did that, neatly leaving the bottom third in income to Mondale and keeping the rest for himself. But it is notable that not only did Reagan bring the decently-off together, he did so by using the populist rhetoric of dispossession—"the people" against "government." Surely that will go down as one of our history's great political feats.

As the *Communist Manifesto* was to the Russian Revolution, so was Kevin Phillips's 1969 book *The Emerging Republican Majority* to Reagan's presidential victories. Phillips, a young aide to President Nixon, was widely considered loony for believing that the South and blue-collar union members one day would, for "populist" reasons, vote solidly Republican. (Now he spends election nights on CBS News, explaining why Ohio just went 60-40 for Reagan.) Phillips has written lately that he doubts the Reagan coalition will hold, and his reasoning seems indisputable. The history of American political parties is mostly one of powerful economic interests at war with each other, and the relative unanimity with which these interests gravitated to the Republican party in the early 1980s probably makes this period a historical exception. More specifically, as Phillips points out, there are potentially major fissures among Reagan voters between those who want government intervention in the economy (like steelworkers and the elderly) and those who don't, and between those who want government to enforce conservative social and religious values and those who don't. In addition, the spinoff of some large group strictly on grounds of self-interested objection to a Reagan policy—for example, "Main Street" business interests who object to the abolition of economic regulations that protected them—is a constant possibility. And it would seem, finally, that power in America will get back in tune with money to the extent that it won't much longer be possible to strike the chord of resentment against the powerful in the middling- and well-off—they'll realize they *are* the powerful.

Democrats

When Reagan and David Stockman, his budget director, were setting out to cut federal spending in 1981, they talked about everyone having to bear the pain equally. This didn't happen—the organized interest groups salvaged their programs—and perhaps as a result, Reagan was able to campaign in 1984 on broad themes almost exclusively. His famous question, "Are you better off than you were four years ago?" defines presidential politics purely in terms of self-interest, but it floats above the morass of interest groups.

In the end, the Democrats also avoided the interest groups, more by sinking below than by rising above them. Throughout the campaign, the party in general and Mondale in particular were preoccupied with who their constituents were and how they should be dealt with. But on election day their one reliable constituency was the poor, especially the black poor. Mondale carried no region, no occupational class, and only one ethnic group, Jews. After the election the thinness of its support remained by far the party's biggest problem.

All discussions of the Democratic party's constituency must begin in familiar fashion, with the "New Deal coalition." This was the fabric that President Franklin D. Roosevelt wove together in the 1930s, seemingly forever—poor people, blacks, Hispanics, white ethnics (such as Poles, Irish, and Jews), blue-collar workers, government employees, small-business owners, farmers, and white southerners. At the time, of course, the country was in an economic crisis of proportions unfathomable today; also, many people in these groups suffered from virulent discrimination on the basis of their heritage. Both of those immediate and urgent conditions have changed and left the Democratic party weaker. Fifty years of prosperity, suburbanization, and assimilation have devastated the ethnic groups' ties to the party. Various strains in the party that grew out of the protest movements of the 1960s and 1970s, which conservatives like to lump together under the name "McGovernism," helped drive away small-business owners and blue-collar workers. The bitter memory of Reconstruction naturally faded over the course of a century, and with it white southerners' Democratic loyalty.

Probably more pernicious for the party, the coalition, like any organization, underwent a process similar to the aging of a bureaucracy. Its members squabbled with each other. The main concern shifted somewhat from external to internal affairs, from selling a cause to the country to bargaining over spoils and turf with each other. What began as matters of belief became matters of self-interest, economic and organizational. The leaders of the various groups in the coalition, especially unions, lost touch with their people. Today it looks as if the real last hurrah of the New Deal coalition was in 1964; although Jimmy Carter in 1976 made it appear that it still held, his appeal was in fact unique. Nonetheless, the coalition dominated the Democratic year in 1984, perhaps for the last time and perhaps only because Mondale was the nominee.

The coalition was at the core of Mondale, so much so that it seemed several times that he knew he should move away from it, but couldn't. He was always an organization man and a loyal protégé, and also an insider. His political home grounds were the extremely effective Democratic-Farmer-Labor party machine of Minnesota and the liberal establishment of Washington. He was totally at home having lunch at the elegant Hay-Adams Hotel with Lane Kirkland of the AFL-CIO, and totally uncomfortable on television. (Nowadays, of course, it's television that delivers votes, not Kirkland.) When it looked in 1981 as if he would have to beat Sen. Edward M. Kennedy, than whom there is no more down-the-line liberal, for the nomination, Mondale underwent a much-publicized "reeducation" whose purpose was to position him away from the undiluted party tradition. But as soon as Kennedy dropped out of the race in 1982, that was forgotten and Mondale became the keeper of the New Deal Democratic flame. So convinced did he seem that the old coalition would work for him that only at the very end of the long election year did he begin to speak with passion about his beliefs, instead of reciting the roster of groups his administration would help.

Mondale was endorsed by the AFL-CIO before the primaries; he also forged strong early links with the cluster of interest groups that are associated with the elderly. He tied himself very closely to these groups—and in effect to a host of policies involving everything from Social Security to national defense to international trade to the tax code. (In a famous incident, he was asked to name one disagreement he had with organized labor; he was speechless.) It was a good strategy for winning the Democratic nomination, given the new Hunt Commission rules that made grass-roots organizing less important and insider endorsements more so, but the question always asked about Mondale was whether he ultimately lost more than he gained from his ties to the party's interest groups. In the immediate sense, they made him seem calculating and led him into obvious errors—trying to put the unpopular Bert Lance in charge of the Democratic National Committee was the act of a man who thinks along back-room lines: "Well, Bert can deliver the South." More broadly, it was clear almost from the start that Mondale was somehow not connecting at all with the great majority of voters.

The sudden rise of Sen. Gary Hart during the primaries—to the point that he was running ahead of Mondale in states where he had no organization at all—was a clear sign of Mondale's lack of fit with the public. By the middle of the primary season, Jesse Jackson had a lock on the Democratic party's black constituency, and Mondale on its union and over-50 constituencies; Hart was free to prospect for support among everybody else. Substantively, his appeal was on the libertarian side of liberal—skeptical, compared to Mondale, of government spending and intervention of almost every kind, either at home or abroad; admiring of the entrepreneurial parts of the country; almost aggressively antiunion; and having no interest in "social issues" such as school prayer and abortion. (Mondale, as a non-peacenik, prounion, pro-welfare-state, culturally conservative Democrat, was exactly what the conservative-centrist wing of the party had been longing for since 1972.) In terms of constituencies, Hart went after and got the affluent and the young, using ad nauseam the word "new" in combination with various nouns.

The most enduring buzz word of 1984, "Yuppies," was hung on Hart, as a way of implying that his voters were not only young, urban,

and professional, but also prosperous, self-absorbed, and uncaring—
somehow less *real* than Mondale's. But that begs a question for the future.
Mondale obviously believes very deeply in the post-New Deal welfare
state, and as a matter of strategy in 1984 he appeared to think that the
way to sell its basic fairness and generosity politically was to bring as
many voters as possible (ideally, a majority) under the umbrella. In
Mondale's America, there would be tens of millions of Americans on
Social Security, unemployment, Medicare, welfare, food stamps, farm
subsidies, trade subsidies, and so on, and the Democratic party would
convince them of the idea that all of these benefits exist together in one un-
breakable package. Those who need extraordinary help at any moment,
such as steelworkers whose plants are closing, would get it without
rebellion in the ranks, because everyone else would realize that they might
need help themselves one day.

Politically, the problem with this vision is that it does not encompass
51 percent of the voters—probably more like one-third. (Mondale's choice
of Rep. Geraldine A. Ferraro as his running mate was, among other
things, an attempt to get to a majority on the basis of female votes, but it
didn't work.) Perhaps the other two-thirds are selfish and don't want to
share their bounty; but more important, perhaps, is that they're annoyed
by the notion that the whole welfare-state apparatus is sacred, that no part
of it can be criticized without the critic's being accused of jeopardizing the
whole thing. They feel, rightly or wrongly, that the government helps not
only the poor but also people who are better off than average, who
happened to have been a necessary part of the New Deal coalition in the
1930s, and therefore got paid off—for instance, affluent retirees. In any
event, it seems clear that even a cohesive alliance of all the beneficiaries of
government can't win a presidential election by itself. It has to attract
sympathizers, and Mondale's failure to do so makes it appear that the
New Deal coalition—and the party itself, as a contender in presidential
elections—is at death's door. Somebody else has to be brought into the
fold.

Technique

In his postelection press conference announcing his retirement from
politics, Mondale noted mournfully that one of his problems as a
presidential candidate was that he's no good on television. Reagan,
everyone agrees, is wonderful on television. This is another way to look
at the election: the better television communicator won, and the lasting
result was to tilt American politics further away from speeches and
substance and more toward 10-second sound bites that play purely to the
emotions.

In greater detail, this line of argument says that Reagan was a pioneer in substituting feelings for issues as the stuff of a presidential campaign. He constantly and expertly associated himself with patriotism: the flag was a constant icon of his campaign, and he was forever pronouncing people "American heroes" and summoning them to the White House to have his picture taken with them. His staff carefully arranged his campaign appearances, first, so that they would look good on the evening news (for instance, if the crowd was sparse the platforms for the TV cameras would be moved forward so that the home audience couldn't tell), and second, so that the networks would be forced to broadcast the administration's "theme of the day" because they were given no other material to work with. In speeches, he used words such as "bright," "future," "optimism," "strong," and "happy" to describe himself and "pessimistic," "gloomy," "dark," "weak," and "past" to describe Mondale and the Democrats.

Reagan's advertising, which was produced by a Madison Avenue all-star team called the Tuesday Group rather than by one of the community of professional political consultants, was in the same vein. The commercials used poignant music and soft, sun-dappled scenes of life in a California small town as a way of conveying what Reagan had done for America. Footage of the candidate himself was in the same genial, nonspecific mood. The makers of the ads quite openly modeled them on successful campaigns for companies, such as Pepsi-Cola and McDonald's, that felt that identifying themselves with a happy America was more effective than making specific claims about their products.

To be sure, all of this is crucially important to understanding Reagan, both as a politician and as a policy maker, but to say that it is an important new development in American politics is nonsense. Was Dwight Eisenhower, courted with equal intensity by Democrats and Republicans, elected president because of his stands on the issues? Was William Henry Harrison or U. S. Grant? Can anyone say what, substantively, John Kennedy's successful campaign pledge to "get America moving" meant? Didn't Gerald Ford in 1976 use music and Pepsi-style imagery heavily in his ads?

The change in campaign technique in 1984 that deserves note is not the lower substance-to-fluff ratio, but the increasing importance of television news. Television is nothing new, of course, but not until this election did its influence seem to overcome that of the print press. Even in 1980 the feeling in the Washington press corps was that the network news operations fairly strictly followed the lead of the big eastern papers, especially the *New York Times* and the *Washington Post*. Presidential candidates paid attention to these papers far out of proportion to their readership because they set the agenda for television's vast national audience.

Today all three networks have new, youngish, aggressive anchormen without significant experience in print journalism. Dan Rather, Tom Brokaw, and Peter Jennings don't feel slightly apologetic about working in television, as the generation of David Brinkley, Howard K. Smith, and Walter Cronkite did. And by 1984 we had lived through four years of a president who aimed much more directly than any predecessor had at getting favorable daily television coverage. It has become common for print reporters to say that the administration just doesn't care about them any more; the pecking order in the White House press room has visibly changed. During a time like the end-of-year maneuvering over the federal budget, when the stories are complicated, print is still the crucial news medium. But in campaigns, when simple thrust and parry characterize the news, television is king.

What this means is more than that politicians who can't deal with television will begin to disappear, which is what Mondale implied. It means that political structures that mediate between candidates and voters will continue to diminish in importance, especially during the fall of a presidential campaign. Endorsements, as Mondale discovered, will matter less and less. Labor unions won't be able to deliver the votes of their members (Mondale discovered that especially). The party conventions will continue on the road to complete superfluity as decision-making bodies, until they are noteworthy only as an opportunity for the parties to advertise themselves free of charge on national television. Eventually the interest groups, which now seem so strong, may suffer a loss of influence, at least in the presidential campaigns. All of this will happen because television lets presidential candidates go directly to the voters; voters react by not wanting to listen any more to the middlemen of national politics, and candidates react by feeling that no longer do they have to deal with those brokers.

There's one other subject pertaining to political technique that occasions endless discussion after every presidential election: the primary system and its inherent biases. Are bosses or grass-roots organizers excessively favored? Do certain states have disproportionate influence? In 1984 there were no seriously contested Republican presidential primaries, and the Democratic ones saw a decline in the grass-roots influence because of the 568 "superdelegates," officeholders and party officials to whom the Hunt Commission guaranteed seats at the convention. But like most changes in the nominating system, this happened because of a shift not in the mood of the nation but in the party rules: Mondale's people helped stack the deck slightly against outsiders on the McGovern-Carter model.

Most likely, future changes in the primaries also will come from future changes in the rules. Until the next election's rules are established, it's impossible to say whether or how the 1984 campaign changed the way one wins a party nomination.

Policy

The presidencies that historians now regard as great coincided with times of crisis—usually war, and if not that, severe economic or political difficulty. By those standards, nothing much happened during Reagan's first term, which only underscores how significant that term was. It is extremely unusual, in the context of American history, for a president to make major changes in the government's policies without any really hard prod from events. Yet Reagan did, and in 20 years he will look, I think, like an important figure in a kind of massive internal reordering of our national priorities that was (we'll know then) either wise or foolish.

Thus the centrality of the federal budget—both sides of it, revenue and spending—to the Reagan administration and to what was at stake in the 1984 election. The budget is a wonderful Rosetta Stone to our society: looking at it reveals both what we want our government to do (or more broadly, what we deem important) and how we want to pay for it.

It is worth tracing Reagan's relationship with the budget in more than cursory detail. As a young man he was a liberal; and then in the early 1950s he made a celebrated conversion to conservatism. He entered the national political scene during the Goldwater campaign and was elected governor of California in 1966. His fiery speeches from those days are full of denunciations of the federal government as too big and too spendthrift. Specifically, Reagan frequently called for a balanced federal budget; said taxes were too high; proposed that participation in the Social Security system be voluntary; opposed Medicare and Medicaid when they were created; and complained about welfare. All these views comprised an intellectually consistent conservative position, but one that never had withstood the test of elective politics and government. Indeed, when he became governor, Reagan himself raised taxes, raised welfare payments, and increased government spending, even while conducting ineffectual but highly publicized budget-cutting drills. As a result, Reagan-watchers from California tended to see him as an extremely skilled politician who talked almost ultraconservative but governed centrist.

It was entirely consistent with this view that although Reagan campaigned in 1980 on a platform of lower taxes, higher military spending, lower domestic spending, and a balanced budget, once in office he would continue to talk about these things but not actually do them. So Reagan surprised the experts in the first half of 1981. He cut taxes by just about as much as he had promised; he raised defense spending by much more than he had promised, more than 25 percent in one year; and he cut heavily from domestic spending. Two parts of his program failed to materialize. First, the notion that the burden of the budget cuts would fall equally on everyone—that the government would undergo a purgation of all its hundreds of special little deals—turned out to be naive. Reagan proposed cuts across a wide spectrum, but the cuts that actually passed were weighted heavily toward poverty programs, the organized middle class having used its political muscle to save programs such as farm price supports, Amtrak subsidies, and student loans. Second, instead of being balanced, the budget went much further out of balance than it had ever been, for the simple reason that Reagan cut far more revenue than spending. Taken together, budget deficits ran more than five times higher than they had under Carter.

Reagan did bear out the old California interpretation of him in one way: when it came to a choice between being politically popular and doctrinally conservative, he always chose popularity. The old view that he most notably abandoned was his hostility to Social Security; the elderly have the highest voter turnout of any group, and according to White House polls most Social Security recipients vote Republican. By 1982 Reagan was presenting himself as Social Security's greatest champion.

In all, the heart of Reagan's first term was that he brought the activities of government into synch with public opinion—taxes and welfare are unpopular and so were cut, defense and the middle-class subsidies are popular and so were increased or spared. The problem is that public opinion on the budget contradicts itself. Extrapolated into policy, it produces a budget that is wildly out of balance, even though the great majority of the country favors, as a proposition, a balanced budget. In fact, on the terms by which Reagan has chosen to operate—namely, don't do anything unpopular—there is no way out of the deficit. That's why Reagan spent 1984 promising that it would go away by itself. In Washington, which worried about the deficit far more than did the general public, there was a surprising degree of consensus about what had to be done about it: the great 1981 tax cuts should be partially or wholly abolished, the defense budget should be cut substantially, and the middle class should have some of its goodies taken away. If that happened, the budget would in fact balance; but every one of those changes would go down hard with the public, so Reagan stayed away from them entirely.

For Mondale the deficit was a terribly difficult issue. On the one hand, it was Reagan's greatest failure as president, a huge and obvious one that made clear the flaws in his beliefs and even in his character. On the other hand, Mondale, as a good Keynesian, had for decades said publicly that deficits (of a different order of magnitude, to be sure) were healthy. Moreover, he didn't very much want to cut the budget. The middle-class goodies were in many cases at the heart of his conception of a noble welfare state that protects the average person as well as the poor. Although he criticized the defense budget, he did so only halfheartedly—the AFL-CIO, his most important backer, likes military spending for pocketbook reasons, and Mondale himself is a cold war liberal. So he was left with two not very good choices: criticizing the Reagan administration's unfairness to the poor and calling for higher taxes. He did both these things, with disastrous political consequences.

Two other themes of Mondale's are worth mentioning: that Reagan was out of touch with the details of government, and that he hadn't conducted any successful arms control negotiations with the Soviet Union. Neither of these seemed to capture the voters, perhaps because both are essentially Washington issues. For better or worse, most of the country doesn't care about the mood of the West Wing or about arms-limitation treaties, which invariably seem incomprehensible. Reagan cheerfully ignored the first charge and negated the second by promising to begin arms talks right away. Meanwhile he talked constantly about taxes, in a way that can only be called demagogic. ("They want every day to be April 15; we want every day to be the Fourth of July.") It must have driven Mondale to distraction that Reagan so blithely explained away the deficit, promised not to raise taxes, urged military strength, and spoke reassuringly to the middle-class beneficiaries of government, all at once. In effect Reagan took the essential logical inconsistency of his 1980 campaign and multiplied it, for the same reason and with the same result—it was popular.

Mondale in fact served indirectly to tighten the Gordian knot of the budget by maneuvering Reagan into ironclad promises not to raise taxes or cut Social Security. He did this by suggesting that Reagan was a mean-spirited, dissembling person. Reagan is deeply attached to his self-image as a nice and truthful man, and these attacks by Mondale got his dander up—never mind that they came from the weakest of challengers. Reagan almost automatically went into his good-man-unjustly-accused mode and, as his budget officials in Washington looked on in horror, essentially gave away the store by promising explicitly that taxes would not be raised or Social Security cut.

Thus while the policy consequences of a victory by Mondale would have been easy to predict (higher taxes, cancellations of a few big-ticket military items, elimination of some business tax breaks, some modest new social programs), to predict with certainty the implications of Reagan's landslide is impossible. By December 1984 the budget was out of balance by more than \$200 billion and the economy, while healthy, was slowing down a bit. The conditions initially set by Reagan were these: he wanted the tax system simplified but didn't want taxes increased; Social Security was not to be touched; defense was to keep increasing. Washington, which usually seethes in the weeks after an election with scheming, jockeying, and speculating over who will get what job, seethed in late 1984 over policy. In effect, the combination of the deficit and Reagan's conditions were like the placement of the pieces on the board in a chess problem, after which an infinity of moves are possible.

One camp began to take shape around Stockman, who wanted to slide past Reagan's conditions and cut defense, raise taxes, and cut Social Security as well as other domestic programs, with the result of a much smaller deficit. Another camp, more ideologically conservative and loosely organized (Reagan's longtime right hand Edwin Meese appeared to be its leader) wanted a new round of spending on defense and no tax increases. The idea was to put enormous short-term pressure on domestic spending, with the hoped-for result being further deep cuts across the board. But that camp also essentially gave up on the deficit, choosing to reduce it to, say, \$150 billion and then hope it didn't produce the dire consequences that many economists predicted. The Senate, Republican but moderate, tended toward Stockman's ideas. So did the Democratic House, but it had a greater interest in seeing the president fail. Reagan was an old hand at getting the legislative branch to "force" him to take the sensible, moderate course, but in the case of the House this would be difficult—it would mean that members would have to run for reelection in 1986 after having voted for a tax increase.

To have tried in the aftermath of the election to predict how this morass would be worked out would have been folly. It makes more sense to approach the consequences of Reagan's reelection in a broader way, by suggesting three axes along which the government will be moving, and then settling, over the next few years. Thinking about them may help frame the issues.

A Conservative-Liberal Axis

It is possible that the elections of 1984 will have essentially ideological consequences for federal policy. If these occur, they will push the government to a point nearer the conservative pole of the axis. In some ways the government can be made more conservative outside of the context of spending and taxing. That already has happened to some extent. Placing ideological conservatives up and down the ranks of the bureaucracy is somewhat difficult because of the civil service laws, but the effects are lasting. Also, the government essentially can stop liberal discretionary activities that have major effects on the society, such as filing antitrust and equal-employment-opportunity suits or strictly enforcing environmental and occupational safety regulations. After eight years the Reagan administration will have appointed scores of federal judges serving lifetime terms, including perhaps a majority of the Supreme Court. It would be surprising, to give just one of many examples, if in 1990 the *Roe v. Wade* abortion decision still stood as the law of the land.

The budgetary consequences of a conservative policy triumph likely would fall into three broad areas: a tax system that is less progressive, a severely reduced welfare state, and a military establishment that gets as much as 50 percent more than presently. None of these prospects should be dismissed automatically. Many conservatives believe that the graduated income tax is a bad idea, that the only real business of the federal government is national defense, and that 9 percent of the gross national product would be a more sensible commitment of resources to defense than the present 6 percent. The most difficult part of the conservative agenda to enact would be huge cuts in middle-class social welfare programs, because they have so many vocal beneficiaries. But it would be politically possible to cut poverty programs further; certainly the policy momentum already has shifted dramatically regarding those programs, so that even liberals don't dare suggest major new government undertakings in the name of helping the poor.

A Needs-Demands Axis

Will the government make its taxing and spending decisions on the basis of what it sees as the nation's needs, or more in response to the power and influence of those who demand government help? Reason says it's preferable to move toward the needs end of the axis, but any democracy will exert a constant pressure in the other direction. So far Reagan has moved us further toward the demands end, because he is so strongly responsive to what the public wants and because in 1981 he put a lot of ostensibly needs-based policies, such as welfare, under fire.

By the end of the first few months of his second term, we will be able to determine with some precision where we are on the needs-demands axis. As 1985 began, Reagan was preparing to submit to Congress a budget that left Social Security intact but cut heavily from other programs with powerful constituencies, such as student loans, Amtrak and farm subsidies, the Export-Import Bank, and veterans' pensions and health benefits. He even proposed a 5 percent cut in all civilian federal employees' salaries. The fate of these cuts will be a neat test of the power of the interest groups, since they have been gearing up for major lobbying campaigns to preserve their programs.

An even fiercer fight was brewing over taxes. In his State of the Union message in January 1984, Reagan had publicly ordered Donald Regan, the secretary of the Treasury, to draw up a tax-simplification plan. Shortly after the election Regan unveiled a tax proposal that, by abolishing a wide range of deductions in order to lower overall tax rates, gored the ox of everyone from restaurant owners to the Metropolitan Opera to steel companies to the AFL-CIO to landlords to the governor of New York. Because there were similar plans being proposed by both Democrats and Republicans on Capitol Hill, it appeared that the issue of tax reform would come up in some form in 1985 and neatly pit the interest groups and their heavy lobbying campaigns against the interests of the average taxpayer. Again, how it came out would say something about the stance of the American government at this moment in history.

The obvious flaw of a demands-based government, if that is what we end up with, is that it doesn't meet our needs perfectly. That may not be as bad as it sounds: our needs may not really be what we perceive them to be at any given moment, and interest group muscling may get us closer to meeting them than one would think. But there's a second consequence that's more ominous in the long run. The more demands-based we are, the less flexible we are. Shifts in who holds power in the country could produce shifts in government spending, but the system would react much more slowly to real shifts in necessity—even, for example, a clear threat to our national security.

A High Deficit-Low Deficit Axis

The fundamental question about the deficit is whether Washington will choose simply to ignore it. That is without question the easiest thing to do. There is seldom great immediate pressure from the public to reduce the deficit by more than a token amount; meanwhile raising taxes and cutting spending each generate considerable pain. Cuts will be more difficult than they were in 1981: on the domestic side, the easy (that is, constituencyless) ones have already been made; on the military side, the service bureaucracies already have committed most of their new resources to big-ticket weapons, which means the administration would face the embarrassment of cutting forces or training, or the political consequences of closing bases or terminating existing contracts. Even the full package of blood-and-gore cuts proposed in Reagan's fiscal 1986 budget submission only amounted to about $40 billion, less than a fifth of the amount of the deficit.

So Reagan may just walk away from the deficit, and we may let him. Then what? It should be acknowledged as a possibility that the high deficits may have no dire consequences. On the other hand, we could experience high inflation again, or high interest rates, or a recession, or high unemployment. A nation can be in a state of constant economic crisis and continue to exist, as Brazil and Israel have shown us, but there is a price. The spirit of national community is bound to fray as the squabbling over resources and federal money becomes a matter of life and death to millions of people. There could be some degree of social disintegration in the cities. The infrastructure of roads, bridges, and railways could deteriorate seriously. It sounds alarmist, somehow, but history justifies worrying in such times about an increased risk of war as a great escape valve for the pressures that have built up in the society, not least of which is the military's need to justify its wartime-level budget in a time of peace and constrained resources.

Even if none of this happens, by moving toward permanent high deficits at this juncture we will have shown a societal preference for unreality, for dealing with extremely difficult problems by trying to wish them away. Historically, nations have made this decision on other issues, quite often with disastrous long-term effects. Perhaps one national vote for unreality won't have consequences, but with the habit formed, the next one may, and the next one, and the next one. The crucial figure in this drama will be Reagan, a second-term president who wants a good verdict from history, but also a politician with a demonstrated affinity for unreality when it is the price of being loved by the public.

Conclusion

By the terms of this exercise—How will the 1984 campaigns and election look in 2004?—it's necessary to look far beyond 1985, even though to do so is necessarily speculative. In terms of government policy, one can at least think about a series of questions that came up during the elections of 1984 and weren't resolved, though they may well have been by 20 years from now. What, first, is the extent of our government's responsibility toward the old and sick? In the weeks after election day, the nation seemed obsessed with a couple of spectacular heart transplant operations that made it seem possible that we might be able to push death back another 10 or 20 years. Should the government bear the enormous cost? Will our society's reverence for human life begin to wane as it demands more and more of the gross national product? The mood in 1984 was summed up during a phone call President Reagan made to William J. Schroeder, the recipient of an artificial heart in Louisville. What did Schroeder have to say to his president? He wanted his Social Security disability check speeded up; Reagan, cheerful as always, promised to get right on it, and did. It's difficult to imagine this scene being repeated in 20 years.

Another difficult long-term question involves the poor. They were curiously absent from the 1984 campaigns, and as the year ended there was strong intellectual momentum building for a further dismantling of the Great Society welfare state—not ostensibly on grounds of its cost, but because it was thought to trap people in poverty. Fifteen years of intense government efforts to bring the poor out of poverty seemed to be coming to an end, and in another 20 years it will be clear, as it's completely unclear now, what the effects of this will be. Will the urban ghettos continue to be an essentially separate society with an entirely different culture regarding work and marriage? For more than a century social observers, writing about a succession of different ethnic groups, have answered this question with a yes, and they have always been wrong; yet right now there seems to be no evidence to support an answer of no.

Finally, and most important of all, is the question of war and peace. America in 1984 was in a curiously contradictory mood on the subject: believing more strongly than it had in decades in the idea of major, continuing increases in military spending during peacetime, and at the same time being attracted by the idea of nuclear disarmament. Reagan and Mondale embraced both sides of the contradiction, but it's hard to imagine its lasting another 20 years. Rarely do two superpowers stay warily at peace for as long as the United States and the Soviet Union have; rarely is a nation willing or able to devote an ever-increasing share of its resources to defense except during a war; and rarely is a military bureaucracy capable of using more and more money wisely when it doesn't have a specific military goal. One power may gradually fade from the arms race, or it may be forced to fade by losing a test of arms. If the first of those happens, and if the power that fades isn't the United States, then in 20 years Americans might look back on 1984 as having been a tense and nervous time. One hopes we won't have to look back on this as our golden era.

11. AN ALIGNING ELECTION, A PRESIDENTIAL PLEBISCITE

Theodore J. Lowi

Herblock caught the spirit of the election in an editorial cartoon just after it was over. A living room television screen shows the words "The End" superimposed above a man, labeled "Campaign of 1984," who is scurrying toward the sunset, suitcases in hand. In the foreground, a viewer toasts his wife with the comment, "Those are the political coattails I've been waiting to see!" [1]

Another presidential election took place on November 6, 1984, the 49th in a series that reaches back almost 200 years. It deserves celebration—the largest bona fide election on Earth, involving enormous stakes, with an outcome so legitimate that some past losers have conceded defeat even before all the polls were closed. To political scientists and other professional election watchers, the process is all the more awesome because it is so commonplace. But to most people it is *merely* commonplace, a boring event mainly to be endured. The voters pack up their troubles in their old kit bags and hope for more interesting choices four years down the road.

The American voters of 1984 have a right to feel let down. They are comparable to the housewife of 1900, who was told that within 20 years the industrial revolution would relieve her of the daily chores of homemaking. The housewife thought the message meant that she would have a full-time maid. What she got instead was a house full of appliances. Similarly, the electronics revolution of the second half of the twentieth century foretold of political debates and participation, a veritable continental town meeting. But instead of politics revolutionizing democracy through the electronic media, commercials adulterated politics. Sadly, the best political analyses of 1984 were those on PBS that brought together a public relations consultant, an advertising agent, and a pollster to discuss the comparative effectiveness of the presidential candidates' 30-second spots.

Real alternatives were at stake in 1984. Ronald Reagan and Walter Mondale are two very different people with two profoundly different visions of good government and the good society. But the campaign filtered out their differences. In June, about two weeks after Mondale had won enough delegates to capture the Democratic nomination, a Gallup poll showed Reagan in the lead by 19 percentage points.[2] The same polling organization found that in the first half of 1984 Reagan's performance as president ("Do you approve or disapprove of the way President Reagan has handled his job as president?") was consistently approved of by 52-55 percent of the respondents.[3] Both sets of figures are close enough to the final 59 percent to 41 percent election outcome to suggest the minimal role played by the campaign in helping voters to decide.

Reagan's victory was an extraordinary nationwide phenomenon. His 59 percent national average was matched within four points in all but 6 of the 49 states he won. Many called it a landslide. To others it was only a minor earthquake whose tremors failed to pierce the outer crust of national politics. But elections do not speak for themselves. The meaning of each has to be constructed from the haphazard collection of fragmentary facts about the campaigns and about the elections that are lying around after the postelection calm has returned.

The Campaign: A Four-Year Stretch

A president's campaign for reelection actually begins even before his first election. It reflects the popular support organized during the first election and the shape and strength of that popular support after three and a half years in office.

Reagan's 1984 campaign, therefore, began when he pieced together his 1980 nomination and election. Probably the most important component of the 1980 victory was the collapse of the Democratic party. For some, the Democrats' collapse can be dated as far back as 1968; for others, 1972. But 1976 is the clincher, if anyone should need one. In 1976 Jimmy Carter ran against the party he wanted to lead and against the government over which he would preside. Carter showed a genius for positioning, somewhere between the Watergate scandal and Americans' traditional antipathy to statism. But his success in the campaign was his undoing as president. By assuming the role of "president of all the people," Carter became obligated to produce results and to stand or fall on the people's judgment of those results—and of him. But he had neither the personal strength nor the popular base to succeed in those terms. Circumstances also went against him, particularly the imported-oil-induced inflation that no president could have controlled.

The Carter campaign and presidency contributed very significantly to the Reagan campaign and presidency in at least three ways. First, the brief Carter era signaled the complete and final electoral collapse of liberalism as a public philosophy. Erroneously labeled the shattering of the New Deal coalition, the Democratic collapse we experienced was that of liberalism itself. Second, the Carter era precipitated what was to become a new national conservatism. Carter's contribution to this was inadvertent in part (his unpopularity set the stage for Reagan's victory), but also positive in that he was the first avowed born-again Christian in the modern presidency and the first to validate small-town Christian morality as the touchstone of national political virtue. Finally, Carter's election in 1976 resulted from the first completely artificial campaign—artificial in that it pieced together a conglomeration of shared public revulsion against Watergate and welfare-state burdens. Carter's was probably the first purely attitudinal constituency, without foundation in a political party. His campaign was built on nothing substantial, and his presidency was more a repellent than a center of gravity.

The Reagan campaign was built to a substantial degree on Carter's 1976 campaign, arising out of morality, antistatism, and small-town Christian values. But Reagan converted Carter's appeals into something more politically positive. For example, although Carter was a truly observant born-again Christian, his faith played almost no political or policy role in his campaign or presidency. It served only to validate the place of Christian morality in national politics. Ironically, although Reagan is a far less observant born-again Christian, religion played a much greater role in his campaign and in his first term as president. It certainly was a sign of the times that in 1980 all three of the major presidential candidates—Carter, Reagan, and independent candidate John Anderson—were avowed born-again Christians. But only Reagan used it as a meaningful, positive political force.

Reagan's campaign also reached beyond this religious base. He combined the white small-town Christians with a host of more cosmopolitan corporate and professional interests through the mythology of the antistate. To the Christians, his antistatism held forth the promise of freedom from national regulation and the renewed empowering of local and state governments in areas of morals and manners that the Supreme Court had taken away from them during the previous two decades. To the more cosmopolitan members of his electoral base, Reagan's antistatism promised freedom from all government, since the only relevant government to the cosmopolites was the national government and its regulatory and redistributive components. There also may have been an element of racism in the antistate attitudes of the cosmopolites in the Reagan camp, but it was probably less important to them than their economic interests. Each side in the coalition fought for the soul of Ronald Reagan, and each side attempted to win by definition. The religious element saw itself making common cause with the cosmopolites against what George Wallace so often had called the "pointy-headed bureaucrats" in Washington. It bided its time for the moment when the real Ronald Reagan would stand up, lead the attack on the Supreme Court, and secure the enactment of constitutional amendments to restore state and local power to regulate morality in ways that the churches alone were too weak to do. For their part, the cosmopolites were willing to accept the alliance in the belief that, when the chips were down, Reagan would betray the religious right.

The Reagan Constituency

In truth, Ronald Reagan was both small-town Christian, cosmopolitan, and more. The composition of the Reagan constituency can be appreciated first by recalling the 1978 "Proposition 13" campaign to cut taxes severely in California: a grass-roots, communitarian, anti-state movement of frustrated middle-class people that organized in opposition to the cost of "social services"—a code concept for income redistribution from the middle class to the poor. Another essential ingredient in the Reagan constituency was the so-called deregulation movement, which within itself combined at least two contradictory viewpoints—the libertarians, who truly and consistently opposed all government regulation; and the conservatives, who opposed most regulation because it was liberal but actually favored an expansion of government power in matters of morality. Yet another element of the Reagan constituency was the "neoconservatives," former liberals turned off by what they felt were excesses both in programs aimed at redistribution of wealth and power and, most particularly, in civil rights programs that had moved from simple desegregation to various types of "affirmative action."

Of all, the most palpable and emotional component of the Reagan camp was the radical right wing, mainly southern evangelical Christians—the Moral Majority—who, perhaps for the first time in history, found common cause not only with libertarians but also with the most conservative elements of the Catholic church. But whatever their varied bases of belief, self-interest, or passion, all of the segments of the Reagan constituency were drawn together and held together by Reagan's explicit and highly programmatic appeals during the 1980 campaign and during most of his first administration—ironically, until the official 1984 campaign itself, when Reagan became a good deal less explicit and programmatic.

Even the most superficial examination of the Reagan constituency reveals profound contradictions. One is tempted at first to compare its disparate elements with those that made up the original New Deal coalition, but there is one great difference: the Reagan constituency's components are separated by ideological differences, while the Roosevelt coalition was pluralistic more along lines of economic self-interest. (This was true even of the difference between the northern liberals and the southern conservatives within the Democratic party, because there were few northern liberals who opposed the southerners on ideological grounds until the 1960s.) The ideological pluralism of the Reagan constituency will become increasingly significant in the second Reagan administration and is likely to tear the Reagan constituency apart once Reagan himself is no longer its center of gravity.

President Reagan did, however, manage to hold this unwieldy constituency together well enough to win comfortably in 1984. This was not easy to do. During the first 30 months of his term Reagan's national approval ratings behaved precisely as did those of his five most recent predecessors *(Figure 11.1)*. This downward tendency exists mainly because virtually every domestic action a president takes is divisive, causing net losses in approval. Reagan's ratings dropped accordingly, despite the great personal affection Americans had for him. But in late 1983 Reagan became the exception among recent presidents in beginning an upward trend months before the election cycle opened. As Figure 11.2 shows, he began his upturn in September, reaching a peak of more than 60 percent in late April 1984 and remaining very high through the November election. Most observers have attempted to attribute the improvement in Reagan's approval ratings to economic recovery. Although there is no denying that the economy improved in 1983, this is an inadequate explanation for Reagan's growing support. In the first place, the economic indicators were barely returning to where they had been in 1981. And note that Nixon's rating also began to move upward during his third year—although not so dramatically as Reagan's—despite the fact that 1971 was the year when the most severe peacetime price controls in history were imposed on the American people. Second, these indicators were moving up gradually, without the kind of dramatic increases that could explain the rapid spurt in Reagan's ratings. Third, and most important, Reagan's approval rating began to climb even as his ratings on specific economic issues continued to be low.

The Harris survey showed, for example, that, in January 1984, 50 percent of the public continued to disapprove of Reagan's efforts to get the country out of recession, and 56 percent continued to disapprove of his handling of inflation. He was burdened with a record-high 70 percent

Figure 11.1 Presidential Approval Ratings from Harry S. Truman to Ronald Reagan: Nationwide Responses to the Gallup Poll Question, "Do you approve or disapprove of the way President _____ is handling his job as president?"

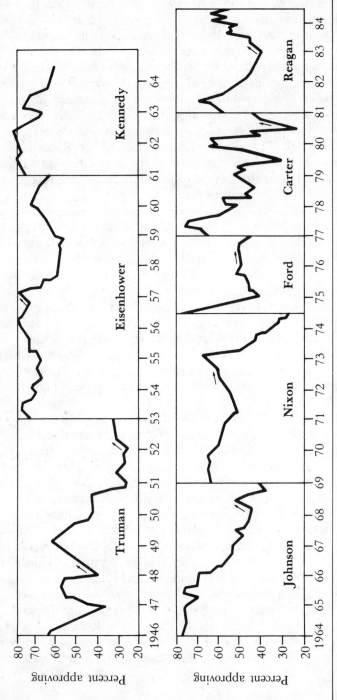

Note: Arrow indicates upward trend in approval rating as presidential election approaches, or, in the case of Nixon and Reagan, well in advance of election.

Source: Theodore J. Lowi, *The Personal President: Power Invested, Promise Unfulfilled* (Ithaca, N.Y.: Cornell University Press, 1985), 14. Copyright © 1985 by Cornell University Press. Reprinted with permission.

Figure 11.2 A Profile of Ronald Reagan's Presidential Popularity, 1983-1984: Nationwide Responses to the Harris Survey Question, "How would you rate the job Reagan is doing as president—excellent, pretty good, only fair, or poor?"

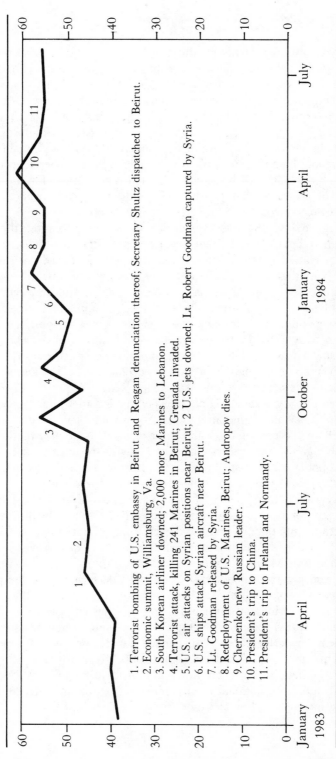

1. Terrorist bombing of U.S. embassy in Beirut and Reagan denunciation thereof; Secretary Shultz dispatched to Beirut.
2. Economic summit, Williamsburg, Va.
3. South Korean airliner downed; 2,000 more Marines to Lebanon.
4. Terrorist attack, killing 241 Marines in Beirut; Grenada invaded.
5. U.S. air attacks on Syrian positions near Beirut; 2 U.S. jets downed; Lt. Robert Goodman captured by Syria.
6. U.S. ships attack Syrian aircraft near Beirut.
7. Lt. Goodman released by Syria.
8. Redeployment of U.S. Marines, Beirut; Andropov dies.
9. Chernenko new Russian leader.
10. President's trip to China.
11. President's trip to Ireland and Normandy.

Source: Theodore J. Lowi, *The Personal President: Power Invested, Promise Unfulfilled* (Ithaca, N.Y.: Cornell University Press, 1985), 18. Data from the Harris survey through regular press releases.
Copyright © 1985 by Cornell University Press. Reprinted with permission.

negative evaluation of his handling of the federal budget and the federal deficit. A 69 percent majority rated him negatively on his efforts to keep people from going hungry, and 73 percent continued to rate him negatively on "helping the unemployed, small business, farmers, and others in economic trouble." [4] About the most that can be said for the economic explanation of the mid-1983 recovery in Reagan's approval rating is that the economic improvement probably helped buoy his administration, smoothing out some of the rough spots in the treacherous presidential track. But it does not provide a sufficient explanation for the dramatic spurts of approval that put him on a different track from that of his predecessors during their final 15 months of office.

Figure 11.2 suggests the specific cause that prompted the upward trend in Reagan's ratings that began in the latter part of his third year: foreign relations—that is, international events associated with the president.[5] Note that although the economy was moving upward at a smooth rate, Reagan's approval rating was developing in a more jagged fashion. Virtually each jump in the rating is shown in Figure 11.2 to be associated with some important foreign policy event. It begins with the six-point boost in May 1983, following the April 18 bombing of the U.S. embassy in Beirut, which killed 40 people, including a dozen Americans. No front-page events in the economy or Congress competed in that period with the Lebanon crisis. The second spurt in Reagan's performance ratings followed the Soviet downing of the Korean Air Lines plane on September 1, 1983. The third came after the U.S. invasion of Grenada—and so on throughout the rest of 1983 and most of 1984. Note also that after each event Reagan's approval rating turned downward until another dramatic foreign policy event pushed it back up. In sum, President Reagan's rise in public approval can be attributed in large part to a succession of foreign policy events with which he skillfully associated himself. This succession of foreign policy events continued into early 1984, at which time another factor came into play, the electoral cycle itself. The trends, noted in Figure 11.1 by the arrows and in Figure 11.2 by the more or less even line that in 1984 began in May and extended into the autumn, show that voters tend to suspend judgment about each president's performance as the presidential election approaches. Although none of the major polling agencies asked the presidential approval ratings question between July and November 1984, most of the responses on related questions suggest that judgment on performance is suspended during the campaign period.[6]

This, in effect, was the Reagan campaign of 1984: a campaign for public opinion, fighting an inherent downward tendency. Success depended upon international events, some of his own making, some totally outside his control, but all associated with him. The economic situation operated more as a setting—indeed, a bad economic situation probably would have hurt Reagan more than the good one helped.

The Democrats

The Mondale campaign of 1984 was typical of the party out of power. As was true of Reagan in 1980 and Carter in 1976, candidates of the out-party begin at the ground floor. This is the concrete, behavioral meaning of the "decline of parties." The new method of nomination, which centers on open competition for individual delegates, encourages a multiplicity of presidential candidates to join in a mad scramble from state to state. It is a struggle among strangers. Presidential candidates enter each state as its primary or caucus approaches, knowing few if any of the leaders or citizens of that state, and campaign for delegates largely through the mass media, telephone banks, and computer-analyzed opinion polls. The delegates they win often do not know the candidate to whom they are pledged or each other. The same pattern is repeated in other states, so that at the national convention the delegates pledged to a candidate have nothing in common but that pledge. The winning candidate's majority is not a coalition at all, but rather a "flux" of individual particles revolving around the center of gravity, the presidential candidate.

Mondale, for all that, was closer to the traditional kind of party candidate than other recent nominees. Indeed, it is a commentary on how far we have changed from the traditional party epoch that Mondale was criticized as "the candidate of the special interests" because he tried to put the New Deal coalition back together. He did not manage to do that, and the effort almost lost him the nomination despite his enormous early lead. Another significant commentary on the 1984 Democratic campaign is the surprise showing of Sen. Gary Hart. The real contender against Mondale was supposed to have been Sen. John Glenn, but three very revealing factors explain why the major contender turned out to be Hart.

First, Hart was closest in style to the Ronald Reagan of 1984. Among the many Democratic candidates, Hart turned out to be the favorite of the media. After Hart's surprise second-place showing in Iowa, the media seized upon his candidacy because surprise is news. From that point on, media coverage itself made Hart the news. But Hart's campaign for new ideas also appealed to a surprising number of voters. He actually displayed few new ideas or policies, but his attraction to these voters was the opportunity he gave them to provide a kind of implicit slap in the face to traditional New Deal Democrats.

The second revealing factor about Hart was that a substantial proportion of his supporters were self-designated independents. In the 14 states that television pollsters studied during the 1984 primary season, one-fourth of the voters in Democratic primaries described themselves as independents. Among self-described Democrats, Mondale averaged 39 percent; among self-described independents, his support dropped to 25 percent. Hart's support was 48 percent among those independents.[7] This helps to explain why Hart showed up stronger than Mondale in the spring "trial heats," polls that hypothetically pitted Hart against Reagan, then Mondale against Reagan. On that basis, many people argued that Hart would have made the stronger Democratic nominee, but the third factor in his success casts a heavy shadow across that.

The third factor is that more than 33 percent of those who supported Hart in the spring Democratic primaries later supported Reagan in the November election. In comparision, only 4 percent of Mondale's primary supporters and 6 percent of Jesse Jackson's switched in November to Reagan. Hart's support may have been the second largest among Democratic candidates, but it also was the least substantial. The Hart voters' attachment to the Democratic party *as a party* ranged from weak to nonexistent.

Another significant element in the 1984 Democratic campaign was the Jesse Jackson phenomenon. But, for all its originality and all of Jackson's magnificent eloquence and dramatic flair, the Jackson movement was mostly significant for its lack of influence on the outcome. Blacks had to confront the fact that they were a captive constituency. Blacks were essential to any Democratic hopes of winning the presidency. They were even more important in the close Senate and gubernatorial races. But black Democrats seemed to have very little influence either at the nominating convention or during the fall campaign. Jackson tried to make peace with the Democratic party but his discomfort showed in his oscillating conduct, which ranged from quiet mutterings, to outright criticism and threats of a bolt, to enthusiastic endorsement.

The Jackson experience leaves the future very uncertain between blacks and the Democratic party, because blacks are unlikely to remain in a quiet corner. One message blacks may have received from the 1984 election is that their embrace of mainstream politics got them nothing and that historically their most important gains have come from movement politics—direct-action politics, politics in the streets rather than the ballot boxes. Another message black leaders may have gotten is that the two-party system is not the only possible path in mainstream electoral politics. A third party is a distinct possibility for blacks and indeed may be a better medium for the charismatic Jackson. A third-party strategy could be adopted as a compromise between direct action and continued participation in the Democratic party. Interestingly, a very warm friendship developed in 1984 between Jackson and John Anderson. It is quite possible that Anderson would have jumped in to campaign for him if Jackson had decided to run as an independent candidate in the South Carolina senatorial race. One of the more emotionally satisfying moments for the two leaders during the 1984 campaign was a very large and enthusiastic joint campaign rally in State College, Pennsylvania. It seems at least possible that a third party could develop out of the parallel frustrations of blacks within the Democratic party and liberals within the Republican party.

In any event, the 1984 campaign was virtually over after the Republican and Democratic conventions. Reagan, the president running for reelection, was the reverse of Reagan the presidential candidate of four years earlier. In 1980 he was specific and programmatic; in 1984 he was vague and evasive. He ran on his record, draping it in the flag. He stood tall, on the shoulders of the Lebanese, the Grenadians, and the U.S. Olympians. He was as moral and as impermeable as the ayatollah of Iran. And Mondale failed accordingly. Try though he did with specific and pointed issues, he failed to pierce Reagan or penetrate the Reagan constituency; indeed, to be more specific he was to be the bearer of bad news, and bearers of bad news are no more welcome today than in the days when death awaited them.

As further evidence of the mass politics of the modern epoch, Mondale's one chance was the televised debates. But the debates are of historical significance mainly because they require a powerful head of state to behave like a mortal, an ordinary political candidate. Otherwise, the debates are merely media events—not debates at all but simultaneous press conferences whose agendas are controlled entirely by the media themselves and whose political significance eventually is determined by the people of the media.

Most important, however, the debates embody the new character of presidential selection as separate from all other political processes in the country. This separation carries over into the president's term of office, in which the president maintains a direct, personal relationship with the millions of American citizens. The only imagery appropriate for this kind of political relationship is *plebiscitary*—such are the developments of presidential selection that we now have a plebiscitary republic with a personal presidency. *Plebiscite* is a harsh term; it evokes the powerful imagery of Roman emperors and French authoritarians who governed on the basis of popular adoration, with the masses giving their noisy consent to every course of action. In the American context, plebiscite is an exaggeration—but by how much? We already have seen it in the nomination process, with presidential candidates attracting a flux of independent particles (called delegates) rather than building a coalition of local and state political organizations. We can see it in the extent to which the parties' presidential nominees run their own campaigns independently of all other campaigns. And we will be able to see it manifest itself in a variety of ways in the election, to which we now turn.

Out of the Polling Booth, Into the Polling Agency

Polling comes from poll, which originally meant head, or crown. The verb means literally the counting of heads, and any method of counting heads would qualify as polling. It all depends on the rules of the polling that are laid down in advance. Traditionally, democracies have preferred to do their polling in elections. But all this is changing. Polling by election is being adulterated by other means of polling, in particular the systematic, scientific, sample survey conducted by various commercial and political polling agencies. Elections, especially the presidential election, now are important far beyond the numerical outcome that ordains the winner. "Who was elected?" is only the first question; "What was decided?" follows immediately upon it. Between them, the results of electoral polling and sample-survey polling constitute a set of facts whose meanings are left to everyone to interpret. Elected officials seek one type of interpretation, one that will give them maximum consent to govern. The defeated seek another, more restrictive, interpretation. One hopes that there are also disinterested analysts who seek only impartial interpretations, interpretations that serve history and good government.

The most important fact about the electoral polling that took place on November 6, 1984, is that Ronald Reagan won the presidential election with a share of the popular vote, 58.9 percent, that has been exceeded only four times since 1860—by Harding in 1920 (60.3 percent), Roosevelt in 1936 (60.8 percent), Johnson in 1964 (61.1 percent), and Nixon in 1972 (60.7 percent).[8] While Reagan's smaller share in 1980 (50.7 percent) could be attributed to very substantial negative voting by Democrats who were disillusioned with President Carter, Reagan's 1984 vote, confirmed by all the sample-survey polls, manifested an outpouring of affection and approval. It was a personal triumph of inestimable proportion.

Other electoral facts, however, must be balanced against Reagan's victory: the results in the Senate, the House of Representatives, and the governorships. In the Senate, instead of gaining as most presidents do, Reagan actually lost two seats, reducing the Republican majority from 55-45 to 53-47. In the House the Republicans gained, but a mere 14 seats—far short of the historical average for landslides, and also short of the 24-30 seats that the Republicans wanted to give Reagan back the "ideological majority" he had enjoyed briefly during his dramatic and innovative first year in office. The Republicans made a net gain of one governor, by losing three and gaining four, making the current lineup 16-34 compared with the former lineup of 15-35.

Another fact underlies the disparity between the presidential results and the congressional and state results: ticket splitting. For 20 years ticket splitting has been widespread and growing. But the extent of ticket splitting seems to have been greater in 1984 than ever before. To pick but one of many possible examples, while President Reagan was winning Delaware by a 60-40 percent margin, the Republican senatorial candidate lost to incumbent Democrat Joseph Biden by the exact same margin, 40-60. For this to happen, 20 percent—and probably more—of the electorate had to split their tickets, assuming that at least a few voters split the other way, voting for Mondale and against Biden.

So far, we have been reviewing mainly electoral results. But we also are justified to review as facts a number of the salient findings of the various sample-survey polls. Table 11.1 portrays the results of the *New York Times*/CBS News exit polls, which were taken as 8,696 voters were leaving the electoral polling places on November 6. A few of those findings deserve special mention here.

It is first important to know that President Reagan led in all sociological categories of voters except blacks, Hispanics, Jews, union members, and people with under $12,500 annual income. Politically, Reagan led among Republicans and also substantially among independents; he led overwhelmingly among conservatives and fairly substantially among those who called themselves moderate. He trailed only among self-designated Democrats and self-designated liberals. This was an extraordinary sweep in its own right. But of equal if not greater interest are those categories in which Reagan enjoyed support greater than his national average of 59 percent. The groups that stand out as being particularly favorable to Reagan are: white Protestants (73 percent), born-again Christians (80 percent), southerners (63 percent, not in Table 11.1), self-designated Republicans (92 percent), and self-designated conservatives (81 percent).

On "the issues" the case for a Reagan landslide is less clear. During the last two years of the first Reagan administration, even as his approval rating was going up, the voters were expressing considerable ambivalence toward his performance on specific economic issues. On election day itself, at least 20 percent of those who reported voting for Reagan said they had "important disagreements" with him on the issues.[9]

These misgivings about Reagan did not show up significantly in the voting for two reasons. First, 20 percent of those who voted for Reagan had "no strong feelings" on the issues one way or the other.[10] Second,

Table 11.1 Voter Preferences on Election Day. Results of the *New York Times*/CBS News Exit Poll of November 6, 1984

% of 1984 total		The Vote in 1980			The Vote in 1984	
		Reagan	*Carter*	*Anderson*	*Reagan*	*Mondale*
—	TOTAL	51%	41%	7%	59%	51%
47%	Men	55	36	7	61	37
53	Women	47	45	7	57	42
86	Whites	55	36	7	66	34
10	Blacks	11	85	3	9	90
3	Hispanics	33	59	6	33	65
24	18-29 years old	43	44	11	58	41
34	30-44 years old	54	36	8	58	42
23	45-59 years old	55	39	5	60	39
19	60 and older	54	41	4	63	36
8	Less than high school education	46	51	2	50	49
30	High school graduate	51	43	4	60	39
30	Some college	55	35	7	60	38
29	College graduate	52	35	11	59	40
51	White Protestant	63	31	6	73	26
26	Catholic	49	42	7	55	44
3	Jewish	39	45	15	32	66
15	White born-again Christian	63	33	3	80	20
26	Union household	43	48	6	45	53
15	Under $12,500 in income	42	51	6	46	53
27	$12,500-24,999	44	46	8	57	42
21	$25,000-34,999	52	39	7	59	40
18	$35,000-50,000	59	32	8	67	32
13	Over $50,000	63	26	9	68	31
35	Republican	86	9	4	92	7
38	Democrat	26	67	6	26	73
26	Independent	55	30	12	63	35
17	Liberal	25	60	11	29	70
44	Moderate	48	42	8	54	46
35	Conservative	72	23	4	81	18
50	Reagan	100	0	0	88	11
31	Carter	0	100	0	19	80
5	Anderson	0	0	100	29	67
	Democratic primary supporters:					
15	Mondale	N.A.	N.A.	N.A.	4	96
11	Hart	N.A.	N.A.	N.A.	34	65
3	Jackson	N.A.	N.A.	N.A.	6	93

Source: *New York Times*/CBS News poll, based on questionnaires completed by 8,696 voters, randomly selected, as they left their polling places.

Copyright © 1984 by The New York Times Co. Reprinted with permission.

nearly half the Reagan voters who had any disagreements with him on specific economic issues felt that he provided sufficiently strong leadership and experience to keep them with him. Although 83 percent of the voters said they thought the economy was in better shape than it had been in 1980, only 40 percent cited the economy as a determinant of their vote. As for specific foreign policy issues, only 2 percent of Reagan's voters and 6 percent of Mondale's identified policy toward Central America, for example, as a major influence on their voting decision.[11]

In the 1984 vote, the general overshadowed and blotted out the particular. President Reagan had run his campaign accordingly. Either his campaign managers had unusual prescience or their campaign brought about the relatively issueless vote, because it was obvious that their strategy was for Reagan to avoid the issues, and in particular to avoid getting embroiled with Mondale in specific disputes over public policy. Mondale was permitted to raise all the issues he wanted, but the response of the Reagan camp was to treat them as if they were simply prophecies of doom and gloom.

Search for Meanings: What Was Decided?

The Reagan victory of 1984 was a personal triumph—broad, nationwide, but shallow. The majority was large but weak. Few members of the Senate or House owe their election to the president, and it seems likely that, after a brief honeymoon, there will be war in the trenches between Reagan and Congress.

Dramatic as they were, the 1981 Reagan accomplishments were the easy ones. Many of his first large cuts in the budget were cuts in the rate of increase for various programs. The reining in of welfare spending was something to which a goodly number of Democrats already were committed; and not all of them were Boll Weevils. The 25 percent tax cut was historic; but tax cuts are not really so hard to accomplish. Nor was the accelerated defense commitment very controversial; Carter's Pentagon budget was already on the increase. Reagan's accomplishments and his effectiveness as a national and legislative leader were substantial, but there are two contrasting facts relevant to 1984. First, the enormous and growing budget deficit gives testimony to the implications of President Reagan's "supply-side" economics approach to public policy, and second, the hard choices are yet to be made: there now have to be real budget cuts instead of cuts in the rate of growth. And if they are to obviate a major tax increase, these cuts will have to be extremely large, unprecedentedly large.

Reagan's postelection plan was to cut domestic spending by $34 billion in fiscal 1986, $60 billion in fiscal 1987, and $75 billion in fiscal 1988.[12] Since all this was to be done without touching Social Security and since there would be no significant reduction in the rate of increase in the defense budget, only about one-third of the budget was left to be cut. The largest single reduction would have to come in Medicare, but almost by definition a number of whole programs also would have to be eliminated, and that requires substantive legislation. Confronting Congress with requests for substantive legislation is a world apart from approaching Congress, as in 1981, with budget cuts, however large. One indication of President Reagan's wish to avoid the legislative route during the first term was in the area of deregulation, a matter of sincere importance to him. Not one proposal was made to eliminate a regulatory program by statute; Reagan preferred to effect deregulation through White House and Office of Management and Budget oversight, slowing down agency rule making and enforcement rather than trying to abolish an agency altogether. Another part of the Reagan agenda that requires substantive legislation is tax reform, which is always more difficult to get through Congress than tax cuts. And if reduction in the rate of increase in defense expenditure is to be substantial, Congress will have to be asked to eliminate one or more entire defense systems instead of counting on the supposed savings through improved management. Nothing in the 1984 election results suggests a mandate for any of these actions.

The time also will come when Reagan must meet his obligations to the religious right. In particular, he will have to make a more sincere effort to enact constitutional amendments that authorize states to allow school prayer and forbid abortion, and legislation to provide tuition tax credits for parents who send their children to private schools. Following the Republican National Convention, the Reverend Jerry Falwell was asked what he expected from Reagan in return for all the support given by the Moral Majority. Falwell replied, smiling, that he expected nothing but was confident that President Reagan sincerely wanted what they wanted.

The advantage to Reagan of the Moral Majority policies is that they add few immediate costs to the budget. The prayer and abortion amendments would simply restore power to the states, requiring no further action or monetary obligation by the national government. Tuition tax credits would drain off federal revenues; but they are a typical "tax expenditure," the kind that do not show up in the budget and that also can be rationalized as taking some of the heat off federal and state governments to spend more on public education. But the political costs of pursuing these policies are very great. Not even the strongest Reaganite believes that the 1984 election gave a mandate for these morality issues. This means that majorities in Congress would have to be built from scratch. The largest number of votes would have to come from the

Republicans, but, as we saw, the existing Republican party is a conglomerate, only part of which is committed fully to the morality issues. Libertarian Republicans do not want the kind of government control that is implicit in school prayer and abortion regulation. Nor do the neoconservatives. This means that a significant number of votes would have to come from congressional Democrats, for the simple majority required for the tuition tax credit as well as for the two-thirds vote required for the constitutional amendments. Merely to state these basic political facts is to predict the outcome. But to keep the religious right in his camp, the president will have to fight the good fight for these proposals, knowing that he will lose time as well as resources that he needs for the truly compelling issues. No matter what happens, he risks alienating some parts of his own constituency.

Reagan's second-term political dilemma fits neatly into the pattern of all his recent predecessors, including his own experience in the second and third years of his first term. Reagan's lame-duck situation is, if anything, worse than that of most presidents. Even as his approval rating drops, as it almost surely will, his efforts to meet the needs of the nation and of his conglomerate constitutency will produce the very controversies around which four to eight Republicans will rise up to succeed him in 1988. These Republican presidential aspirants will be joined by the large number of Senate and House Republicans who are up for reelection in 1986 and whose own future is more important to them than the success of their lame-duck president.

These speculations on Reagan's second term amount to a short-term assessment; it is the long term that should concern us most. For pollsters and journalists with publication deadlines, the long term is about 48 hours. For politicians, the long term is measured in units of two, four, and six years—electoral time. For the academic, the long term is measured in institutional time. The main concern of the rest of the chapter is the institutional implications of the Reagan reelection.

A Confirming Election: The Plebiscitary President

Despite its several distinctive features, the 1984 election was in one important sense a confirming election. It confirms the plebiscitary presidency, which has been emerging with increasing clarity and strength during the past two decades. President Reagan is both a recipient of this new institutional tradition and an important contributor to it.

First and foremost, the results of the election demonstrate the existence of two separate constituencies, one for the presidency and one for Congress and state and local offices. As observed earlier, the spread between support for Reagan and support for other Republicans was enormous. The president's constituency is a personal constituency involving a direct and unmediated relationship between the president and the mass public. To a tremendous extent voters take into account the personal attributes of the presidential candidates, particularly when one of those candidates is the incumbent president. Reagan's personal attributes were more politically significant than those of other recent presidents who ran for reelection—Carter, Ford, Nixon, and Johnson—but the distinction is only one of degree. Personality and personal attributes are far more important than party in presidential elections. On the whole, the reverse is closer to the truth for congressional and state and local elections, which explains the extent of split-ticket voting and split electoral outcomes.

Another indicator of the existence of two separate constituencies is the extent to which the separation has been institutionalized into two sets of campaign organizations, one set for the congressional and state and local offices and one for the presidential campaign. As partisan as President Reagan seems to be, he made every effort to separate himself from party when it came to running for reelection. James A. Baker, the White House chief of staff, and Ed Rollins, Reagan's campaign manager, both said publicly weeks before the election that their main job was to re-elect the president and that Reagan would not promote House and Senate candidacies until the last two or three weeks of the campaign. It was fairly widely recognized that the Reagan campaign was run from the White House and not from the Republican National Committee, even though the RNC recently has become a very impressive management operation. It has been highly successful in raising money and redistributing it to state and local Republican candidates who have some chance to win. Nevertheless, the separateness of Reagan's 1984 presidential campaign not only was recognized but was the subject of very considerable complaint by some of his strongest supporters. Robert Michel, the House minority leader, stood up soon after the election to blame President Reagan's personal campaign for the Republicans' disappointing showing in the House elections:

> He never really, in my opinion, joined that issue of what it really means to have the numbers in the House. . . . Here the son-of-a-buck ended up with 59 percent and you bring in [only] 15 seats.[13]

Columnists Jack Germond and Jules Witcover observed that "the danger in the Reagan sweep is that future presidents and their political strategists, having seen the stonewall and the isolation booth work for Nixon and Reagan, will make it standard operating procedure. . . ."[14] It was already standard operating procedure before Reagan.

The consequences of the plebiscitary presidency are so important that I have devoted an entire book to them.[15] Suffice it to say here that the tremendous pressures on the president that derive from this direct and personal relationship with millions of voters are incessant and highly concentrated. Figures 11.1 and 11.2 suggest that for his high performance rating to survive the second term, President Reagan will have to be lucky enough to have four more years of prosperity and a succession of international events that are sufficiently important to buoy his approval ratings and sufficiently short-lived not to drag on for long, which would frustrate voters and lower their approval of him. The probability of that happening is low. Thus, even if Reagan should continue to enjoy the affections of Americans, his general approval rating cannot long remain impervious to their expectations. As his approval rating declines, he will be under greater pressure to find international events with which to associate himself, for, without a buoyant rating, he will find it increasingly difficult to lead Congress and accomplish his extremely important legislative goals. The risk of the president's manipulating American public opinion by triggering international events is grievously dangerous.

An Aligning Election: Conservatism versus Liberalism

To stress the personal character of Reagan's 1984 victory is not to argue that it was without significance beyond Reagan himself. Many observers are tempted to treat 1984 as a "realigning election." Briefly, a realignment can be defined as a fundamental shift in voter affiliations that tends to last through a number of succeeding elections. For the better part of two decades, students of American elections have been looking for a "critical realignment" of the parties to compare with the realignments of 1896 and 1932. Despite its landslide proportions, the election of 1984 does not qualify as such a critical realignment, because the Republican victory failed to penetrate local and state electoral patterns. In truth the voters now prefer specialization to realignment. Republicans have won four of the last five presidential elections and six of the last nine, without being able to win control of both chambers of Congress since 1952. Unconvinced that a realignment has occurred in modern times, many professional observers began some time ago to speak of party *de*alignment, meaning that the parties have been weakened so badly that there are no remaining lines of partisan affiliation left to be crossed or redrawn. I share that view but hope to develop a more positive characterization of what has occurred, which I call *alignment*.

The elections of 1980, followed by the elections of 1984, clarified a line of distinction between the Republican party and the Democratic party that had existed, although less clearly, for several decades. At least since the critical realignment of 1932, the Democratic party has been the more liberal party and the Republican party the more conservative. But each had substantial ideological wings that tended in the other party's direction: liberal Republicans, conservative Democrats. Reagan clarified the line of ideological distinction. The theorists of dealignment are correct when they argue that, organizationally, party lines are weak unto disappearance. Nevertheless, there are two enormous clusters of partisanship, and the two Reagan elections clarified greatly the nature of those two clusters, reducing both the leftward dispersion of the Republican cluster and the rightward drift of the Democratic cluster. Although Reagan's popularity with almost all groups of voters in 1984 tended to overshadow this distinction, consider again those groups in Table 11.1 with which Reagan made his biggest gains: self-defined conservatives, already high at 72 percent support in 1980, jumped to 81 percent in 1984; self-defined Republicans, up from 86 percent to 92 percent; the most conservative Christians (white, born-again Christians), up from 63 percent in 1980 to 80 percent in 1984. And it was the most liberally inclined groups of voters who resisted the Reagan tide: self-designated liberals, up from 60 percent for Carter in 1980 to 70 percent for Mondale in 1984; self-designated Democrats, up from 67 percent for Carter in 1980 to 73 percent for Mondale in 1984; people earning under $12,500 or less in annual income, up from 51 percent to 53 percent; Jews, up from 45 percent to 66 percent; and blacks, up from 85 percent to 90 percent. While one would hesitate to suggest that America has become an ideologically polarized society, it is safe to say that the ideological cores of the two parties are a great deal more distinct and farther apart than at any time before.

To say that 1984 is an aligning election is not to suggest that the alignment can last indefinitely. The cleaner and sharper the lines of ideological demarcation between the two clusters of partisanship, the less capable of accommodation in government the two parties will be. Already there are signs of discomfort on the part of many hitherto loyal Republicans, including Republican members of Congress, with the newly ideological character of the party. There is even more obvious discomfort among many Democrats, who fear that the Democratic party has become not just a liberal party but a labor party. One possibility is that the two parties will return to their more blurred and accommodationist positions. The probability of that scenario would increase if a less conservative Republican won the party's presidential nomination in 1988. Another possible scenario is the emergence of a third major political party, combining the liberal wing of the Republican party with either the right-of-center, "Yuppie" component of the Democratic party or the left-of-center, mostly black Jackson constituency. This is fertile ground for the likes of John Anderson. Its probability is drastically reduced by state electoral laws that favor the two-party system. But if liberal Republicans grow sufficiently uncomfortable within a white, Christian, Sun Belt party, and if the Democrats continue the futile effort to rebuild their party around a core of organized labor, sufficient interest in reform of electoral laws could develop by the end of this decade. That would produce a true realignment.

The Legacy of Ronald Reagan: R.I.P.

Ronald Reagan will end his second term having failed to leave the legacy he seeks—a conservative majority party and a national government built on conservative lines. In the first place, Reagan will fail for the same reasons all five of his most recent predecessors failed. The presidency has become an impossible job, not because individual presidents have been of smaller stature than in the past but because the presidency has become too big and expectations of presidential performance have grown too high. The plebiscitary presidency is such that even modest successes look like failures. After a brief honeymoon period in 1985, President Reagan's approval ratings are highly likely to begin the familiar downward trend. This will both reflect the stalemate he will confront in Congress and contribute to that stalemate.

A second reason why Reagan will fail to leave a conservative legacy in politics and government is the thinness of his popular base. Although larger than in 1980, the 1984 Reagan victory was not the victory of a conservative majority but of a Reagan majority. Sadly for conservatives, charisma cannot be passed from its possessor to others. A review of the relationship between Reagan's voter base in the election and the fundamental policy decisions he will have to confront as president strongly confirms the basic incompatibility of the two. Reagan has pieced together a conglomerate constituency that is not comparable to the Roosevelt conglomeration, because of one critical difference. Roosevelt's was a real coalition, made up not only of interest aggregates but also of strong state and local party organizations. Moreover, the interest aggregates and party units were able to live together in a mutually beneficial relationship fed by governmental policies. In contrast, the Reagan conglomeration is just a conglomeration. There are interest aggregates, but the party component has been weakened in the decades since the 1930s. Even more significant, there is a much stronger ideological component in the Reagan conglomeration, which means that government policies are as likely to divide as to integrate.

The third reason why there will not be much of a conservative Reagan legacy is that liberalism is too well entrenched in the national system of government. This includes the welfare state and the regulation of capitalism; it involves the ironing out of the most egregious disparities among states and regions and the most egregious departures from racial and economic equity. The liberal electoral majority collapsed during the 1970s, making way not only for Reagan's conservatism but Carter's conservatism before that. But that is a far cry from making way for a fundamental change in the liberal national government. Reagan could put on the brakes in liberal government, but he could barely turn the steering wheel, much less reverse direction. Let it be recalled once again that President Reagan had only one good year in his first administration. Beginning early in 1982, despite his continuing personal popularity and despite his undoubtedly valid reputation as a legislative leader, the history of the rest of his first term was one of war in the trenches.

Acknowledging these limitations, what would it take for Reagan to leave any sort of legacy? Success does not require that he repeal the New Deal. In fact conservatives would wish to maintain or restore some New Deal legacies, not the least of which are presidential power and administrative discretion. At a minimum, success will require that Reagan institutionalize his political conglomerate, making it into a real coalition. Since inevitably the business of Reagan's hoped-for conservative revolution will be incomplete at the end of his second term, President Reagan and the conservative core of his administration will have to create a popular base and an organizational structure that will last a decade or more beyond the end of his second term, so that the agenda of national political discourse will continue as though Reagan were still president. The question then becomes: What will it take to organize a political coalition that will outlast the charismatic, personal presidency of Ronald Reagan?

Precisely because Reagan lacks the traditional party structure, he will have to bind his conglomerate of interests together all the more tightly around their prospects of satisfaction from government. First, to solidify the support of his white Christian constituency, Reagan will have to make a sincere and concerted effort to get the prayer and abortion amendments adopted. He will not actually have to secure their adoption, but the effort will have to be serious even at the risk of alienating other parts of the Republican conglomerate.

Second, Reagan will have to join the Moral Majority segment to other conservative and libertarian elements of his conglomerate through the appointment of ideologically suitable federal appellate judges, particularly to the Supreme Court. Here Reagan will have to show success as well as effort. Because he has only a bare Republican majority in the Senate and lacks an ideological majority, it will be extremely difficult for him to nominate exactly the kinds of judges he wants without risking Senate rejection. This will become even more difficult if judicial vacancies do not occur in the first two years of his second administration, because he could very well lose his Republican majority in the Senate after the 1986 elections. Thus, the judges he nominates will have to be so far above reproach that moderate senators will confirm the appointments despite their ideological purity. But without the ideological purity, the judiciary would not serve as the integrative force that the Reagan coalition needs.

Finally, if Reagan is to institutionalize his 1984 victory into an enduring coalition, he will have to win the adoption of programs that will tie the parts of his conglomerate together through self interest. To further this end Reagan has the vast resource of the defense budget to tap. Defense spending could be the connective element for a Reagan coalition that public works programs were for the Roosevelt coalition. But although virtually everyone in the Reagan administration is a hard-liner on defense and military policy, there are at least two different kinds of hard-liners— the instrumentalists and the moralists. The differences between them are obstacles to unity within the Reagan coalition. The instrumentalists mistrust the Russians as an adversary whose basic interests conflict with those of the United States, and against which an impressive deterrent is an absolute necessity. But with the deterrent, instrumentalists believe, the Russians can be successively contained and democracy has a chance to flower, perhaps even to win in the end. The moralists believe that the West is almost certain to lose because of the Russians' absolute commitment to their communist system and their willingness to sacrifice individuals for the collective will, in contrast to a Western system made up of individuals concerned mainly with their own comforts. Still another limitation on Reagan's ability to use the vast patronage of defense contracts to fuse his coalition is that he does not have the majority in Congress that Roosevelt enjoyed when he used other forms of government patronage to cement the New Deal coalition together. In fact, the Democrats have enjoyed over the years a tremendous amount of access to major financial and industrial interests precisely because of their ability, through congressional committees, to manipulate the defense budget.

Two other Reagan policies would, if judiciously implemented, promote the integration of a Reagan coalition: tax indexing and the tuition tax credit. Tax indexing has certainly given those of the middle and upper-middle class a big stake in maintaining a Republican or any other administration committed to preserving indexing. The tuition tax credit, if adopted, would give the less prosperous, truly conservative interests a much stronger tie to a Republican administration and a Reagan coalition. This is the one policy that ties together conservative principles and self-interest most comfortably.

If President Reagan does succeed in getting a better Republican-conservative grip on the defense contracting system and in adding tuition tax credits to tax indexing, he definitely will have in his possession a fund of patronage resources to equal those of President Roosevelt. And it is reasonable to assume that he would have the wit and wisdom to use them as cement for his coalition. But even if that happens what would be the outcome? The Reagan coalition would amount to nothing but an embrace of the principles on which the old liberal coalition and the liberal national government were built. In other words, big government would continue to be the necessary condition for national political success. Indeed, President Reagan's main contribution would turn out to be that he gave some of the nation's more conservative interest groups a bigger stake in national government than they ever had. What an ironic turn of events! Instead of getting a smaller national government with more functions devolved to the states and localities, the Reagan coalition, to last beyond Reagan itself, would add to big government the loyalty of a set of groups previously distrustful or downright antagonistic.

One is tempted to say that such a Reagan coalition would answer interest-group liberalism with interest-group conservatism. But that would be proposing a distinction without a difference. Having emptied supply-side economics of all meaning with a gigantic defense budget, a gigantic deficit, a gigantic annual debt service payment, and a set of gigantic commitments to "tax expenditures" through tax indexing, tuition tax credits, and a variety of investment incentives, President Reagan's legacy would turn out to be just another version of statism—interest-group liberalism with an opening to the right.

Notes

My thanks to Kathleen Frankovic, Benjamin Ginsberg, Martin Shefter, and Joel Silbey for their contributions to this essay.

1. Herblock, *Washington Post,* November 8, 1984, A26.
2. Gallup poll released June 17, 1984.
3. Gallup poll released August 5, 1984.
4. All of the figures in this paragraph are from the Harris survey press release of January 2, 1984.
5. George C. Edwards III argues that significant international events usually do not push up the president's approval ratings. However, this turns out largely to be an artifact of Edwards's analysis. He chose as his threshold for a "significant rallying event" a full 10 percentage point increase in approval

immediately following the event. This very high threshold enabled him to eliminate the Bay of Pigs as a rallying event because John F. Kennedy's public approval increased by slightly less than 10 percentage points. It also enabled Edwards to eliminate other important events, such as the 6 point increase in Dwight D. Eisenhower's approval after the U2 spy plane debacle, the 7 point increase following Richard Nixon's trip to China, the 4 point increase after the Nixon-Vietnam peace agreement was signed, the 9 point increase after Gerald R. Ford's *Mayaguez* incident, and the 4 point increase that Jimmy Carter briefly enjoyed after his vain attempt to rescue the Iranian hostages in 1980. Edwards, *The Public Presidency: The Pursuit of Popular Support* (New York: St. Martin's Press, 1983), 247. Edwards offers no compelling argument for taking the 10 percentage point threshold. Considering that almost all domestic events *depress* rather than rally approval ratings, *any* increase in approval ratings ought to be taken as interesting and not insignificant. Not every international event associated with the president will push up approval ratings, but international events are the only events that do push up the ratings.

6. The continued buoyancy of Nixon's 1972 and Ford's 1976 ratings can also be explained on this basis. One interesting review of the poll responses can be found in *Time*, November 5, 1984, 21.

7. William Schneider, "Independents Seen Squarely with Reagan," *National Journal Campaign Monthly*, June 1984, 1.

8. *Congressional Quarterly Weekly Report*, November 10, 1984, 2894.

9. *New York Times*/CBS News poll, November 11, 1984, A30.

10. Ibid.

11. Ibid.

12. *Congressional Quarterly Weekly Report*, December 8, 1984, 3090.

13. Quoted in Richard Viguerie, "Reagan's Campaign Double-Crossed the GOP," *New York Times*, November 12, 1984, A19. See also *Congressional Quarterly Weekly Report*, November 10, 1984, 2898. Michel was speaking before the election count disclosed that the Republicans gained 14 House seats, not 15.

14. Jack W. Germond and Jules Witcover, "On Reagan's Second-Term Plans, the Public 'Ain't Heard Nothin' Yet,'" *National Journal*, November 10, 1984, 2176.

15. Theodore J. Lowi, *The Personal President: Power Invested, Promise Unfulfilled* (Ithaca, N.Y.: Cornell University Press, 1985).

CONTRIBUTORS

Robert H. Birkby is professor of political science at Vanderbilt University. His articles have appeared in the *Midwest Journal of Political Science,* the *Western Political Quarterly,* and the *Texas Law Review,* among others. He is the author of *The Court and Public Policy* (1983) and is writing a biography of Supreme Court Justice James Clark McReynolds.

Richard Davis is a doctoral candidate in political science at Syracuse University. A former college public relations officer, he currently is doing a study of the nature of mass media coverage of American political institutions.

Benjamin Ginsberg is professor of government at Cornell University. He is the author of articles in the *American Political Science Review* and other professional journals. His books include *Poliscide,* with Theodore J. Lowi (1976), and *The Consequences of Consent: Elections, Citizen Control, and Popular Acquisitions* (1982). He is writing a book about the role of public opinion in democratic politics.

Erwin C. Hargrove is professor of political science at Vanderbilt University. His books include *Presidential Leadership, Personality and Political Style* (1966), *The Power of the Modern Presidency* (1974), *The Missing Link: The Study of Implementation of Social Policy* (1975), *TVA: Fifty Years of Grassroots Bureaucracy,* with Paul Conkin (1984), *The President and the Council of Economic Advisers,* with Samuel Morley (1984), and *Presidents, Politics, and Policy,* with Michael Nelson (1984). He is writing a book about domestic policy making in the Carter administration.

Stephen Hess is a senior fellow at the Brookings Institution. A former official in the Eisenhower and Nixon administrations, he is the author of *America's Political Dynasties* (1966), *The Republican Establishment,* with David S. Broder (1968), *The Presidential Campaign* (1974), *Organizing the Presidency* (1976), *The Washington Reporters* (1981), and *The Government/Press Connection* (1984). He is writing a book about the Senate and the press.

Gary C. Jacobson is professor of political science at the University of California, San Diego. His books include *Money in Congressional Elections* (1980), *Strategy and Choice in Congressional Elections,* 2d ed., with Samuel Kernell (1983), and *The Politics of Congressional Elections* (1983). Most recently he has written a series of papers on the electoral activities of national party organizations and political action committees and on other aspects of congressional election politics.

Celinda Lake, who was the chief analyst for Peter D. Hart Research Associates Inc. assigned to the Mondale-Ferraro campaign, serves on the staff of Rep. Pat Williams. She has worked for the Center for Political Studies at the University of Michigan and currently is writing on voting behavior, campaign strategies, the gender gap, and women candidates.

Nicholas Lemann is national correspondent for the *Atlantic* and a contributing editor of the *Washington Monthly.* He is the author of *The Fast Track* (1981) and *Out of the Forties* (1983).

Paul C. Light is director of research at the National Academy of Public Administration. As an American Political Science Association Congressional Fellow, he served with Rep. Barber B. Conable, Jr., and with Sen. John Glenn and the Glenn presidential campaign committee. He is the author of *The President's Agenda* (1982), *Vice-Presidential Power* (1984), and *Artful Work: The Politics of Social Security Reform* (1985). He is working on studies of hazardous waste, presidential appointments, and the politics of economic forecasting.

Theodore J. Lowi is John L. Senior Professor of American Institutions at Cornell University. In a survey of the members of the American Political Science Association he was chosen as the political scientist who made the most significant contribution to knowledge during the

1970s. His books include *At the Pleasure of the Mayor* (1964), *The Pursuit of Justice,* with Robert F. Kennedy (1964), *The Politics of Disorder* (1971), *Poliscide,* with Benjamin Ginsberg (1974), *The End of Liberalism: The Second Republic of the United States* (1969; 2d ed., 1979), and *The Personal President: Power Invested, Promise Unfulfilled* (1985).

Michael Nelson is associate professor of political science at Vanderbilt University. A former editor of the *Washington Monthly,* he has written articles for the *Journal of Politics, Public Interest, Virginia Quarterly Review, Saturday Review, Congress and the Presidency,* and *Harvard Business Review,* among others. He has won writing awards for his articles on classical music and baseball and is coeditor and coauthor of *The Culture of Bureaucracy,* with Charles Peters (1979), editor of and contributor to *The Presidency and the Political System* (1984), and coauthor of *Presidents, Politics, and Policy,* with Erwin C. Hargrove (1984). He is writing a book about the origins and development of American national bureaucracy.

Gary R. Orren is associate professor of public policy at the John F. Kennedy School of Government at Harvard University. He has been active in presidential nomination politics both as director of polling for Sen. Edward Kennedy in 1980 and technical adviser to the Hunt Commission. The coauthor of *Equality in America: The View from the Top,* with Sidney Verba (1984), he is writing a book on the future effects of new media technologies on politics, government, and democratic values.

Thomas E. Patterson is professor and chair of political science at the Maxwell School of Citizenship and Public Affairs of Syracuse University. His articles have appeared in *Public Opinion, Journal of Communication, Annals,* and other journals, and his books include *The Unseeing Eye: The Myth of Television Power in National Elections,* with Robert D. McClure (1976), and *The Mass Media Election: How Americans Choose Their President* (1980). He is writing an introductory text on American government and conducting a study of mass media systems in advanced democratic nations.

Paul J. Quirk is assistant professor of political science at the University of Pennsylvania. The author of *Industry Influence in Federal Regulatory Agencies* (1981) and coauthor of *The Politics of Deregu-*

lation, with Martha Derthick (1985), he is working on a study of public policy making as negotiation.

Martin Shefter is associate professor of government at Cornell University. His articles have appeared in *Political Science Quarterly, Public Interest, Politics & Society,* the *Sage Electoral Studies Yearbook,* and numerous edited volumes. His book on the political sources and consequences of New York City's fiscal crisis is being published by Basic Books in 1985.

INDEX

ABC News poll - 106 (chart)
Abortion - 22, 202, 232, 240, 242, 246, 292, 293
AFL-CIO - 263, 270
  Defense issues - 146
  Democratic delegates - 71
  Johnson support - 28
  Labor legislation - 9
  Mondale support - 54, 56, 61, 203, 264
Aged - 105
Agriculture
  Farm subsidies - 272
  Postwar policies - 3
Alabama Democratic Conference - 61
Aid to Families with Dependent Children (AFDC) - 201
Alabama primary - 50, 54
  Campaign spending - 51
  Candidate spending limits - 46
Alignment. *See under* Presidential elections
American Bar Association Committee on the Federal Judiciary - 243-244, 247, 251
American Enterprise Institute - 9, 195
Amicus curiae, government as - 241, 242, 254, 255
Amtrak - 272
Anderson, John B. - 297
  Constituency - 290 (chart)
  Election influence - 14
  Election returns - 131 (chart)
  Possible Coalition with Jackson - 286-287
Armed Services Committee (Senate) - 139
Arms control. *See* Nuclear weapons; Soviet Union
Arms Control Export Act - 6
Arrington, Richard - 61
Askew, Reubin
  Foreign policy - 145, 146
  Political alignment - 16

  Primaries - 28
Atomic weapons. *See* Nuclear weapons
Babbitt, Bruce - 212
Baker, Howard - 29, 154, 165
Baker, James A. - 294
Baker, Russell - 114
Bankruptcy courts, restructuring - 252
Barkley, Alben - 154
Barrett, Laurence I. - 165
Bay of Pigs - 136
Bayh, Birch - 29
Berelson, Bernard - 122
Bickel, Alexander M. - 248
Biden, Joseph - 212, 289
Birkby, Robert H. - 239-258
Blackmun, Harry - 239, 243, 244, 246
Blacks
  Civil rights - 3
  New Deal coalition - 1, 25
  1984 voting - 68
  Political alignment - 12, 107, 260, 262, 263, 286
  Vietnam participation - 4
Bob Jones University v. United States - 241
Brennan, William - 239, 242, 244, 245
Bradley, Bill - 212
Brinkley, David - 267
Broder, David - 74
Brokaw, Tom - 267
Brown, Jerry - 63
Brownell, Herbert - 246
Budget deficits - 89, 97, 102, 230
  Carter presidency - 196
  Economic cause - 159
  Ford presidency - 195
  1980 primary race - 164
  Reagan presidency - 156, 166-167, 173-174, 202, 203, 207, 208, 209, 273-274
Bumpers, Dale - 212

Burger, Warren - 239, 243, 244, 249-250, 257
Bush, George, 240
  Debate - 103, 151
  Foreign policy experience - 96, 139
  1980 campaign - 29, 78
  Task Force on Regulatory Relief - 199
  Tax issue - 176
Business Roundtable - 9
Butz, Earl - 135
Caddell, Patrick - 58, 204
California primary - 35
  Campaign spending - 51
California, University of, at Berkeley - 4
Cambodia invasion - 134
Campaign issues. *See under* Domestic policy;
 Foreign policy
Campaign spending - 42-52
  Candidate limits and delegates - 45, 47, 48
   (charts)
  Delegate committees - 51
  Federal matching funds - 43, 77-78
  Fund raising - 43-51
  Media influence - 52-55
  1984 nomination period - 49 (chart)
  Relation to outcomes - 50 (chart)
  Republican party - 71, 77
Campbell, Angus - 142
Carswell, G. Harrold - 247, 248
Carter, Jimmy - 165, 215, 239
  Constituency - 261, 290 (chart), 296
  Court appointments - 239, 250, 251, 252
  Defense spending - 198, 200
  Domestic policies - 196-198, 202, 204
  Economic policy - 160, 161
  Election returns - 131 (chart)
  Foreign policy - 198, 200, 209
  Fund raising - 44, 78
  Hostage crisis - 135-136
  Mondale role - 68, 73, 203
  1976 campaign - 42
   Foreign policy issues - 134-135
   Nomination - 29
   Political alignments - 13
   Primaries - 42
   Strategy - 82, 278
   Vice presidential selection process - 70
  1980 campaign - 71
   Debate - 99
   Ethnic vote - 137
   Foreign policy issues - 135-136, 144
   Media coverage - 118
  As party outsider - 205
  President of preparation - 196-198
  Presidential approval ratings - 72, 282
   (chart)
Castro, Fidel - 132

Caucuses. *See* Party caucuses; Primary elec-
 tions and caucuses
Center for Political Studies - 140
Central Intelligence Agency (CIA) - 6, 137,
 139
  CIA Nicaragua manual - 103
Chase, Samuel - 242
Child nutrition - 200, 201
China
  Atomic power - 133
  Nixon initiative - 110, 134
Church and state. *See* Religion
Chrysler Corporation - 68, 147
Church, Frank - 63, 154
Civil rights
  Court appointments - 240, 241
  Movement - 3
Civil Rights Act of 1964 - 241
Clean air legislation - 8
Clean water legislation - 8
Colorado State University - 4
Commentary - 195
Committee for Economic Development - 155
Committee on the Present Danger - 200
Common Cause - 7
Communist Manifesto - 262
Congress
  Committee hearings - 223
  New Politics alignment - 8, 12
  1984 campaigns - 220-225
  1986 elections - 234-236
  99th Congress prospects - 229-234
  Presidential coattail effect - 215-237
  Reagan legislative program - 199-203
Congressional Budget Office - 176
Connally, John - 50
Connecticut campaign spending - 51
Conscience of a Conservative (Goldwater,
 Barry) - 132
Conservatism vs. Liberalism - 295-297
Conservative-Liberal Axis - 271-272
Constitution, U.S.
  Amendments to overturn Court decisions -
   242
  Conduct of elections - 31-32
  Supreme Court role in interpretation - 249
Consumer legislation - 6
Converse, Philip - 74
Coolidge, Calvin - 74, 193
Council of Economic Advisers - 167
Cox, Archibald - 7
Cranston, Alan
  Campaign strategy - 80
  Foreign policy experience - 145
  Media coverage - 114
  Political alignment - 16

Primaries - 28
Cronkite, Walter - 267
Cuba
Bay of Pigs - 136
Castro takeover - 132
Reagan policy - 208
Cuomo, Mario - 61, 69, 212, 239
Dahl, Robert A. - 241, 249
Darman, Richard G. - 164
Davis, Lanny - 76-77
Davis, Richard - 111-127
Debates
1976 campaign - 13
1980 campaign - 99
1984 campaign
Media coverage - 120-122
Presidential - 84, 99, 100-103, 150-151,
177, 287
Vice presidential - 103, 151
Totals (chart) - 41
Defense, Department of
Arms control - 210
Procurement procedures - 209
Defense budget
Carter policy - 198, 200
Hart policy - 17
Mondale policy - 205
Reagan policy - 20, 22, 107, 162, 200, 201,
232, 271, 291, 299
Defense industry
Contracting system - 300
Establishment - 2
Political alignment - 11, 20
Delegates. *See also* Democratic party
Candidate share - 36-40
Delegate committees - 51, 78-79
Fairness Commission - 42
Selection - 32, 33, 34 (chart), 35, 65, 76, 77,
78
"Superdelegates" - 33, 35, 40
Democratic National Committee - 264
Democratic National Convention - 69-71
Balloting (chart) - 64
Democratic party. *See also* New Deal; New
Politics
Boll weevils - 200, 291
Collapse - 278
Delegate selection reforms - 32, 33, 34
(chart)
Electoral strategies (1972-1984) - 10-18,
205-206
1984 nomination - 64, 69-71, 145-148, 203-
205
Nominating process - 11, 64, 69-71, 112
Party identification, constituency - 66, 84-85,
200, 262-265

Post-1984 strategies - 71, 211-212
Public opinion and foreign policy - 144
Reagan legislative program - 199-200, 202-
203
Deregulation - 292
Dole, Robert - 29, 109, 166, 167
Domenici, Pete V. - 166
Domestic content legislation - 147
Domestic policy - 129-154
Campaign issues - 20-23, 99, 129, 139
99th Congress agenda - 229-232
Reagan budget cuts - 162, 291
Dukakis, Michael - 212
Economic policies. *See also* Budget deficits;
Taxes
Democracy and - 178-182
Keynesian economics - 2, 157, 160, 169
Macroeconomics - 156, 157, 159
Microeconomics - 156
Neo-Keynesian economics - 157, 160
1984 campaign - 89-90, 107, 109, 170-178
99th Congress agenda - 233
Reagan policy - 155, 162-168, 168-170
Supply-side economics - 21, 157, 163-165,
199, 208, 210, 211, 237
Economic Recovery Program - 162
Education
Compensatory - 201
School prayer - 22, 202, 207, 232, 242, 292,
293
Race and sex discrimination - 25, 241
Student loans - 99, 272
Tuition tax credits - 24, 232, 292, 293, 299
Edwards, George C. III - 300-301
Eisenhower, Dwight D. - 266
Age issue - 210
Congressional coattail effect - 216
Delegate credential challenge - 78
Economic policy - 160
Election returns - 131 (chart)
Foreign policy issues - 130-132, 141
Military background - 139
1952 nomination - 29
Presidency of consolidation - 193
Presidential approval ratings - 282 (chart)
Supreme Court appointment - 246
El Salvador, U.S. involvement - 146, 200
Electoral college - 31, 56
Emergency Price Control Act of 1942 - 242,
256
Emerging Republican Majority (Phillips,
Kevin) - 262
Employment programs, public - 195, 199,
201
Entitlement programs - 196

Environment
Deregulation - 207
Legislation - 6
Policies - 201
Ethnic vote - 62, 137, 146
New Deal coalition - 1, 163
Party participation - 262-263
Equal Rights Amendment - 6, 256
Executive orders, Supreme Court and - 241
Export-Import Bank - 272
Fairness Commission - 42
Falwell, Jerry - 240, 292
Federal courts appointments. *See* Judiciary
Federal Election Campaign Act (FECA)
Delegate committees - 51, 79
Federal matching funds - 43
Limits on fund raising and spending - 43-44,
51
Federal Reserve Board - 157, 161, 162, 259
Federal Trade Commission (FTC) - 199
Feldstein, Martin - 167, 168, 176
Ferraro, Geraldine
Debate - 103, 151
Economic strategy - 174
Media coverage - 118-120
Nomination - 18, 28, 30, 70, 96, 205, 265
Voter concern - 107-108
Firefighters Local Union No. 1784 v. Stotts -
241
Florida primary - 35, 54
Campaign spending - 51
Congressional and local elections - 219
Food for Peace - 139
Food stamps - 196, 199, 201
Ford, Gerald R.
Defense spending - 198
Détente - 201, 209
Economic policy - 160, 195
Election returns - 131 (chart)
1976 campaign, 71
Campaign committee - 135
Campaign spending limits - 78
Foreign policy issues - 134-135
Nomination - 30, 86
Political alignments - 13
Primaries - 261
Office of president - 189
Presidential approval ratings - 282 (chart)
Supreme Court appointment - 239, 251
Foreign policy. *See also under presidents by*
name
Campaign issue - 129-154
1952 election - 130, 141
1956 election - 130-132, 141
1960 election - 132, 142
1964 election - 132-133, 142

1968 election - 133-134, 142-143
1972 election - 134, 143
1976 election - 134-135, 143
1980 election - 135-136, 143
1984 election - 99, 103, 109, 145-152
99th Congress agenda - 231-232
Presidential vote and (1952-1984) - 140-144,
148-152
Foreign Commitments Resolution - 6
Foreign Relations Committee (Senate) - 139,
154
Fortas, Abe - 244, 247
Freedom of Information Act - 7
Fulbright, William - 9
Fund for a Conservative Majority - 45
Gallup poll
1980 campaign - 135
1984 campaign - 31, 91, 96, 100
Presidential approval - 171, 172
Reagan's foreign policy initiatives - 148
Gannett poll - 102
Gender gap - 17, 25, 105
Georgia primary - 54
Campaign spending - 51
Candidate spending limits - 46
Gergen, David - 189
Germond, Jack - 294
Gingrich, Newt - 210, 237
Ginsberg, Benjamin - 1-25
Glenn, John - 285
Campaign spending - 45 (chart)
Campaign strategy - 56, 57-58, 80-81
Foreign policy experience - 145
Iowa caucuses - 53
Media coverage - 120
Political alignment - 16
Polls - 172
Primaries - 28, 93, 115
Goldwater, Barry M. - 215, 247, 259
Constituency - 260
Election returns - 131 (chart)
Foreign policy experience - 139
1964 campaign - 29, 132, 142
Goodman, Robert - 60, 147
Governorships - 288
Grant, U. S. - 266
Great Society - 4, 190, 193, 196, 211, 221, 228
Grenada invasion - 148, 149, 200, 205, 209,
284
Gromyko, Andrei - 149
Gross National Product (GNP) - 162, 169,
171, 176, 179, 211
Grove City College v. Bell - 241, 254
Habeas Corpus Act of 1868 - 242, 256
Harding, Warren G. - 74, 103 (chart), 193,
288

Hargrove, Erwin C. - 189-213
Harriman, Averell - 139
Harris, Seymour - 139
Harris survey
  1982 midterm election - 171
  1984 campaign - 150, 281
Harrison, William Henry - 266
Hart, Gary - 239, 264
  Campaign spending - 45 (chart), 46-51
  Campaign strategy - 56, 58-59, 60-63, 65, 82
  Delegate share - 36, 38, 40, 41, 77, 78
  Economic themes - 204-205
  Foreign policy experience - 145, 147
  Foreign policy position - 146
  Group support - 68
  Intermestic issues - 147
  Iowa caucuses - 53
  Media coverage - 53-55, 114, 116, 117 (chart), 118, 123
  1984 primaries and caucuses - 28, 36, 38, 40, 41-42, 53, 58-59, 60-63, 93, 115, 203-205
  Outsider candidacy - 30
  Political alignment, constituency - 16, 17, 18, 81, 205, 264-265, 285-286
  Post-1984 prospects - 212
Hart, Peter - 151
Harvard University - 4
Haynsworth, Clement F. - 247, 248
Health and safety legislation - 6
Health insurance hearings - 9
Heclo, Hugh - 163
Helms, Jesse - 225, 231
Herblock - 277
Heritage Foundation - 9, 195, 200
Herter Committee (House) - 139
Hess, Stephen - 129-154
Hollings, Ernest
  Defense spending - 202
  Foreign policy experience - 145
  Political alignment - 16
  Primaries - 28
Holmes, Oliver Wendell - 249, 257
Honduras, U.S. involvement - 146, 149
Hoover, Herbert C. - 193
Hoover Institute - 195
House of Representatives
  Presidential coattail effect - 216-224, 216 (chart)
  Ticket splitting - 288-289
Housing assistance - 199, 201
Huddleston, Walter - 225
Hughes, Emmet John - 130
Humphrey, Hubert H.
  Election returns (chart) - 131
  Foreign relations experience - 154
  Mondale support - 68

  1960 campaign - 29, 32
  1968 campaign - 30
    Campaign spending - 77
    Foreign policy issues - 133, 134
    Nomination - 112, 134
    Political alignments - 10
  1972 campaign - 29
Hungarian uprising, 1956 - 132
Hunt, James B. - 33, 225
Hunt Commission - 28, 33, 35, 36, 40, 41, 73, 76-77, 264
Illinois primary - 35
  AFL-CIO role - 61
  Campaign spending - 51
  Cook County Democratic machine - 61
  Media coverage - 54-55
Indiana primary - 40
  Campaign spending - 51
Industrial policy - 15. *See also* Labor
  Regulatory legislation - 8
Inflation. *See also* Stagflation
  Carter administration - 278
  Democratic position - 158
  Johnson administration - 4
  Reagan administration - 22, 90
Infrastructure needs - 274
Interest groups - 2-3, 68, 136
Intermestic issues - 138, 145, 147, 153
Internal Revenue Service (IRS) - 201
Iowa caucuses - 35, 42, 50, 118, 164, 285
  Campaign spending - 51
  Campaign strategies - 58-59
  Candidate spending limits - 44
  Media coverage - 52
Iran hostage crisis - 135-136, 143
Israel
  Suez Canal - 132
  U.N. vote - 137
  U.S. embassy - 146
Jackson, Henry
  Campaign fund raising - 44
  Foreign policy experience - 139
  1972 campaign - 29
  1980 campaign - 29
  Political alignment - 16
Jackson, Jesse
  Campaign spending - 45 (chart), 49, 50
  Constituency - 67 (chart), 70, 81, 264
  Delegate share - 36, 39, 40, 41, 63, 64, 77
  Foreign policy experience - 145, 147
  Foreign policy position - 146
  Jewish vote - 60, 146-147
  Media coverage - 119
  1984 candidacy - 28, 30, 203-205

Campaign strategy - 59-60
  Primaries and caucuses - 28, 38
  Possible Coalition with Anderson - 286-287
Jacobson, Gary C. - 215-237
Jefferson, Thomas - 242
Jennings, Peter - 267
Jepsen, Roger - 225
Jewish constituency - 60, 137, 146-147, 262-263
Johnson, James - 80
Johnson, Lyndon B.
  Campaign spending - 77
  Civil rights campaign - 3
  Congressional coattail effect - 215, 221, 228
  Economic policy - 160
  Election returns - 103, 104 (chart), 131 (chart)
  Foreign policy issues - 4, 132, 139
  1960 campaign - 29
  1968 campaign withdrawal - 71, 86, 112, 133
  Office of president - 189
  Preprimary endorsements - 28
  President of achievement - 190, 192
  Presidential approval ratings - 282 (chart), 288
  Supreme Court appointments - 239, 251
  Vietnam War - 4
Jordan, Hamilton - 80
Judiciary. *See also* Supreme Court
  Federal appointments - 250-253, 272, 298
  New Politics alignment - 7, 8, 12
  Reagan influence - 272, 298
Judiciary Committee (Senate) -214, 247-248
Justice, Department of - 241. *See also* Solicitor General
  Federal court appointments - 252
  Supreme Court cases - 241
Kaagan, Larry - 137
Kefauver, Estes - 30, 75
Kegley, Charles - 138
Kemp, Jack F. - 195, 210
Kemp-Roth tax bill - 164
Kennedy, Edward
  National health insurance - 9, 197
  1980 campaign - 28, 29, 135, 136, 263
    Political alignments - 14
  1984 campaign - 28, 56
Kennedy, John F.
  Bay of Pigs - 136
  Campaign spending - 77
  Civil rights campaign - 3
  Congressional coattail effect - 221
  Economic policy - 160
  Election returns - 131 (chart)
  Foreign relations experience - 154

1960 campaign - 29, 132
  Presidential approval ratings - 282 (chart)
  Primaries - 75, 112
  Religion issue - 132, 142
  Supreme Court appointment - 243
Kennedy, Robert F. - 43-44, 112
Kent State University - 4
Kentucky senate election - 225
Kessel, John - 56
Key, V. O. - 137
Keynesian economics - 2, 157, 160, 169
Khrushchev, Nikita - 133
Kirkland, Lane - 263
Korean Air Lines disaster - 284
Korean War - 4, 209
Labor. *See also* AFL-CIO
  Antidiscrimination suit - 241
  Defense issues - 146
  Democratic delegates - 71
  Domestic content legislation - 147
  Mondale support - 51, 54, 56, 61, 203, 264
  New Deal coalition - 1
  1984 voting pattern - 105
  Political alignments - 11, 15, 16, 197, 203, 263, 267
Laffer, Arthur - 163
Lake, Celinda - 83-110
Lance, Bert - 61, 70, 264
Landon, Alf - 103, 104
Lazarsfeld, Paul - 122
Lebanon, 209
  Terrorist bombings - 98, 148, 284
  Troop removal - 149
Lederman, Susan - 142, 143
Lee, Rex - 241, 253-255
Lemann, Nicholas - 259-275
Lewis, Anthony - 189, 240
Light, Paul C. - 83-110
Lippmann, Walter - 113, 115
Lodge, Henry Cabot
  1972 candidacy - 29
  Vice presidential candidacy - 129
Lodge, Henry Cabot, Sr. - 245
Los Angeles Times - 113
Los Angeles Times/NBC poll - 81, 102
Lowi, Theodore J. - 3, 277-301
Luken, Thomas - 223
Lurton, Horace - 245
Maine caucuses - 45, 59
  Campaign spending - 51
Macroeconomics - 156, 157, 159
Manatt, Charles - 70
Marshall, Thurgood - 239, 242, 244, 245, 248
Making of a President (White, T. H.) - 132
Marshall Plan - 5, 139, 260
Martilla, John - 58

Massachusetts primary - 40, 54
 Campaign strategies - 58
 Candidate spending - 46, 51
Matsu - 132
Matthews, Donald - 52
McCarthy, Eugene
 Foreign relations experience - 154
 1968 presidential race - 29, 30
 Primaries - 112, 133, 137
McConnell, Mitch - 225
McGovern, George S. - 216
 Black vote - 12
 Committee hearings - 9
 Election returns - 131 (chart)
 Foreign policy experience - 139, 145
 Foreign policy issues - 11, 146
 Iowa caucuses - 53
 1972 presidential race - 29, 42, 72
 1984 candidacy - 28, 42, 59
 Political alignments - 11, 16
 Vietnam War - 134, 143
McGovern-Fraser Commission - 7, 11
McReynolds, James Clark - 246
Media. *See also* News media
Medicaid - 196, 201
Medicare - 102, 196, 201, 265, 292
Meese, Edwin - 271
Michel, Robert - 294
Michigan primary - 35
 Campaign spending - 51
Microeconomics - 156
Michigan caucuses - 61
Military Reform Caucus - 204
Mississippi senate election - 225
Minnesota
 Political constituency - 263
 Senate elections - 225
Mondale, Walter F.
 Campaign spending - 45-51
 Campaign strategy - 63, 65, 80, 88, 92-95,
 203, 205-206, 285
  Economic - 173-178, 269-270
  Nomination campaign - 56-57, 60-63, 65
 Carter identification - 68, 73, 94, 203
 Debates - 99, 100-103, 150-151, 177
 Defense spending - 205
 Delegates - 39, 40, 41, 77, 78
 Economic policy - 173-177
 Election returns - 103-108, 106 (chart), 131
 (chart)
 Endorsements - 56-57, 61, 68, 270
 Ferraro nomination - 70
 Foreign policy issues - 94-95, 99, 145, 146,
 150-151
 Fund raising - 46, 51, 56, 77-79

Group support - 66, 67 (chart). *See also
 under* Labor
Iowa caucuses - 53
Israel, U.S. embassy in - 146
Media coverage - 54, 55, 114, 116-118, 117
 (chart), 118, 265-267
1984 campaign
 Calendar - 41-42
 Nomination - 18, 30, 148, 203, 205
 Public support - 31, 81
 Strategy - 265, 267, 269-271
1984 caucuses - 36, 38
1984 primaries - 28, 36, 37, 93-94
Nuclear weapons - 92, 95, 150
Party identification - 84-85, 87
Political alignments, constituency - 15-18,
 197, 261, 265, 285, 296
Supreme Court issue - 239, 240
Tax proposal - 97, 175, 178, 205
Television skills - 75
Moral Majority - 280, 292, 298
Mullins, Dennis - 246
Murdock, Norm - 223
Murphy, Frank - 244
Muskie, Edmund
 Environmental hearings - 9
 Foreign relations experience - 154
 Media coverage - 120
 1968 campaign - 10
 1972 campaign - 29, 53
MX missile commission - 210
Nasser, Abdel - 132
National Education Association (NEA) - 56,
 71, 203
National Organization for Women (NOW) -
 16, 56, 70, 71, 203, 205
**National Republican Congressional Com-
mittee** - 218
National Women's Political Caucus - 71
NATO. *See* North Atlantic Treaty Organiza-
tion
Nelson, Michael - 129-154, 189-213
Neoconservatives - 280
Neo-Keynesian economics - 157, 160
Nevada caucuses - 54
New Deal
 Philosophy - 190
 Political coalition - 1, 3, 23, 92, 211, 263
 Presidential coattail effect - 215, 228
New Freedom - 190, 193, 228
New Frontier - 4
New Hampshire
 Campaign spending - 51
 Candidate spending limits - 44, 45-46
 1968 primary - 133
 1980 and 1984 primary reforms - 35

1984 primary - 27-28, 36, 42, 60, 115-116
Primary media coverage - 52-54
Senate elections - 225
New Jersey primary - 35, 36
Candidate spending - 49, 51
New Mexico primary - 40
New Politics - 1
Electoral strategies
1968 campaign - 10
1972 campaign - 11-13
1976 campaign - 13-14
1980 campaign - 14
1984 campaign - 15-18
Environmental and consumer legislation - 6
Regulatory effect - 6
Vietnam opposition - 6
Women's movement - 16
New Right intellectuals - 195
New York primary - 35
Campaign spending - 51
Candidate spending limits - 46
Strategy - 61, 62
New York Times - 7, 28, 113, 115, 124, 199, 266
New York Times/**CBS News polls** - 23, 66, 67 (chart), 70, 97, 99, 101, 102, 103, 151, 176, 177, 289
Newman, Edwin - 101
News media
Influence - 52-55, 111-127, 182, 265, 266-267
New Politics alignment - 7-8, 12
Newscast coverage - 112-113
Newsweek - 240
Nicaragua
CIA manual - 103
U.S. involvement - 137, 146, 149, 200, 205, 208
Nixon, Richard
Arms talks - 134, 209
China visit - 134
Congressional coattail effect - 216
Defense spending - 198
Détente - 201
Domestic policies - 193
Economic policy - 158, 160
Election returns - 103, 104 (chart), 131 (chart)
Foreign policy experience - 110, 139
1960 campaign
Foreign policy issues - 132
Vice presidential selection - 129
1968 campaign
Campaign spending - 77
Foreign policy issues - 133
Nomination - 29

Vietnam War - 133-134, 143
1972 campaign, Vietnam War - 134, 143
Office of the presidency - 189
Political alignments - 19-20
Presidential approval ratings - 281, 282 (chart), 288
Supreme Court appointments - 239, 243, 251, 257
Watergate scandal - 7, 135
Nomination process - 27-82. *See also* Delegates
Calendar - 41
Delegate selection - 31-33, 34 (chart), 35-36, 40-42
Early front runners - 29
Evolution - 31
Fairness Commission - 42
Hunt Commission - 27, 33
Long-term influences - 30, 65-69
Media coverage, influence - 52-55, 79-80
Money - 42-46, 48-52
Outsider candidates - 29, 33, 74
Primaries and caucuses - 32-42
Short-term influences - 30-65
Strategy - 55-65
Norris, George - 75
Norris-LaGuardia Act of 1932 - 242, 256
North Atlantic Treaty Organization (NATO) - 2, 133
North Carolina congressional elections - 235
North Vietnam
1968 campaign issue - 133-134
Tet offensive - 133
Northern Securities Co. v. United States - 257
NOW. *See* National Organization for Women
Nuclear weapons
Arms-control talks - 134, 231, 270
Campaign issue - 132
Chinese development - 133
Mondale policy - 92, 95, 150
Reagan policy - 110, 150-151, 207, 208, 209-210
Strategic Arms Limitation Treaty - 134, 209
Strategic Defense Initiative - 24, 87
Voter concern - 107
Nunn, Sam - 212
Occupational Safety and Health Administration (OSHA) - 199
O'Connor, Sandra Day - 239, 243, 244, 245, 247, 248
Office of Management and Budget
Budget deficits - 167, 178
Deregulation - 292
Program analysis - 209

Ohio primary - 35, 40
  Candidate spending - 49, 51
Oil
  OPEC price increases - 5, 195, 196, 261
  Suez Canal seizure - 132
Oklahoma caucuses - 54
O'Neill, Thomas P., Jr. - 74-75, 200, 230
OPEC. *See* Organization of Petroleum Exporting Countries
Organization of Petroleum Exporting Countries - 5, 195, 196
Orren, Gary R. - 27-82
Ortega, Katherine - 240
Parker, John J. - 247
Party caucuses, history - 32. *See also* Primary elections and caucuses
Party conventions, history - 32, 69
Patterson, Thomas E. - 111-127
Peace Corps - 139
Penner, Rudolph - 163
Pennsylvania primary - 35, 36, 61
  Campaign spending - 51
  Candidate spending limits - 46
  Delegate shares - 77
Percy, Charles - 82, 224
Peters, Charles - 123
Phillips, Kevin - 262
Political action committees (PACs) - 9, 51, 219
Political Control of the Economy (Tufte, Edward R.) - 155
Pollsters, polls - 288
  Economic influence - 171, 172
  Election analysis - 277
  1980 campaign - 106 (chart), 135, 137, 143, 290 (chart)
  1984 campaign
    Bush-Ferraro debate - 103
    Clergy endorsement - 97
    Exit polls - 81, 106 (chart), 289, 290 (chart)
    Generational effects - 66, 70
    Preprimary - 57, 62
    Reagan vs. Hart - 81
    Reagan vs. Mondale - 31, 81, 84, 91, 96, 99-102, 106 (chart), 150, 151, 278, 290 (chart)
  Presidential approval (charts) - 282, 283
  Reagan's foreign policy initiatives - 148
  Tax issue - 176, 177
Polsby, Nelson - 134
Pomper, Gerald - 142, 143
Powell, Lewis - 239, 243, 245
Presidency
  Of achievement - 190-192, 194
  Of consolidation - 193, 194

  Of preparation - 193-194
  Relationship with Supreme Court - 240-242
Presidential elections
  Election returns, 1952-1984 - 131 (chart)
  Foreign policy dominance - 129-154
  Nomination process - 27-82
  Political realignments - 1-25, 295-297
Price, David E. - 76
Primary elections and caucuses. *See also state names*
  Candidate expenditures - 44-52
  Delegate selection (1912-1984) - 34 (chart)
  Evolution - 32-33
  Generational effects - 65-68, 69, 81-82
  Group support - 67 (chart)
  "Loophole" - 32-33, 35, 77
  Media coverage - 52-55
  1984 Democratic results - 27-28, 37 (chart), 38 (chart)
  Reforms - 32-41
  Strategy - 55-65
Progressive movement - 32, 81
Prohibition movement - 6
Public Interest - 195
Public Liaison Office, White House - 86
Public Presidency: The Pursuit of Popular Support (Edwards, George C. III) - 301
Public works projects - 6, 15
Puerto Rico - 35
Quemoy - 132
Quirk, Paul J. - 155-187
Rainbow coalition - 59-60
Rather, Dan - 267
Reader's Digest - 240
Reagan, Ronald
  Age issue - 210
  Budget proposals - 272
  Carter preparation for - 198
  Campaign financing - 45, 77-78
  Campaign spending - 71
  Campaign strategy - 72, 89-92, 206-207, 266-268, 279
  Congressional coattail effect - 207, 215, 217-220
  Constituency - 31, 259, 261-262, 280-281, 284-285, 289, 290 (chart), 293-297. *See also* Polls, pollsters
  Debates - 30, 121, 150-151, 177
  Defense spending - 179, 199, 200, 202-203, 207, 208, 269
  Domestic policies - 20-21, 199-200, 201-202, 206-207, 208, 268
  Economic policy - 21, 89-90, 161-168, 199-200, 207, 211-212, 262, 268, 269
  Election returns (chart) - 131

Foreign policy initiatives - 148-150, 200, 201, 208-209, 284
Foreign policy issues - 135-136, 143
Incumbency advantage - 85-88
Lebanon issue - 98
Media coverage - 119, 121, 122-124, 266
1976 campaign - 30
1980 campaign - 29
99th Congress agenda - 229-234
Nuclear weapons - 95, 110, 150, 270
Party identification - 84-85
Political support - 74-75, 90-91, 189
President of achievement - 198-203, 206
Presidential approval ratings - 281, 282 (chart), 283 (chart), 288
Second-term prospects - 206-211, 291-293, 297-300
Social services - 20, 199, 201
Supreme Court appointments - 239-246, 249, 251-253, 256, 272
Tax legislation
    First term - 20, 162-163, 199, 208
    Proposals - 176-179, 271
Realignment. *See under* Presidential elections
Reconstituted Right - 1
Election strategies
    1968, 1972 campaigns - 19-20
    1980, 1984 campaigns - 20-23
Regan, Donald - 167, 168, 273
Regulatory legislation
New Politics movement - 6
Reconstituted Right - 21
Rehnquist, William H. - 244, 256
Reich, Robert -204
Religion
Campaign issue - 132, 142, 279
Mondale campaign - 96
Political realignment - 9
Supreme Court seats - 244
Republican National Committee - 294
Republican National Convention
1960 - 129
1984 - 71-72
Republican party
Campaign spending - 71
Delegate selection reforms - 76
Electoral strategies (1968-1984) - 19-23
Nomination (1984) - 71-72
Party identification - 84-85
Public opinion and foreign policy - 144
Reagan second-term factionalism - 210
Reston, James - 133
Rhode Island primary - 40, 54
Rockefeller, Jay - 212
Rockefeller, Nelson

Campaign spending - 50
Foreign policy experience - 139
1964 campaign - 29, 133
Roe v. Wade - 246, 272
Rollins, Ed - 294
Roosevelt, Franklin D. - 74, 222
Campaign spending - 77
Congressional coattail effect - 228
Election returns - 103, 104 (chart)
New Deal coalition - 1, 3, 23
New Deal philosophy - 190
President of achievement - 190, 192, 200
Presidential approval ratings - 288
Supreme Court appointments - 239, 245, 248, 257
Roosevelt, Theodore - 74, 75, 78, 194, 197, 245, 257
Rose, Jonathan C. - 252
Salinger, Pierre - 134
SALT. *See* Strategic Arms Limitation Treaty
Schlesinger, Arthur, Jr. - 139, 202
Scranton, William - 133, 139
School prayer - 22, 207, 202, 207, 232, 242, 292, 293
Schroeder, William J. - 274
Scowcroft Commission - 210
Scranton, William - 29
SEATO. *See* Southeast Asia Treaty Organization
Senate election results
1952 - 224
1956-1984 - 216 (chart)
1980 - 198-199, 224
1984 - 224-229, 226-227 (charts)
    Ticket splitting - 288
Republican control - 198-199, 224
Seymour-Ure, Colin - 118, 125
Shefter, Martin - 1-25
Shriver, Sargent - 139
Silent Majority - 19-20
Smith, Al - 74
Smith, Howard K. - 267
Social programs - 22, 279. *See also* Domestic policy
Social Security - 22, 92, 99, 102, 201, 210, 264, 265, 271, 272, 291
Social Security Administration - 254
Solicitor General - 242, 253-255
Southeast Asia Treaty Organization (SEATO) - 2
Soviet Union - 275
Arms talks - 95, 200, 207-208, 209, 270
Hungarian uprising, 1956 - 132
Khrushchev resignation - 133
Reagan defense buildup - 200, 207-208
Stagflation - 5, 161, 195, 196

Stanton, Frank - 8
"Star Wars" antimissile program. *See* Strategic Defense Initiative
Statutes, federal, Court invalidation of - 241
Steeper, Frederick - 135
Stein, Herbert - 161, 163
Stevens, John Paul - 244
Stevenson, Adlai - 216
   Domestic policy issues - 139
   Foreign policy experience - 139
   Foreign policy issues - 130-131
   1952 campaign - 30
   1960 campaign - 29
   Nomination - 112
   As party outsider - 205
Stockman, David - 101, 167, 168, 195, 199, 236, 262, 271
Stone, Harlan Fiske - 257
Strategic Arms Limitation Treaty (SALT) - 134, 137, 209
Strategic Defense Initiative - 24, 87, 95, 232
Stratton, William G. - 129
Student loans - 99, 272
Suez Canal - 132
Sun Belt region - 260
"Sunshine" laws - 7
Supply-side economics - 21, 157, 163-165, 199, 208, 210, 211, 237
Supreme Court
   Appointments - 239-253, 256, 272, 298
      Criteria - 243-247
      Role of Senate - 247-248
   Checks on Congress - 249-250
   Government cases - 241, 242, 253-255
   Impeachment of justices - 242
   New Politics alignment - 8
   Relationship with president - 240-242, 248-250, 272, 298
   Watergate decision - 7
Symington, Stuart - 29, 154
Taft, Robert - 29
Taft, William Howard - 78, 194, 257
Taxes - 158
   Indexing - 299
   Mondale proposal - 97
   99th Congress - 230-231
   Reagan policies - 20, 24, 162-163, 176-179, 198-200, 271
   Tuition tax credits - 24, 232, 292, 293, 299
Television - 75, 265-267. *See also* News media
Texas, congressional and local elections - 219, 225, 235
Third World, U.S. involvement - 3
Thornberry, Homer - 247
Thurmond, Strom - 247
Thurow, Lester - 204, 173

Time - 240
Trade, international - 89
Treasury, Department of the - 43, 167
Truman, Harry S. - 112, 226, 194
   Presidential approval ratings - 282 (chart)
   Supreme Court appointment - 248-249
Tuesday Group - 266
Tufte, Edward R. - 155, 158, 173
Tweed, William "Boss" - 27
Udall, Morris - 29, 79
Unemployment - 90, 158, 166, 168, 169, 207. *See also* Stagflation
United Nations, Israel vote - 137
University of Michigan, Center for Political Studies - 140
Veterans' pensions and health benefits - 272
Vietnam War - 192, 209, 261
   Cambodia invasion - 134
   Congressional hearings - 9
   Hanoi bombing - 134
   1968 presidential campaign - 142
   1972 presidential campaign - 134, 143
   Tet offensive - 133
Volcker, Paul - 259
Voting Rights Act - 201
Vrdolyak, Ed - 55
Wallace, George C. - 5
   Election returns - 131 (chart)
   As party outsider - 205
   Political alignment - 19
   Voter appeal - 9
Walters, Barbara - 136
War Powers Act - 6
Warren, Earl - 246, 257
Washington caucuses - 54
Washington, George - 239, 244
Washington Post - 7, 113, 266
Washington Post/ABC News poll - 91, 92, 95
Watergate scandal - 7, 135, 196, 278, 279
Weaver, Paul - 113
Welfare programs - 199
Welfare reform - 196
Wharton Econometrics - 172
Whip Inflation Now (WIN) -195
White, Byron - 239, 243, 244
White, Theodore H.
   1956 presidential election - 131
   1960 presidential election - 132
Wicker, Tom - 240
Wildavsky, Aaron - 134
Willkie, Wendell - 74, 205
Wilson, Woodrow
   Campaign spending - 77
   New Freedom program - 190, 193
   Outsider candidacy - 74
   President of achievement - 192

Supreme Court appointment - 246, 251, 257
Witcover, Jules - 294
Wittkopf, Eugene - 138
Women. *See also* Abortion; Equal Rights
Amendment
  Gender gap - 17, 25, 105
  Rights - 92

Woodruff, Judy - 118
World War I - 192
World War II - 192
Wright, Jim - 74
Yankelovich, Daniel - 137
Yuppies - 105, 264-265, 296